The Messenger

Prophet Muhammad and His Life of Compassion

THE MESSENGER

Prophet Muhammad and His Life of Compassion

Reşit Haylamaz
Y. Alp Aslandoğan

TUGHRA
BOOKS
New Jersey

Published by Tughra Books
335 Clifton Ave.
Clifton, NJ, 07011, USA
www.tughrabooks.com

978-1-59784-932-6

Library of Congress Cataloging-in-Publication Data

Names: Haylamaz, Resit, author. | Aslandogan, Yuksel A., author.
Title: The messenger : Prophet Muhammad and his life of compassion / Resit
   Haylamaz ; Y. Alp Aslandogan.
Other titles: Buzdan dagları eriten sefkat günesi. English
Identifiers: LCCN 2018023901 (print) | LCCN 2018024929 (ebook) | ISBN
   9781597849746 | ISBN 9781597849326 (pbk.)
Subjects: LCSH: Muhammad, Prophet, -632--Biography. | Muhammad, Prophet,
   -632--Character. | Compassion--Religious aspects--Islam.
Classification: LCC BP75.27 (ebook) | LCC BP75.27 .H38813 2018 (print) | DDC
   297.6/3 [B] --dc23
LC record available at https://lccn.loc.gov/2018023901

Contents

Foreword 7

Preface 9

Introduction A Prophet in Grief 13

Chapter 1 Mercy in the Face of Violence 29

Chapter 2 Never Give Up On Anyone 91

Chapter 3 The End of Hatred and Enmity 227

Appendix 247

Index 335

Foreword

There is a new interest in discovering the ethos of Islam and the life lessons of Prophet Muhammad (peace and blessings of God be upon him) driven, unfortunately, by the tragic events of the early twenty-first century. This book serves this interest in significant ways. First, it narrates the life of the Noble Prophet, shedding light upon segments of his life that are either neglected or glossed over in conflict-focused biographies. The narrations in this book revolve around various strategies to avoid conflicts, the use of diplomacy and other methods, and approaches to reconciliation in the aftermath of conflicts. In narrating these events, the book helps the readers broaden their perspective on the life of the Messenger of God and better capture the ethos of his life. Indeed, both Muslims and non-Muslims may benefit from this understanding at a time when violent extremist groups such as ISIS are causing carnage with their brutality while dressing their totalitarian ideologies in Muslim garb. The book exposes the hypocritical and willful deception of radical groups which cherrypick incidents and sayings from the Prophet's life, decontextualize them and abuse them to serve their perverted ideologies.

The book reveals a number of striking facts, including the following:

Prophet Muhammad, upon whom be peace and blessings, never killed or even attempted to wound anyone during these clashes although he was at times seriously wounded, being obliged to resort to his sword against his sworn enemies only for self-defense. Indeed, the Prophet of Mercy pardoned them, including even those who had made attempts on his life.

Despite subjugating early Muslims to various forms of oppression, including physical harassment, confiscation of property, torture and execution, the Muslims later brought its population of over 10,000 under control with a loss of only 16 lives. The Noble Prophet did his utmost to secure a peaceful surrender of Mecca and succeeded. Meccans were spared retribution, forgiven, and not forced to accept Islam.

Important in understanding certain actions and statements of the Messenger of God and his Companions is the consideration of the culture, traditions and "normal" behaviors of that time. These actions and attitudes of the Muslims of this era can only be understood properly in their context and in relation to the behavior of their contemporaries who were mostly stern idolators. Pulling the actions and statements of early Muslims out of their historical and cultural context is a great disservice to Islam and humanity. The world of the early Muslims was seventh-century Arabia, which was full of barbarity and brutality. What may appear to be a harsh attitude or punishment today was either the norm or was an ameliorated form of a harsher punishment of seventh-century Arabia. Until Islam established itself as the primary influence in their lives, the early Muslims were influenced heavily by their former culture and traditions. So, especially during the early period of their life as Muslims, their actions are not necessarily a consequence of their religious sentiment. To understand what was induced by their Muslim identity as opposed to their identity as members of their society, we have to contrast their actions and statements with those of their non-Muslim contemporaries. One example is the application of punishments that are considered harsh and cruel today. Again, these can only be understood in relation to the norms of the day, and based upon a holistic study of the Qur'an, the Prophet's life and indications of where they were taking the society. The cases of polygamy and war captives can be understood in this light. The book also sheds some light on the methods used by the Noble Prophet to win the hearts of his contemporaries, to prevent and resolve violent conflicts and to repair relationships when conflicts did occur. However, this book is by no means an exhaustive list of all the steps God's Messenger took to conquer the hearts of almost all inhabitants of the Arabian Peninsula and turn them from die-hard enemies into devoted faithful friends. Despite his being the individual whose life is most minutely recorded throughout human history, all of the actions, strategies, and words of God's Messenger have not been transmitted to our day. Nevertheless, it is our opinion that the material presented in this book will be enough to dispel many myths about the life and message of the Noble Prophet, who is described in the Qur'an as "a mercy to all the worlds."

Preface

The Messenger of God is, for Muslims, in every aspect of his life, an unfailing guide that we need to follow meticulously. He was sent to the world as a Messenger for all who would live and breathe on earth until the Last Day and led a full life with the potential to solve every possible problem. His days of Prophethood are akin to compressed files; with each page that is opened, new windows and doors are opened, and new alternative solutions presented, which are commensurate with our intention and clarity of vision.

Within a period of twenty-three years, God's Messenger laid the foundations for the edifice of Islam to stand until the end of time, and left openings in the face of the structure that would give access to every century. That is to say, the answer to every possible kind of problem to be experienced until the end of time is to be found in the twenty-three-year Age of Happiness that was his Prophethood. However, the solution to these problems is contingent upon our discovery of the openings in question extending to us from that world whose foundations were laid in those days, and upon our ability to enter them and take positive strides forward.

The first and most fundamental threshold we must cross is a comprehensive acquaintance with his world. But this is not enough on its own, for every individual is a child of the age in which they live and so the second threshold at this juncture is the importance of being well-versed in the particular era in which we live. It is necessary to raise our awareness in both areas for the solution of the problems of our day with the same Prophetic methods. This way we will act upon the practice of the Prophet consciously by drawing parallels with his time and better fulfill the requirements of the present time. From this perspective we see that our world has often witnessed the predicaments of our people, who have been unable to properly interpret their own times despite their knowledge of the Age of Happiness, and unfortunately we continue to repeat the same mistake today. We continue to waste the opportunities bestowed upon us by God, with a dissipation akin to the squandering of our inheritance, and we lose, sea by sea, all that was accumulated, drop by drop, over centuries.

Access to this rich Prophetic legacy and the solutions he provided for both individual and social problems in the past is only possible if we follow the path of the Noble Prophet. At the same time, this is not a matter that can be realized merely by exclaiming, "But I am traversing the path!" Just as we need to have uniformity in goals, so we need to feel the same pangs, to take the same determined attitude, to make the same acuteness the animating spirit of our lives, to seek the same nearness to God through remembrance of the Beloved of God, to apply the same methodology, to display the same resolution and patience, to show the same treatment to everyone even when it sears our hearts, and in short, to take a throughly Prophetic approach. For our efforts will only gain widespread acceptance and our service will only bear fruit as long as we travel along that Prophetic way.

We have often witnessed the swift bankruptcy of alternative resolutions that spring from human thought. Those who have been able to generate long-term solutions have always been the heroes of this Prophetic way. The present is no different from the past, and the heroes of tomorrow will undoubtedly come from among the faithful followers of this Prophetic way.

Thus, we urgently need to commit ourselves to this endeavour, to cast aside glib slogans and to become active in every sphere of life, to be free of the affliction of imprisoning the Qur'an in a narrow space as though it comprised only a few verses, to examine the twenty-three-year Prophethood of God's Messenger beyond the incidents of Badr and Khaybar, and in short to reacquaint ourselves with the Messenger of God as a Prophet who embraced his addressees in all aspects, with every step that he took outside the mosque, as well as within it.

We need to keep in mind that it is the human being who gives rise to problems in the first place and where humans are approached with the intention of enabling them to reach their individual perfection, every kind of problem can be resolved. However, this task that the Qur'an presents to us in the stories of a great number of Prophets is perhaps the most difficult task in the world. But it is not impossible. The Messenger of God demonstrated to us through his own lived example that for every problem there is a solution and bequeathed us a legacy in the form of a path replete with solutions. Therefore, there is a path leading to the heart of every human being, even Abu Jahl; what matters is adherence to the principles and prerequisites of the path concerning its discovery and conventions.

The book explores the contact of God's Messenger with the Meccans in particular, and aims to understand the methodology and procedure of the past in order to solve the problems of today. It is a work which seeks to discover the principles upon which Prophet Muhammad, upon whom be peace and blessings, acted for a period of twenty-three years, despite his coming to the world at a time when troubles were mounting, and to comprehend the particular strategies he used in solving these problems in their entirety.

The work comprises three major sections. The lengthy introduction provides a summary of events in Mecca starting from the pre-Islamic era and aims to understand why its people, who for forty years referred to God's Messenger by the honorific "the Trustworthy" (al-Amin), changed all at once and turned him into the target of their hatred and hostility. Section One presents the Prophetic stance in the face of all manner of violence and conflict, and examines at length the ways that the Messenger paved to win over people's hearts under the most difficult conditions. Showing by specific examples the significance of the "atmosphere of service" which accompanies reconciliation, peace, dialogue and human contact under a variety of circumstances, this section seeks to discover the impeccable world of God's Messenger by means of re-evaluation, re-examination, definition and new interpretation. Since violence and war could not possibly unite with the benevolent world of the most merciful human being to walk the earth, this section examines why a perception of violence developed that is contrary to the reality, and it draws attention to the chasm between this perception and the truth. The section also elucidates in detail the kinds of initiatives God's Messenger took in order to affect the hearts of his addressees, even at times when, after all the events that had transpired, negative feelings threatened to predominate over reason and sound judgment.

Section Two discusses how transformation was achieved in the Age of Happiness. It attempts to set out the broad arena in which the Prophetic methodology was employed and to articulate the meaning of its steps for our day. This section, which can also be understood as the method and manner of softening hearts and being purged of all problems, is important in that it relates to us how the problems of today's world can be solved. It describes the milestones of transformation and sheds light on the principles we need to follow with a Prophetic sensitiv-

ity in order to serve others; it lays down succinctly the precise foundations upon which the luminous world of tomorrow may rise.

The third and final section centers on the conquest of Mecca and
contains a discussion of the fruit of twenty-one years. It depicts the Messenger's personal visits to those who had not responded favorably to his
call. Here we see the birth of a new spring with the Sun of Mercy rising
again over Mecca, and the melting away of the barriers built up until
this time. This outcome did not come easily, but Mecca was won over
en masse. Behind this, without a doubt, lay great effort, patiently woven,
stitch by stitch. At the same time, this was a triumph with no losing side.
Even those came who had been until very recently the leading actors of
hatred and animosity, and, what is more, they took their distinguished
places on the stage of history as the heroes of compassion of the future.

A critical detail ought to be noted here: we see the Messenger of
God bidding farewell to his Companions at a time when he had reached
the final, happy outcome. Addressing the throngs at the plains of Arafat, he laid before them his knowledge and experience of the past twenty-three years, reminded them of the particular paths and methods
through which such an outcome is obtained, and placing the future in
their hands, he reunited with his Lord soon after his Farewell Sermon,
thus ascending to the lofty horizon of his own spirit. His declarations[1]
reverberating in Arafat and the lofty name of Muhammad, upon whom
be peace and blessings, are for us glad tidings of the luminous world
of the future, as well as a sacred trust reminding us of our duties and
responsibilities.

Today, too, God's Messenger seeks safe hands to take over and protect this trust.

INTRODUCTION

A PROPHET IN GRIEF

A Prophet in Grief

It is not possible to grasp the overreaction of the Meccans to the beginning of the Prophethood of God's Messenger without considering the period before his Prophethood, for a complete contradiction is evident between the attitude of the Meccans before and after its annunciation to the Noble Prophet. For an accurate reading of the Meccan years it is necessary to understand the underlying reasons that the Meccans suddenly became his greatest enemy, when previously they had always referred to him by the honorific "the Trustworthy."

Qusayy ibn Kilab,[2] sixth-generation ancestor of the Noble Prophet, made a series of important changes in the administration of Mecca that he took over from the Khuda'a, and reinstated a Ka'ba-centered life in Mecca. He virtually built Mecca anew and so as to establish on solid grounds the major and minor pilgrimages that had continued since the time of Prophet Abraham. He set up the tribes in new lodgings, starting with the Ka'ba surrounds and placing the tribes with greater male populations around the Ka'ba, while those with fewer male members able to fight were housed towards the valleys. The rationale behind this arrangement was to organize Mecca so as to be able to offer a thorough and faultless service to those who came for pilgrimage. To this end, each tribe was assigned a duty:[3] providing food and water to the pilgrims (*rifada* and *siqaya*),[4] command of troops in war (*qiyada*), possession of the keys and control of the Sanctuary (*sidana*), guarding the Ka'ba (*hijaba*), inter-tribal affairs or legation (*sifara*), carrying the standard in battle (*liwa'*), carrying the war banner (*uqab*), the tent in which donations for public emergency were collected (*qubba*), determining the value of pecuniary liabilities (*ashnaq*), presidency of divination (*aysar*), offerings to the Sanctuary (*amwal muhajjara*), bridling (*a'inna*), government (*hukuma*), use of an assembly for deliberation (*nadwa*), and consultation (*mashwara*). Each tribe controlled one or more of these services.[5] A council referred to as the Dar al-Nadwa was established for which eminent figures were selected from each tribe to take important decisions, and the Meccan administration began to be run from this council. Naturally, the president of this council was Qusayy ibn Kilab himself, a powerful administrator and the conquering commander of Mecca.

From the institution of this administration onwards, the Meccan tribes began to compete in good works and the superiority of the tribes over one another came to be measured in their acts of charity and the services they provided. However, even though this sense of benevolence was felt in the first generations, feelings of hatred and animosity reared their ugly head in the succeeding generations; base feelings of ambition and rivalry replaced the competition to do charitable works. As a matter of course, this atmosphere also brought with it conflict and commotion and opened the door to major dispute between the tribes. Most of these problems arose between the Banu Hashim, who had the final say in matters of Meccan administration, and the Banu Umayya and Banu Makhzum, whose strength was growing. On two occasions, when the tribes could not find a compromise, they applied to an arbitrator. In both cases the arbitrators ruled in favor of the Quraysh. So critical was the situation that as a result of the arbitration (*munafara*) conducted between Umayya and his uncle Hashim, the former was forced to pay a compensation of fifty camels and banished from Mecca to live in Damascus[6] for a period of ten years.[7] This was, no doubt, a vital event which rendered permanent the rift between the two families.[8]

During this increasingly tense period, the Banu Umayya and Banu Makhzum's occasional attempts to take over the administration of Mecca failed. The chief reason for this failure was the great leadership of 'Abd al-Muttalib and his powerful resistance, like that which Abraha faced when advancing on Mecca with his army to destroy the Ka'ba. 'Abd al-Muttalib's manner and bearing during this period, and the role he played in the rediscovery of the well of Zamzam following three successive dreams, consolidated Meccan Chief 'Abd al-Muttalib's position and invested his administrative and political power with a divine dimension. Before his might, the Banu Umayya and Banu Makhzum were forced to delay their takeover attempts. However, the struggle was not over and their efforts to influence and dominate the Dar al-Nadwa continued. Upon examination of the expressions they used when dispatching their envoys to Abyssinia, it becomes apparent just how adept the Abu Jahls of the day were in setting the groundwork for influencing the people and the particular methods they employed to this end. As is known, the Meccans instructed the envoys they sent in pursuit of the migrant Muslims to speak with the dignitaries and clergy before meeting the Abyssinian

King, and only after winning over their hearts with the expensive gifts they brought with them, were they to appear before the King. Their purpose was to put pressure on the King in a matter on which everyone else had reached consensus and to achieve their desired outcome, without risk and with relative ease.

An intensification of such activity is evident during the time of Abu Talib who succeeded 'Abd al-Muttalib as the chief of Mecca, with those in alliance against the Banu Hashim holding more sway. Although Dar al-Nadwa membership had its own set rules and criteria, these rules were not applied when it came to their own men but applied rigidly to those they wanted to exclude. For instance, while no one under the age of forty was given membership of the Dar al-Nadwa, they accepted Abu Jahl amongst them at just thirty years of age. It would appear that the most important figure who designed and planned the future of Mecca in line with his own will was Walid ibn al-Mughira, to whom the Qur'an draws attention in this regard.[9]

When conditions in Mecca had ripened and the time had come for the final move, an unexpected incident transpired and Muhammad the Trustworthy was given the mission of Prophethood. For those who had set their eyes on the seat of Mecca and made preparations for a coup d'état, this was unforeseen and from that moment on everything changed. The Messenger of God, whom they had hitherto called The Trustworthy and of whom they could not speak highly enough, was declared the greatest enemy of all. For them, he was now the greatest obstacle on the path to the seat of Mecca and the first barrier that needed to be removed. In declaring him the enemy, they did not consider his forty-year history of trustworthiness, and the situation was viewed ruthlessly through their own self-interest. As Said Nursi states, in politics along these lines, where visions are blurred and emotion holds sway, even Satan would see the person siding with him as angel, and an angel would see one who is on what they pronounce to be the opposing side as Satan. Consequently, they could not see the Embodiment of Mercy upon whom even the angels looked with admiration. Abu Jahl, who had begun to see himself as future leader and head of Mecca, openly and repeatedly expressed this. For instance, when he once walked through the streets of Mecca accompanied by Mughira ibn Shu'ba, he crossed paths with God's Messenger, and God's Messenger said, wanting to seize such an opportunity and invite him to belief, "O father of Hakam, I invite you to belief in God. Could you too not believe in God and His Messenger?" But Abu Jahl took his usual insolent attitude and said to the Messenger of God, "O Muhammad! When will you abandon speaking ill of our idols! If your purpose in doing so is that we testify before God in the other world that you have duly conveyed to us the message with which you were sent, do not weary yourself, for I will be your witness. But do not inconvenience us at the present time (and leave us to ourselves). Indeed, even if I know your words to be true, I can never believe in your Prophethood."

In the face of the impudence of Abu Jahl, who did not possess any concern for the other world, God's Messenger preferred to remain silent and departed so as not to heighten the tension. Watching him walk off from behind, Mughira ibn Shu'ba turned to Abu Jahl and asked, "What is your true opinion of him? Do you not indeed believe in his Prophethood?" After darting a glance at him as if to say, "Of course I do," he said, "By God, I know his words to be true. But we compete with the Hashemites in everything. Until this time, they have boasted of guardianship of the Honored Key to the Sanctuary. They have laid claim to the Nadwa (council), and we raised no objection. They asserted their right to be the standard-bearer, and we let it pass unchallenged. They assumed the duty of providing the pilgrims with water, and again we did not object. They provided food, and so did we, so much so that we were constantly neck and neck. And now they begin to boast of having a Prophet! By God, this I cannot endure at all."[10]

Abu Jahl's view was not merely one he voiced on the spur of the moment but one he made clear in the presence of others also; while affirming God's Messenger's Prophethood, he did not hesitate to openly state that a sense of rivalry necessitated him to stand against him. His words subsequent to what he saw and heard along with Abu Sufyan and Akhnas ibn Shariq for three consecutive nights are of the same nature. Each of the three, secretly and independently of the others, went out by night to listen to the Messenger of God as he prayed. Each hid at a distance from him, wanting to see him more closely as he observed the prayer and recited the Qur'an. They were full of curiosity but they did not want the others to know what they were doing, and thus preferred the dark of the night to do this, when everyone else had retired to their homes. Hence, none knew where his companions were sitting.

The sight was indeed a great one; the most beloved of God, rising like the sun at the House of God with the language of his heart and the tongue of his immaculate demeanor, met with his Lord and experienced a union at the Ka'ba that was a scene to behold. They watched in admiration and listened at length; the Qur'anic recitation they heard were like drops of mercy pouring forth in the heat of summer. They were so engrossed that they did not even notice how quickly time passed. They spent the night listening to him. When God's Messenger eventually completed his prayer and his recitation of the Qur'an at the Ka'ba ceased, they dispersed, each setting out for home. They walked with hurried and uneasy steps, anxious in case somebody might see them. But the trio, who had gone to great lengths to ensure that nobody saw them, came face to face. Even though they did not concede that they had lent an ear to the voice of their conscience, they were embarrassed upon seeing one another. With heads down, overcome by guilt, they reproached one other and said that they should never do such a thing again. "For if one of the flippant fools sees us in such a state, suspicion will be aroused in their mind, and they will do the same."

It was easy to say, but it was impossible for them to forget the scene they had just witnessed and to ignore what that they had heard. A truth constantly lingering in their minds resounded within them. There was no way to prevent the feeling flowing forth from within; after all, what would come of going and listening just one more time?

In truth, each of them was thinking the same thing, independently of the others. They returned, therefore, the next night and passed the night watching and listening again. When they met again on the way home later that night, embarrassment was visible in their every gesture. Even if their change of color could not be seen in the dark of the night, they had all seen a manifest reality. The chagrin in their voices in particular communicated just how defeated they were before this truth that they could not bring themselves to admit. How could they? They were each as surprised as the other.

They promised each other just as they had done on the first night: they were not going to come and listen to Muhammad again. On no account would they put themselves through such embarrassment again.

Perhaps Abu Jahl's heart had not yet become stone, Abu Sufyan's democratic side was predominating, and Akhnas ibn Shariq had not yet become as driven by evil as in the years to come. The three cronies, who thought that their friends would not come to the Sanctuary again after being cautioned for two nights in a row, stopped at the Ka'ba again on the following night; when darkness fell and the streets were all but empty, they again set off to listen to God's Messenger.

What is more, they stayed until the early hours, and when dawn broke, they set off back home again, confident that they would not be seen, when the three ran into each other once more at the very same spot.

They could not believe it. They would bear enmity against and oppose him and vow that they would never come again, yet they had also hastened to listen to him, giving each other the slip for a third time. They then began to reprove one another and vowed to the death that such a thing should never happen again, no matter what. They gave a solemn promise that they would never return.

The next morning, Akhnas ibn Shariq took his staff and rushed to the house of Abu Sufyan. "Tell me the truth, O father of Hanzala," he said. "What is your opinion of what you have heard from Muhammad?"

Abu Sufyan was guarded in his speech; he did not want to reveal his true colors to the friend from whom he could not hide his position for long. He thought it would be safer to get his opinion first, and therefore asked him a question in reply to his question: "And what is your opinion on the matter?" Akhnas ibn Shariq chose candor and said, "I believe what he has come with to be truth."

Cautious from the very beginning, Abu Sufyan breathed a sigh of relief, turned to him and said, "O father of Tha'laba, by God, to this day, I have heard many things whose meaning I do not know, nor what was intended by them. Now, I have a pretty good idea of what is meant by these particular words." He had scarcely finished his words when Akhnas interjected, "I feel precisely the same! But these are unlike any of them!"

Thus, they affirmed the truth of God's Messenger and acknowledged the veracity of the message with which he came. However, it was not all that easy to make this manifest and announce it, as there was the opposing figure of Abu Jahl.

Then, Akhnas ibn Shariq left Abu Sufyan's house and headed straight for Abu Jahl's place, to discuss the same things with him. "O father of Hakam," he began, "what is your opinion concerning all that you have heard from Muhammad?"

"And what have I heard anyway?" he said first, wanting to make light of the matter. But Akhnas was determined. "O father of Hakam," he repeated, "what is your actual opinion of Muhammad? Is he a man of truth or is he lying? Don't hold back. Look, there is no one else present to hear what you have to say."

Abu Jahl realized that he could not escape with an evasive answer. He had been caught out and it was clear that he could get away with nothing less than being straightforward. He first took a deep breath and then said the following:

"By God! Muhammad is telling the truth; he never speaks a single word of untruth. But it grieves me to think of the Banu Qusayy's possessing the right to raise the war standard and their services of the well of Zamzam, their ascendancy in serving food to the visiting pilgrims, on top of their claims to Prophethood. Now, can you imagine what will become of the Quraysh if they obtain exclusive possession of such a distinction as Prophethood? We have always been rivals with the Banu 'Abd Manaf for ascendancy and in honor; they fed the poor, and so have we. They assumed the burdens of others, and so have we. They have been generous and enabled others to benefit from the resources at their disposal, and we too gave others a share in our wealth and property. Just when we had finally caught up with them, and we were like two horses of equal speed, they now claim to have among them a Messenger to whom revelation comes from the heavens. And when, pray tell me, shall we ever attain anything of the like? By God, we will never believe in him, nor shall we affirm him."[11]

Even though the voice of his conscience told him otherwise, with his emotions driven by interests and politics, Abu Jahl was seeing black as white and white as black. From this moment on, there was no way of his seeing the truth. Because of the tarnishing of their consciences under the sway of hatred and animosity, it had become impossible for Abu Jahl and his fellows to heed advice and it was as though their hearts had become hardened, shut tight, never to be reopened. For them, this was akin to fleeting breezes blowing in the coldest time in winter; even though they blew gently from time to time, storms immediately followed and the breezes were replaced by deluges that swept away everything before them.

At the same time, Abu Talib's position in the Dar al-Nadwa was weakening considerably, despite his continuing chieftaincy, and Abu Jahl and his minions began to grow in influence as a direct consequence of the groundwork they had laid over the years. Similarly, 'Abbas, another uncle of the Prophet who represented the Banu Hashim at Dar al-Nadwa, was no longer able to make his voice heard in this prevailing climate. More precisely, from that day forth the Dar al-Nadwa turned into a center of operations where those who joined forces against a "common enemy" took decisions, fabricated lies for the purpose of influencing the masses, and where long-running strategies to defame and discredit God's Messenger first and foremost, followed by all believers, were discussed and resolved upon.

At a time when tribal life took its fiercest form, the Dar al-Nadwa sustained the oppressive mentality of the chieftains, and in an Age of Ignorance, in which the words that fell from their lips were deemed law, others did not have the luxury of having a mind of their own. What the tribal chief said was absolute truth, and there was an unnamed dark and brutal caste system. As a result, from that moment virtually all Mecca became a sort of Dar al-Nadwa radiating rancor and hatred; with every kind of violence and suppression, including verbal abuse, insult and invective, censure, oppression, attacks, deathtraps, ultimatums, overthrows, banishments, and various insurrection attempts, almost every day Mecca witnessed a new scenario or stratagem from the Abu Jahls of the era. Tension and disturbance was in the air almost every day of the Messenger's thirteen years in Mecca. Moreover, this tension was not limited to those creating the tension, but billowed over the whole community. Thick barriers were raised between God's Messenger and the rest of society to conceal the qualities that were the expression of his virtue such as mercy, compassion, gentleness, and mildness.

Of course, the believers were not guided by the Meccans, but by the Messenger of God himself. However, the lengths to which the Meccans of the era went in evil and malice is important for us in that it highlights how God's Messenger treated them in spite of everything they did, what methods he employed in reaching out to the Meccans in their animosity, hatred, rage and violence of all descriptions, and the means he used in transforming the people of the time, who were obsessed with killing, into devotees of letting live. For the most part, it is this aspect of the matter which holds importance for us with respect to solving our present problems by means of his methodology.

The sorrowful Messenger

The Messenger of God felt much grief in the face of all that was blindly done despite the manifest nature of the truth and was deeply distressed for those who were clearly being dragged into a terrible end and for those dragging others, the mass of the population included, in the same direction. God's Messenger made use of every possible opportunity to take them by the hand and to help them to reach the shores of salvation; he did not want to leave behind a single person with whom he had not sat and conversed, to whom he had not extended a hand, and whom he had not taken aboard his ship to guide to deliverance. From the fourth year of his Prophethood in particular, when the Message began to be openly conveyed, this course gathered greater speed and the Messenger of God visited everyone who came to Mecca, sitting with them and inviting them to belief. To this end, he spent his days in the markets of Dhu al-Majaz, Majanna, and 'Ukaz, waiting for visiting pilgrims to Mecca, addressing everyone with whom he made contact, and trying to divert from the wrong path those who were blindly falling prey to idolatry. He had a single aim: that all the living and breathing servants of God come to know their Creator and thus open the door of eternal salvation by means of His mercy.

This was, of course, an aim that the Meccans of the day, who were concerned with nothing save their own worldly future, could not possibly understand, and they immediately flew into action. Abu Jahl and Abu Lahab emerged as the main actors; both of them tried to prevent even a single person from being affected by God's Messenger. More particularly, the Prophet's uncle, Abu Lahab, was the dominating presence in those marketplaces. Even when Abu Jahl was nowhere to be seen, he committed himself to finishing the matter and kept close track of his nephew. Probably, Abu Jahl gave Abu Lahab priority in these settings due to his being the Prophet's paternal uncle and thus tried to create doubt in the people: "How can someone be trusted whose own uncle opposes and campaigns against him?"

They visited everyone that God's Messenger visited and claimed that he—God forbid—was not speaking the truth, labeling him as a Sabean[12] who divined from heavenly bodies. While acknowledging the power of his words, they tried to explain them away as magic and ascribed them to soothsaying.

They knew very well themselves that none of their falsehoods would hold, but what did this matter to the Abu Jahls? With their misinformation and lies they built a wall around God's Messenger and allowed no one to pass.

Years later, a Kinanan merchant vividly reported a similar incident:

"I saw the Messenger of God at the trade fair of Dhu al-Majaz addressing the people saying, "O people, say, 'There is no deity but God' and be saved." Right behind him was Abu Jahl, splattering dirt and dust upon him as he walked, yelling at the top of his voice, and following him at every step. He frightened the people saying, "O people, let not this man deceive you in regards to your religion for he wants you to renounce worship of the idols of al-Lat and al-Uzza." The Messenger of God, however, paid no mind to him, sought rather to pull away from him, and solemnly went on his way."[13]

Burning with the hope of finding a face acquainted with the truth on the hot grounds of the market and bearing all kinds of trouble from others, the Messenger of God did not judge on the basis of another's hatred and enmity and always did as behooved him.

In describing the difficulties he endured in striving to affect the heart of yet another person, another merchant from the 'Amiri tribe reported:

"During the Age of Ignorance,[14] *I heard God's Messenger say, 'O people, say 'There is no deity but God,' and be saved.'" Some of those surrounding him and trailing him spat on his blessed face and others threw dirt and dust upon him. Some among them were hurling insults and obscenities at him, when at the middle of the day, a small girl came to him with some water in her hand. God's Messenger took the water and after washing his hands and face turned to the girl and said, "Dear daughter, fear not for your father for none can overcome or debase him." I asked those beside me who she was and they said, 'She is Zaynab, the daughter of God's Messenger.' She was then a bright-faced young girl approaching her teens."*[15]

In those days, going from door to door saying, "O people, say 'There is no deity but God,' and be saved,"[16] was the main aim and activity of God's Messenger. He first called people to the One and only God, and did not even insist on their recognition of his own Prophethood as a precondition (on the path of truth).[17] However, had he only said, without meeting any acceptance, "Come, O people, there is God! There is life after death! There is reckoning and you will be brought to account for all that you do in your worldly lives," then he would still have fulfilled his mission. For when describing his position, the Qur'an states that the Messenger's sole mission was to convey the message,[18] and that this in no way implied or included forcing people to accept the message with which he came.[19] Yet he embarked upon an endeavor to save the lives of those who made attempts on his life, and to render luminous the darkened worlds of those who were facing a death of eternal damnation, and, as indicated in the Qur'an, almost ruined himself with grief, sorrowing after them, for their turning away from his Message.[20]

He expected nothing in return, but his close friends and family members who become acquainted with Islam early on supported him in his cause and acted with him at every step along the way. His wife Khadija, for instance, prepared food almost every single day, and 'Ali and Zayd went from street to street inviting the Meccans to dine with them. Even though there was always someone at the meal who would put a damper on the occasion, God's Messenger addressed the mind and reason of the people for whom he organized these meals and appealed directly to their feelings and hearts. He tried to soften their hearts with gifts and by taking the first step himself, cleared one by one the potential stumbling blocks in the path of his addressees. This was repeated to such an extent that the day came when the fortune of the wealthy Khadija, which had been acquired through years in international trade, was all but spent. By ten years after the beginning of God's Messenger's Prophethood, there was left no trace of her former wealth. Khadija, who shouldered three years of harsh boycott and exile side by side with God's Messenger, passed away as a person who laid everything she had out in the way of God. Where, then, did this wealth go? It was, no doubt, spent on the stomachs of such ungrateful individuals as Walid ibn al-Mughira, 'As ibn al-Wa'il, Abu Jahl, Abu Lahab, 'Uqba ibn Abi Mu'ayt, Utba, and Shayba.

It is indeed interesting that despite all their opposition and vehemence, these Meccans did not turn down this invitation. This means that they could not ignore the trustworthiness of God's Messenger and, despite their hostility, did not close the door entirely. Had one of them not spoken out each time to destroy the positive atmosphere, the hearts of some of them would have softened, and they could have been able to use their free will to stand where they ought to have stood.

But this did not happen. This had not happened during the times of previous Prophets. So it was not to be in this period either. That light would suppress darkness was clear, but bearing patiently the period of burden was yet another expression of fulfilling causes and doing what was necessary for a given end. For if everything in that era had developed at an extraordinary pace, a model could not have emerged that succeeding generations could use as an example. This change and transformation that followed a natural course of development was to leave behind it a tried and tested methodology that could be applied in every age and era, and so it was.

In return for this sacrifice and effort, the Meccans responded with more intensity each day and constantly took the path of violence. This was, after all, their only alternative where they were unable to produce reasonable arguments against the beauty and goodness that God's Messenger brought. These darkened souls, who rendered the day dark for themselves by merely closing their eyes, supposed that they could draw a veil over the sun with brute force.

Naturally, this did not happen either.

Reading well the growing tension and friction, God's Messenger left to their own devices the Meccans who had lost the capacity to act in a rational manner, until the time they could adopt a more reasonable stance. He had done the same thing before; the Messenger of God did not wish to be a part of the escalating tension, and so as not to cause any further vexation to the Meccans, who could not tolerate the presence of his Companions, he sent the latter to Abyssinia before leaving Mecca himself for Medina.

He had begun sending his Companions to Medina months before, gradually, in order to avoid more disastrous circumstances. On no occasion did he fling the Meccans' lack of acknowledgment for all the sacrifices made for them in their face, or accuse them of ingratitude. Despite the fact that they had long since deserved much worse, he never displayed indifference to a single individual. Just as there was never room in his world for "kicking someone when they're down," there was also no room for ruling anyone out completely. Despite the presence of the Helpers in Medina, whose numbers grew with every passing day, not once did he lose sight of Mecca, and he emigrated on that day with the intention that he would one day take them aboard too. Perhaps for them this meant purification from such negative feelings, a settling of the emotions that until that day had taken their mind and reason under their sway, and, in a sense, this departure constituted time for thought and consideration. As can be seen, it was again God's Messenger who took the first step in solving the problems of those who constantly created tension. From the outside, this could have been viewed as a step back, but as a result of this step, he acquired the opportunity to take new steps in reaching his addressees in their entirety.

This was exactly what happened. Sent with the purpose of opening doors and building bridges between people, God's Messenger did not abandon the doors that had opened bit by bit and the bridges that had been built inch by inch; on the contrary, when emigrating he set off by opening new doors and building new bridges. He caught the Meccans by surprise yet again, for he appointed his nephew 'Ali as his proxy in the city, to restore to their rightful owners all that the Meccans had entrusted to him as "The Trustworthy One"; taking a great risk, he left 'Ali that night, in his own bed.

How strange it was then that his departure did not result in things settling down for the Meccans, for they were even troubled by his living and breathing. Eventually, they gathered their armies and advanced upon him to destroy him together with his Companions.

CHAPTER 1

MERCY IN THE FACE OF VIOLENCE

Mercy in the Face of Violence

In the thirteen years that he lived in Mecca, the Messenger of God faced every kind of oppression, but not once did he retaliate in kind. The Qur'anic verses sent down during the revelation that began with Hira commanded justice and fairness even if the Prophet's addressees had far overstepped the mark, and pointed to patience as the sole recourse in such circumstances.[21] He was the Prophet of mercy,[22] and he always treated his opponents with mercy. Although he faced persecution at their hands, he exerted himself almost to his own detriment and sought to take them also into his atmosphere of mercy.[23] There was no room in his world for causing harm, nor returning harm with harm.[24] Whatever the circumstances, the Messenger of God always did what became him.

He guided his Companions in the same course of action;[25] no one who had been hurt, attacked, whose property was pillaged, or whose life was endangered retaliated. They were not on the same level as the Meccans who had made violence their second nature because, from the outset, God's Messenger advised everyone, Abu Dharr,[26] Abu Bakr[27] and 'Umar[28] first and foremost, to act with restraint and prudence, and no one was to react, to return in kind the wrong done to them, or to become a party to violence. It was again God's Messenger who showed them exactly what stance they needed to take, assuring them, "The most beloved of you to me, and the closest of you to me on the Day of Judgment, are the best of you in character. Those among you who talk with affectation, are given to boasting, and who offend others with their words and actions, will be the most repugnant to me and farthest from me on the Day of Judgment."[29] He described gentleness and mercy as actions beautifying a person, and violence and crudeness as actions making them repugnant.[30] When such Companions as 'Abdu'r-Rahman ibn 'Awf came to him and said, "O Messenger of God, while we were honored in our days as polytheists, we are held in contempt and despised as believers," and thus requested permission to retaliate, God's Messenger said, "I have been commanded to forgive the people and not to fight them." In so doing, he did not permit them to take retributory action.[31] This was, after all, God's decree; Gabriel had come to him and had said, *"(Even so, O Messenger) adopt the way of forbearance and tolerance, and enjoin what* is good and right, and withdraw from the ignorant ones (do not care what they say and do)" (Al-A'raf 7:199). When Archangel Gabriel revealed this verse, God's Messenger turned to the angel of revelation and said, "O Gabriel, what is the meaning of this?"

"O Muhammad," Gabriel replied, "God commands you to forgive those who have wronged you, give to those who deprived you, and keep relations with those who have severed their ties with you."[32]

Was it at all possible for God's Messenger to do anything but hearken immediately to God's command?

What is more, for those who wanted to exact retribution for the persecution to which they had been subjected, Gabriel came on another occasion to declare that permission had not been granted: "*Surely God defends strongly those who believe. Certainly God does not love any treacherous, ungrateful one*" (al-Hajj 22:38).[33] For this reason, God's Messenger constantly exhorted his Companions at a time when the Meccans could not yet brook their presence, instructing them to observe even their most innocent posture, their prayer, in the uninhabited quarters of the city's outskirts.[34] This was because he was the representative of the way expressed in the words, "By the Name of Him in Whose Hands is my soul, I will accept anything they ask of me, provided it does not violate the ordinances of God."[35]

He did not merely utter these words, but actualized them. There was no room whatsoever in his world for responding in kind to threats, insult, and violence. The sole protest that God's Messenger uttered in the face of such ordeals was, "O Banu 'Abd Manaf, what kind of neighborly treatment is this!"[36] In fact, this stance was the Qur'anic commandment, and he himself was an embodiment of the Qur'an. God warns His Messenger, first and foremost, followed by all the believers, declaring:

(*So, O believers, as a requirement of the wisdom in, and purpose for, your life of the world,) you will surely be tested in respect of your properties and your selves, and you will certainly hear many hurtful things from those who were given the Book before you and those who associate partners with God. If you remain patient (are steadfast in your Religion, and observe the bounds set by God in your relations with them) and keep within the limits of piety (in obeying God, and in your conduct toward them), (know that) this is among meritorious things requiring great resolution to fulfill.* (Al Imran 3:186)

It was, no doubt, God's Messenger who was the first to translate this ordinance into action. As Usama relates, the Messenger of God was always patient in the face of torment and persecution by the Meccan polytheists and the People of the Book, never reacted, and even went a step further, forgiving the thankless souls of the age in spite of everything they did.[37]

Almost every day of his thirteen years in Mecca he faced a brandnew stratagem, experienced an ordeal that distressed or pained him, and was subjected to all kinds of tactics to prevent and thwart him; however, he patiently endured all the oppression and torment and bore every kind of tribulation with determination.[38] Despite all the difficulty and hardship, he perpetually suppressed his feelings with his willpower and never once surrendered his reason to his emotion. He displayed a formidable example of patience; this was, however, a patience which was outwardly constant, while in essence active. When Mecca's conquest is taken into account, for most of his addressees, this period lasted for exactly twenty years. When examined from this perspective, there is no doubt that God's Messenger is the most patient individual that human history has ever witnessed.

To be sure, this is not a matter which the people of our day, who get angry and fly into a rage at the smallest wrong, can readily understand. Such a stance might today be viewed as a lack of identity, meekness, or even a want of character, and a retaliatory or disproportionate response might be viewed as virtue. However, a harsh reaction serves no other purpose than to magnify the problem or to burn bridges with those addressed. In addition, in the hands of people who act in full awareness of their actions, the methodology of the Noble Prophet serves as a strategy that will carry them far ahead in terms of future interests. No doubt these instances where God's Messenger took a step back carried him hundreds of steps forward. The fruit of his actions was that he built bridges with all people and solved every kind of problem by winning over their hearts.

In fact, an individual who aspires to serve all humanity cannot act on impulse and alone. Especially one who seeks to reach everyone in the name of guidance and conveying the message cannot walk the same path as one who talks impulsively, who supposes they are guiding and reaching out to others by hiding behind their self-generated slogans, or who aimlessly wander the streets. The burden of one with an aim is heavy indeed, and they are only able to shoulder such a load by treading the Prophetic path. The Messenger of God aimed to win over the hearts of all those he addressed, sought to change to the path of Paradise the course of all those being dragged in droves into the Fire, and wanted to remove all the obstacles to their salvation. For severing communication is the greatest obstacle in conveying the matter to the addressee, and conflict, violence, and war constitute the biggest cause of such severance. You cannot convey anything to a person with whom you are in conflict. Especially if you have hurt them or if they have lost their loved ones in the conflict, then you have burnt all the bridges and condemned your addressee to the blindness of emotion. Such situations trigger defensive emotions and suppress reason and judgment, and those who act upon strong emotions such as fear or hate have next to no chance of making the right decision. So, by stepping back despite all the difficulty he faced, God's Messenger constantly sought to appeal to their mind and reason and aimed to prevent their falling prey to their emotion and feeling.

On a more practical level, let us now examine a relevant scene from the Meccan period. The Abu Jahls of the day spotted God's Messenger performing his Prayer at the Ka'ba and went into action; they wanted to carry out yet another operation in the name of their denial and thus intimidate all those around him.[39] Seeking a partner in crime, Abu Jahl asked, "Is there not a stouthearted youth among you to bring the entrails of a camel sacrificed by So-and-so last night and throw them over Muhammad as he prostrates in prayer?" Making eye contact with 'Uqba ibn Abi Mu'ayt, Abu Jahl motioned for 'Uqba, the agent of brigandage, to take him up on the challenge. The latter then went to the specified address and returned soon after with the camel entrails that he carried with the help of his men. He threw the entrails, along with all their filth, onto God's Messenger. This was the treatment they deemed suitable for God's most beloved, when he was closest to Him, and at God's House. They then stood on one side shrieking with laughter. They supposed they had done a good job and were now savoring the moment.

Were we to perceive this as a simple historical incident, we would not be able to fully appreciate the worth of the Prophetic stance. Let us, therefore, try to empathize and take a closer look at the issue. Suppose that we are observing the Daily Prayer in the courtyard of the famous Blue Mosque in Istanbul. Somebody comes and does a similar thing to us in front of everyone's eyes. The people then gather around us in hysterical laughter. What would we do?

Look at what the Messenger of God did: he continued his worship. Meanwhile, his household was informed of the situation and one of his daughters[40] rushed to the Ka'ba. Seeing her father in such a state grieved her greatly, and she invoked God's wrath upon the perpetrators. God's Messenger comforted her. He turned to her and said, "Grieve not, dear daughter, for God will not forsake your father."[41] Subjected to this tribulation, God's Messenger was consoling his daughter who felt great sorrow at what had befallen him.

How much time elapsed from the moment the entrails were thrown on top of him to his getting up and leaving? Eyewitnesses to the event did not possess today's means of communication to call his residence and inform his household of what had happened. It was clear that one of those present thought of going there and letting his family know. The family members rushed to the Ka'ba upon hearing the news. When the distance between the Ka'ba and the house and the time needed for a person to get ready and leave the house is taken into account, this means that a period of at least ten minutes elapsed. Now let us once again put ourselves in his place and ask, which one of us would do what he did?

God's Messenger was still there. He neither threatened those around him, nor hurled threats such as, "I may not be able to do anything today, but I'll show you tomorrow." He did not gnash his teeth, cast vengeful glances and look hostilely at them. Instead, he turned to his Lord and contented himself with referring them to Him. "My Lord," he said. "I leave the Quraysh to You! My Lord! I leave Abu Jahl ibn Hisham, 'Utba ibn Rabi'a, Shayba ibn Rabi'a, Walid ibn 'Uqba,[42] Umayya ibn Khalaf, and 'Uqba ibn Abi Mu'ayt to You. Surely only You can devastate them."[43] He then rose and made his way home.[44]

Endurance

The Messenger of God made no concessions in his manner even during his most trying and sorrowful times, and approached his addressees, who did not hesitate to cause him the greatest pain, with mercy even when he shed the most tears. At the city of Ta'if, to which he went in hope, he faced the violence of their mobs and was pelted with stones for close to three kilometers. Zayd ibn Harith, who accompanied him, was drenched in blood. He was perhaps experiencing one of the most grueling days of his life.[45]

In spite of this, the Messenger of God took shelter beneath a tree and began offering the much loved Prayer that he had referred to as, "the light of my eye." Clearly, there is a need to turn wholeheartedly to the True Possessor of strength and power at such times. That is to say, fine-tuning one's bearing in this way is a prerequisite for freeing oneself from human weaknesses and being imbued with a celestial hue. Perhaps all these events were a message to his community, to prevent their acting in anger and haste. Following the two units of Prayer that he offered, he raised his hands high and broke out in supplication and entreaty. Zayd was stricken with awe before the circumspection and patience that he saw in God's Messenger and listened carefully to what he was saying:

"To You, my Lord, I complain of my weakness, my want of resources and the humiliation I am made to receive,

O Most Merciful of the Merciful!

You are the Lord of the weak and the powerless,

And you are my Lord.

To whom do You leave me?

To a distant stranger who receives me with hostility? Or to an enemy You have given power over me?"

Thus, voicing his state to the Divine Court, God's Messenger collected himself right at this point; it was as though he felt he had said something that he should not have said, and it was almost as if he himself was troubled by these words that he uttered. He then raised his hands even higher towards the heavens and continued his supplication:

"As long as You are not displeased with me, I care not what I face. Your favor is all that matters to me.

I seek refuge in the light of Your face, by which all darkness is illuminated and the affairs of both this world and the next are set right, lest I incur Your wrath or become the subject of Your anger.

To You I submit, until You are well pleased.

There is no power and no might save in You."[46]

The Messenger of God had not even finished his supplication when truthful Gabriel suddenly appeared by his side accompanied by the angel of the mountains. It was clear that the entreaty of the grieved Messenger had shaken the highest heavens and God had sent the two angels to his aid. "O Muhammad," he said, "indeed God has full knowledge of what your people said to you and what they did after turning away from you. And He has sent to you the angel in charge of the mountains that he may do to them whatever you please." The appointed angel greeted God's Messenger and added, "Should you so wish, O Muhammad, I will crush them between these two great mountains."

The world was witnessing a mercy and compassion with no precedent, since the very beginning of its existence. This was the extraordinary singularity of the Prophet of Mercy. His choice was unquestionably to mean a great deal for those to come after him. He turned to the angel and said, "No!" And his justification for such a decision was also remarkable: "Rather, I hope that God raise from their offspring servants who worship none but Him and who do not ascribe to Him any partners."[47]

This was the distinction of an absolutely lucid disposition and a willpower subordinating its every step to the ideal of letting live. Unable to conceal his astonishment before such profoundness, the appointed angel exclaimed, "How benevolent and compassionate you truly are, just as your Lord has described you."[48] Surely, in so doing, he sought to call to mind the Qur'anic verse (which means), *"There has come to you (O people) a Messenger from among yourselves; extremely grievous to him is your suffering, full of concern for you is he, and for the believers full of pity and compassion"* (At-Tawbah 9:128). Thus did he draw attention to the two attributes with which God invested and honored him, and demonstrated precisely what a paragon he was of mercy and compassion.

We see a continuation of this same Prophetic attitude at Uhud, where his blessed teeth were broken, two metal pieces pierced his temples, he lost a further two teeth to remove these metal pieces,[49] seventy of his Companions were slaughtered, and a smell of blood came from every direction. On that day, as he wiped the blood which dripped down his face onto his beard, he said, "How can such a people attain salvation who color the face of their Messenger with blood and break his tooth, while he only calls them to God?" Indeed, on that day Uhud was witness to heart-wrenching scenes. To be sure, this was a scene unbearable for the Companions: blood trickled down the face of the very Messenger for the sake of whose cause they had devoted their lives. There were those who approached him wanting to share his sorrow and those who wanted him to entreat God and curse those who put him through such grief, saying, "Raise your hands and invoke God's wrath upon them, O Messenger of God!" But God's Messenger, the Prophet of mercy and compassion, did not yield to their request even under these circumstances. While wiping from his face the blood which flowed towards his beard, he turned to them and said, "I was sent not to curse the people, but to call them to mercy."

Meanwhile, Archangel Gabriel came to his aid once again, just as at every other important juncture, and brought with him another new message. God informed His Messenger that this was not an affair at the disposal of mortals by declaring, "*(O Messenger, you are a servant charged with a certain duty, therefore) it is not a matter for you whether He turns towards them in mercy (to accept their repentance for their unbelief, and grants them faith) or punishes them because they are wrongdoers*" (Al Imran 3:128), and thus affirmed the truth of His Messenger's stance. At the same time, this meant that those who on that day broke his teeth and wounded him, perpetrating a savagery which made even beasts look innocent, would one day change and be transformed, and gave the glad tidings of their leaving their feelings to one side, returning to the course of sound judgment and reason, and thus repenting.[50] This was what God's Messenger sought in the first place, and he immediately raised his hands and began beseeching God exclaiming, "My Lord!" He had all but forgotten his own pain, at the thought of the anguish and agony that awaited such ingrates at the unspeakable end of the Fire. He lowered his head and said, "Forgive my people, for they do not know!"[51]

We see yet another example of the Prophetic bearing again at Uhud, at his seeing the grievous situation of his uncle, Hamza. Having lost sight of Hamza, the foremost man sought on the battlefield, God's Messenger asked 'Ali to find his uncle who was also his milk brother. 'Ali found him in a place known as Batn al-Wadi and came straight to God's Messenger to let him know. God's Messenger hastened to him. It was a heart-wrenching scene indeed that met him, for Hamza's belly had been gashed open, his liver plucked out, his nose and ears cut off, and his body mutilated. Moreover, this was not something perpetrated against Hamza alone; sixty-nine of the seventy Companions killed on that day shared Hamza's fate.[52] Sixteen women coming onto the battlefield from behind the Meccan army, which had launched an onslaught against Uhud like savage wolves, swooped down on the slain like ravenous beasts and mutilated the bodies of the Uhud martyrs with knives and daggers. They even went as far as to string the ears, noses and limbs of the dead to hang them around their necks as necklaces. Hind, Abu Sufyan's wife, wore Hamza's limbs around her neck. Upon receiving the news that the black slave Wahshi, who had long been seeking an opportunity for his emancipation, had killed him, Hind gave him the necklace she was wearing as a reward. She then followed him, did what she did, and strung Hamza's limbs on a cord to hang them around her neck instead.

Such brutality was there at Uhud on that day that even commander of the day, Abu Sufyan, could not defend or take responsibility for it. Prior to leaving the battlefield, he called out to God's Messenger, "O Muhammad, today you will find among your dead some who have been mutilated. I neither ordered nor approved of this."[53]

The Messenger of God, however, was grief-stricken and in tears. This was perhaps the time that God's Messenger wept the most. He had long forgotten his broken tooth, and could no longer feel the pain in his temples. Before such a blood-curdling scene, he was at first about to say, "And seventy of your men..."[54] However, this was not in line with the Divine will. God enjoined the Prophet of Mercy to act with the utmost compassion and mercy. For at Uhud, Gabriel appeared once again and revealed, "*If you have to respond to any wrong, respond (only) to the measure of the wrong done to you; but if you endure patiently, it is indeed better for the patient.*"[55]

God's Messenger looked for something with which he could cover Hamza's body. A Companion from the Medinan natives came forward, removed the garment he was wearing and draped it over Hamza, but this was not enough to cover his whole body. Thereupon, a second garment was brought and, in this way, arguably one of the most brutal sights in human history was covered up.

Meanwhile, when God's Messenger saw that his paternal aunt Safiyya bint 'Abd al-Muttalib had arrived, he called out for those present to take care of her lest she see her brother Hamza in that state. Even though her son Zubayr stood in front of her as a result, and wished to prevent her from seeing his uncle, Safiyya pushed her son aside and said, "Be off! For I am not here to see you right now!"

Continuing to call out from behind her, Zubayr said, "Mother! The Messenger of God orders you to go back!" Upon hearing these words, she inquired as to the reason for this and then added, "I have heard that my brother was mutilated.[56] Though I cannot bear the thought of what has happened, I shall be resigned to it and will endure it with patience."

When Zubayr related his irrepressible mother's state to God's Messenger, the latter turned to Zubayr and said, "Leave her." In immediate consequence, Safiyya, a pillar of fortitude, came to her brother Hamza's side and entreated God for him at length. She repeated the words, "Surely we belong to God (as His creatures and servants), and surely to Him we are bound to return,"[57] and asked God for his forgiveness.

Among the Companions witnessing this scene were those like Abu Qatada who could not contain themselves and invoked God's punishment upon the Quraysh for what they had done. Despite the intensity of his own emotions and despite his arguably weeping more than he had at any other time in his life, the Prophet of Mercy turned to Abu Qatada and said affectionately:

"O Abu Qatada, surely the Quraysh are a people of trust. Whoever exceeds the limit in relation to them, God will deal with them. The time may come, provided God grants you a long life, when you will make light of your deeds in consideration of their deeds and servanthood, and when you will rue your not having done more."[58]

The meaning of this was clear: God's Messenger, an embodiment of Divine mercy, viewed all those he encountered as his potential Companions, even in the most difficult situations, and he thus precluded any step that would deprive them of that outcome. Moreover, the message that Gabriel brought when he came to their succor, echoed the same course of action, confirming the righteousness of the Prophet's stance:

It was by a mercy from God that (at the time of the setback), you (O Messenger) were lenient with them (your Companions). Had you been harsh and hard-hearted, they would surely have scattered away from about you. (Al Imran 3:159)

There is no doubt that this stance of the Messenger of God was not one specific to that particular time. Even when he obtained the opportunity years later to punish those responsible for the atrocity at Uhud, he did not allow anyone to touch them, and opposed those who said on the day of Mecca's conquest, "Consider the Quraysh finished from this day forth!"[59] For the message that Gabriel brought was unmistakable: "*If you have to respond to any wrong, respond (only) to the measure of the wrong done to you; but if you endure patiently, it is indeed better for the patient"* (An-Nahl 16:126).[60] As a matter of course, this injunction is for all believers.

War and the Prophetic stance

This was the true reason underlying the Prophet's aversion to conflict, his not becoming a party to violence, and his walking away from any arena of fighting: there was no room for war in his world. Why, then, did battles occur? What were their underlying causes and what kind of course was taken from the moment they became imminent? What was the Prophet's strategy when fighting became inevitable and what was his attitude during battle? Which steps were taken in the aftermath, aimed at healing the deepening wounds, and with what outcome? Unless we find answers to these questions and resolve the matter on realistic grounds, there is no way of grasping the actual dimensions of the subject. Let us now try to comprehend these elements.

Causes of violence and perception of war

It is most regrettable that up to our day the life of God's Messenger has been repeatedly related with the main focus on its military dimension. This has given rise to the perception of him as an individual constantly at war and at odds with everybody. This misconception is no doubt grounded in the heroic or warrior culture (*ayyam al-'Arab*) which was prevalent in pre-Islamic Arabia. "Heroism," one of the fundamental values of the day, was one of the key causes of the customary conflict, constituted a means for superiority that the victors exaggerated and glorified in their stories, and was a central subject of their poetry and rhetoric. They would measure their time according to battles and victories and would draw attention to them as the bedrock of their superiority. They went to such lengths in this that when they could not find an example of heroism from their own day to relate, they would refer to their forebears and pride themselves on the exploits of the long dead, pointing to their graves as proof of their own distinction.[61]

Thus, the very first people addressed by Islam were raised in such a culture. When a period of battle starting with Badr inevitably began fifteen years later, the heroic deeds exhibited in the battles became a focal point of later scholars and the singularity of God's Messenger could not be adequately recognized. Naturally, the situation was considered from the perspective of enmity, the reason for the battles in the first place, as well as the hostility felt towards those who knew no limits in oppression and tyranny, and so the Prophetic compassion was overshadowed by the anger felt towards the Abu Jahls of the day. On the other hand, each of the Prophet's Companions performed heroic deeds the likes of which had never been seen before. In short, there was a plethora of such heroic deeds, and triumph at the end too. Thus, those looking at Badr from the perspective of this victory and the heroic qualities seen, preferred to express these singularities which moved them to tears, in lieu of taking a more holistic view of the matter in their descriptions. The most salient demonstration of this is the fact that the vast majority of the early works relating the life of God's Messenger contain separate books entitled "*maghazi*" (military expeditions).[62]

The prevalent attitude in later periods was no different. Continuing through the centuries, this attitude is current in current media and film production, with action and tension sought-after elements for watchability, so a similar perception regrettably forms in the minds of today's generations. Of course, the role of radicalism, examples of which are regrettably observed from time to time, must not be forgotten in the rise of this perception.

The duration of the battles

In stark contrast to God's Messenger's long Prophethood of close to 8,000 days[63] the military campaigns where he was forced to engage in active conflict, such as Badr, Uhud, and Hunayn, did not carry over to a second day. It is evident that these major battles occupied only half a day or less.

Badr was a battle that ended just as quickly as it had begun. A consideration of its beginning, the number of men on both sides, its phases, and outcome reveal that it did not take longer than a total of three hours. Battle loomed on the second day of the month of Ramadan[64] and transpired on the Friday[65] corresponding with the seventeenth day of Ramadan. Three days were spent in Badr after the battle, followed by a return to the city of Medina. It can be said that from the moment it became a subject of discussion up until the return to Medina, and including the process of resolution concerning the prisoners of war, a maximum of twenty days passed.

Uhud was no different; while the battle began in a similar way to that of Badr, on the basis of the descriptions from those who witnessed it firsthand, and taking into account the vicissitudes experienced on the day, it was a battle that did not exceed five hours. At Uhud, which began when the sun rose above the horizon, God's Messenger offered the Noon Prayer where he was receiving treatment for his wounds, despite the events that unfolded. Following the departure of the Meccan forces, he laid seventy martyrs to rest, returned to Medina, and led the Evening Prayer in the Prophet's Mosque. In view of the fact that seventy of the seven hundred Companions accompanying God's Messenger were martyred and twice this number critically injured, and considering as well the effort exerted to obtain the necessary tools for digging and the carrying out of the burial procedures, the total duration of the battle can be more clearly seen. Also, the sources expressly state that it took place on the morning of that day.[66]

While separate confrontations took place at what was known as the trench, or *khandaq*, there was no battle *per se*;[67] The Confederate (Ahzab) forces[68] arrived and, after waiting for approximately twenty days,[69] were forced to return empty-handed. The Second Badr,[70] which was an open invitation by the Meccans after Uhud, was a course upon which God's Messenger initially embarked with the purpose of battle, but from which they returned without skirmish, as the Meccan forces failed to turn up.

Instances of direct conflict apart from this include Hunayn. Consideration of its events and battle site reveals that it ended within a matter of hours. Personally, I am of the view that, like Badr, it did not exceed three hours. When the initial ambush and pursuit of the enemy is also taken into account, it is estimated that this period was no more than four hours.

Ta'if, which was in a sense a continuation of Hunayn, remained a siege, and despite the objections of the Companions, God's Messenger withdrew, aborting the siege just at the point it could have allowed for a favorable outcome. His withdrawal, however, paved the way to winning over the entire Ta'if population, and when weapons were sheathed, hearts freely and voluntarily opened to Islam.

As concerns Tabuk, to which God's Messenger set off having thoroughly completed his battle preparations, this too ended without confrontation due to the retreat of the Byzantine Romans. Tabuk thus stands as a significant milestone where the Muslims returned with treaties that were the fruits of peace.

The mobilizations against Banu Qaynuqa, Banu Nadir, Banu Quray-za, and the Khaybar siege were not battles, but could each be considered counter-terrorist operations against insurrection attempts. As is the case today, every form of governance maintains a firm stance against such activities and clamps down on terrorist groups, for there was a legitimate leadership recognized by each of these tribes. But later these tribes engaged in armed insurrection against the same leadership which had been formed with their complete contractual agreement. Thus, it was incumbent upon the Prophet as the elected leader of the Medinan community to quell these acts of open revolt against civil authority. In any event, no armed uprising against a state in our day is called "warfare" or "battle," but is always referred to as "terrorism." Moreover, when the causes for these conflicts are examined in detail, they were conducted against either an uprising, revolt, or due to violation of a treaty, assassination, conspiracy, armed insurgence, collaboration with foreign powers against their own administration. Such activities also included banding together with various powers for the formation of armed networks. And these were happening while these tribes were parties to the alliance they had formed with God's Messenger after the Migration. They turned in rebellion and armed attack against the leadership they were party to and that they themselves had established. On top of that, they turned a deaf ear to the envoys and messages sent by the Prophet to settle the agitation, cooperated treasonably with forces that were open enemies, and instigated all-out assault. It is also important to note that these uprisings did not take place all at the same time. They remained local, were not transformed into a war of religion, and never involved an entire mass of people being targeted.

Furthermore, the position of the other Jewish groups who remained loyal to the treaty during this process is also different. They did not respond favorably to their belligerent coreligionists and kinfolk who sought help from them, and viewed the matter as being their own issue. Rebellions were unsettling seventy percent of the city, including most of the other Jewish tribes, thus the Medinan leaders exercised their most natural right of self-defense. The situation was resolved by means of the sieges in as short time as possible, not allowing it to become a permanent problem for Medina.

A closer look at the general strategy used during the sieges reveals that remarkable care was taken to avoid bloodshed. The clearest demonstration of this is the fact that not a single woman or child was killed, despite a complete siege of the citadels in which they sought refuge. This was the main reason for the extended duration of the sieges in the first place: their surrender without the use of arms was the aim, and the matter was resolved with minimal losses. For instance, in the siege of the Banu Qaynuqa, who had instigated the insurrection attempts, no was one killed other than one of the Prophet's Companions who was martyred at the outset and the Jew that this Companion killed in that fight. Other sieges were no different; despite the fact that the Banu Nadir had attempted to kill the Messenger of God, their surrender was achieved almost entirely without use of the sword, while in the siege of Banu Qurayza, only two Companions were martyred.[71] One of these was Khallad ibn Suwayd ibn Tha'laba, who was killed when a millstone was thrown on him from one of the citadels as he rested in the shade of a tree. At Khaybar, however, where more intense encounters took place and which took close to one month, despite direct fighting and face-to-face combat, only fifteen Companions were martyred,[72] and ninety-three Jews were killed.[73]

At the ends of the sieges, the demands of the tribes were taken into consideration despite their defeat, they were not treated as captives, all their wealth and possessions were not seized, and they were addressed directly once more, with new agreements being made with them. What is more, the Banu Qaynuqa and Banu Nadir tribes in particular, who had instigated the insurrection, were permitted to migrate elsewhere, with as many possessions as they could carry with them.[74]

The Banu Khaybar, whose hatred and animosity had built up and intensified over four years and who had begun preparations for an attack against Medina by joining forces with other tribes such as the Banu Ghatafan, were treated differently despite their capture. Although they had been defeated, this was overlooked and a new agreement was made with them. In return for fulfilling their financial obligations, they could remain and cultivate their lands. What is interesting here is that this agreement, which no other victorious military commander of the day would ever have agreed to, was repeated with the Jews of Tayma', Fadak, and Wadi al-Qura. So from that day forth Medina left nearly four years of tension behind, and people began a natural and unaffected life of coexistence, with their respective Muslim and Jewish identities. So much so that on the day of God's Messenger's demise, his armor was in the possession of a Jewish merchant by the name of Abu al-Shahm as security for the measure of barley he had purchased on credit from him, so that he could serve his guests with it.[75]

An examination of these sieges in the historical records indicates that Banu Qaynuqa fell after fifteen days, Banu Nadir after six,[76] Banu Qurayza after fifteen, and the siege of Khaybar took less than a month, despite their fortified citadels, the gates of which they reinforced many times over.

The other campaigns discussed to date in almost every book under the heading "Ghazwa" (expeditions attended by the Noble Prophet), such as Abwa' (Waddan), Buwat, Dhu al-'Ashira ('Ushayra), Sawiq, Hamra' al-Asad, Banu Sulaym (Kudr), Buhran, Dhat al-Riqa', Dumat al-Jandal, Banu Lihyan, Ghatafan (Dhu Amarr), and Dhu Qarad (Ghaba), were not battles in the sense we understand them today, but constituted border reconnaissance and security operations of the newly founded State of Medina, and were conducted in order to secure and maintain the peace and public order. In any case, none of these involved a military campaign with heated combat as these expeditions essentially served to deter the imminent insurrection of mobs; this way, the beginning of an era where such actions would not go unpunished was declared. As a result, peace and harmony was established in a region where chaos had reigned for the past 120 years; this development on its own was nothing short of miraculous, one which nobody prior to that day could even have imagined. Moreover, this was not the sole aim of these expeditions; agreements were made with tribes en route, and the peace did not remain confined to the borders of Medina, but spread to a wider region. We do not know with whom exactly God's Messenger made contact, which leaders he met, and the precise steps he took in order to build a peaceful future. With respect to Medina, however, when we examine the results obtained from these operations over a decade, it is certain that he must have taken quite significant steps not recorded in history and of which we remain unaware.

To refer to Hudaybiya and the minor pilgrimage performed later in lieu of that which the Meccans prevented ('Umra al-Qada') as military campaigns or "battles" would be a grave injustice indeed, for all the Companions were in the ritual state of *ihram* and were unarmed. What is more, they had with them the sacrificial animals that they had so marked. Such was the blamelessness of the sight in question that it brought even the representatives of the enemy to reason. God's Messenger repeatedly reminded the envoys he sent to the Meccans as well as the spokesmen coming from Mecca of the same notion—that they were unarmed and came in a state of consecration with their sacrificial animals—and reiterated that their purpose was not war but purely worship. In fact, no form of conflict was experienced at Hudaybiya, nor during the minor pilgrimage made up the following year, despite all the tension and provocation, and they returned peacefully to Medina after fulfillment of all the intended acts of worship.

As for the conquest of Mecca, this was an encounter that was realized with great care to avoid bloodshed. In outcome, it was by no means a "battle," but resembled a happy season of reunion between relatives that had been separated for years on end. Even though twelve thousand people entered the city with its population of around ten thousand, vigilance, warning, and careful follow-up ensured that there was no resistance, other than the brisk encounter at Khandama through which Khalid ibn al-Walid entered the city. The Messenger of God advanced all the way to the Ka'ba in less than an hour. The general attitude of the Meccan populace at the time, the displays of endearment of the Meccan women and children, and the quiet withdrawal of the city's inhabitants to their homes, all demonstrate that there was nothing warlike in the encounter in the city. In other words, as a result of the Prophetic approach, the individuals of Mecca had long been conquered in spite of all the separating distance and adversity of conditions. The Prophet came to put a name to the conquest that had already been realized, and having done so, he set off back to Medina. Furthermore, the Messenger of God confirmed this in his manner and bearing. Signaling from the outset that he would not remain in Mecca but return to Medina, he shortened all his prayers, offering them two at a time, according to the requirements for a traveler. This was the greatest indication that he would stay in his hometown, Mecca—the city which contained the treasured Ka'ba—for a very short time (fifteen days at the most for a traveler).

The same applies to the expeditions (*sariyya*), in which God's Messenger himself did not take part but sent his Companions, as to the campaigns (*ghazwa*) in which he himself was present. At a time when brute force was virtually the only determining factor, when there was no authority to respond to the call of the weak, and when rules were established only by those who possessed power, these expeditions served as law enforcement mechanisms aimed at showing that old habits of authority were no longer tenable, and that offenders would most certainly be punished. As with the campaigns, the key function of the expeditions was to widen the circle of security by making agreements with the tribes they encountered.

These are, of course, the most striking reasons for the campaigns and expeditions. In fact, all the social ties destroyed with respect to Badr were rebuilt in as little as six years, and a people who were bound by no rule in their hostility were transformed into heroes of love. When this enormous transformation is taken into account, it becomes clear that these expeditions and campaigns had a great many other aims with respect to guidance and conveying the message. If we look at that period considering the fact that in our day particularly brothers are against brothers and taking into account the security gaps in the regions deprived of state authority and grappling with war, then it quickly becomes clear just how necessary and appropriate were the existence of such teams at the time. With the total of seven campaigns[77] and the seventy-three reconnaissance operations,[78] thirteen of which were attended by the Prophet himself, God's Messenger gained total command of the region he directly addressed, within as little as ten years. He thus established such an environment of safety and security that in a region where travel had until then been perilous even for the trade caravans having all the security measures, women could now travel unattended. When the people living at the time witnessed the actualization of what God's Messenger had heralded[79] in the early days of Mecca, they could not hide their joy and deemed this too a proof of God's Messenger's Prophethood.[80]

When the Age of Happiness in its entirety is examined in this light, and calculating the time of the military campaigns and expeditions of God's Messenger, Badr and Uhud included, a most striking outcome is revealed: with the exception of Mu'ta which continued through the second day,[81] this period of active conflict, in total, does not occupy a full day. Even when Mu'ta is included, this total time emerges as a maximum of three days. When compared to close to 8,000 days of Prophethood, this fact explicitly demonstrates just how inadequate and erroneous is the approach of confining the life of God's Messenger merely to a discussion of battles, when Islam is an extraordinary civilization whose foundations were laid and edifice constructed in the 7,997 days outside the military expeditions and campaigns. What is more, even in cases where active warfare took place, this was dependent on clearly defined and set rules, and such occasions were periods oriented more towards enabling others to live than to killing, and where a sweeping compassion prevailed.

By way of further elaboration, when we take into account such factors as the preparatory stages which took place from the moment battle was at issue, the time for travel, the exertions to dissuade the enemy from war, the time for commanders to arrange their formations for battle, the battle itself, waiting three days on the battle site in the aftermath, the burying of those killed, the return home, and the finalization of the process concerning war spoils and prisoners of war, it becomes evident that warfare occupied the Prophet's agenda for a total of roughly 79 days. If we are to include the Second Badr and Tabuk where there was no military encounter or fighting, then battle took up a total of 144 days during the entire Age of Happiness. With the activities of the security teams in which God's Messenger did not take part but sent his Companions, and the siege maneuvers directed at subversive terrorist activities, a total of 392 days is obtained; the greater part of this time, however, was spent on the road in journeys that took weeks on end, or in the sieges that were drawn out to prevent the loss of human life.[82]

The total loss of life during this period of ten years, despite this number of operations, sieges and encounters, is also striking: 108 casualties on the Muslim side and 111 dead in enemy ranks. Including the conquest of Mecca, sieges and expeditions on top of this give a total 217 martyrs[83] and 287 people known to have been killed on the opposing side.[84] With the delegation of 79 Companions who were ambushed and treacherously killed, along with those upon whom the penalty of death was imposed for committing certain crimes,[85] this number becomes 296 and 701 respectively. Accordingly, the total loss on both sides is 997.[86]

In no subsequent war in human history has there been so little loss of life, nor any ideology, state or civilization formed with so few casualties. In order to recognize the strategy and precision that God's Messenger exhibited in this field, and the extraordinary civilization that God's Messenger wove with the thread of the ideal to enable others to live, one need only compare this with the grievous scenes appearing before us throughout history wherein not just troops but millions of civilians, above all women and children, have been lost.[87]

The causes of the battles

None of these were God's Messenger's battles. He was not the one who took the first step, and he employed all the rules of diplomacy to stop these conflicts. A closer analysis of the places where the battles took place demonstrates that this was a natural consequence. Uhud and Khandaq today are part of the city of Medina, but in those days Badr was approximately 350 kilometers away from Mecca and 120 kilometers from Medina; the battle came after the inhabitants of Medina got wind of the Meccans' scheme to attack the city and systematically exterminate all its inhabitants, women, children and all. What is more, from the moment the potential for battle became clear, envoys were sent to put a stop to this course that would give rise to unnecessary bloodshed among relatives, and message upon message was sent to Abu Jahl's army requesting them to turn back. This is clear demonstration of the fact that the Meccan army attacked at every possible opportunity. To be more precise, the Messenger of God was never on the side that went on the offensive, but always on the defensive.

Badr was the polytheist Quraysh's plan of mass extermination. Uhud was the assault to avenge their heavy defeat at Badr, while Khandaq was the final onslaught, attempted with the alliance of all the tribes. But all three maneuvers came to naught and Islam could not be eradicated.

The conquest of Mecca came into question with the indiscriminate killing by the Meccans of 23 women, children and the elderly from the Khuda'a tribe, allied to the Muslims. In the wake of these murders, which constituted a clear breach of the Hudaybiya Treaty, God's Messenger sent envoys to the Meccans and presented them with set options. The Meccans rendered the treaty signed two years earlier null and void by continuing to act with pride and arrogance, even going so far as to attempt to kill the envoy and, with the same attitude of defiance, refusing to accept any of the options. The conquest of Mecca, through which God had promised victory, transpired on the basis of this lawlessness.

Hunayn was the result of their chagrin following Mecca's conquest and the thought that their turn would come. In the battle, everything that moved—women, children, camels, cattle, sheep—was incorporated in the army and the Hawazin came to Hunayn and put their all into the attack.

However, the battles in Medina, which began with the Banu Qay-nuqa and ended with Khaybar, were regional uprisings against the state aimed at regaining the old system the tribes had established with their easy money and the influence they had lost, and this could only be possible with the tribes' complete support. Because it was turning into an armed insurrection and they were procuring weapons and becoming set on war, the Medinan State responded in self-defense and quelled these respective uprisings. Among these tribes, the Banu Qurayza is rather different; during the adverse events experienced with the other two tribes God's Messenger sat with the Banu Qurayza once again and renewed the treaties with them.[88] Moreover, until the Prophet's emigration to Medina, the Banu Qurayza was a tribe to which the other Jewish tribes paid no importance and which they did not regard as their equal, and it was God's Messenger who raised their status and brought them onto an equal footing with all others.[89] What is more, even as the trench was being dug, there was no concern whatsoever about them and God's Messenger had confidence in them as he did in his Companions, and he left the trench on the Medinan side despite those sharing their views being on the opposing side. In spite of all these gestures, the Banu Qurayza made contact with the Confederate forces and, what is more, betrayed the Muslim forces from the very beginning of the siege. Throughout the month-long siege, they supplied the Confederate forces with food and weapons, strengthened their hand with the intelligence they provided from the inside, and organized attacks against the defenseless women and children who remained in the city. Consequently, when the siege came to an end and the Confederate forces left, Archangel Gabriel came and, indicating that this flagrant treachery ought not go unpunished, communicated to God's Messenger that he was waiting for God's Messenger and his Companions where the Banu Qurayza lived. God's Messenger, who by this point had taken off his armor and was washing his face, took his Companions with him and went to the quarter of the Banu Qurayza. The Banu Qurayza not only betrayed the agreement they signed with the Prophet for the defense of the very city they were living in, but also refused to accept his arbitration. Instead, they chose Sa'd ibn Mu'adh, the leader of Aws tribe which were allies with the Banu Qurayza, to decide their fate. Sa'd passed a ruling based on the Mosaic Law (as described in Deuteronomy 20: 10-14), which was the capital punishment of the adult males.

The chief evidence that peace was fundamental to all these maneuvers and that there was not even the slightest imbalance in the scales of justice was that as a result of this tension that had continued for at least three and a half years, treaties were signed once again with all the Jewish tribes living in Medina, and that, in burying all the ill-feeling and negativity of the past, a completely new and peaceful existence began and lasted again for about three and a half years until the demise of God's Messenger. It is to be regretted that today, instead of seeing that God's Messenger solved every kind of problem and looking at this last phase of his life, we look at the slice of time in which problems emerged and constantly create problems rather than solutions. What is vital is to focus on the situations where problems were resolved and the particular manner of their resolution and to solve the problems of our day with the same Prophetic methods.

Verification and diplomacy

Another example of Prophetic discretion exhibited from the moment the potential for conflict arose was the way he verified the reports he received; God's Messenger would immediately send one of his Companions or a delegation to the relevant place and ask them to gather intelligence from within, wanting to be certain of the truth of the information he received so as not to leave any room for error. We see this same sensitivity in virtually every problematic arena beginning with Badr. For example, to the Banu Qurayza, who acted treacherously in the course of the Khandaq episode, he dispatched a delegation led by the two leaders of the Aws and Khazraj tribes, Sa'd ibn Mu'adh and Sa'd ibn 'Ubada, and including such Companions as 'Abdu'llah ibn Rawaha and Khawwat ibn Jubayr, advising them the following:

"Now go forth and learn the truth of the news that has come to us from them. If these reports are indeed correct, then do not inform me of this openly upon your return, but in a way that only I can comprehend your meaning. However, should you find the Banu Qurayza loyal to the pact between us (and the rumors to be thus groundless), then you may openly declare your findings."[90]

In so doing, he laid the groundwork for the strategy to be built upon this information. This same discretion was used in all problematic situations.

When it became clear that the reports agreed with the information received earlier, the Prophet's next measure was undoubtedly diplomacy. In this case, he would assign envoys to convey his message to those in authority and to attempt to dissuade them from conflict. From the moment news of Badr had been received, the Messenger of God warned that brother would take up arms against brother and father against son, and strived to talk them out of meeting face to face in deadly conflict. Understanding the Prophet's intentions correctly, Khadija's nephew Hakim ibn Hizam[91] approached 'Utba and said, "O Abu al-Walid, you are an elder of the Quraysh and their lord, and command their obedience. Would you not want to do that for which the people would praise you until the end of time?"

'Utba, who was himself constantly wavering,[92] was stunned by this most unexpected proposal and asked, "What do you mean to say, O Hakim? What is that you speak of?"

"Return with the people (to Mecca)," Hakim said, "and take upon yourself the responsibility of your ally, 'Amr ibn Hadrami." 'Utba was very straightforward and among the most outspoken of the people, and Hakim's suggestion was what needed to happen in any case. Accepting the reasonableness of the suggestion, 'Utba turned to Hakim ibn Hizam and said, "All right, I will do so, but only on the condition that you help me in return. It is true he is my ally. I will surely assume responsibility for his blood money and restore the caravan that was taken, or you can testify against me about that. And you go to Ibn al-Hanzaliyya (meaning Abu Jahl),[93] for I do not fear that anyone else will object to the idea of the people's return."

Making a new move at the field at Badr, 'Utba was about to take a historic step. He turned to those around him and began his address, "O people of the Quraysh," he said, "by God, you will achieve nothing by meeting Muhammad and his Companions in battle. Even if you should fight and defeat him, how will you be able to look one another in the face when you have killed the son of your paternal or maternal uncle or a member of your clan? You had better turn back and not come between Muhammad and the rest of the Arabs. For should they defeat him, this will be in line with your wishes, and if not, no harm will come to you from him for you have not done to him what you would have wished to do. To be sure, I see those among you this very moment who are determined to fight to the death, while it is not possible for you to overcome them. Still, it is not too late, and this propitious decision is yours to make. Now, go back!"

In uttering these words, he assumed that he needed to acknowledge the accusations that would be leveled against him by those he addressed and continued, "My people, if you should so wish, you might bind this affair on my head and blame it on my cowardice; it is no matter. Yet you know full well that I am by no means the most cowardly of you."

When the Messenger of God saw 'Utba from afar calling out to the Quraysh forces from upon his mount and summoning them to turn back, he too turned to his Companions and said, "If there is any good in this host opposing us, it is surely in that rider of the red camel, for should they follow his advice, they would have done what is best."[94]

Meanwhile, Hakim ibn Hizam approached Abu Jahl, who was readying his coat of mail and sharpening his sword. He conveyed to him 'Utba's greetings of peace and related to him the situation. He hoped that Abu Jahl too would give up on this cause and wanted them to return together, safe and sound. But this was not what happened. Flying into a rage at what he heard, Abu Jahl hurled threats and accused those who were backtracking of cowardice and treason. In the firing line was 'Utba, the figure who was weakening morale. "It appears," he said, "that his lungs were filled with fear when he saw Muhammad and his Companions. No, by God, we will not return until God has judged between Muhammad and us. Never mind 'Utba. He is not a man to do such a thing. What really troubles him is the fact that he sees Muhammad and his Companions so few in number that the meat of one slaughtered camel would suffice them, and he speaks thus for fear that harm will come to his son, who is among them."[95]

Abu Jahl found fault with 'Utba's lack of guile and was changing their course back again. But this was not enough for him. Furious, he formulated alternative schemes to steer things in the direction he desired. It did not take long and by exploiting a handful of men willing to sacrifice their lives in his cause, he transformed the atmosphere of Badr, which had just been turning towards peace, into the cold climate of war once more.

Hearing of Abu Jahl's treacherous outburst, upon a course of certain death, 'Utba began to abuse Abu Jahl in return. He swore at him, hurling insults, and retorted, "He will soon find out whose lungs are full of fear, mine or his!"

Even at times when calls for death rose from the Meccan ranks, God's Messenger the peerless representative of complete mercy stretched out to the Meccans a renewed hand of mercy. He sent 'Umar as an envoy, proposing to stop the battle that had not yet begun. In his message, he said, "Lay down your arms and return (to Mecca)! I would have preferred someone other than you to have come and assumed responsibility for this affair, and it is better for you that I assume control of the affair from someone other than you."

The first to respond to the message brought by 'Umar was Hakim ibn Hizam, who stepped forward and made an impassioned appeal to those around him: "He proposes justice, so accept it. For you will not be victorious over him, if you insist on fighting after what he proposes." However, all the strings on that day were in the hands of Abu Jahl. He turned to those around him, as though wanting to frustrate Hakim's plea, and said, "By God, we will not return now that God has given us this opportunity and until we have completely outmaneuvered and cornered them."[96]

As can be seen, the final hand of mercy extended was not accepted either. Such individuals as 'Utba and Hakim ibn Hizam who witnessed this would henceforth servilely await Abu Jahl's commands.

At the same time this was a shining demonstration that everything that could have been done was done, that all local avenues were exhausted, and that there was no further step that could be taken in the name of diplomacy.

Recourse to causes

It is well established that the Messenger of God always had recourse to causes and, therefore, as he had not ruled out the probability of war, he had prepared his Companions for it. In any case, the power that he needed to retain was meant to serve as a deterrent and this was in line with the Qur'anic commandment.[97] The application was also in strict conformity with this injunction. When steps towards preventing war proved fruitless, he resorted to the necessary causes. After this juncture, God's Messenger organized his Companions, ensured that they were battle-ready,[98] gave them the necessary instructions,[99] and did justice where a counteroffensive against an attacking force was called for. But here, too, we see a notable difference: before us stands a Prophet who hurts no one, who conceals his tactics so he can deal with the situation without bloodshed,[100] and who approached with compassion even those who attacked to kill him. Despite all the crises he weathered and his defending himself against those attacking him, there was not a drop of blood on the sword he carried with him.[101] Despite all the fighting and onslaught, he did not shed the blood or take the life of even a single person. Even when he came face to face with death, he did what behooved him and merely intended to subdue an attacker who came to kill him, ensuring that he aimed at a part of his body that would not cause a fatal injury.[102] While self-defense is one of the five fundamental principles that God demands from every Prophet and Messenger,[103] a person who dies in the struggle to protect their life and property is considered a martyr.[104] Thus, in this case, God's Messenger could have killed the person who came to kill him and no one could have said anything in this regard. In addition, defending oneself when faced with such a threat is obligatory, while acting otherwise is tantamount to suicide. But even here the Messenger of God did not think of killing and neither smashed the attacker's head to pieces, nor thrust the spear in his hand into their heart.

We see the first and only example of this at Uhud. Ubayy ibn Khalaf, who was taken prisoner in the aftermath of Badr, vowed to himself on the day that he paid the ransom for his release that he would begin preparations as soon as he returned to Mecca and would kill the Messenger of God. He did as he promised and came to Uhud completely ready for the task. He lay in wait. Just at that moment, the cavalry forces that found the opening they had been waiting for following the mobilization at Archers' Hill attacked from behind and the Companions, who had begun to think that they had gained victory, were caught in crossfire. Meanwhile, God's Messenger had become aware of the situation and warned his Companions saying, "I fear that Ubayy ibn Khalaf will come from behind me, so be sure to tell me if you see him approach." Indeed, shortly thereafter, Ubayy appeared in armor, mounted on his horse, and with a group of men by his side. "Where is Muhammad?" he shouted in open challenge. "If he lives today, then consider me dead!" Although a few people tried to prevent him, they could not. "Leave him,"

God's Messenger said, "Give him way." Ubayy charged God's Messenger, shouting out profanities and insults. God's Messenger took Harith ibn al-Simma's spear from his hand. Those who saw him in that state for the very first time frantically fled in all directions. He then thrust the spear into Ubayy, who was about to strike a fatal blow.

Ubayy fell to the ground with the force of the spear and began rolling about, bellowing, "By God, Muhammad has killed me!" He was an important figure, so those who rushed to his aid could not understand the reason why he was moaning. For there was scarcely a wound, let alone one that could kill him. They asked him why he was making such a fuss when there were those who were more seriously wounded than him and they had not made a sound. "Don't say that," he protested. "By Lat and 'Uzza, had all the people of Dhu al-Majaz been struck with its like, they would all have surely perished. Did he not say when in Mecca, 'I will kill you?'[105] By God, he'd have killed me today even if he had struck me with his spit."

Ubayy did not die that day, nor the following day. But he died a thousand deaths every moment, waiting for death to come, for no matter how much they opposed the Messenger of God, they knew that what he said would most certainly occur as they had never once seen him speak a single word of untruth. Then this too would transpire as predicted, and Ubayy too would die. Ubayy's meeting with the Angel of Death occurred on the return to Mecca. When they had reached the place called Sarif,[106] he was all but spent, and it is there that he died. It is not known whether his death was a result of fear or cerebral hemorrhage.[107]

The first and only such incident in the life of God's Messenger was this incident with Ubayy ibn Khalaf and it was nothing but self defense, a natural reflex response and an obligation required of every living being. However, the singularity here ought not to be overlooked but given more detailed consideration: a Prophet confirmed by Divine revelation was no doubt one who achieved his goal perfectly. The Messenger of God was the leader and sultan of all the Prophets and Messengers. Had he wished to kill Ubayy that day, he could have easily done so. It is important to note that even here, he merely sought to prevent Ubayy from achieving his goal. By aiming his spear at Ubayy's shoulder, God's Messenger stopped his attack with minimum harm to his body.[108] So as Ubayy lost his balance and fell to the ground, God's Messenger had both fulfilled his duty of defending his own person, as well as demonstrating what set him apart, as a Messenger sent out of mercy. Even while protecting his own life, he strived to minimize the harm to the aggressor.

God's Messenger even accorded *aman*, or a pledge of security to those who came to kill him, let alone killing them. For instance, he had turned to his Companions at Badr and said, "I have learned that some men of the Banu Hashim, and others, have been forced to march against us against their will, having no desire to fight us. Whoever of you meets one of the Banu Hashim, let him not kill him." Furthermore, he continued, "If any of you should meet Abu al-Bakhtari ibn Hisham ibn al-Harith ibn Asad, he should not kill him."[109]

There were other names granted protection on that day, such as Hakim ibn Hizam. What is more, God's Messenger did this despite the objections of those around him.[110] The earth was arguably witnessing such a stance for the very first time. Although they were eager and ready to fight courageously against the relentless enemies of Islam, God's Messenger did not allow anyone to lay a finger on them, and took them under the Prophetic protection, even under war conditions. At a point where nothing could be seen for the dust and smoke, Abu al-Bakhtari, who had been granted protection from God's Messenger, nevertheless engaged in a sword fight to protect his friend Junada and was killed by the Companion Mujadhdhar. Mujadhdhar ibn Dhiyad was at a loss as to what to do. In the end, hanging his head, with shame manifest in his every manner, he came to the Prophet. Informing God's Messenger of the situation, he said in a low voice, "O Messenger of God, By Him Who has sent you with the truth, I tried so hard to make him give himself up so that I could bring him to you, but he insisted on fighting, and so I had to fight him."[111]

This was a heightened sensibility exhibited by a sensitive soul raised in the educational climate of the Prophet of Mercy who was sent to enable others to live. The same sensibility was evident on that day in all who were nurtured in the same climate.[112]

War discipline

The Messenger of God established inviolable and clear-cut rules for situations where diplomatic measures were met with violence, where the rule of law was flouted, and where conflict thus became inevitable, and he followed developments closely and meticulously in order to implement these rules in the smallest detail. We can clearly say that just as the rules that he put in place in his time were a first, humanity has yet to arrive at these principles, which were not merely declared at that time, but which also found their vivid expression in practice.

The rules for warfare that God's Messenger established are as follows:

"Go forth in the Name of God and against those who deny God and rebel against Him, but do not wrong anyone. Do not break your pledge and do not oppress. Do not kill women and children, and do not kill those who are devoted in their places of worship. Do not cut down trees or destroy date orchards. Do not destroy any buildings."[113]

However, he did not merely express these in words but, as indicated by Anas, reminded the people of them as the indispensable rules and conduct for war and reiterated them. Anas[114] relates that whenever God's Messenger dispatched a detachment to a certain place, he instructed them as follows:

"Go forth in the Name of God, trusting in Him and upon the religion of His Messenger. Never kill the old verging on death, young infants, children, or women. Do not transgress the bounds. Gather all that falls to your lot on the battlefield, be the representatives of peace and always do good, for God loves those who do good to others."[115]

Similarly, another relevant narration reads:

"Set forth in the Name of God, against those who deny Him, in the path of God, but do not wrong or oppress others and do not mutilate the dead. Do not exceed the bounds and do not kill children or those occupied in their cloisters."[116]

The meaning of these Prophetic directives is clear: you are only permitted to fight against those engaged in active combat and, beyond this, are not allowed to harm civilians, whoever they may be. You cannot even harm vegetation or trees, let alone civilians.

Let us ask ourselves at this point in which war of our era can such sensitivity be seen? We witness with bitterness the men and women, children, and the elderly—civilians in general—killed in wars in different parts of the world, victims who are the subject of news reports almost every day. If we take pride in the point we have reached in civilization, it is impossible to justify our innovations in the bloodcurdling field of weapons of mass destruction, our investments in guided missiles for killing people, and our setting aside budgets hundreds of times larger for weapons manufacture than for support and development of human beings. Who knows just how many more weapons, from the chemical to the biological, continue to be produced not merely for deterrance or defense, but to show what can be done with them through the pharaoh-like dictatorships, tyrannical oppressions and Nimrod-like stratagems that rear their ugly heads from time to time. Even a cursory glance at the regions through which the cold face of war has passed is enough to reveal the cries and lamentations of women and children, the ceaseless tears of the elderly, and the complete decimation of the places of worship that have been targeted despite their being humanity's most powerful call to peace. Furthermore, the impact of the destruction in our day does not remain confined to those affected now, but threatens future generations like a virulent disease inherited down the ages.

Let us now look at the Prophetic sensitivity anew: the rules that the Messenger of God established, which we still cannot fulfil even today, were not merely set out in theory, but were actually put in practice, and by adamantly responding to any who violated them, God's Messenger kept a close check until all these rules became second nature and ingrained in every believer.

There are many examples from that period. Once, violating the terms of the Hudaybiya treaty, the Meccans attacked the Khuda'a tribe, who were allied with God's Messenger, and killed 23 people in one night—women, children and the elderly, without discrimination. The tribe then came to Medina to inform the Messenger of the unjust treatment they had suffered, upon which an envoy was sent to Mecca and the Meccans presented with a clear range of options. But paying no mind to any of these, the Meccans instead attempted to kill the Prophet's envoy, and their reckless attitude continued without ceasing. God too had made a promise, and God's Messenger moved forward towards the conquest of Mecca with his Companions. On the other hand, when the Meccans proved almost completely unresponsive to God's Messenger, who had made use of all available means to reach out to the Meccans, even generating new reasons to make contact each time, God's Messenger as good as told them that he would go to them instead. Rising anew on the Meccan horizon, he wanted to extend to them a helping hand. So meticulous was he in this that no one could mistake that his sole aim was to realize the complete conquest of Mecca without even the slightest harm coming to anyone.

Meanwhile, the Khuda'a tribe, the Messenger's own allies, had begun clashing with the Hudhayl, paying no heed to all the warnings given, and had shed blood. As soon as God's Messenger was informed of this, he turned his back to the Ka'ba so as to face the people and, after praising God, rebuked them saying, "O people of the Khuda'a, stay your hands from killing. By God, this is too much!" He then uttered the following momentous words: "I will surely pay the blood money for the man that you have killed. How prone this Khirash is to killing![117] Were I to kill a believer in return for a disbeliever, I would surely have killed Khirash on this day." He then turned to the people and said the following:

"O people, God made Mecca a sanctuary when He created the heavens and the earth, and the day He created the sun and moon and put down these two mountains. It will remain a sanctuary by virtue of the sanctity God has bestowed upon it until the Day of Resurrection. It is not lawful for anyone who believes in God and the Last Day to shed blood therein, nor to cut down trees, nor uproot its grass or vegetation. It was not made lawful to anyone before me. Nor will it be made lawful to anyone after me, and it was not made lawful for me except for a short period of time. It has now regained its former sacredness. Let those who are present convey my words to those who could not be here today. Should anyone say, 'The Messenger of God also fought in the sanctuary,' say, 'God permitted His Messenger to do so for a given period, but He does not permit you.'

"O people, those most inclined to flouting the Divine Law are those who kill another in the Sanctuary, those who intend to kill any person other than the killer, and those who seek to shed blood unjustly, motivated by feelings of revenge that remain from the Age of Ignorance.

"Whoever kills from this time forth, his people have a choice: if they so wish, they can have the blood of the killer or the blood money, should they want this instead."

Through this sermon, the Messenger of God made clear his unwavering stance towards the rights of human beings and announced that from this point on, for the welfare of society, he would take even sterner action against those who broke the law.[118]

Another example is from the conquest of Mecca. During the entry into Mecca by four different routes, God's Messenger heard commotion coming from Khalid ibn al-Walid's point of entry and, upon closer observation from a place called Adhakhir, saw the glimmer of swords and people fleeing in all directions. Indicating this scene, he asked those next to him, "What is this glimmer?" and added, "Did I not forbid you from fighting?"

"O Messenger of God," they said, "Khalid ibn al-Walid was attacked and had he not been attacked, he would not have fought. O Messenger of God, he neither meant to disobey nor oppose you, but merely fought those who mounted resistance against him."

This was the way they related the truth of the event and vindicated the actions of their friends who had been forced to defend themselves. However, when God's Messenger was informed that some people were killed during the tumult, he was deeply angered at what Khalid ibn al-Walid[119] had done, raised his hands in entreaty, and thrice exclaimed, "My Lord, I am innocent of what Khalid has done!"[120]

The Prophet maintained this discipline. We see the same on the day of Hunayn in the clash with Malik ibn 'Awf, the commander errant who was troubled by the conquest of Mecca and feared that what was then a threat might be an even greater danger in future; he threw his all into the resistance, sent everything and everyone to the front—livestock, women, and children included. When the Prophet's eye was caught by his Companions with drawn swords in front of the women and children who were forced to the front, he called out to those next to him, "What is the matter with people that they go killing even the children?" He then added, "Children should never be killed!"

It is important to note at this point that these women and children were not civilians residing in their homes, but had traveled approximately seventy kilometers, coming all the way to Hunayn with the troops, and in active combat on the front line with arrows, spears and swords in their hands.

Presumably unable to fully grasp the profundity of this message, Usayd ibn Hudayr, who was with God's Messenger, asked, "O Messenger of God, are they not the children of polytheists?"

Outwardly, there was nothing out of the ordinary in the killing in the culture of the time and what generally occurred on battlefields. There was, therefore, no obvious mistake. However, there was an entirely different meaning in the Prophet's stance, and this meaning needed to be brought to light. This question had to be asked so that everyone until the end of time could become acquainted with this truth and establish it as a key principle in their lives.

The valley of Hunayn witnessed the Prophet's indignation: the veins on God's Messenger's neck became swollen (in anger), and he said, "Are not the best of you the children of polytheists?"

Usayd ibn Hudayr and all those with him were stupefied; these words cut them to the quick. Indeed, none of their parents had believed until very recently. Moreover, on that day, the valley of Hunayn received hundreds of Companions whose fathers died while still polytheists. And had not the message brought by Archangel Gabriel[121] communicated the same thing? The Messenger of God had once again spoken in all honesty and frankness, but he did not stop there: "There is none born but is created with their true nature and they remain thus until they begin to express themselves with their tongue." God's Messenger emphasized that it is the parents who typically make them follow the religion of their forefathers.[122]

In saying this, God's Messenger reminded them that what mattered most was that they be busy with the ideal of letting others live and supporting people. In drawing attention to an incident that no one could forget, at a most critical time, he left an indelible mark. Which Companion witnessing this exchange could raise his sword against a woman or a child from that day forth? Furthermore, outside the incident involving Khalid ibn al-Walid,[123] not a single woman or child was killed in any of the other battles which took place during the Age of Happiness, even though at sites of active combat such as Badr, Uhud, and Hunayn, there were women and children present among the enemy forces. Despite the fact that they had come to the battlefield as combatants and notwithstanding their taking up arms, no woman or child was killed, and not a single civilian was harmed.[124]

There is no doubt that this Prophetic stance,[125] which continued from the very beginning, was widely talked about until there was no one left in the Arabian Peninsula that had not heard of it. One striking example was experienced among the Banu Qurayza. There was a Jew by the name of Hakam who realized that their actions were war crimes and amounted to flagrant treachery, and who later, during the siege, foresaw the outcome and shared it with his beloved wife Nubata, with whom he was deeply in love and did not wish to part. She looked at her husband in deep sorrow and said, "Indeed you will be separated from me." He said to her, "By the Torah, it will be as you say." He then indicated to his wife a way that she too could be killed along with him (as it was not for the Muslims to kill women):

"You are a woman and you will not be killed. You should throw a millstone down upon them. Indeed, we have not killed one of them yet (thus warranting their retaliation). And, in any case, we will not have the chance to kill any of them after this. You are a woman and if Muhammad defeats us he will not kill women."[126]

As can be seen, just as Hakam knew that God's Messenger did not kill women,[127] he was also sure that God's Messenger would never act contrary to the law. This is why he called on his wife to commit murder and in this way be killed along with him. He hated the thought of her being taken prisoner and wanted her to be killed for the crime. Together, the two of them took a millstone to the top of the fortress of al-Zabir ibn Bata, and threw it down from above the fortress, on top of the Prophet's Companion Khallad ibn Suwayd, and thus killed him. It was, of course, Hakam's wife Nubata who actually dealt the fatal blow and who was to face the consequences for her actions.[128]

The true source of appeal

So meticulous, so unerring, and so full of compassion was the Prophet of Mercy that he did not shed the blood of even a single person. In that case, what did he do when he was forced to fight? Let us examine this.

God's Messenger was a model of perfection in reliance on God as well as in having recourse to causes. He thus demonstrated that one's connection with God must not be neglected even at the most critical times and, as such, entreated God in supplication until the morning on the eve of Badr,[129] for before them stood an enemy that was three times their number. Turning to God especially at these times, when battles were won and lost by force of numbers, was clearly of the utmost importance. This was, after all, the secret to a small community's prevailing over those many times their size. For there was no power that could not be overcome by relying on God and submitting to Him. Hence, he opened his hands and beseeched the Creator and the True Cause of All Causes:

"My Lord, Leave me not to my own devices. My Lord, I beseech You for the fulfillment of Your promise and the bestowal of Your favor. My Lord, should this small band of Muslims be destroyed here today, there will be none left to worship You on earth."[130]

So sincere was he in these words and so completely absorbed was he in his petition that each time he raised his hands towards the heavens, the mantle that he was wearing fell down from his shoulders. Abu Bakr picked up the mantle and placed it back on the Prophet's shoulders while saying, "O Messenger of God, this prayer of yours to your Lord will suffice you. You have appealed to your Lord extremely pressingly, and He will fulfill for you what He has promised you."[131] Shortly thereafter, the Noble Prophet turned to those around him with a beaming countenance, his face shining like the full moon, and said:

"Glad tidings to you, O Abu Bakr! This is Gabriel appearing in a yellow turban, taking the reign of his horse, and poised between the heavens and the earth. When he descended to earth, I lost sight of him for a short time. He then appeared to me once more from the peaks of Badr, saying, 'God's help has come in response to your prayer and invocation.'"[132]

With perfect purity of poise and in full consciousness of being in the Divine presence, the angels descended to Badr.[133] The forces against one who was deeply absorbed in the Divine presence were in effect waging war against God Himself, and the end of those who wage such a war was clear from the outset.

With jubilation visible on his face as he stepped out of his tent, God's Messenger still experienced difficulty standing up in his armor, while at the same time reciting the following Qur'anic verse to all those around him:

(Let them know that) the hosts will all be routed, and they will turn their backs and flee. Indeed, the Last Hour is their appointed time (for their complete recompense), and the Last Hour will be more grievous and more bitter. (Al-Qamar, 54:45-46)[134]

'Ali, who was drawing water from one of the wells of Badr at the time, witnessed three strong gusts of wind one after another, the likes he had never seen before, and was utterly bemused by them. God's Messenger shed light on the situation not long after: Gabriel had come with the first gust, Mika'il with the second, and Israfil with the third. Each archangel came with a further one thousand angels and this figure was to later reach five thousand.[135]

This was manifest grace. God had supported His servant who acted as being in His presence required, against the army of Abu Jahl, who had come with the presumption that his forces would exterminate everyone in their path and then revel in their victory.[136] From this moment on a celestial aroma of victory filled the air at Badr. Those favored with Divine confirmation and support conducted themselves in the consciousness of their standing and acted in complete reliance upon an insuperable power.[137]

There were further Prophetic tidings at a time when there were smiles of joy on all faces. The Messenger of God informed his Companions, "I am as though beholding, at this very moment, the precise places where the chieftains of the enemy will be killed. So and so will be killed here, so and so here, and so and so here."[138]

He himself had strapped on his sword and was poised for battle against the enemy. At the forefront in every undertaking, God's Messenger demonstrated to his Companions exactly how to stand against the Meccan army, which refused to hold back and insisted on fighting. At one point, he threw a handful of dust at the Meccan army, saying, "May their faces be ruined." He then blew the remaining dust in his palm in their direction and said, "O Lord, cast fear into their hearts, and make their steps stumble." He also instructed his Companions to stand firm and close ranks.[139] This was the result of the unity of spirit and matter. The battle was about to start.

From this moment on God's Messenger was going to follow developments from his tent. What, then, did he do in his tent?

Indicating that he went to the tent of God's Messenger worried about God's Messenger in the heat of the battle, 'Ali states that he found the Prophet in prostration each time, engrossed in supplication and entreaty. 'Ali even says that he went to the tent three times in the three-hour battle and that he witnessed the same scene each time. So much so that when he came to the tent at the end of the battle, he found God's Messenger again in the same posture, imploring God with the words, "O my Lord, the All-Living, the Self- Subsisting One (by Whom all else subsist)!" It is remarkable that this state continued until the moment the Meccan army left Badr.

By this stance, God's Messenger demonstrated the importance of connection with one's Lord in order for the fulfillment of the promised victory. It was as though he said the following to those who saw him on that day and all those who would subsequently witness this scene:

They have allied against you to destroy you completely and are advancing upon you with resources that you cannot possibly overcome. If you seek to survive unscathed, then this is the door to which you need to turn and the true source of appeal. If you do not fail in your servanthood to God, then He will watch over His servant. Those who display enmity to a servant with such consciousness of servitude to Him will have God to contend with. And the lot of one who wages war against God is utter ruin![140]

Indeed, God declares in a sacred tradition (*hadith qudsi*), "Whosoever shows enmity to one of My friends (someone devoted to Me), I shall be at war with him."[141]

The meaning of this sacred tradition is clear: there is no doubt that one who touches a person God declares to be His friend gets burnt.

Badr is the finest example in this regard. The enemies of God who rejected all the Prophet's offers and thought of nothing but bloodshed met with incalculable ruin and devastation. For them Badr was a battle that had as good as ended before it had even begun, for they so readily came crashing down like rotten trees. It was as if those they could not see were coming and finishing them off one by one. It was as though they faced an unseen army, and this army devastated the Quraysh.[142] The Muslim army that they had hitherto belittled and underestimated had doubled in size in their eyes. They recalled the fate of Abraha's army. But it was all too late.[143]

The Meccan army fleeing in great fear left in its wake seventy dead and seventy prisoners of war. And what is more, most of the dead were from their leadership cadre.

Recovery

Badr had transpired and finished despite the reluctance of God's Messenger. After this, hatred, animosity, and bitter hostility peaked in Mecca in young and old, man and woman. All ties had been destroyed, and all the fruits of Prophetic endeavor acquired through blood, sweat and tears were destroyed. Fifteen years of effort were squandered because of the ambition and obstinacy of the Abu Jahls of the age and, on top of that, this ambition and obstinacy had in turn destroyed themselves. As for those left behind, a hostility, the like of which had never been seen before, reared its ugly head. They declared that they would not avail themselves of earthly pleasures until they exacted revenge, and swore that they would not approach their wives, nor seek shelter in the shade, until they made the Muslims pay the price for Badr.

These people, for whose deliverance from the Fire, God's Messenger had troubled himself almost to death, had now come even closer to the Fire, and the bonds that he had established to reach out to them had also been destroyed. The cost of Badr had been high indeed for the Meccans.

No doubt God's Messenger too was deeply saddened by this. This is precisely why he had not wanted to confront them for fifteen long years, and it was always he who pulled back so as not to sever the ties that were ready to snap in a climate of conflict. He had given warning, sent envoys and conveyed a great many messages, but he could not prevent father from confronting son and brother from confronting brother. And now, there was a completely new situation at hand.

So what did God's Messenger do from this moment on? He saw to protecting the lifeless bodies of these men who had come to kill him along with his Companions, to bury them in the sands of Badr, to feast and make merry over their graves, but who themselves had died instead. He did not leave their bodies to waste, but buried them all at Badr,[144] even personally overseeing the burial of twenty-four of them, all leaders of the Quraysh. In doing so, he called each of them by name, as if to say, "What good was it!" His purpose in addressing them thus was in all likelihood his sadness at the eternal departure of these men—for nothing—who had fallen prey to their greed and ambition.

But why did God's Messenger do this? What was the meaning of his actions? Why is the term *Ahl al-Qalib* (People of the Well) used mistakenly in reference to this incident? And why would people, even the scholars, simply ignore the philosophical facet of the issue?

To begin with, even at a point where all the bonds had been broken, everything positive had turned bitter, visions were shaken and dreams shattered, and where relationships had hit rock bottom, God's Messenger made steps to rebuild everything anew, again allowed his boundless heart to speak, demonstrated that a believer can never fall no matter how shaken they may be, and showed in his own person that this storm too would ultimately be weathered. From the standpoint of those they buried there, he did what was required by respect for human dignity and saved their corpses from becoming carrion for wild beasts. In this was indisputably a great message for the kith and kin left behind: the leaders, fathers, brothers, or relatives that they abandoned in their flight were attended to by God's Messenger whom they had taken as an enemy and set upon. The fruits of this would be seen in time and whoever was left behind from those buried at Badr that day would, in as short a time as six years, leave their old hostilities aside and come to the Prophet's assembly of mercy.[145] These people that he buried at Badr on that day became seeds, as it were, planted in the earth in spring. These later sprouted, grew trunks, put forth branches, produced foliage, and then blossomed, and God's Messenger subsequently gathered all their fruits when the time came. Only those who acted on the spur of their ambition and emotion died and were buried at Badr on that day, and the hearts of all those left behind were won over.[146]

It may prove useful at this point to ponder this matter: at a time where there were none of the communication channels of today such as television, radio, newspapers, magazines, books, the internet and social media networks, where the only communication medium between human beings was one-to-one contact, this absolute transformation, despite all the difficulties posed by the distance between Mecca and Medina, was nothing short of a miracle.

On the other hand, Badr was a place where one strange thing after another happened. Next to God's Messenger as he was burying the leading figures of Mecca stood 'Utba's son Abu Hudhayfa. It was a sad sight. His father 'Utba, his uncle Shayba, and brother Walid were being buried at the hand of the compassionate one against whom they had fought to the death, laying everything they had on the line. What is more, they had died as unbelievers and were headed towards eternal torment.

The Prophet of Mercy was always aware of his surroundings, however, and when he noticed Abu Hudhayfa's inner sorrow showing on his face, he said, "*It seems that you are saddened by the fate your father met today.*" He sought to stand by Abu Hudhayfa at such a trying time and offer his support.

Indeed, he spoke the truth for Abu Hudhayfa was truly grief-stricken. He turned to God's Messenger, who was consoling and comforting him in his distress and said:

"No, O Messenger of God! I do not lament or doubt the justice of my father's fate. I have known him to be a mild-mannered, good man, and I had hoped that his wisdom and virtue would one day lead him to Islam. But when I saw what befell him, despite all the hope I had entertained for him, it was for this that I was sorry."

This was a community that knew well precisely how it was to approach each issue, in the name of a collective consciousness. Abu Hudhayfa was more grieved at his father's inability to free himself from Abu Jahl's influence and thus losing him for all eternity, than at his father's death. With that, God's Messenger consoled Abu Hudhayfa and prayed for him.[147]

Three days passed. Before readying his horse and setting off, the Messenger of God went once more to the place where Abu Jahl and his men were buried and began calling each of them using their honorific titles saying the following:

"O so and so, son of so and so.

O Abu Jahl ibn Hisham! O Utba ibn Rabi'a! O Shayba ibn Rabi'a! O Umayya ibn Khalaf! Would it not have been easier to have obeyed God and His Messenger? Have you found what your Lord promised you to be true? We have found what our Lord promised us to be true.

How evil were your people to His Messenger! You denied me when the people confirmed me. You drove me into exile when others gave me refuge. You fought against me when others came to my aid.

And God has made you taste the worst punishment for all the evil you have inflicted. While I was assured of what I was saying, you accused me of lying; you called me false, while I was faithful and true!"

Astonished, his Companions said, "O Messenger of God, do you speak to the dead?"

"Yes," the Messenger of God replied, "for they now well know that the promise of their Lord has fully come to pass."

On this, 'Umar added, "O Messenger of God, you address them thus after three days. You speak to lifeless bodies that have no souls. They are dead and their bodies have decayed."

Teaching his community much in his every state and manner,

God's Messenger turned to 'Umar and spoke clearly and distinctly, as though to teach all those who were to hear these words: "You do not hear what I say better than they do. Indeed, at this moment they hear what I say, except that they are unable to answer me."[148]

This incident is known in Islamic history as *Ahl al-Qalib* (People of the Well) and it is most unfortunate that the Prophetic compassion was overshadowed by this term. It is clear that the greatest underlying factor here is the scholars' approach to the matter from the perspective of the prevailing *ayyam al-'Arab* (heroic) culture and the anger felt towards the Abu Jahls of the day by those who recorded events. Our indignation towards the people who were the driving force behind Badr and who were the main source of fifteen years of hardship and suffering has eclipsed these Prophetic steps that were aimed at healing, and we have passed down a description of events using a phrase which comes to mean, "the people thrown into a well," whereas on closer scrutiny, we see that God's Messenger took the best possible course of action on that day. In the absence of modern earthmoving equipment and even the most basic digging tools, and in a harsh setting, he placed the dead in a large pit and had them covered with earth. The question of the possibility of sending someone to Medina to bring digging tools can come to mind at this point. However, at the time, a single person's going from Badr to Medina and returning to Badr with the necessary tools and implements meant a total travel time of at least five days, even using the fastest possible mode of transport. In that case, there would be no bodies left intact and the stench would have made staying on at Badr impossible. Similarly, digging a grave for each individual was out of the question when digging was hard manual work, and those present had just survived a battle. When God's Messenger entrusted seventy of his Companions to Uhud about a year later, he placed two or three people in a single grave,[149] covered them with earth, and then left for Medina, even though Uhud is only five kilometers from Medina and even women were able to go to Uhud repeatedly, in order to provide support to those stationed there. Had there been the option to bury each martyr in a single grave or had such a need been felt, this would surely have been done at Uhud, where the necessary tools and equipment could easily have been brought.

One final note is in order before concluding this discussion of the Prophetic stance in the face of war: the Messenger of God won over the hearts of everyone who marched upon him with their armies to deter him from his mission and against whom he was thus forced to fight. Despite the deep wounds inflicted on the front line, he treated all of these within a short time, changed the views of yesterday's representatives of hatred and enmity, found the roads leading to their hearts, and transformed those who would not forgo their swords into compassionate teachers and representatives of his cause.

Former adversaries become devout teachers

It was the Meccans who confronted God's Messenger at Badr, Uhud, and Khandaq, but at the end of the course of events that had begun with Badr and ended with conquest, there was not a single person remaining who did not believe. Despite all the people martyred and killed, all the wounds had healed in as little as six years. The channels closed by high emotion and passions were opened anew, and a reunion on the plane of reason and sound judgment was experienced.

The actors of Hunayn were from the Hawazin, but their end was no different to that of the Meccans. After Ji'rana they, too, accepted Islam. The outcome of the siege of Ta'if, which came to pass in connection with Hunayn, was the same. Following the unfinished siege, all the city's inhabitants freely announced their acceptance of Islam.

This means that even under the worst conditions—in battle—the Messenger of God exhibited a stance that was so effective that it transformed those people with whom he made contact, showed compassion that eclipsed all adversities, and ultimately forged a change that was as good as bringing people back to life.

It stands to reason that all of this cannot possibly have been achieved with a hostile attitude towards people or by acting impulsively. His life, then, is not made up of military campaigns. What is more, it becomes clear that the subject discussed in books about his life under the heading "Ghazwa" is not truly synonymous with what we term "war" or "battle." For implied in "battle" in our day, are the negative connotations of a dark world where bloodshed is rife. However, even aspects of his life which have so far been referred to using the term *ghazwa* are luminous, full of compassion, and are centers of virtue wherein human dignity is protected to the utmost degree.

In any event, our examination of his life from such a narrow perspective up until today has meant that we have not found and could not formulate new solutions to today's problems. No doubt the greatest evidence of this one-sided approach is the fact that the early books of Islamic history were devoted merely to a discussion of battles, and were referred to with the name "Maghazi." As mentioned earlier, the meaning of this is clear: people concentrated their attention on battles and the heroic deeds displayed in those battles. Naturally, they found many heroes and recounted the valor and bravery exhibited by each Companion. A microscope was focused on a small area, so to speak, and as a result the impression developed that what was under the microscope was all there actually was. But as mentioned earlier, Badr was an event that took roughly three hours. Moreover, this three-hour process did not consist merely of active combat and killing. It appears that despite the fact that God's Messenger experienced them in their entirety, we today have taken a certain portion of his experiences and, to our great loss, have neglected the rest in our history books.

Prisoners of war

When God's Messenger was forced to fight, under the strain of the imposed conditions and with his diplomatic approaches going unanswered, his treatment of prisoners of war was also very different. He did not mistreat them as did others, did not injure their human dignity, did not hurt them, and always treated them in a way which befitted him. He sought whatever means he could find to release them, showed them most unexpected acts of kindness, addressed them in pleasing words, and asked his Companions to adopt the same type of conduct and sensitivity.

The first incident which raised the issue of prisoners of war was the military expedition of 'Abdu'llah ibn Jahsh. As 'Abdu'llah ibn Jahsh waited at Nakhla with his companions, he encountered a caravan that was carrying materials and equipment for the Quraysh who were preparing for battle. 'Uthman ibn 'Abdu'llah and Hakam ibn Qaysan were taken captive after the ensuing clash.[150]

When 'Abdu'llah ibn Jahsh returned to Medina with his prisoners, God's Messenger first censured them saying, "I have not commanded you to fight during the sacred months!" He then opted to suspend any action in relation to the two captives and the goods carried by the caravan.[151] Meanwhile, he met with the two prisoners and invited them to Islam. Learning of this, some of the Prophet's Companions suggested that these efforts were in vain, and proposed that the captives be killed.

There was no room for this attitude in the world of the Prophet of Mercy. He opened his heart to the captives, whom he approached with compassion, and addressed their hearts as well as their reason. Thus, he invited those harboring enmity under the influence of Meccan propaganda, to open their minds and called them, too, to journeying across the emerald hills of Paradise.

It turned out just he had anticipated. Before long, one of the captives, Hakam ibn Qaysan accepted this Prophetic invitation and embraced Islam. Witnessing this, the Prophet of Mercy turned to his Companions and said, about how they ought to consider the matter from now on, "Had I taken your advice and killed him (in anger), he would now have been of the Fire."[152] These words vividly illustrate the extent of the Messenger's compassion, while even the shadow of mercy and compassion did not fall upon the world of the Meccans, for they killed the Muslims they got their hands on in the wickedest possible way and in the spirit of festive ritual. Khubayb ibn 'Adi and Zayd ibn Dathinna's experiences following the Raji' incident, in the events leading up to their death, is the most salient example of this. The Meccans, who had been dealt a great blow at Badr and who returned from Uhud without having obtained what they had hoped for, sought to exact revenge on these two Companions, and they wanted everyone to partake in this "festivity." They first imprisoned both of them, then took them to a place called Tan'im, and brutally killed them.[153]

God's Messenger endeavored to enable human beings to lead lives as human beings, without the slightest change to this general attitude and method in later periods. He never judged on the basis of the mistakes and wrongdoing of others and one of his unchanging characteristics from the very beginning was always to treat others with mercy, compassion and mildness. His attitude towards those prisoners remaining from the army who came to Badr with the aim of killing him and his Companions and then celebrating their victory was no different. On the contrary, he showed them the same mercy and benevolence. God's Messenger divided up among certain families among his Companions the seventy captives from the Battle of Badr—the very first encounter with the Meccans at whose hands they had faced relentless persecution for fifteen years. He repeatedly instructed them to, "Treat the captives well,"[154] and made it very clear that he expected his Companions to show the same conscientiousness that he showed. Yet again, he did not leave these words unfulfilled, but translated them into action. We see God's Messenger on that day, for instance, providing some of the captives like 'Abbas with fine clothing.[155]

When distributing the captives among the families, we see him displaying a remarkable sensitivity. He chose those families who could show concern for them and entrusted the captives, who were grieving the deaths of their friends at Badr, who were shaken by the pain experienced at the front, and whose pride had been hurt by their capture, to those people who could win over their sensitive hearts. For instance, to the care of the mother of believers, Umm Salama, who was a member of the Banu Makhzum, he entrusted Khalid ibn Hisham, a chieftain of the same tribe and full brother of Abu Jahl who was killed at Badr,[156] and another member of that tribe, Umayya ibn Abi Hudhayfa.[157] Everything was new. It was obvious that the Messenger of God wanted the captives to feel secure in the company of their relatives, and he wanted to please their relatives, in turn, by letting them watch over their kinsfolk. Upon hearing that her paternal cousins had come to her home, Umm Salama went to God's Messenger and asked him, "O Messenger of God, the sons of my uncle seek to visit me and I to receive them. They request that I attend to some of their needs and assist them at this difficult time. But I do not like to do that until I have sought your permission." God's Messenger responded to his wife, who was as yet unaware of his strategy, "I do not disapprove of any of this. Do as you see fit."[158]

So sensitive, so receptive, and so benevolent was he in this regard that in order to prevent any harm coming to these prisoners who had killed the family members or relatives of his Companions, he instructed, "Let not anyone among you exchange his prisoner with his brother's with the intent of killing them."[159] It was as though he had charged each of his Companions with the care and responsibility of each of them or a few of them, and was exhorting his Companions as to exactly how they should behave, in order to break the ice between them. It filled him with trepidation to think that harm might come to them, and he warned his

Companions from the beginning, so that no one would get hurt. For example, of Sa'd ibn Abi Waqqas, whose brother[160] was martyred at Badr, God's Messenger said, "Do not inform Sa'd about the killing of his brother, for he will kill all the prisoners in your hands."[161] Not content with his own care and attention, he called his Companions, who had been shaped by the culture from which they came, to adopt the same sensitivity. In the prevailing culture killing was commonplace. Indeed, had they killed the Badr prisoners on that day, there was no higher authority who could call them to account for it. As an inhabitant of this cultural environment, Sa'd ibn Mu'adh made no effort to hide his view that they had needlessly shouldered the burden of these captives and that they needed to kill them and thus free themselves at once. When the Messenger of God noticed Sa'd's disapproval at the taking of prisoners, he said, "It seems, Sa'd, that you disapprove of what the people are doing," and thus warned him. In doing so, God's Messenger demonstrated that irrespective of some among them who held such views, no one would be killed, and that he considered those taken captive at Badr as being entrusted to their care.[162] In his world, as much delicacy was to be shown towards prisoners of war as was shown in safeguarding trusts. Their predicament was not to be exploited, nor their rights violated, no wrong was to be committed that would injure their human dignity, and they would always be treated with goodness and benevolence.

After all, was it possible for God's Messenger to make a request that the Companions would not put into effect right away? The Companions had made putting the Prophet's wishes into practice to the letter their foremost aspiration and from this moment on, they thought of their captives before their own selves, and offered the best of whatever they had to their captive first. They did this to such a degree that while they made-do with dried dates for food, they fed their captives the best foodstuffs that they had to offer. The Prophet's son-in-law Abu al-'As ibn al-Rabi',[163] who was among the captives on that day and was later to embrace Islam, describes this scrupulousness and delicacy:

"*I was with a group of the Ansar when they captured me after the battle of Badr. When it came to mealtimes, they would give me bread and themselves eat dates on account of the Messenger of God's command. They had less bread and more dates with them. As soon as any one of them found a morsel of bread in his hand he immediately gave it to me. Feeling ashamed, I would give it back to one of them, only to have it come back to me soon after.*"[164]

Mus'ab ibn 'Umayr's brother 'Aziz ibn 'Umayr was also among the captives. He said, "I was in a group of the natives of Medina when they brought me from Badr. When they took their lunch and supper, they gave me bread in preference to themselves while they ate dates, because the Messenger of God had enjoined them concerning us, 'Treat the captives well.' I would feel ashamed and give it back to one of them, but he would return it to me without touching it."[165]

A further detail concerning the Companions' sensitivity is reported by Khalid ibn al-Walid's brother Walid ibn Walid ibn al-Mughira.[166] He was to become Muslim as a result of the kind treatment he received and described this fastidiousness saying, "They made us ride, while they themselves traveled on foot."[167] It is interesting to note that three of the uncles of Walid ibn al-Walid, the speaker of these words, had been slain[168] at Badr on that day and yet another was taken prisoner.[169] The situation of the others was no different. As well as their leaders, their closest of kin had died at Badr, and most of those who escaped had returned to Mecca with deep wounds. Those who could not flee, however, fell into captivity and their pride was wounded.

Every Meccan young and old, woman and man receiving the bitter news, while they may not have been at Badr themselves, swore oaths that they would taste of no worldly pleasures until they obtained their revenge and all together began preparations for the next battle.[170]

However, the steps that God's Messenger took at Badr were not limited to those outlined above. Noticing that the hands and feet of the prisoners were bound, he called one of his Companions and ordered him, "Untie all the captives," and thus afforded the captives the treatment of people who were free while events were still so fresh.[171]

Suhayl ibn 'Amr, the prominent orator of the Quraysh tribe, who resented his son 'Abdu'llah for joining the Muslim ranks and who had incited the Meccan army to fight, was also among the prisoners. Seeing Suhayl among the captives, 'Umar eagerly asked the Prophet for permission to punish him severely.[172] But the Messenger of God did not agree, for he was sent not to kill, but to let live. As if to instruct 'Umar in the exact nature of this ideal, he turned to 'Umar and said, "Leave him, O 'Umar, for it may well be that one day his actions will please you."[173]

'Umar, who had shot up in anger, re-sheathed his sword.[174]

The Messenger of God wanted to add one further gesture and favor for the captives who were encountering such a practice for the very first time. However, he first wished to raise the issue with his Companions and thus involve them. The Messenger of God asked them, "What is your opinion concerning these captives? Even if most of them were formerly your brothers, God has left it to you to decide their fate."[175] Abu Bakr was of the same opinion as the Prophet.[176] Such Companions as 'Umar[177] and 'Abdu'llah ibn Rawaha,[178] however, thought differently. They were presumably affected by the fifteen-year ordeal in Mecca, their state of mind on the return from Badr, and the emotions triggered during battle; the idea that the captives should be killed dominated.

Clearly, the Messenger of God was not pleased with this attitude and he withdrew from their company without comment. The Companions discussed amongst themselves the decision that God's Messenger would take. Some of them supposed that he would act upon Abu Bakr's view and release them on ransom. Others thought that he would judge on the basis of 'Umar's views and put them to death. A third group felt that he might adopt the idea of 'Abdu'llah ibn Rawaha to light a big fire and cast them into it. Soon after, God's Messenger returned to them and said, "Assuredly God softens the hearts of some until they become the softest of soft, and He hardens the hearts of some until they become harder than stone. You, O Abu Bakr, are like the archangel Mika'il, who is a herald of God's Mercy. Among the Prophets, you are like Abraham, who said, '*So, he who follows me is truly of me; while he who disobeys me, surely You are All-Forgiving, All-Compassionate,*' and like Jesus, who said, '*If You punish them, they are Your servants; and if You forgive them, You are the All-Glorious with irresistible might, the All-Wise*'" (Ibrahim 14:36; al-Ma'ida 5:118).

He then turned to 'Umar and said, "You, O 'Umar, resemble Gabriel among the angels, who delivers God's just punishment to His enemies, and among the Prophets you are like Noah who said, '*My Lord! Do not leave on the earth any from among the unbelievers dwelling therein!*' (Nuh 71:36) and like Moses, who said, '*Our Lord! Destroy their riches, and press upon their hearts, for they do not believe until they see the painful punishment.*'"[179] He then addressed both of them saying, "Were you both to concur on a matter, I would not object to it."[180] He had scarcely finished speaking, when the voice of 'Abdu'llah ibn Mas'ud was heard, "O Messenger of God," he exclaimed, "Let Suhayl ibn Bayda' be an exception, for he is considering becoming a Muslim."[181]

This was exhilarating news and the countenance of God's Messenger was as radiant as the full moon. In utter joy he repeated, "Let Suhayl ibn Bayda' be an exception!"[182] These words made 'Abdu'llah ibn Rawaha go weak at the knees. He was terrified. Later, relating his experiences on that day, he was to say, "I was never so afraid as when I heard God's Messenger say, 'Let Suhayl ibn Bayda' be an exception,' as I feared that stones would rain down upon me from the heavens for the words I uttered before God and His Messenger."[183]

The matter was about to reach the point God's Messenger desired. Those unable to grasp the main objective until that point also came to understand the essence of the matter through this process. They had begun to realize that what mattered was not killing, but paving the way for enabling human beings to live as human beings. At the same time, God's Messenger was slowly and painstakingly raising an ideal community even under the most adverse conditions. Instructed by Gabriel, the Prophet offered the choice to punish the captives for their previous crimes or release them for ransom and the Companions chose the latter, despite the risk of facing the same people as combatants again and the risk of losing their lives.[184]

They were making a monumental choice indeed. The meaning of this was, "Let us die, so long as they are saved." This was the difference in being a Companion. This was, at the same time, something witnessed for the very first time in human history. To be sure, the Qur'anic verses revealed until that time, which encouraged forgiveness and emphasized calling people wisely and with kindness,[185] were instrumental in this choice. Acting upon emotion and responding in anger were being left behind and pardoning everyone as a soul that has become one with the Qur'an became second nature to every believer. It was, of course, the Messenger of God who was the exemplar in this regard, and on that day he ruled in favor of the captives being released for ransom.

The first prisoner to be released was Abu Wada'a. His son Muttalib was the first to slip away to Medina,[186] despite all the warnings of the Meccans, and after paying a sum of four thousand *'uqiyya*,[187] took his father with him back to Mecca.[188] In a sense, this set the sum to be paid for release. Nonetheless, flexibility was the normal practice and they were lenient to those who could not muster this, further reducing this amount.[189]

Then there were those impoverished individuals who had nothing whatsoever to give and it did not take long for the Prophetic benevolence to find a solution to this too. Those who could not pay the set amount had to teach ten young Muslims to read and write in exchange for their freedom.[190]

There was yet another group in need of support, like 'Amr ibn 'Abdu'llah, who was also known as Abu 'Azza. They neither possessed money, nor were they able to teach reading and writing. God's Messenger did not leave him without help and released him on the understanding that he would not inveigh against Islam and take part in hostilities against the Muslims again.[191] Sa'ib ibn 'Ubayd, 'Ubayd ibn 'Amr, Sayfi ibn Abi Rifa'a Mutallib ibn Hantab ibn al-Harith, and Rabi'a ibn al-Darraj ibn al-'Anbas were also released on these conditions.[192] This situation was arguably a first in human history. Their period of slavery, the marks of which they had begun to accept and which they thought would remain with them for the rest of their lives and be the lot of their descendants too, ended within a matter of days. Instead of servitude to others for a full stomach, or being sold at the market, they were returning to their hometown, where they could make a fresh start.[193] On that day, God's Messenger was also to set free 'Amr, the son of Abu Sufyan, who held Sa'd ibn al-Nu'man hostage in exchange for his son. Abu Sufyan had captured Sa'd upon the latter's Minor Pilgrimage to the Ka'ba.[194]

The Messenger of God also favored Jubayr ibn Mut'im, whom he noticed among those who came to claim their prisoners. With a view to inviting him to Islam, God's Messenger said, "If your father Mut'im ibn 'Adi had been alive, I would have freed all those Qurayshi prisoners on his behalf."[195] This was because Mut'im ibn 'Adi was one of the rare notables of Mecca who stood out for his benevolence. He had protected God's Messenger[196] from the Meccan polytheists on his return from Ta'if and was one of the handful of honorable figures who took the crucial steps which ultimately ended the three years of exile and boycott.[197] This simultaneously signified a kind of expression of condolence, as Mut'im ibn 'Adi had died around seven months prior to Badr.[198] Jubayr, who was to become a Muslim following Hudaybiya,[199] was later to pinpoint his witnessing the Prophet's Prayer and hearing his recitation of the Qur'an for the very first time as the moment his life began to change. He was also later to describe this as the first instance of his heart's softening and inclination towards Islam.[200]

The Prophet's gestures did not stop there, but rather continued one after the other. He also freed Suhayl ibn 'Amr, who had inveighed against Islam at every opportunity for fifteen years and was one of those who financed the forces that came to Badr. Mikraz ibn Hafs stayed in Medina in his place and returned to Mecca after Suhayl's ransom had arrived.[201] Qutayla bint al-Harith, the daughter of a fierce opponent of the Prophet, Nadr ibn al-Harith who made a practice of following God's Messenger wherever and to whomever he went for the purpose of destroying the positive climate that he had established, wrote a letter to God's Messenger after her father was killed at Badr. When God's Messenger read her elegy, he was deeply moved and wept so profusely that his beard became wet with his tears. Such weeping was for a man who constantly provoked the Meccans against him and who had devoted his life to destroying everything pertaining to Islam.[202]

Thus, the hearts of the captives softened when they witnessed such extraordinary magnanimity and kindness. Their hatred and animosity was at the very least ameliorated, with the enmity of some even being completely replaced with feelings of affection. Suhayl ibn Bayda',[203] Nawfal ibn al-Harith,[204] Walid ibn al-Walid,[205] Sa'ib ibn 'Ubayd,[206] Muttalib ibn Hantab,[207] Hajjaj ibn Qays,[208] 'Abdu'r-Rahman ibn Mashnu',[209] Musafi' ibn 'Iyad,[210] Abu Rafi',[211] 'A'idh b. al-Sa'ib,[212] and Bijad ibn al-Sa'ib[213] were those whoprofessed their acceptance of Islam there and then.

Among those returning to Mecca the same day, 'Umayr ibn Wahb[214] and his son Wahb ibn 'Umayr[215] and the youth[216] that Abu Sufyan had sent to Medina to assassinate the Prophet had also become Muslim. The sources indicate that when 'Umayr ibn Wahb, who was introduced to the radiant countenance of Islam and who had the opportunity of seeing the Messenger of God directly, returned to Mecca, he contributed to many people accepting the faith.[217] Meanwhile, figures such as 'Abdu'llah ibn Suhayl ibn 'Amr[218] and 'Umayr ibn al-'Awf[219] who came all the way to Badr only to change sides, also took their place among Muslim ranks.[220]

Similarly, among those taken captive, Suhayl ibn 'Amr,[221] 'Aqil ibn Abi Talib,[222] Abu al-'As,[223] Khalid ibn Hisham,[224] Khalid ibn Asid,[225] 'Adi ibn al-Khiyar,[226] Abu Wada'a ibn al-Subira,[227] 'Abdu'llah ibn Ubayy ibn Khalaf,[228] Sa'ib ibn Abu Hubaysh,[229] Nistas,[230] 'Abd ibn Zam'a,[231] Qays ibn al-Sa'ib,[232] and Abu 'Aziz bin 'Umayr[233] would comprehend this difference and, putting aside a lifetime's vain ideal, would profess their belief in Islam.

As a consequence, it becomes evident that in the aftermath of Badr—the conflict that God's Messenger did everything he possibly could to prevent but that he could not convince his enemy to avoid—a period unparalleled in human history was beginning. For in this time, under the most intense conditions, the hearts of at least sixteen people were won over within roughly ten days. This is twenty-three percent of seventy captives and is the same as the total number of people who became Muslim in the thirteen-year Meccan period.[234] Eleven of these were prisoners, two were those who defected before the battle even started and joined the Muslims, and two were the assassins sent to Medina to avenge the defeat at Badr. Furthermore, those who embraced Islam through the efforts of 'Umayr ibn Wahb after his return to Mecca,[235] and Hakam ibn Qaysan who was taken captive during the Nakhla expedition and became Muslim, are not counted in this figure. Taking these into account too, the number of those who came to God's Messenger and professed their belief within two or three months was at least twenty.

As we have seen, God's Messenger generated new openings even during a period that was on the surface atrocious. In so doing, he personally demonstrated that hearts could be conquered even at a time when emotions were in a heightened state of negativity. This goes to show that there is a mercy so great as to melt hatred and animosity as great as mountains, treat the deep wounds inflicted in hearts and indeed heal all wounds. They saw this boundless compassion that they had hitherto been unable to see, noticed this glorious mercy that they had not noticed before and, changing sides against all odds, they chose the straightest path even at a time when all roads had become so convoluted. The message that this conveyed to those who could not make the same choice on the day is self-evident. No matter how defeated by their emotions were the Meccans, who were accepted in a completely unexpected way before everyone's eyes, they were beginning to realize that doors were opening for them. They witnessed firsthand the treatment they would receive when they would join the Muslims in the future. After all, they had seen the small but gradual stream of people who had made use of this opportunity in the lead up to Mecca's conquest.

Without question, the Prophet's attitude continued unchanged. He released prisoners without ransom[236] and always did what behooved him, as opposed to following established custom. For instance, God's Messenger welcomed the Tamim delegation that had come to Medina to retrieve their prisoners and caused him much vexation with their crudeness.[237] In spite of everything, he sat with them at length and set the captives free. Witnessing his magnanimity on that day, Aqra' ibn Habis and his fellow tribesmen accepted Islam.[238] When Juwayriya bint al-Harith, who was taken captive after the encounter with the Banu Mustaliq, embraced Islam, the Messenger of God took her in marriage. The Companions who witnessed the marriage said, "How can we enslave the in-laws of God's Messenger?" and set all the captives free. Before such a courteous gesture, the Banu Mustaliq naturally softened and all together embraced Islam.[239] Moreover, Juwayriya's father and leader of the Banu Mustaliq, Harith ibn Abi Dirar, hid two of the camels he had taken all the way to the 'Aqiq Valley as ransom for his daughter and entered Medina alone. When he appeared before the Messenger of God, he responded to him saying, "And tell me, where are the two camels that you hid in such and such place at the 'Aqiq Valley?" Upon the Prophet's relating to him this, which no one else knew, Harith too accepted Islam.[240]

The Banu Qurayza, with whom God's Messenger had consolidated ties by drawing up a new agreement during the tension experienced with the Banu Qaynuqa and the Banu Nadir, sided with the Confederate forces and collaborated with them to attack from the inside during the Battle of the Trench. As a result of this treasonous conduct, they were besieged and close to one thousand people were taken prisoner. The Messenger of God announced that those who produced the required ransom within the specified time would be released, no questions asked. Affluent Jews such as Abu al-Shahm did not want to miss out on such a favor and bought the freedom of many of their relatives.[241] Furthermore, seeing that the captives were being kept under the sweltering sun, God's Messenger immediately intervened and said, "Do not punish them both with the heat of the sun and the glow of the sword."[242] We also see the Messenger of God, the Pride of Humanity, exhorting his Companions to ensure that children were not separated from their mothers saying,

"Do not separate the mother from her children until they have reached maturity."[243] He said, "Whoever separates a mother and her child, God will separate them from their loved ones on the Day of Judgment."[244]

Yet another Prophetic warning concerning prisoners of war was about the treatment of women and that no harm should come to them. When Rayhana bint Sham'un from the Banu Qurayza became Muslim, God's Messenger forgot all his troubles and experienced great happiness.[245] When the sister of Hatim al-Ta'i, who was then renowned for his generosity, was taken captive, he provided her with clothing and an allowance, and sent her to her homeland, accompanied by some of his Companions.[246]

In another example of God's Messenger's good treatment of captives, security teams dispatched towards Najd captured a chief of the Banu Hanifa, Thumama ibn Uthal, and brought him to Medina, tying him to one of the mosque's pillars so that he could not escape. God's Messenger approached him and asked, "What are you expecting, O Thumama?" "I am expecting good, O Muhammad. For if you should kill me, you would have killed one who has already shed the blood of another,[247] and if you should set me free, you would have favored and obliged one who will be grateful. If it is wealth and possessions that you seek, then ask of me whatever you wish and it shall be granted to you."

The Messenger of God went to him again the following day and asked him once more, "What are you expecting, O Thumama?"

"What I (have already) told you," Thumama replied. "Should you set me free, you would have shown kindness to and obliged one who will be grateful. But, should you kill me, you would have killed somebody who has already shed blood. If it is wealth and possessions that you seek instead, you will be given as much as you should wish."

God's Messenger left Thumama alone that day also, only to come to him on the third day and repeat the same question, to which he received the same response from Thumama. It appeared that Thumama, who repeated the same things that were established practice, was not able to comprehend the Prophet's purpose. Hearing the same statements from Thumama a third time, God's Messenger ordered his Companions, "Release Thumama." Just as Thumama was expecting to lose his head or receive a hefty demand, he was set free without expectation of anything in return. This left Thumama stupefied. He ruminated over this, but he could not for the life of him imagine how such a courtesy could be shown. There was no longer anything binding him in Medina, for he was free and could return back home. But he felt as though he had become attached to Medina. He was free of the enslavement that restricted his actions and movement, but had become the captive of God's Messenger who had treated him so.

Thumama disappeared for a brief period, in which he withdrew to a grove of date palms and performed the major ritual ablution. He returned to the Prophet's Mosque with water dripping from his head, approached the Messenger of God in due reverence, and said, "I bear witness that there is no deity worthy of worship but God, and I also bear witness that Muhammad is His servant and His Messenger." He was voicing his innermost convictions. However, he did not content Himself merely with this. "O Muhammad," he continued, looking God's Messenger directly in the face, "until this moment, there was no face on earth I disliked more than yours, but now your face is the dearest and you are the most beloved of all to me. There was no religion more hateful to me than yours, but it is now the dearest of all to me. There was no place more detestable to me than this place, but it is now the most beloved place on earth to me." With yet another person awakening to the truth, there was none happier, none more at ease than God's Messenger.[248]

A great many other examples of the sensitivity of God's Messenger concerning war spoils and captives can be offered, as one who was sent to enable human beings to live as fully human and who demonstrated this to the rest of humanity in his person. There is, however, a scene exemplifying his utmost delicacy which warrants mention, for a failure to do so in this discussion would be an injustice to his painstaking care.

Despite Malik ibn 'Awf's launching a deadly onslaught with a sizable army, God's Messenger inflicted a decisive defeat on his army at Hunayn. He then fled and sought sanctuary in Ta'if. Left behind him on the battlefield were twenty-four thousand camels, more than forty thousand sheep, and around four thousand *'uqiyya* of silver. There were also six thousand prisoners, the majority of whom were women and children. The Messenger of God once again exhorted his Companions concerning women, emphatically warning against laying hands on them. Archangel Gabriel had come on this day too, reaffirming the need for such delicacy.[249]

God's Messenger had come to Ji'rana on the return from Ta'if and despite the days that had passed, had not divided up the captives nor the spoils in question. There were even those who were troubled by this long delay.

Wishing to spend this time in the best possible way, God's Messenger sent his Companion, Busr ibn Sufyan, to Mecca to purchase new clothes for the prisoners at Ji'rana. It was clear that he wanted to make the most of this time. Under the Prophet's strict instructions, Busr immediately set off for Mecca and returned to Ji'rana with enough clothing for all the captives. This was yet another new practice: the women and children expecting to be sold at the slave market were fitted out with new clothes and the hearts of these people who had been forced to the front line and exposed to peril by their own leader were won over.[250]

Then, a Hawazin delegation of fourteen people led by Zuhayr ibn Surad was seen to be approaching Ji'rana. Among them, was the Prophet's foster uncle, Abu Burqan. They had realized that the incessant conflict and fighting would get them nowhere and had embraced Islam. "O Messenger of God," they said, "we are of noble origin and we are kinsfolk. The disaster which has befallen us is not unknown to you. Please show us favor, so that God may bestow favor upon you."

The Prophet's initial response was to inquire about their foolhardy commander. "What happened to Malik ibn 'Awf," he asked the delegation. When the delegation replied, "He fled and took refuge in the fortress of Ta'if along with the Thaqif," God's Messenger said, "Inform him that if he comes here as a Muslim, I will return to him his family and property and give him an additional hundred camels."[251] He had sent Malik ibn 'Awf's family to Mecca in any case, to lodge in the house of his paternal aunt Umm 'Abdu'llah bint Abi Umayya, so that special attention be shown to them. Seeing the Messenger's earnestness, the Hawazin delegation said, "O Messenger of God, they are our lords and are dearest to us," upon which God's Messenger replied, "Indeed I desire the best for them."

The Prophet's Companions watched the unfolding of events in sheer astonishment. Thus, underlying the Messenger's delaying the matter and not hastening to render judgment concerning the war spoils and prisoners taken from the Hawazin were certain things of which they had been unaware. That the Messenger of God would approach the captives affably was clear from the very moment he distributed clothing made of cotton and linen to every one of them.[252] And now, men who had just a few weeks earlier wielded swords at them, had come of their own free will and expressed their acceptance of Islam. Then, their spokesperson Zuhayr ibn Surad turned to the Prophet and said, "O Messenger of God, among the captives are your paternal and maternal aunts and those who suckled and looked after you. Had our women played similar roles to Harith ibn Abi Shimr or Nu'man ibn al-Mundhir, and were we to be in the same predicament with them as we are with you, we could have hoped for their favor and kindness. And yet you are the most honorable of men."

The poet Zuhayr was later to employ this same power of expression in his poetry and voice his purpose through verse. Moreover, this was a development that God's Messenger expected and he first said, "All that was due for myself and the family of 'Abd al-Muttalib is yours." He would thus lead his Companions in yet another practice, in voluntarily relinquishing their own share, again taking the first step himself. The Quraysh who witnessed this said, "And all that falls to our share belongs to God and His Messenger," thus renouncing any claim to the spoils. After hearing this, God's Messenger asked, "Which is dearer to you, your women and children or your wealth and possessions? The most beloved speech to me is the most truthful. So choose one of the two alternatives: either the captives or the property, as I have been waiting for you and have thus delayed their distribution."

Before such unanticipated magnanimity, the Hawazin delegation said, "O Messenger of God, if you are giving us a choice between our captives and our property, we choose our captives."

This was a surprise to God's Messenger, but he was going to do this before everyone and in a manner which allowed for its recognition and acceptance by public opinion. This is why he directed them saying, "Come to me after I lead the Noon Prayer, declare your acceptance of Islam in the midst of the worshipers and say, 'We are your brothers and sisters in faith and call upon the Messenger of God to intercede with the Muslims for us and the Muslims to intercede with the Messenger of God for us concerning our women and children.' I shall then publicly declare that I relinquish my share and ask that they relinquish their share also." He also advised them in the manner of reciting the Declaration of Faith and gave them pointers as to how they were to address the people following the Prayer.

The Noon Prayer was offered, and the time came to put God's Messenger's strategy into action. The Hawazin delegation stood up and requested permission to speak. No sooner had they been given permission than their spokesmen began presenting their intentions, as the Messenger of God had advised. Addressing the Companions directly, they petitioned them for the restoration of their prisoners. A new page was being turned before everyone's eyes. At the completion of their address, God's Messenger turned to the people, first praised and glorified God, and then said, "Your brothers are here having repented and I deem it proper to return their captives. So, whoever of you wishes to do the same of their own accord, let them do so. And whoever wishes to keep their share until we give to them from the very first spoils that God may bestow upon us, than let them do so."

The Prophet's Companions possessed keen discernment and had long since grasped the subtlety in his words. He wished to set the captives free. Thus, they proclaimed in unison, "This would please us also, O Messenger of God." They were relinquishing any claim to their own share. But the Messenger of God did not want this acceptance to be limited merely to those present in the mosque, and he sought for this to be embraced and espoused by wider society as a whole. This is why he added, "We cannot know at present which of you have agreed and which have not; so go back to your homes and discuss the matter amongst yourselves once again. Then let your representatives convey to us your decision."

Before long, the representatives of the Helpers and the Migrants returned to the Messenger of God to inform him that all of them had readily agreed. They said, "Anything that is lawfully ours belongs to the Messenger of God and is hereby relinquished." There was no one left among the Companions on that day who did not accept, with the exception of Aqra' ibn Habis representing the Tamim, Banu Fazara chieftain 'Uyayna ibn Hisn, and 'Abbas ibn Mirdas, speaking for the Banu Sulaym. They maintained that they would not relinquish their right and stated that their tribes would not act otherwise. On account of this, God's Messenger pledged six camels from the first war spoils that were acquired, for every captive that they set free, and everyone except 'Uyayna ibn Hisn consented. 'Uyayna would not budge. About such meaningless insistence and greed for worldly wealth, God's Messenger would entreat God with the words, "O Lord, diminish what falls to his share."[253]

Meanwhile, the Hawazin delegation had relayed the Prophet's message to their chieftain Malik ibn 'Awf and had informed him that anyone could return and take advantage of this general amnesty. Malik was overcome by anxiety. He feared that the Thaqifs might learn he had been assured that his family and possessions would be restored to him if he returned as a Muslim, and that they might therefore imprison him in the fortress to prevent his escape. He secretly had a camel prepared and had it sent to Dahna, instructing the slave he sent with his mount to wait until he arrived there. He himself stole out of Ta'if by night and headed straight for Dahna. No one noticed his departure. Upon reaching Dahna, he mounted his camel and made straight for Ji'rana. He went immediately to the Messenger of God, overcome with shame, but fully aware that he was only now beginning to take his first step towards true happiness. The Messenger of God rejoiced at his arrival and returned Malik's family and possessions to him as he had promised, and the additional hundred camels. Malik ibn 'Awf attempted to express in verse his gratitude for this generosity and earnest hospitality. He spoke of his never having seen the likes of God's Messenger in goodness and generosity and endeavored to describe his making known in advance, one by one, events that would happen in the future.[254]

CHAPTER 2

NEVER GIVE UP ON ANYONE

Never Give Up On Anyone

While he was forced to migrate, the Messenger of God did not forsake the Meccans, or write them off because of the thirteen-year suffering and persecution to which they subjected the Muslims. Despite being warmly and wholeheartedly embraced in Medina, he always kept Mecca in mind. At a time when there were limited resources, distance was a major barrier, and the only means of communication was the letter or courier, he found ways of reaching all the Meccans and was able to enter Mecca eight years later having won over all their hearts without exception.

In fact, the Messenger of God did not make contact with people merely through speech, but adopted many different strategies, using the resources at his disposal, and undertook a broad range of activities to reach his addressees. When we look at his life from this standpoint, we see that his communication of the message and guiding others was not just a matter of going to visit them and relating his objective, but was a longer process in which he made contact with them in every way he could. A consideration of the climate that was established in Mecca following Badr reveals that the conquest of the city in as little as six years could not have been possible otherwise. The complete transformation, so quickly, of a city where hatred and animosity were at a peak and all its inhabitants—young and old, male and female—lived and breathed revenge cannot be explained in any other way. For they now put on a pedestal the individual and idea that they had until only yesterday viewed as their chief enemy, and they now welcomed with open arms the people they had not wanted in their city.

God's Messenger's life is arguably the most thoroughly documented life in human history. Still, his every action, confirmation, and word has not been recorded. An examination of his life from this vantage point indicates that for him to have reached each and every one around him within a space of twenty-three years, he must have used many other methods aside from those already known. Indeed, the conquest of Mecca is symbolic. What was realized on that day was not merely a particular event, but a long process that had come to fruition. A wider perspective reveals that God's Messenger entered the city freely and without any opposition. The resistance put up at a single location during an entry into the city from four directions was local and limited to particular individuals, and when they realized that they would not be able to hold out, they fell apart and were each forced to flee in different directions.

It seems that new channels had been found to the hearts of those who had lived and breathed hatred and animosity for the past six years, and who had vowed that they would taste no worldly pleasure until they exacted revenge. Enmities had been all but wiped away through new and altogether different strategies, with seedlings of love planted in their place. This was not a random result. Behind this surely lay the initiatives of a Messenger who constantly sacrificed of his own self for others, used all the resources at his disposal for the benefit of those he addressed, initiated new ways of making contact with them, patiently endured all hardship and affliction to come from them, and offered them food and gifts. Even at times when the Meccans were heightening the tension and closing themselves off entirely from him, he forged new relationships with them and opened new doors. When they were subjected to trials and tribulations, he offered them assistance and attended to their needs, suffered every kind of difficulty caused by those sabotaging the process, and implemented who knows how many other strategies to affect even the most troubled of hearts.

One of these Prophetic strategies was the existence of Companions who concealed their Muslim identity and remained in Mecca. As can be gleaned from particular verses and Prophetic Traditions the Messenger of God had certain Companions keep their Muslim identity secret[255] for various reasons and had them undertake certain activities of which only he and they were aware. It also appears that he charged some among them with certain duties and directed them. They remained among the polytheists, despite their belief, established close relationships with them, and thus tried to soften their hearts towards Islam. They strove to keep them on the course of fairness and reason by showing them hospitality and presenting them with gifts, and kept God's Messenger informed of all developments. The Qur'an explicitly refers to this when describing the causes of the peaceful and victorious return from Hudaybiya:

And had there not been (in Mecca) believing men and believing women whom you did not know and therefore might have trodden down, and thus something undesired might have afflicted you on their account (for what you did) unknowingly, (God would not have restrained your hands from fighting. (Al-Fath 48:25)

The Companion 'Abdu'llah ibn 'Abbas states that the people mentioned in the following verses are precisely such people:

O Lord! Bring us out of this land whose people are oppressors (An-Nisa 4:75), and

As to those whose souls the angels (charged with taking the souls of people) take in the state of wronging themselves (by continuing to live in unbelief, without suffering to migrate to a land where they would be able to attain faith): They (the angels) ask them: 'What situation were you in (so that you were not with the believers)?' They say: 'We were under such oppression in this land that we could not find a way to faith.' They (the angels) say: 'Was God's earth not wide enough for you to migrate in it?' Such are those whose refuge is Hell: how evil a destination to arrive at! Except those truly oppressed among the men, and the women, and the children altogether without means and not guided to a way (to migrate, and including those who, in their lifetime, have not had a means to be guided to faith). For those (while their circumstances are unchanged, it is expected that) God will not hold them accountable and will excuse them. Assuredly God is One Who excuses much, All-Forgiving. (An-Nisa 4:97–99)[256]

While 'Abdu'llah ibn 'Abbas indicates that both he and his mother are among those described in this verse,[257] Ikrima, the freed slave of Ibn 'Abbas and one of the most prominent scholars of the successors of the Companions, gives the same interpretation and states that Ibn 'Abbas was one of the people in this category.[258]

The people mentioned particularly in the first verse cited are not those people referred to in the literature as the *mustad'afin* (the helpless and dispossessed) who could not migrate due to lack of means, or those whose movements were restricted due to slavery or because of imprisonment or forced confinement by a family member and who thus had to remain in Mecca, for their identities, as well as the reasons for their inability to migrate are known.[259] So those mentioned in the Qur'anic chapter titled Al-Fath are the unknown heroes who laid the foundations of conquest from the very beginning, shouldered the burden and faced the hardship and suffering of this path, led a life bent under the yoke of longing and separation, and whose names we cannot even know.

This is surely a projection of Prophetic mercy. He did not ignore those people whose hearts he could not win over in the thirteen-year period where he strived his utmost to reach them. Rather, he went to Medina having laid the groundwork for continuing this contact after the migration. The unfavorable reactions he had seen from them for thirteen years could do nothing to stifle the sorrow he felt at their heading towards death as polytheists. In spite of everything, God's Messenger continued responding to them with compassion, and although he remained in Medina, continued his contact with them by means of the hidden heroes he left behind among them.

There were, no doubt, other objectives of this strategy, including receiving information beforehand about all kinds of violence planned by the Meccans, reducing challenging environments and heated situations as much as possible, and taking measures to foster reason and sound judgment. Other objectives include formulating counter-strategies to ensure that the process was achieved with minimal losses, and so avoiding bloodshed and greater blood loss. When we look at the lead up to the Conquest, it can even be said that one of the initiatives was simply to make people responsible for each other's care and welfare.

Underlying all these tactics is again "mercy." The Messenger executed a long-term strategy and intended that the masses, whose views were blurred by the stirring up of public opinion, would sustain the least possible damage until the day that they could see the truth more clearly.

As plural in Arabic indicates more than two, it can be understood from the Qur'anic statements that these people numbered at least three, both women and men. Moreover, there is no question of an upper limit. The meaning of this is that in Mecca at the time, there were many such women and men. In any case, the verses on this subject provide an account of the logic and reasoning behind the peace made at Hudaybiya, rather than relating their exact number and the tasks they undertook. Hence, the verse was revealed after Hudaybiya, and Mecca is the place described as having such people among its inhabitants. As for Hudaybiya, it is the name given to the course of events in which the Messenger of God—notwithstanding all the tension and provocation that continued for close to twenty days—demonstrated the principle, "Whatever terms the Quraysh propose today in which they ask me to show kindness to kindred, I shall accept."[260] After all the envoys he had sent, God's Messenger wanted to send 'Uthman also, and charged him with two important tasks. One of these concerned these unknown heroes. God's Messenger told him the residence places of these believers in Mecca and instructed him to go to them and inform them of the need to endure and be patient for a little longer.[261] For they had rejoiced upon hearing that the Messenger of God was only about 25 kilometers away, and began the anxious wait for him, in the hope that the years of longing and separation would come to an end. But now he was to turn back after signing a truce. In other words, at a time when they yearned for reunion, their hopes would be dashed and they would experience great sorrow instead. It was precisely so that they would not experience such sorrow and dejection that the Messenger of God sent 'Uthman to them and told them that they needed to endure this process for a little longer.[262] Otherwise, the people of whom even God's Messenger's closest Companions, including Abu Bakr, 'Umar, and 'Ali, had no knowledge, would become a target purely because of their being in Mecca, and Muslim might unwittingly kill Muslim.[263]

We see God's Messenger relating a similar detail to Walid ibn al-Walid, when sending him to Mecca to deliver from torture his brother Salama ibn Hisham and maternal half-brother 'Ayyash ibn Abi Rabi'a. Sending him alone to Mecca at such a critical time, he said:

"O Walid, set out for Mecca and hide in the house of the blacksmith by the name of so-and-so for he has become Muslim. Then try to find 'Ayyash and Salama. Tell them that you are my envoy and that I have commanded them to come to me. Inform them that God will assuredly provide them with aid and ease on this path."[264]

The names that God's Messenger provided to 'Uthman at Hudaybiya and the name of the Muslim blacksmith are still unknown to us. The meaning of this, however, is apparent. This demonstrates that the Messenger of God had strategies and practices that he did not disclose even to those closest to him. To discuss every vital or confidential matter openly can result in frustration and disappointment, even death.

The identities of these people indirectly referred to in the Qur'an, the names of whom God's Messenger revealed to 'Uthman and about some of whom we can only conjecture, are for the most part unknown. Furthermore, an examination of relevant narrations illustrates that these people were unknown even to one another, with the knowledge of each of them restricted only to their own area of concern. In describing these days, Junayd ibn Subai', whom we know to be one of them, says, "We numbered a total of nine, two of whom were women."[265] It is not possible for this figure to remain limited to that provided by Junayd, as according to the Qur'an the men and women each need to number at least three people, with no maximum. Another narration reads, "We were nine people, three of them women."[266] It is quite possible that those mentioned in these two narrations were responsible for looking out for each other or undertaking a joint activity. That is, the matter was carried out in complete secrecy, maintained in some cases even between husband and wife. For instance, Jimash ibn Qays ibn Khalid made preparations to join the resistance during Mecca's conquest, vowing that on no circumstances would they allow Muhammad free entry into Mecca. He rushed to his house as soon as he had heard the call of the like-minded Meccan chiefs and began preparing his weapons.[267] The following exchange, which took place between Jimash and his wife, who had accepted Islam earlier and had withheld this information from her husband and who noticed this change in him, vividly portrays the state of affairs:

"Why all this preparation? Why are you preparing what I see?"

"On account of Muhammad and his men."

"By God, I do not think that anything can stand in the way of Muhammad and his men."

"We shall see! I shall even bring one of them back as a servant, to wait on you!"

"Woe unto you! Do not, whatever you do, set out to do such a thing and dare to fight Muhammad! For, by God, had you seen Muhammad and his men, you would not have acted thus and would have quickly backed down."

"We shall see!"

After reciting lines of verse, Jimash set off and met up with Safwan ibn Umayya, 'Ikrima ibn Abi Jahl, and Suhayl ibn 'Amr at Khandama, and took up position with them there. A skirmish followed with the forces under the command of Khalid ibn al-Walid. Swords drawn, they swore that they would not allow them entry into Mecca.

Naturally, the outcome was not as they had anticipated, as they faced no less than Khalid in al-Walid. It did not take long for them to realize that there was no way out, and they all took flight. Scattering in all directions, some shut themselves up in their houses, others took to the mountains, while others still left Mecca, making for other towns and cities.

Jimash, however, came home covered in wounds, weary and trembling, banging on the front door. Seeing her husband in such a state, his wife understood immediately what had happened. It was now her turn, and she said to Jimash, who was utterly wretched, "So where is the servant that you promised me? I have been waiting for you since the morning."

Running for dear life, Jimash had long forgotten his promise of a servant. He said to his wife angrily, "Forget it! Quick, lock the door behind me!" Then, he turned to poetry once more. Laying the blame on Safwan ibn Umayya, 'Ikrima ibn Abi Jahl, and the others, he spoke of how they fell apart and scattered, how each of them scampered in different directions in fear, and detailed their crushing defeat.[268]

From all this we can conclude that these heroes maintained secrecy to the highest degree. There is constant activity, but no one is aware of the activities of another. Those who are aware are only aware of what falls into their area of activity and only know what they have found out in that drawn-out process. The limited number of narrations on the subject also serves to illustrate that each part of the process occurred well away from the knowledge and awareness of others. So much so that these heroes who resided in Mecca did not even know one another, let alone the believers in Medina.[269]

The most striking name among them was the Prophet's uncle 'Abbas.[270] He held a crucial role in Mecca from before the years of the Messenger's Prophethood. He represented the Banu Hashim as a natural member of the House of Assembly (Dar al-Nadwa), and held the Quraysh's office of providing drinking water and other refreshments to the pilgrims (*siqaya* and *'imara*).[271] After the commencement of God's Messenger's Prophethood, however, the Dar al-Nadwa became the central place where the Meccans came together to deliberate, plan, scheme, and develop strategies in the name of unbelief—their headquarters, so to speak. Being a member, 'Abbas had a natural right to enter this place as he pleased. Presumably at the directive of God's Messenger, he maintained his position here despite having accepted Islam, and without ever revealing his new identity. When describing this situation in later years, 'Abbas' slave Abu Rafi', as one of those who knew him best, stated that 'Abbas and his family had become Muslim early on, but had concealed this.[272] That 'Abbas' wife Umm al-Fadl is referred to in the key sources as the first woman to accept Islam after the Prophet's wife Khadija[273] also corroborates Abu Rafi's view. It is also reported that God's Messenger set Abu Rafi' free when he brought God's Messenger the good news of 'Abbas and his wife's acceptance of Islam.[274]

'Abbas' attitude and stance from the very beginning also reinforces this idea. The following account of 'Abbas' old friend 'Afif ibn Qays, who came to visit him in the early days of Prophethood, is noteworthy:

When I was a merchant during the Age of Ignorance I came to stay with 'Abbas ibn 'Abd al-Muttalib at Mina. While I was sitting with him, a man in the prime of life came out, looked toward the sky where the sun hovered above, and then stood for Prayer. Then a woman came out and stood for Prayer behind him. Then a youth just past the age of puberty came, and stood praying with them. I said to 'Abbas, "Who is this?" He said, "This is my brother's son Muhammad ibn 'Abdu'llah ibn 'Abd al-Muttalib, who alleges that God has sent him as a Messenger. None save this woman and this youth have followed him in his religion. But he says that the treasures of Chosroes and Caesar will be opened to him." "And who is this woman?" I asked. "This woman is his wife Khadija bint Khuwaylid," he said. When I asked him, "Who is this youth?" he calmly replied, "This youth is his uncle's son 'Ali ibn Abi Talib." "And what is it that they do?" I asked, to which he answered, "They are performing the Prayer."[275]

We see 'Abbas—who some sources report as having become Muslim during the period of nascent Islam—in a panic on the day of the Pledge of 'Aqaba. Concerned that God's Messenger whom they had looked out for until that day would leave for Medina, he said:

O people of the Khazraj,[276] you all know well the position that Muhammad holds among us. Though we may think differently about him, we have protected him from our people. He lives in honor and security among his people, but he is now to turn to you and join you. If you think you can be faithful to what you have promised him and withstand what is to befall you as a consequence, then assume the burden you have undertaken. But if you are going to leave him to his enemies and abandon him after he has gone with you, then leave him now, for he is respected and safe in his own land.[277]

As can be seen, 'Abbas asked them over and over again if they knew the exact implications of the invitation they had extended to God's Messenger. His purpose was to make it clear that an invitation in theory was merely the beginning of what was to come, and to ascertain whether or not they would protect the Messenger of God whatever may come to pass.[278]

In one of the letters he wrote to God's Messenger after the Migration, he mentioned that he wanted to come to Medina, but the Messenger of God said, "O uncle, remain where you are, for it is better that you stay in Mecca. This is, for you, an excellent jihad."[279] Furthermore, by indicating that his uncle would be the last person to migrate to Medina, the Messenger of God defined the exact time frame for 'Abbas' mission in Mecca.[280] Looking at the Prophet's words on that day from the latter period, it is possible to understand them as signifying, "You will remain in Mecca until the day of its conquest." Indeed, this was what happened. Hearing that God's Messenger had left Medina with a view to conquest, 'Abbas too left Mecca and met him along the way. Seeing his uncle, God's Messenger said, as though reminding him of his prophecy, "Just as I am the last in the line of Prophets, so too shall you be the last to migrate."[281] In just this way, 'Abbas was the last person to migrate from Mecca to Medina.

The greatest proof of 'Abbas' true identity in the early period is undoubtedly the course of events at Badr. Looking at the bigger picture, one can see that the leading name which drew the Meccans' suspicion, from Abu Jahl first and foremost, was 'Abbas. This was because he noticed that the Medinans knew their every step, and they had thus begun to harbor suspicions about one another. They realized that God's Messenger was informed of every matter they had deliberated upon and planned, and concentrated their efforts on possible suspects. However, as they had no solid proof, they could do nothing and were unable to resolve the matter. Badr, for them, was a valuable process where the battle lines would be drawn. This is why they especially forced those they supposed were close to the Messenger of God to fight, wanting to learn their 'true colors' on the military front.[282] The only exception to this was Abu Lahab, for in the eyes of the Abu Jahls of the time, Abu Lahab was a certified unbeliever who was close enough to use the same toothpick, even though Abu Lahab was a paternal uncle of God's Messenger just like 'Abbas was. When Abu Lahab, of whose place in their own ranks they entertained no doubt, said that he would not go to Badr, but would send in his place

Abu Jahl's brother, 'Asi ibn Hisham, who owed him four thousand dirhams, they raised no objection whatsoever.[283] However, when the names of individuals of whom the Meccans were suspicious, such as the Prophet's uncle 'Abbas, 'Ali's brother 'Aqil, his other brother Talib, and another one of the Prophet's nephews Nawfal ibn al-Harith, came into question, they responded in a very different way. For they suspected that some of them had already embraced Islam and that others would be sympathetic to Islam if left to their own devices. Their attention was focused on the Prophet's uncle 'Abbas and his relatives, the Banu Hashim in particular. Hence, 'Abbas was left with no other option but to go to Badr. On top of that, we see that the Quraysh strove to find this out from the very beginning. For example, when setting off for battle on that day, they turned to the wealthy individuals of Mecca for the preparation of their forces. In doing so, they passed the entire financial burden of all those who participated in Badr onto the shoulders of ten individuals and one of these was naturally the Prophet's uncle 'Abbas.[284] Those unaware of the Prophet's strategy, such as Abu Hudhayfa, even said, "Are we to kill our fathers and our sons and our brothers and our families, and spare 'Abbas?" For among Abu Jahl's forces coming to Badr on that day were his father, 'Utba, his uncle, Shayba, and his brother, Walid.[285]

When these words reached God's Messenger, he called 'Umar and said, "O Abu Hafs,[286] ought the face of the Messenger's uncle to be marked with the sword?"

God's Messenger's bearing in saying this, the expression on his face, and his general manner were read clearly by such Companions as 'Umar and they too were troubled. He offered to punish the utterer of this statement. But God's Messenger did not agree. On no account would anyone be punished for voicing their views. There was no such concept in his world. What is more, this was not a case of a matter being discussed with malice. It was crucial that people expressed their opinions for the truth to be revealed. In addition, these differences would be dissolved upon entering the melting pot of Islam, where all become one, and when the time came, everyone would be united around the absolute truth, and this was what ultimately happened. Those 'Umar thought were showing signs of hypocrisy at Badr each acquired the status of being the object of 'Umar's admiration, and faithful companions of God's Messenger.[287] So full of remorse was Abu Hudhayfa for his words concerning the Prophet's uncle 'Abbas that he feared their spiritual repercussions and said, "I never felt safe afterwards on account of those words which I spoke that day, but I hoped that martyrdom might expiate them." He was ultimately to find at Yamama the martyrdom he sought.[288]

Like fire, war is something easily begun but very difficult to control. Consequently, in a highly-agitated arena like that, things can spiral out of control and many a deviation and departure from what is right and proper can occur with it. 'Abbas found himself within precisely such tumult at Badr, to which he came very reluctantly, despite all the Prophet's warnings, and was taken prisoner.[289]

On the first night the captives were brought to Medina, the Messenger of God lay awake the whole night, unable to sleep. When his Companions who noticed this asked him the reason, he said, "I heard the writhing and moans of 'Abbas." So one of the Companions immediately rose to his feet and untied 'Abbas. Following all developments very closely, God's Messenger later asked his Companions why he could not hear 'Abbas' cries of pain any longer. The Companion who had untied 'Abbas' hands and feet stepped forward and said, "I untied him, O Messenger of God." These words were enough to put a huge smile on the face of the Prophet of Mercy. He was evidently very pleased with this action. However, he was a strategic leader just as he was a Prophet who was the representative of justice. He therefore instructed the Companion who had untied 'Abbas, "Go and untie all the captives."[290] In this way, those who had not been able to see the compassionate face of Islam until then would now be able to behold it, while at the same time ensuring that 'Abbas was not granted preferential treatment.

God's Messenger at one point inspected the captives with a group of his Companions. At this stage, one of the Companions jumped forward to say that the time had come, after the victory at Badr, for the renegade Qurayshi caravan. The Messenger's uncle 'Abbas, who was among the captives at the time, heard this remark also and, raising his voice in reply, said, "This would not be lawful for you."

This surprised everybody. This was strange indeed, for he had been taken captive and yet was speaking up, without hesitation or equivocation, on a subject with which most others would not interfere. The Messenger of God then asked, "And why is that?" This was presumably directed at showing to those who were accurately able to read developments and thus see the Prophetic strategy and the distinctiveness of 'Abbas. "Because," 'Abbas began, in response to this question, "God has promised you one of 'two', and He has bestowed on you already what He has promised."[291] Indeed, this was true, for the Qur'an declared:

Even when God had promised you that one of the two hosts (the trade caravan and the Meccan army approaching) would fall to you, you still wished that other than the powerful, armed one should fall into your hands—whereas God willed to prove the truth to be true by His decrees and make it triumphant, and uproot the unbelievers (by causing their leaders to die). (Al-Anfal 8:7)

In this way, God had pledged either the trade caravan, or the Badr victory. Now, given that He had favored them with a victory at Badr, it was not fitting that they pursue the trade caravan and show ambition in this regard. God's Messenger turned to 'Abbas and said, "You speak the truth."[292]

Considering that this Qur'anic verse of which 'Abbas makes mention was revealed during the pursuit of Abu Sufyan, who had left Damascus with his caravan and was close to Badr, the situation changes completely. For 'Abbas is aware of a Qur'anic verse that was revealed only ten days ago.[293] What is more, at that point, he was with the Meccan forces that were on their way to Badr. Clearly, this points to communication between the unknown believers of the time and God's Messenger, such that 'Abbas was aware of a newly revealed Qur'anic verse. Not only was he aware of the verse, but he grasped its meaning, and was the first to object when the idea of following the trade caravan was raised following Badr.

Around this time, God's Messenger and the Companions began to discuss what would be done with the Badr captives. God's Messenger, who tried to share the credit for his every step with his Companions, asked such leading Companions as Abu Bakr and 'Umar for their views. Abu Bakr was of the view that they should be forgiven, while 'Umar held that they ought to be put to death. 'Abdu'llah ibn Rawaha was harsher: "O Messenger of Allah," he said, "as far as I can make out, there is abundant wood and twigs in this valley. Gather them there and set fire to the valley."[294]

Needless to say, 'Abdu'llah's approach was due in large part to the fifteen years of persecution and suffering in Mecca and to the reason for their coming to Badr in the first place. He thus thought that this was what the captives had long since deserved. Of course, Prophetic mercy could not in any way accept this suggestion, which arose from heated emotions. It was a blood-curdling proposal, and no sooner did 'Abbas hear it than he again intervened and indicated its wrongfulness, saying, "You have severed the ties of kinship!"[295]

At one point, relations on his mother's side had approached God's Messenger wanting to intervene, and said, "O Messenger of God, allow us not to take the ransom of our maternal cousin, and to thus set him free."

"No," he said, and added, "You are not to leave even a single *dirham* of it."[296]

The consultations ended and the time came to release the captives for ransom. The Messenger of God demanded four thousand *dirham*s from his uncle 'Abbas. There was a plan of action that 'Abbas had not yet been able to fully comprehend and he said, "O Messenger of God, I was a Muslim."[297] He was right in his own way. For fifteen years he had put up with the Meccans and had gritted his teeth and borne all manner of trial and affliction. He had been forced into coming to fight and with a bleeding heart he came; on top of that, he had been taken captive and his pride was wounded. Moreover, treating those people with whom he had become close friends to meals and tempering their ferocity with gifts were all matters requiring financial means. What is more, there was no one in Mecca to help him with these undertakings. And now God's Messenger was on the verge of taking the wealth that he had kept in reserve too. But the Messenger's strategy was altogether different, and so he turned to 'Abbas and said, "God knows best concerning your Islam." Then he continued, "If it is as you say, God will reward you for it. So pay your ransom. You must ransom yourself, your two nephews, 'Aqil ibn Abi Talib and Nawfal ibn al-Harith, and your confederate, 'Utba ibn 'Amr, the brother of the Banu al-Harith ibn Fihr, for you are a wealthy man."[298]

These were suggestions that shook 'Abbas, for he was still unaware of the Prophet's strategy. What is more, while he had appealed for a reduction in his financial obligation, God's Messenger now demanded from him the ransom money for four people. With a glimmer of hope, he said to God's Messenger, "But I have nothing with which to pay." However, this, too, was to prove fruitless. God's Messenger would signal that all paths were closed, and that 'Abbas should no longer insist, saying, "Where is the money that you left in Mecca with Umm al-Fadl, and no one else was present with you two when you said, 'If I am killed, then 'Abdu'llah is to have so much and al-Fadl is to have so much'?"

'Abbas was thunderstruck: "By Him Who sent you with the Truth," he said, "I bear witness that you are indeed the Messenger of God. For this is a thing that none except Umm al-Fadl and I knew."[299]

In addition to this, there are accounts that 'Abbas requested that the twenty *'uqiyya* he brought with him should be credited towards his ransom, to which God's Messenger replied, "No, that was something which God gave to us by means of you."[300] So 'Abbas realized that he was surrounded on all sides after Badr and was forced to pay ransom for himself, as well for three others.[301]

On the day that news of the Badr defeat reached Mecca events were quite dramatic. Hearing of the disastrous outcome, Abu Lahab flew into a rage. The bringer of the news began to relate how they had suffered a devastating blow at the hands of people they did not know, describing everything in the minutest detail, down to their mounts and turbans, and 'Abbas' slave, Abu Rafi', could not help but blurt out, "By God, those were the angels!" This revealed the allegiance that he had kept hidden until that day and Abu Lahab swooped upon Abu Rafi' to vent his rage on him. 'Abbas' wife, Umm al-Fadl, realized that one of the Meccan chiefs was looking on and was infuriated by Abu Lahab's beating a slave in the absence of his master. She therefore took hold of a tent pole and brought it crashing down upon Abu Lahab's head and, in that way, was able to protect Abu Rafi's secret. For Abu Lahab, stunned by the might of the blow, died a few days later without being able to share what he had learned on that day.[302]

Situations indicating 'Abbas' Muslim identity were certainly not limited to Badr. Scrutiny of the mission that 'Abbas fulfilled afterwards in Mecca reveals that this was a conscious Prophetic strategy. At Uhud, a most critical point, God's Messenger received letters from Mecca, and the author of those letters was without question 'Abbas himself.[303] What is more, it is worth stressing that while a letter under normal circumstances could only arrive in six days at the earliest, sources document that it took three days on the Mecca-Medina route for 'Abbas' letter to reach God's Messenger.[304] It is also apparent that the Messenger of God dispatched expeditions and campaigns along the Meccan route early on, in order to ensure safe passage, and that by signing agreements with the tribes en route, he was prepared for any surprises. Clearly this implies an uninterrupted journey realized via transfers along the way, with rested camels and camels that were travel-ready.

The content of the letter is also worthy of note. It informs God's Messenger of the discussions and deliberations in Mecca, what kind of strategies were developed, the nature of the forces gathered and its participants, the expected time of the attack, and the general atmosphere in Mecca. It also added a note on the urgency of action and the need for preparations to be complete before those of their opponents.[305] 'Abbas' letter reads:

The Quraysh have gathered to advance upon you, so do what you must when they come to you. Complete your preparations before them and act before they do. They are headed towards you, and number three thousand. They lead two hundred horses, and have seven hundred armor plates and three thousand camels, and they have taken all their weapons with them.[306]

This is the chief reason for individuals such as 'Abbas remaining in Mecca. In this way, God's Messenger formulated new strategies to ensure that the masses marching upon him in vengeance were able to return without harm or with minimal losses. To be more precise, the Messenger of God sought to send 'Abbas, who served as his eyes and ears, to Mecca once again, and in so doing, dispel all the suspicions entertained by the Meccans, and so strengthen his hand.

We see 'Abbas, who was devoted to his nephew's cause, was particularly sensitive when God's Messenger went to Khaybar. Harping on this move, the Meccans disseminated lies and misinformation as part of their psychological warfare, and began to announce that the Messenger had been defeated at Khaybar. Already full of apprehension, 'Abbas is said to have languished and fainted in response to this unfavorable report.[307]

When 'Abbas finally caught wind that his nephew had left Medina for the conquest, he understood his mission in the city was complete, and thus set off, their paths crossing in Juhfa. When the Messenger of God saw him, he said, as though wanting to remind him of what he said to his uncle the day he sought permission to migrate to Medina, "Just as my Prophethood is the last in the line of Prophethood, so too is your migration, dear uncle, the last migration."[308] This expression of favor was at the same time an indication that Mecca would embrace Islam and that the door of migration would henceforth be shut. Thereafter, God's Messenger sent 'Abbas' load to Medina[309] and set out to Mecca for the conquest, taking 'Abbas with him.

While there were many causes and factors in the conquest of Mecca, it can be argued, in light of all this information, that perhaps the most important figure in the backdrop to the conquest is the Prophet's uncle 'Abbas.[310] The course of events changed based on the intelligence he provided. The Messenger of God took steps to enable violence to be replaced with mercy, instead of those in which violence bred violence, and the most arduous circumstances were endured with minimum damage.

Ties of kinship

Another one of God's Messenger's strategies was to open new doors where all doors had been closed one by one, and to form new ties with his addressees. Those who stood against him and confronted him with their hostility until their dying breath were all united in their ties of kinship also. Almost all of them were descendants of Qusayy ibn Kilab. Though these people, known as the 'Quraysh' on this account, later branched into separate sub-clans, they were essentially kindred. At a time when tribal life predominated, which bound them even closer together, such a connection was not one that could be bought for all the money in the world. A person who was related to a fellow clan member was related to their entire clan. They were thereafter treated as "one of the family," and all the clan's members conformed to this social norm.

Sharing a common ancestral origin, the Meccans thought to furnish security for their future through similar alliances. From this perspective the opponents of God's Messenger were establishing new bonds of kinship with each other and striving to forge new and dynamic power relationships. For instance, Abu Sufyan's sister, Umm Jamil, was married to the Prophet's uncle, Abu Lahab.[311] Walid ibn al-Mughira was married to Lubaba bint al-Harith, who was at the same time 'Abbas and Safwan ibn Umayya's sister-in-law. Suhayl ibn 'Amr was married to Abu Jahl's daughter, Hunfa', while 'As ibn al-Wa'il was married to the daughter of Hisham ibn al-Mughira. Similarly, Umayya ibn Khalaf married his son,

Safwan ibn Umayya, to Fakhita,[312] daughter of Walid ibn al-Mughira, while Abu Jahl married his son 'Ikrima to Umm Hakim, the daughter of his brother Harith ibn Hisham.[313] Abu Jahl's brother Harith ibn Hisham was married to Fatima bint al-Walid, the daughter of his uncle, Walid ibn al-Mughira, and also sister of Khalid ibn al-Walid.[314] In an environment where the bonds of kinship were so closely intertwined, Safwan ibn Umayya, 'Ikrima and his brothers, as well as Khalid grew up as brothers.[315]

There is no doubt that the parallel practices of God's Messenger played a part in the softening of the hardest hearts of the time. This was also divine guidance. The Qur'an, which reduced the number of women a man could marry according to the customary practice in pre-Islamic Arabia, and encouraged monogamy, allowed God's Messenger to marry several women in order to influence all his addressees within as little as twenty-three years. When his first wife, Khadija, died after 25 years of marriage, the Messenger of God made use of his subsequent marriages to build close ties at a time when all the doors on which he knocked were slammed shut in his face. Moreover, it is not possible to suppose that the marriages of God's Messenger, who stated, "God has assuredly willed that I marry only those who are of Paradise,"[316] and who took every step in line with the Divine injunctions, could have been realized except by God's permission. Within this context, he states, "Each of my marriages and those of my daughters was conducted as a result of Divine permission conveyed to me through Gabriel."[317] In this way he was able to meet, on the basis of kinship, with people who were otherwise unapproachable, and it was in these encounters that the hearts of those who had been consumed with hatred and enmity were softened. The marriages of God's Messenger functioned as a bridge in his communication with them, and served to relax the atmosphere as well as legitimize his steps in their eyes. He extended hospitality towards them, invited them to his wedding feasts so his marriages united people, and sent them gifts, drawing attention to their affinity. In a culture where maintaining the ties of kinship held great importance, he found opportunities to converse with them through visiting them or hosting them at his home. In this way the Messenger of God established a close connection with those whose hostility had been most intense, and ensured that their animosity was soon transformed into mildness and affection. The most salient example of this is his marriage with Umm Habiba the daughter of Abu Sufyan, at a time when the latter's audacity and effrontery was at its height.

Marriage to Umm Habiba

Tension in Mecca had reached its peak. The unrivaled chief and representative of this tension, especially in the post-Badr period, was Abu Sufyan. As fierce as a bird of prey, he made all imaginable attempts to end the life of God's Messenger, even sending a contract killer to Medina for that purpose. He was the one behind the brutality at Uhud, and it was he who held the position of commander at Khandaq. It was precisely in this period that Gabriel came to God's Messenger and revealed to him the following verse:

(When you obey God in His commands and prohibitions,) it may be that God will bring about love and friendship between you and those of them with whom you are in enmity. God is All-Powerful, and God is All-Forgiving, All- Compassionate. (Al-Mumtahana 60:7)

The timing was striking: at a time when hostility was most intense, this verse announced that this hostility would fade away and, what is more, foretold that it would be replaced by love and affection. There was more good news: it affirmed that this transformation was possible by God's power, and that such love and friendship could only be attained by forgiveness, acceptance, humility, avoiding retaliatory attitudes, and by compassion. This verse also echoes other Qur'anic statements that describe deep fellowship between those who were in fact once enemies,[318] and prescribe the necessary steps to realize this message. The unmistakable message is that even the staunchest enemies will one day come face to face with reality and lay down their arms, and in defiance of the past, lead the rest of their lives as heroes of love.

For God's Messenger did not harbor any enmity at all towards any other. His enmity was directed at enmity itself. So those who acted in enmity were, more often than not, the Meccans, and at the helm as their leader was none other than Abu Sufyan. While he was not present in person at Badr,[319] he was the commander of the forces at Uhud and Khandaq. He was also the protagonist in various skirmishes that took place between these two events. In the verse mentioned, Abu Sufyan clearly stands as the fulcrum of the enmity that is to be transformed into affection in the near future. The verse also indicates that not just Abu Sufyan's enmity, but all manner of enmity would be eradicated when the compassion in the latter part of the verse would be rendered the essence of one's occupation and when the path would be trodden with active patience. The hearts of the Meccans would then be filled with love instead of hatred.[320]

Naturally, the establishment of love is possible only through knowledge, for one is indeed an enemy of what one does not know. The Abu Sufyans of the era showed hostility because they did not know God and His Messenger, and did their best to avoid such knowledge. In this sense, the verse pointed to Abu Sufyan as the first objective for the believer in achieving this acquaintance. The most potent way of ensuring this acquaintance, as mentioned at the outset, was through kinship.[321] The scholarly Companion 'Abdu'llah ibn 'Abbas, honored with the special prayer of God's Messenger and extolled by the epithet the Sage of the Community (*Hibr al-Ummah*), offers an account of these events:

The marriage of the Messenger of God to Umm Habiba was conducted after the revelation of the verse, "*It may be that God will bring about love and friendship between you and those of them with whom you are in enmity. God is All-Powerful, and God is All-Forgiving, All-Compassionate*" (Al-Mumtahana 60:7). Mu'awiya thus became the maternal uncle of the believers.[322]

Not only did the Messenger of God understand the verse's implications, but he also took pains to put the words of the Qur'an into practice. The marriage took place in the following manner:

Having received a message from Gabriel, the Messenger of God sent his Companion 'Amr ibn Umayya to the Negus, or King, of Abyssinia, giving him two letters to present to the sovereign. In one of these letters, God's Messenger invited[323] to Islam[324] the new Negus, successor to the throne of Negus al-Asham ibn Abjar, who had sixteen years earlier welcomed Ja'far and his friends to Abyssinia. In the second letter, God's Messenger requested that the Negus wed him to Ramla bint Abi Sufyan,[325] whose husband[326] had died and left her alone with her daughter in Abyssinia.[327]

Abu Sufyan was pleased[328] upon learning of his son-in-law's death[329] and from the moment he received the news entertained the hope of his daughter Umm Habiba's speedy return to Mecca. However, the latest report reaching him had it that Muhammad the Trustworthy had taken his daughter in marriage. He was dumbfounded yet again. Indeed, he knew Muhammad the Trustworthy, and even felt a certain closeness to him in terms of kinship.[330]

But as he had set his hopes on the moment when he could let bygones be bygones and welcome his daughter with open arms once again, it was not at all easy for him to stomach his daughter's marriage to the person he deemed his archenemy, and upon whom he had advanced with his forces. Despite this news making the powerful Meccan chief's blood boil, he was not naïve: he knew he could do nothing about it. This is why he merely remarked, "A suitable match!" He then added the proverbial phrase, "A noble camel can't be bridled."[331]

By this marriage, God's Messenger also became brother-in-law to Safwan ibn Umayya, another one of his fiercest enemies. Safwan was married to the sister of Umm Habiba, Umayna bint Abi Sufyan.[332]

What has been related thus far concerns the central objective of the Prophet's marriage to Umm Habiba and the manner in which it took place.[333] Let us now take a look at what happened to Abu Sufyan after the marriage took place. Abu Sufyan, who was also a prominent merchant, began seeing Medina differently, especially on his travels to and from Damascus. The trade route passed through Medina and residing in this city was his very own daughter Umm Habiba. As a result, he began coming up with various excuses to call upon his daughter whenever he had the chance. He was now frequenting the house of the man whose sight he could not bear, especially after Badr. Needless to say, he encountered a great many new things on each of these visits. Until that day, he had closed all doors to Medina, except the one that led to hate, while now he was beginning to discover it, not through the accounts and construal of others, but through his personal observations. For instance, on one of his Medina visits, he called upon his daughter Umm Habiba. Naturally, he expected respect from his daughter, but was met instead with a reaction he did not expect at all. When he wanted to sit down on a mattress, Umm Habiba promptly pulled the mattress out from under him and did not allow him to sit down on it. In astonishment, he exclaimed, "Dear daughter! I hardly know if you think that I am too good for the mattress or that the mattress is too good for me?"

The answer Umm Habiba gave her father only increased his shock: "It is the mattress of God's Messenger," she said. "I just deemed you unworthy to sit on it, for you are an idolater, and are impure. This is why I did not want you to sit on the mattress of the Messenger of God." His shock was compounded. "O daughter," he said, "how you have changed for the worse since I saw you last!"[334]

It was true that his daughter had changed a great deal. This change had brought her to her true essence and had enabled her to be a slave to the All-Merciful, whereas Abu Sufyan was still doing the incomprehensible. This is why she turned to her father and said, "On the contrary! God has honored me with Islam. As for you, father, you allow yourself to worship stones, mere idols that have power neither to see nor hear."[335]

Only just beginning to find himself, Abu Sufyan had now taken a completely new course. Every episode he experienced, every sentence he heard, and every person he spoke to was toppling the sacrosanct idols within his world one by one. Now, he too could discern that everything spoken in Mecca for the past eight years was nothing but a lie.

This marriage was thus the beginning of a new era. It simultaneously served as one of the breaking points in the lead up to Mecca's conquest, as God's Messenger had opened a crucial door at a time when all doors had been shut one after the other. God's Messenger, too, would pass through this door like Abu Sufyan, and was to build new bridges to the Meccans, beginning with the family of Abu Sufyan.

After this marriage, Abu Sufyan's policy began to change. He was no longer consumed by hatred, and did not utter threats of death in fits of rage. His character changed a great deal so that he could sit down and talk. The glad tidings conveyed in the Qur'an were thus beginning to bear fruit, and an eighteen-year enmity was rapidly melting away in the warmth of this closeness. The "Perfect Embodiment of the Qur'an," whom God had confirmed with Divine revelation, was reaping the fruits of every step that he took. This was not, of course, a step that was intended only for Abu Sufyan. Before long, Abu Sufyan's other daughter, Durra,[336] joined her sister in Medina without the knowledge of her father, and embraced Islam.[337]

The Messenger of God, the Pride of Humanity, was building a new future, brick by brick. He had used a strong mortar in building the foundations of the Meccan conquest that would be realized several years later; Abu Sufyan was to play a critical role in the smooth surrender of the city.

There was also the matter of Mecca itself. The leader that the city's inhabitants had viewed as a "hawk" until that time was now exhibiting an altogether different attitude, a completely transformed identity when it came to Medina in particular. Even though they put pressure on him to return to his former ways, it proved fruitless, and they resorted to bypassing him in certain matters. Khalid ibn al-Walid, 'Ikrima, Safwan ibn Umayya, and Suhayl ibn 'Amr in particular, had emerged as a deadly foursome in opposition and animosity towards Islam. They were, for instance, those who stopped God's Messenger at Hudaybiya. It was also they who kept the compensatory pilgrimage under their firm control and followed it most closely.[338] Nevertheless, God's Messenger was trying to win them over too.

Marriage to Safiyya

When looked at from the aforementioned perspective, it quickly becomes apparent just how pivotal was the marriage of God's Messenger to Safiyya.[339] She was the daughter of Huyayy ibn Akhtab—the most intractable figure among the Jewish communities the Prophet was in contact with at the time. Her father was a chief of the Banu Nadir. He made fighting with God's Messenger his life's mission, and by inciting his tribe, caused their ultimate banishment from Medina. During this period of exile, he settled in Khaybar, only this time to provoke the people of Khaybar into active revolt against God's Messenger. Perhaps his greatest attack was when he traveled with a group of Jews first to Mecca and then to all the other tribes and clans, uniting all of them to form the Confederate forces, with a promise of worldly gains and glory.[340] His hopes were great for the venture, in which everyone other than the Muslims mobilized and advanced upon Medina. Besides, judging by appearances, there would be nothing left standing in Medina, merely by their marching through. Moreover, it was Huyayy himself who persuaded the Banu Qurayza into fighting—the same Banu Qurayza who had remained faithful to their truce right up until the Confederate forces surrounded Medina and with whom God's Messenger had renewed agreement in this time. He went to the house of Ka'b ibn Asad to impel him to renounce the agreement with God's Messenger, and while not successful to begin with, managed to persuade him after much insistence. Banu Qurayza thus raised the flag of rebellion.[341] No doubt, it was also Huyayy who led the way in inveighing against the Messenger of God and injuring him personally with his insult and invective.

Relationships that had followed a normal course until Badr[342] slowly began to take a tense turn, and as a result of this, some Jewish tribes then began rising against the State of Medina. These clashes, however, remained local. Under the control of God's Messenger they never turned into a battle between Judaism and Islam, even though certain tribes were engaging in armed insurrection against the state, and there was a defensive reflex by the state. Here, too, the first response of God's Messenger, after investigating the truth of the reports, was diplomacy. He sent emissaries, more often than not going in person for deliberations, explaining the futility of the uprising and the severity of its consequences, and thus trying to dissuade them from pursuing their ambitions. Despite all the efforts to deter them, they refused to change. When they carried the matter too far, the Companions advanced against them and God's Messenger resolved the matter to defend the state.

This process culminated in Khaybar. Given that Khaybar took place in the seventh year after the Migration in the month of Safar,[343] the period of conflict with the Jews can be said to have lasted for close to four years. Khaybar was to prove a turning point in relations with the Jews, where the tension experienced would come to an end, strained relationships would be mended through new agreements, and relationships were restored to a normal plane, free of latent hostility or distrust. However, those God's Messenger addressed then were human beings too, and in this period continuing for close to four years, sensitivity increased both on the part of the Jews and on the part of the Muslims, and even the smallest shortcomings began to be viewed as great wrongs.

Just as after Badr, the Messenger of God began repairing relations, which required extra sensitivity, and took a step that neither side expected—he married the daughter of Huyayy ibn Akhtab, the most difficult figure. This marriage had several facets. Putting all the troubles behind him, God's Messenger personally demonstrated to the Muslims that enmity cannot be shown to anyone because of their Jewishness. By also showing the Jews the boundlessness of his heart, he proclaimed to them that the door to reconciliation remained wide open for them.[344] Finally, he took the opportunity to demonstrate how the wives and daughters of the defeated should be respected and protected by the victorious forces.

Safiyya, daughter of Huyayy ibn Akhtab, and the daughter of her uncle were among those who were taken prisoner at Khaybar. After her father,[345] and then her husband, Kinana ibn Abi'l-Huqayq, had been killed at Khaybar, she was anxious about what might become of her along with the other captives.

After the battle, Dihya al-Kalbi asked the Messenger of God for one of the captives and God's Messenger agreed. Dihya, an emissary of the Prophet and in whose form Gabriel often appeared to God's Messenger, went to the captives and chose Safiyya for himself. One of the Companions witnessed this and immediately approached God's Messenger and said, "O Messenger of God, you gave the noblewoman, the daughter of Huyayy ibn Akhtab, chief of the Banu Qurayza and Banu Nadir, to Dihya, while she befits none but you."

Such was the discernment of the Companions, who had been molded by Divine revelation and educated by God's Messenger himself. They were right. Such a preference also meant the conquest of Khaybar through the heart. So God's Messenger called Dihya and asked that he choose another one of the captives for himself instead. He then called Bilal, and requested that they be brought to his presence.[346]

Bilal rushed to Safiyya, who had been anxiously observing developments, and informed her that the Messenger of God had sent for her. As soon as she heard, she remembered a dream she had had years earlier. She had even reminded her husband of it before Khaybar, and he had struck her for it.[347] Furthermore, the Messenger of God was the talk of virtually every Jew, her own father and uncle above all, and now he was summoning her.

So that they could reach God's Messenger sooner, Bilal took a short cut through the battlefield. Naturally, strewn across the field were the vestiges of the skirmish. Seeing the corpses of two Khaybarites on the way, her uncle's daughter let out a scream and began throwing soil all about her. God's Messenger, who saw the scene, called out, "O Bilal!" God's Messenger was crushed with sorrow. He continued, as though to teach his followers a lesson in kindness, an ounce of which he himself had never received, "Have you no compassion, that you brought these women past their dead?"[348]

When Safiyya appeared before God's Messenger, he presented Islam to her. He merely explained and left her free to choose whether or not she would accept it. This was not the only option he presented her with. He informed her that he would take her in marriage in the event of her acceptance of Islam, but should she refuse, she would be set free and sent back to her people.

Everything about him clearly demonstrated that he was the Last Prophet expected to come at the end of time, the one foretold in the Scriptures. While he was a victorious commander, he was addressing one the captives directly and conversing with her. What is more, instead of saying, "Should you refuse, I will make you pay," he said, "I will release you and send you back to your people." Only a Prophet could have exhibited such rectitude.

"O Messenger of God," she began, "I long desired to embrace Islam before you invited me to accept it and wished to affirm your Prophethood. I no longer have any concern with Judaism, nor any connection to it. You leave me free to choose between unbelief and Islam and I choose God and His Messenger. God and His Messenger are dearer to me than my freedom and than my returning to my people."[349]

These were, at the same time, expressions that indicated the profundity of her knowledge, and God's Messenger first set Safiyya free and then took her as his wife. The daughter of the most intractable figure in Medina and one of those captured, "Zaynab"[350] suddenly found herself one of the Mothers of the Believers. Her dream had come true and she had, at this moment, forgotten all her cares.[351] What is more, upon their arrival in a place two nights' distance from Medina, the Messenger of God gave a wedding feast as a sign of his marriage to Safiyya and asked her to invite those close to her.[352] When the preparations began for the return to Medina at the end of the feast, the Companions saw God's Messenger covering Safiyya with a cloth, and down on his knees, waiting to help her to mount her camel with ease. Safiyya then placed her foot on his thigh and got up on her camel.[353]

An interesting incident took place before this: when they were inside the Prophet's tent at nightfall, God's Messenger heard the sound of footsteps approaching outside. Considering how close the individual had come, God's Messenger believed it was someone coming to appeal to him in a particular matter. God's Messenger stepped out of his tent before the person could come any closer. Abu Ayyub al-Ansari, the spiritual guide and pride of the city of Constantinople (present-day Istanbul), was standing guard, armed with his sword. Seeing him, God's Messenger asked, "O Abu Ayyub, what is the matter?" "O Messenger of God," he said. "I feared that harm would come to you from this woman for her father, her husband, and her people were killed at Khaybar, and she was until just recently in a state of unbelief. I was afraid for you on her account and so kept watch."[354]

This was typical of the Companions. They took responsibility upon themselves for any situation; in this case, Abu Ayyub considered what might happen if the Messenger were left alone with a woman whose closest relations had only recently been killed, and he came to stand sentinel outside the tent. At the same time this reflected the attitude of the Companions towards Safiyya's tribe. They were vigilant because they had received blow after blow from her tribe and were as cautious as they could possibly be. This was a delicate situation and God's Messenger raised his hands and beseeched God, "My Lord, guard Abu Ayyub just as he came here with the intention of spending the night guarding me."[355]

What happened next? The other wives of God's Messenger did not take kindly to his marriage to the daughter of a Jew who had constantly escalated the tension for the past four years. There were those who criticized her purely because of her Jewish origin and who condemned her for her connections. They viewed differently someone who had entered the boundless atmosphere of God's Messenger and whom he had taken into his intimate sanctuary as a member of his household. On top of that, highlighting the close ties of kinship of their own fathers and ancestors, they said that they were closer to God's Messenger, and that Safiyya was more distant from him. What is more, her relatives had done all that they could to exacerbate that distance. When some of his wives even claimed to have superiority in the eyes of God's Messenger due to their relationship by descent as well as through marriage, God's Messenger became angry and said to her, "When they speak to you or dismiss you, say, 'How can you fare better than me when my father is Aaron and my uncle, Moses?'"[356]

During one of his journeys, the Messenger of God took Safiyya to accompany him and at one point Safiyya's camel became unruly and ran away. God's Messenger turned to another of his wives who also accompanied him on the journey[357] to ask, "Safiyya's camel has run away. What about giving one of your camels to her?" She replied, "Give my camel to that Jew?" Hearing such hate-filled words coming from someone so close to his inner sanctum, God's Messenger was greatly angered and severed his relations with her for two or three months.[358]

In the early days of her arrival in Medina, Safiyya was a guest in the home of Haritha ibn al-Nu'man, where all the women of the Ansar came to visit her and expressed their admiration of her beauty. 'A'isha had also come, her face veiled. Seeing her leave, God's Messenger approached her and, referring to Safiyya, asked her, "How did you find her, O 'A'isha?" When he received the reply, "I found her to be Jewish," he was very saddened by this and said to 'A'isha, "Do not speak such words, for she has become a Muslim and quite a fine one at that."[359]

Against Abu Bakr's daughter, 'A'isha, and 'Umar's daughter, Hafsa, the Messenger of God supported the daughter of Huyayy ibn Akhtab, his inveterate enemy amongst the Jews. Because of his marriage to Safiyya, the phobia of the Jews that had begun to form among the Companions was abated, and being Jewish was no longer a justification for enmity. For the Jews too were now relatives of God's Messenger. As his wives were "*Mothers of the Believers*" (al-Ahzab 33:6), the Companions began to view the Jews as maternal uncles and aunts.

There was also the dimension of this marriage that concerned Safiyya's family and relatives.[360] Following the wedding, some of those who at once found themselves within the atmosphere engendered by this closeness came to the Last Messenger, for whom they had been waiting for years on end, and professed their belief in Islam.[361]

The following question ought to be asked at this juncture: Why, at a time when every woman aspired to be wed to God's Messenger, did God's Messenger marry the daughters of Abu Sufyan and Huyayy ibn Akhtab, the very two men who went out of their way to cause him every kind of offense and injury? And what is more, when both of them were now unprotected having lost their husbands.

The meaning of this is crystal clear: it was the Messenger of God who took the first step and made the first sacrifice in order to put a stop to problems that were escalating. Just when relationships had reached break point, he made a move that was as novel as it was completely unanticipated.[362]

Had we been able to take similar steps today as three or five families and enabled the intermarriage of our children with those who deem us enemies, in lieu of hurling insults at one another in the public arena, then we would have solved most of those "chronic" problems that have cost thousands of lives and that have caused immeasurable fortunes to go to waste. Alas! In any case, when the path taken is not a "Prophetic" one, the road that is traveled will amount to nothing more than running around in circles.

Juwayriya

Another one of the marriages God's Messenger conducted that helped conveying his message was with Juwayriya. Juwayriya was the daughter of the chief of Banu Mustaliq, Harith ibn Abi Dirar. When her father was engaged in preparations for an offensive against Medina with all the forces he could muster, God's Messenger had information gathered about their movements and activities, and acted before he had the chance to attack the city and defeated him. Juwayriya was among those captured and she had fell to the lot of one of the Companions. She made a contract with her captor for her release, according to which she was to pay a hefty sum and be set free.[363]

At one point, she summoned all her courage and came to God's Messenger to plead her case. "O Messenger of God," she said, "indeed, I am a Muslim woman and I bear witness that there is no deity (to be worshipped) but God and that you are the Messenger of God. I am Juwayriya, daughter of Harith ibn Abi Dirar, the leader of my people. The troubles that have befallen me are not unknown to you. I fell to the share of Thabit ibn Qays ibn Shammas and his cousin. Thabit released me from his cousin with a portion of his date orchards in Medina (in payment). Thabit concluded an agreement concerning me that I have no power to fulfill. To that, however, I agreed of my own accord. Nothing forced me to it except that I hoped help to come from you, that you would assist me in obtaining my liberty."

God's Messenger asked her, "Would you like that which is better than that?" Surprised by such a response, she said, in nervous excitement, "What is it, O Messenger of God?" He said, "That I pay the amount stipulated in the contract and that I marry you."

She was insightful a woman as not to miss out on such an opportunity being offered her, without her paying even a single coin. "Yes, O Messenger of God," she said, "I accept."[364]

God's Messenger now sent for Thabit ibn Qays and informed him of his wish to pay Juwayriya's ransom in full and take her as his wife. The Messenger's offer pleased Thabit immensely. He had already supposed that the daughter of the Banu Mustaliq chief befitted God's Messenger.[365] God's Messenger was just about to take another Prophetic initiative in healing their hearts and rebuilding their wounded pride. Thabit said, "By my father and my mother, she is yours, and without recompense."

In spite of this, the Messenger of God paid the amount to Thabit that had been agreed upon in her contract, released Juwayriya, and then married her.

The events that unfolded after this are of great importance. News of the Messenger's marriage quickly spread among the Companions, and every Companion who heard about it viewed their captives as the Messenger's relations by marriage. The Banu Mustaliq, whom they had only just faced on the front line, and when they had least expected it, had suddenly become related to God's Messenger.

How could the relations of the Messenger of God ever be looked upon and treated as captives? As mentioned in the discussion on prisoners of war, Juwayriya not only freed herself from captivity, but was the means for the liberation of all her people. For all the Companions began releasing their captives and displayed yet another example of magnanimity never before seen in human history. Purely for the sake of this kinship, one hundred families were set free and, availing themselves of the blessings of this auspicious marriage, declared their acceptance of Islam. Upon learning of these developments from the daughter of her uncle, Juwayriya glorified God and praised Him for allowing the freedom of her people to be secured through her.

'A'isha was to later refer to this transformation that came about through Juwayriya, with the words, "I know not a woman who was a greater blessing to her people than she," and she went on to say that a hundred families were released out of respect for the Messenger's relationship to them through marriage.[366]

Interestingly, even though her father Harith ibn Abi Dirar, who had such a narrow escape on that day, lost his reputation and personal property, he sprang into action a few days later to free his daughter, and came to Medina bringing his remaining camels with him. He intended to give, in exchange for his daughter, however many camels were demanded in ransom and take her and return back home. When he reached 'Aqiq Valley, he began looking at his camels over and over again, for he was about to voluntarily surrender his remaining wealth. This gnawed away at him, and the two camels he admired in particular he set aside, hiding them in one of the passes of the valley. He planned to give the other camels for his daughter's ransom and, upon his return, retrieve these two camels and go home with them.

When he eventually arrived in Medina, he went to God's Messenger with his daughter's ransom and said, "Muhammad, you have taken my daughter captive; here is her ransom!"

The Messenger of God was sorry to see the state of the man who until scarcely one month earlier had very different aspirations. He looked at the camels that Harith offered in return for his daughter's freedom and said, "And where are the two camels that you hid in such-and-such pass in the valley of 'Aqiq?"

Harith was at a loss for words. He had hidden the camels in a desolate place and, what is more, there was not a living soul around to see what he had done. How, then, could Muhammad the Trustworthy possibly have known about the existence of these camels? No, this was not a matter that could be known by any mortal. This demonstrated that Muhammad the Trustworthy indeed acted upon Divine revelation after all. Following a dazed interlude, he turned to God's Messenger and after his daughter and his people, he too declared, "I bear witness that you are the Messenger of God!"[367]

The Prophetic strategy had conquered yet another hardened heart. This conquest was not to be limited to Harith; in spite of all the tribulations they faced, his entire tribe was to come before God's Messenger and deliver themselves to his atmosphere of mercy.[368]

Other wives of God's Messenger

When considered from this perspective, the same question applies to all of the wives of God's Messenger, as all of the Mothers of the Believers were members of their respective tribes and clans—to whom God's Messenger addressed himself—and all had their parents, their uncles, siblings, and other relations. These ties were the most powerful points of contact in society. Through his wives, the Messenger of God aimed to reach a tribe, a city, and a nation, and in time achieved his objective. Each of the Mothers of Believers served as bridges connecting him to their own communities.[369] As the central theme of our discussion is not the marriages of God's Messenger, we looked at his marriages with Umm Habiba, Safiyya and Juwayriya to give the reader some idea in this regard. Whichever of his wives is taken into consideration, the same fact emerges, that he reached a great number of people through them. For instance, Maymuna, whose marriage to God's Messenger was proposed by his uncle 'Abbas, was one of the few people who had ties of kinship to a great many people in Mecca. Abu Sufyan's mother Safiyya bint Hazn ibn Bujayr al-Hilaliyya was her paternal aunt.[370] Her mother Hind bint 'Awf ibn al-Harith was known as the most honorable woman among Arabs at the time, by virtue of her descent.[371] She was one of ten sisters,[372] and on the day that God's Messenger married her, he became at once related to nine tribes simultaneously. He became brother-in-law to Walid ibn al-Mughira and Ubayy ibn Khalaf, and established connections with their relations, and as a result to their deceased ancestors, and drew the attention of the pair once more. Although God's Messenger was in Medina at the time, he brought his relatives in Mecca closer to one another and laid before them a new path by which they could overcome their preconceptions and prejudices. This was because the children of Walid ibn al-Mughira, Ziyad ibn 'Abdu'llah and Ubayy ibn Khalaf, Khalid ibn al-Walid first and foremost, and the children of 'Abbas, Ja'far and 'Abdu'llah ibn Jahsh were cousins through a maternal relationship. The marriage of God's Messenger to Khalid ibn al-Walid's maternal aunt, Maymuna,[373] was pivotal to his acceptance of Islam. The marriage took place during the Compensatory Pilgrimage. Through it, God's Messenger sought to give a banquet to the Meccans, who had just the year before prevented him from performing the lesser pilgrimage (*'umra*) and who, even then, had allowed him to stay at the Ka'ba for only three days. But he could not get them to accept. As always, he did not fail to do what fell to him to do.

He sent for Walid ibn al-Walid[374] and asked him, "Where is Khalid?"

Like the others, Khalid too had taken to the hills to observe what they deemed to be "humiliation," over the three days where a lot was squeezed into a very short time. As a result, Walid replied, "I know not, O Messenger of God. I have not had the chance to speak with him."

Yet, there were things that God's Messenger had knowledge of. And so the Messenger of God began describing Khalid ibn al-Walid in the presence of his brother, referring to everything from his intelligence and bravery to all his other virtues. Praising him to the skies, it was as though making a legend of him, depicting him as the ultimate hero. He then asked, "Will he still not come?" And added, "A man like Khalid cannot remain ignorant of Islam for long." He then paid compliment to him saying, "And were he to come, we would certainly have honored him and preferred him to others."[375]

With God's Messenger's departure, Walid ibn al-Walid wrote a letter to his brother Khalid, saying, "Despite the fact that you have left no adversity that you have not inflicted on us, God's Messenger asked me about you on his return. While I could not relate anything to him about you, he said a great many things about you."[376]

When this letter, in which the Messenger's statements concerning his brother were conveyed, eventually reached Khalid, the situation was to be altogether altered. A letter had come to him from the very place that he had hitherto chosen to observe from afar and upon which he had only marched sword in hand, and its gracious contents became imprinted on his heart. He read it again and again. What kind of logic was this? What kind of magnanimity and humanity was this? The person for whose downfall and ruin he worked for twenty years, now bestowed on him compliments as though he had been following his every step, and called him with a view to conferring distinction upon him.

First, he went to Abu Sufyan and said, "Come, let us go together." But he was not yet ready, or perhaps there were other things that he still needed to do in Mecca, as part of his mission. He then knocked on the door of his brother-in-law,[377] Safwan ibn Umayya. He, too, refused.[378] Subsequently, he made arrangements with 'Uthman ibn Talha to set out to Medina together. They met up with another traveler on the way, 'Amr b. al-'As, and together, the three of them came to God's Messenger, to the luminous world of Islam.

The role of Umm Salama in 'Amr's acceptance must not be overlooked, as he was a member of the Banu Makhzum—Khalid ibn al-

Walid's tribe.[379] Walid ibn al-Mughira was his paternal uncle.[380] In other words, he and Khalid ibn al-Walid were cousins through a paternal uncle. At the same time, the Banu Makhzum was also the tribe of the Abu Jahl, and by connection, of 'Ikrima.[381] Umm Salama was also related to Zama'a ibn al-Aswad. She was the sister of his sister-in-law, Qurayba bint Abu Umayya.[382]

Assistance

Following the Qur'anic verse revealed after the Battle of the Trench and heralding the coming of a time where love reigned supreme, was the verse which declared that God did not forbid the believers to deal kindly with those who did not fight them on the basis of their religion and who did not drive them out of their homes. The verse ended with the declaration that God loves those who deal kindly and justly.[383] After the revelation of this particular verse, God's Messenger immediately moved into action and, by marrying Ramla bint Abi Sufyan (Umm Habiba), took a step towards putting an end to all manner of hostility. The time had now come for the second step. Given that all hostility was to end, all his attention was focused on the Meccans.

The news since Uhud was not very positive for them; trade was slow. On top of that, the Meccans were suffering the scourge of famine. The people were struggling to make a living and writhing under financial trouble and hardship. Despite being the ones who had challenged God's Messenger when leaving Uhud, calling out, "O Muhammad, you were victorious at Badr, while today at Uhud, we have defeated you. The matter thus remains undecided. We shall meet again at Badr next year, where the victor will be determined," panic set in when the time approached, and they resorted to all manner of means to avoid going to Badr. Meccan leader Abu Sufyan, who was at the same time at the head of the city's forces, was of the view that they should not be the side taking the first step and thus made plan after plan to prevail upon Medina. So as not to be the reneging party, it most certainly had to be God's Messenger, and not they, who failed to come to Badr.

For all Abu Sufyan's exertions, God's Messenger still set forth for Badr when the time came, with his Companions, 1,500 strong, on the basis of Abu Sufyan's call at Uhud. Even though Abu Sufyan wanted to cancel this challenge within this period, he was unable to do so in a manly fashion. He sent frequent messages without letting on that he did not want to go to Badr, and always on account of others, wanting God's Messenger to be the one who did not turn up. He wanted to say to those around him, "Do you see? We were to face them once again at Badr, while they got scared and could not come! Victory is ours!" And he was to win a battle, in his own way, without lifting a finger. This is why he could not say that they had better give it up. Now, he heard of the Messenger's heading from Medina in the direction of Badr with his Companions, and was tormented at the prospect of disaster.

Desperate, he too set off with an army of two thousand men, but was well aware that he was heading for defeat. There was no way that an army made up of all these troubled, destitute members who could not even see to their own needs, could ever win battle. Attempting such a venture, the end result of which was clear from the beginning, was unreasonable to say the least. To him, this undertaking spelled the end of the Quraysh. He advanced, but a fear that ate away at him held sway. When he eventually reached Marr al-Zahran and they encamped by the Majanna well, he addressed his men, saying, "O people of the Quraysh, turn back! Only a plentiful year will suit us wherein we can pasture our animals on the herbage and drink their milk, whereas this year is a year of drought. How can we be expected to fight during such famine? Indeed, I shall return, and so must you."

So they did. As though expecting this call, the Meccan army returned in high spirits. Moreover, as they had slaughtered camels on their way to Badr for food, the Meccan army had to make do with barley soup. This is why the Meccans called this army the Barley Army (Jaysh al-Sawiq).[384]

Their situation only worsened with each passing day. Out of hunger, they began to eat bones and carrion, their eyes lost their luster, and they began to see even the clear blue sky as clouded over. Meanwhile, their animals had also come to the brink of death. It was on one of these days that they sent Abu Sufyan to God's Messenger to petition him to pray for rain. "Muhammad," said Abu Sufyan, "you enjoin the people to keep good relations with their kin, whereas your people are now dying. Entreat God for them that He may deliver them from their hardship."

This was indeed a strange predicament. They mobilized all the resources at their disposal for his downfall on the one hand, while turning to him for assistance at a time when they were facing annihilation, on the other. Even within this contradiction, there were the workings of Prophetic mercy: God's Messenger had not burnt the bridges linking him to anyone, even under the worst of conditions, and did not shut the door in anyone's face, with the hope that they might one day return. Now they had come and, though they did not believe in him, were begging God's Messenger to beseech God to help them.

The Messenger of God now raised his blessed hands for them, and asked that His All-Merciful Lord deliver the Meccans from their tribulations, have mercy on them and send them rain. Then came the rain clouds. The Meccans had received a mercy that would gladden them and ease their hearts, for it was pouring with rain.[385]

Even though they were favored with Divine grace through the Messenger's prayer, they failed to appreciate this blessing, let alone recognize the true worth of that Prophet of Mercy, and once again returned to their former state. Needless to say, the punishment for such ingratitude was a return to their former days, and before too long, days of famine began again for the Meccans, and they were thus inflicted with manifold Divine punishments.[386]

Several years passed, and the Messenger of God set forth to Khaybar to solve yet another problem. With a conquest that came after drawn-out sieges, he returned to Medina with abundant wealth.[387]

Contrary to expectations, God's Messenger did not divide up the spoils gained from Khaybar among his Companions. He had the great wealth loaded onto camels and sent it to the Meccans who had caused trouble for twenty years without interruption. The Companion 'Amr ibn Umayya was driving the camels, while those to whom the aid was sent were the Meccan ringleaders of unbelief, such as Safwan ibn Umayya and Suhayl ibn 'Amr. Among them, 'Ikrima, Safwan ibn Umayya, and Suhayl ibn 'Amr could not tolerate even a wind blowing from the direction of Medina. They led the way in denial and vehement hatred of Islam and the Muslims. In spite of this, a fortune was heading for Mecca from Medina on the backs of camels. In this aid, for instance, were 500 dinars (of gold coin), which was great riches at the time.[388]

Human history was again witnessing a first. While he himself was repeatedly injured, God's Messenger never once caused injury. To those who dealt blow after blow to him, he responded with not even the slightest aggression, but always treated them with benevolence and compassion. Now he was doing the same thing. He extended a hand to those who were eager to destroy him and was sending them a huge fortune in order to save them from the dire straits in which they found themselves.

The intended outcome, however, was not achieved. Even though they were suffering and dizzy from hunger, they turned down the aid, and sent it straight back. Suhayl ibn 'Amr, in particular, was furious. While they were well aware of the great need of those around them, they could not bring themselves to accept assistance from the very place against which they had until now directed unbridled acts of violence and hate.[389] This generous offer was, nonetheless, a most poignant message that struck a deep chord. Judging by the past, they knew well that not just anyone would offer them such help. Although they were not at all interested in accepting the offer, they saw the distinction of God's Messenger once again, and knew they were the recipients of yet another honorable act.

God's Messenger was saddened to see the aid that he sent come back. But he did not give up, and sent the same contents back to Mecca, with one notable difference, as this time, both the recipient and the method had changed. 'Amr ibn Umayya led the camels, along with their load and a letter from God's Messenger, directly to Abu Sufyan. Abu Sufyan received the letter from God's Messenger and began reading it: "I send you all of this in exchange for the leather you have in Mecca."

Failure to consider the Prophetic sensitivity here would lead one to overlook the tactfulness in this letter. Note that after the return of the aid that God's Messenger sent, he changed his method and presented the aid he wished to send as an exchange, trade or barter. This was, after all, how business was generally conducted at the time. To veteran merchant Abu Sufyan he said, "Take these and send me leather in exchange." Abu Sufyan was well versed in this language and responded favorably to his offer, distributing these goods to their correct destination in spite of his former actions.

The following question may well arise at this point: During this time, Abu Sufyan was the Prophet's father-in-law, and this proximity gave rise to his softening and adopting a more reasonable position with respect to Islam and God's Messenger. Why then, did God's Messenger feel the need to alter his method instead of sending these goods as aid? The answer, however, is clear: Had God's Messenger sent this contribution as "aid," the Meccans would have disdained Abu Sufyan immediately and would have questioned his character, honor, and dignity. And even if he were to work wonders, they would no longer care to listen to him. They would have completely dismissed the leader, whom they had already begun to disregard when it suited them, after his daughter Umm Habiba's marriage to the Messenger of God, and they would never have followed him again. However, in Mecca's seamless transformation was a vital mission that Abu Sufyan would fulfill. The Messenger of God therefore changed his method—as an expression of mercy and in consideration of the situation of the Meccans — for a brand new offer which would strengthen Abu Sufyan's hand.

Receiving this offer, Abu Sufyan's eyes shuttled between the wealth-laden camels and the letter in his hand. He was moved. He began by saying, "May God have mercy on the son of my brother and reward him with abundant good. For he has fulfilled the dues of kinship and has seen to our welfare." Abu Sufyan then distributed all of it to Mecca's poor.[390] Then came the time to send the leather, and Abu Sufyan fulfilled God's Messenger's request. He also wrote a letter of response to God's Messenger informing him that he had dispatched the leather that he had specifically asked for.[391]

With these supplies that came to their rescue at a time they most needed it, the hearts of the Meccans were conquered once more. To be more precise, the steps that God's Messenger took each time in a different way yielded results, and the conquest of their hearts flowed throughout the community.

That is to say, one of the most effective ways of penetrating hearts, solving problems, or winning people over, is to be with people during times of difficulty, not hurting them even if one is hurt oneself, returning evil with acts of goodness, and being with them with every resource at our disposal, so as to revive lifeless hearts. As the steadfast representative of this method, God's Messenger saw the hatred and animosity of those he addressed melt a little more with every passing day, and awaited the paradisiacal future that would appear on the path on which he took these steps. His waiting took the form of "active patience"; who knows what actions he endured while waiting.

International diplomacy

The Meccans, who looked for any opportunity to kill him and mobilized all possible means to overshadow all the good with which God's Messenger came, still appealed to him when they faced a situation that they could not overcome. We saw an example of this in the prayer for rain that they sought from him at a time when they were suffering drought and famine.[392]

The chief of Yamama, Thumama ibn Uthal, who was set free and who put aside his hatred and became Muslim as a result of the honorable treatment he received in captivity, came to Mecca with the Messenger's permission, seeking to complete the lesser pilgrimage that he had been unable to do earlier.[393] He presumed that Mecca was a safe place and thought that all those who entered it would be assured of safety as well. But the matter was not at all as he thought. The Meccan polytheists cornered him, took advantage of the situation, and made an attempt on his life. Not only did they prevent him from performing his worship at the House, they wanted to kill him and make an example of him.

They were just about to realize their aim when one among them warned that this action would come at a high price for them. This was because Yamama was the source of grain sold in Mecca and this killing would spell hunger and destitution for the already famine-stricken Meccans.

Thumama survived on that day, but he viewed the Meccans with hatred and detestation and affirmed that he would not send them even an ounce of grain henceforth. And he did as he said he would. The supply of grain from Yamama was cut off and the Meccans faced great hardship.

Abu Sufyan, who had shouldered every kind of responsibility for the Meccans, traveled to Medina to appeal in person to God's Messenger to intervene in the situation. He had no doubt that Thumama would listen to the Messenger of God. A complete solution to the matter thus rested in Medina and this was why Abu Sufyan came.

He first provided a brief summary of the situation and then sought help from the Messenger of God, requesting his personal mediation.

He received the exact treatment he expected. God's Messenger took him seriously and reciprocated by responding favorably to his request. He immediately sent a letter to Thumama, the chief of Yamama, asking that he lift the embargo against Mecca.

Was it at all possible for God's Messenger to make a request and for his Companions not to comply? This letter that he received from the Messenger of God made Thumama forget all his troubles and the transporting of grain to Mecca resumed. From then on, Mecca would be free from the fire of hunger and days of hardship, and would return to its former days of ease through the Messenger's mediation.[394]

It was as though things had settled between Mecca and Medina, with new pages opened each day by the messages God's Messenger conveyed through his actions. As a result of this meeting, the Meccans, who had until this day produced imaginary enemies and were reluctant to set foot on Muslim lands, would now be able to freely conduct the trade they had planned in the Syria surrounds and would be able to travel in safety without any occasion for concern. Abu Sufyan was surely at the head of those who benefited from this arrangement.

Gifts

It is also evident that God's Messenger used the resources at his disposal as gifts in order to dispel the animosity of his addressees, and alleviate the tension between them so that he could meet and converse with them on friendly terms. In describing this characteristic of God's Messenger, Anas ibn Malik says:

"*Sometimes a man would come to ask something worldly of God's Messenger, but his opinion would change before nightfall, by which time Islam would have become dearer to him than the world and all that it contains.*"[395]

Again, illustrating this aspect of God's Messenger, Anas relates a personal anecdote:

"*Whenever the Messenger of God was asked for a thing by a person in the name of Islam, he would give it. A man once came to him and he gave him a flock of sheep scattered between two mountains. When he returned to his people, he said to them, 'O people, accept Islam, for Muhammad gives to a degree that allows no fear of poverty.'*"[396]

Just as he gave gifts to those around him, the Messenger of God also sent gifts to tribal chiefs and rulers in his surrounds. Muslim sources report that when sending back to their lands the envoys who came to visit him in Medina, he saw them off with bundles of presents. For instance, when members of the Hanifa and Tha'laba delegations wanted to return to their homes, the Messenger of God ordered that five 'uqiyya (of silver) be awarded to each of them.[397] To all the members of the Murra delegation he gave twelve 'uqiyya,[398] and to 'Abdu'llah ibn al-Ash'ath he gave twelve 'uqiyya.[399] He granted delegations from the tribes of 'Uqayl ibn Ka'b and Ja'da a valley and tract of land in which there were springs and date palms, informing them separately of this in writing.[400] Just as he sent those coming from Sulaym away with gifts,[401] he presented the ambassador of the Qushayr ibn Ka'b with clothes and asked him to distribute these among his people.[402] He affectionately patted the face of Khuzayma ibn Sawa' from the Muharib delegation and sent him back with gifts, as he did all the other delegation members.[403]

We also know of his sending gifts to the Negus, who gave his Companions a kind reception in Abyssinia, protected them and who refused to send them back to Mecca despite all the Meccan pressure. Our sources even provide accounts that the last of these gifts included essences and perfumes. But the Negus had passed away before this gift reached him, and upon their return to Medina, God's Messenger gave some of these to Umm Salama and the others to the rest of his wives.[404]

Even more striking is the fact that God's Messenger was grieved when he did not have anything on his person that he could give as a present and that he showed this distress to his addressees. For example, following the envoy and letter that the Messenger sent to Byzantine King Heraclius, the ruler reciprocated, sending an envoy from whom he requested information on three matters.[405] God's Messenger was at Tabuk at the time. God's Messenger wanted to give a present to the envoy,[406] who reached him at the well of Tabuk to present Heraclius' letter,[407] but was unable to find anything close at hand to give him. God's Messenger said to the envoy, "Indeed you are the messenger of a people and have claim over us, but we are at present travelers who are on the move, and possess nothing with us that we can present to you as a gift." 'Uthman intervened at this point, giving some cloth to the envoy on behalf of God's Messenger. In addition to this, the Messenger of God turned to his Companions and asked whether there were any among them who would treat the envoy to a meal, to which one of the Medinan natives responded.[408]

The Prophet's paternal cousin, 'Abdu'llah ibn 'Abbas, who was known as the ocean of knowledge, indicates that exchanging gifts is a Prophetic legacy and relates that God's Messenger said, "Honor and give gifts to the foreign delegations as you have seen me doing."[409]

Compliment and prayer

Another of the methods used by the Messenger of God in reaching out to people and winning their hearts was showing affection to those he addressed, paying compliments to them, and allowing them to feel that he was with them during their times of difficulty by means of prayer. For example, he affectionately patted the face of Khuzayma Ibn Sawa',[410] the Muharib envoy whom he showered with gifts when seeing him off, and after paying a compliment to a representative from the delegation of the 'Amir ibn Sa'sa'a in greeting him, he said, "You are of me and I of you."[411] In much the same way, he addressed the twenty-member Rabi'a and 'Abd al-Qays delegation, complimenting them and saying, "Welcome to you all. What a good people are the 'Abd al-Qays." He paid particular attention to Munqidh ibn Hayyan, patting him on the face, and turned to 'Abdu'llah al-Ashajj among them, praising him with the words, "You possess two characteristics loved by God: forbearance and dignity." He hosted this delegation, honoring them with feasts for ten days.[412]

Upon the arrival of the Murra delegation, he offered a supplication for their respective towns. To the members of the Fazara delegation, he inquired after the condition of their towns and after hearing of the hardship that they were enduring, ascended the pulpit and prayed to God for them.[413]

In the case of 'Adi ibn Hatim, who came to God's Messenger as a Christian, when God's Messenger saw him, he stood up, held him by the hand, and led him to his own home. Here, he continued his courtesy to him, providing him with a cushion to sit on, while he himself sat on the hard ground. He then talked to 'Adi at length about Islam, dealing with all his potential reservations, and answering all his questions. God's Messenger informed him of the luminous future of Islam, spoke of the atmosphere of safety and security that would be established on earth through Islam, and invited him to Islam also.[414]

We see that God's Messenger, who was ever a representative of restoration and revival, was not open to demands for destruction and ruin.

For instance, Tufayl ibn 'Amr who once came to God's Messenger informed him that his own tribe, the Daws, had abandoned their association with Islam and showed an inclination to return to their former days. He then asked God's Messenger to invoke God's wrath upon them. Upon hearing this, God's Messenger exclaimed, "The Daws is on the verge of ruin," and instead of cursing them, said, "O Lord, grant guidance to the people of Daws, and bring them (to Islam)."[415]

Furthermore, God's Messenger is known to have prayed not only for the believers, but for the polytheists also, who had not yet been able to recognize the luminousness of this world.[416] It is well known that the second 'Umar in his famous supplication, "O Allah, strengthen Islam with one of the two 'Umars" was none other than Abu Jahl himself, whose actual name was 'Amr ibn Hisham.[417]

Welcoming the "other"

Another way in which God's Messenger affected people's hearts was to enable them to enter his own atmosphere, to share the space that they had characterized as "other," and, thus, to come to realize the beauties within. The objective of all this was to eliminate negative preconditioning, to free reason and logic from the pressure exerted by emotions, and to be able to welcome them in settings where they could become more closely acquainted with the culture that they had identified as their "enemy." When the life of God's Messenger is looked at from this perspective, it becomes evident that he realized with ease one by one, despite the harsh stance of his addressees, practices that people today would have difficulty accepting. He extended hospitality to them in his own mosque, despite others' objections, and made sure they did not feel those objections in the slightest. He even allowed Christians to perform their services in the Prophet's Mosque, which can be considered the first mosque of Islam. While he was a Messenger who was sent to abolish all former falsehood and corruption, he did not place before them any obstacle that would prevent them from freely practicing their beliefs.

An example of this occurred when members of the Thaqif delegation came to Medina in the ninth year of the Migration, during the month of Ramadan, to meet with the Messenger of God. The Messenger of God had a tent pitched for them inside the Prophet's Mosque.[418] There were those among the Companions who deemed this situation odd. This was because the members of the delegation had not yet become acquainted with the radiant countenance of Islam and had not yet become Muslim. Some Muslims came to God's Messenger asserting that they were polytheists, and that they could not stay in the mosque in that state. To those who objected, God's Messenger said, "Indeed, nothing makes foul the earth."[419] Thereupon, Mughira ibn Shu'ba,[420] who belonged to the same tribe, intervened and requested that his people come stay with him at his home. God's Messenger, however, did not share his view and said, "I will not debar you from receiving your people, but do so in a place where they can listen to the Qur'an."[421]

Taking the first step himself, he sent his Companion Mughira ibn Shu'ba to the Najran Christians, and later sent a letter inviting them to Medina. As a result of these developments, a sixty-member Christian delegation set off from Najran to meet with the Messenger of God in Medina.[422] Even if their reason for and approach to the visit was different, God's Messenger received and hosted them in his own space, had a special tent pitched within his mosque for them, and allowed them to conduct their worship therein. He even obviated the objections of some of his Companions to their offering their religious services facing the east and enabled them to perform their worship just as they wished in this space that was Islam's second most important place of worship, as well as his base.[423]

Not making people feel guilty

Another point that God's Messenger observed in his communications, especially when dealing with people who caused a lot of problems, was not to disclose what he knew about others, even if everything was obvious to him. The same thing applied for his Companions. He did not permit them to talk in such cases, did not approve of demands to punish them even when their evil plots became manifest. The most striking instance of this was the hypocrites who revealed themselves particularly after Uhud.[424] The Messenger of God never confronted the hypocrites who deserted him at the most critical stage of the Battle of Uhud and who emboldened the enemy by demoralizing the believers. Not once did he use their shortcomings as an excuse, or hold their faults against them, and he always treated them in accord with their outward identities, as though no problem were ever experienced with them. The same was also true for the crimes they committed in subsequent periods. God's Messenger did not resort to punishing them despite their blatant treachery, slander, threats, and insults, nor did he sanction any demands for their death in retaliation for all their manifest crimes. In the period when 'Abdu'llah ibn Ubayy slandered the Mother of the Believers, 'A'isha, and stirred up trouble, 'Umar sought permission from God's Messenger to kill him, which God's Messenger categorically denied. Instead, he ordered the army to march towards Medina, to eliminate any opportunity for discussion, and set off on a journey of close to twenty-four hours. Once the truth was divulged with the revelation of the Qur'anic chapter *al-Munafiqun* (The Hypocrites), to the very sentences 'Abdu'llah ibn Ubayy denied, the same individual began losing his supporters one by one. God's Messenger then said to 'Umar, indicating him:

"Do you see, O 'Umar, had I allowed you to kill him when you sought permission from me to do so, he would have become a hero for those who now seek his ruin."[425]

In the same incident, the son of the notorious hypocrite came to God's Messenger and expressed his concerns about the rumors that his father might be put to death. But the Messenger of God assured him that his father would be dealt with kindly.[426]

As is evident, the Messenger of God did not adopt the course of punishing even the leading figure in an episode that caused him so much anguish and deep distress, and the Messenger did not have him killed despite his guilt being confirmed by Qur'anic revelation, and while there were those who wholeheartedly sought to do so. He thus indicates exactly how even seemingly inextricable matters can be solved with deliberation and careful consideration.

Once witnessing people speaking of the hypocritical orientation of one such person in their absence, he immediately intervened. Voicing a favorable opinion of the person, God's Messenger thus cleared him of accusation and blame before others.[427]

Although he knew those who had schemed against and attempted to kill him during the Tabuk campaign, he concealed his knowledge, closed the door to those who came to him with the suggestion of killing,[428] and in this way waited for the time when these opponents too would melt away within the peaceful atmosphere of Islam.

He led the funeral prayer of the well-known hypocrite, 'Abdu'llah ibn Ubayy, who was behind every kind of wickedness and whose position virtually all the Companions knew. God's Messenger even placed his mantle over him.[429] Like Abu Jahl, perhaps this figure too passed over to the Hereafter with his former identity; however, as a result of the practices of God's Messenger in his dealings with them, he won over the hearts of practically everyone in their circles and as with all his other affairs, solved the question of hypocrisy from its source.

Familiarity with his audience

The Messenger of God knew his audience very well whether on an individual, or familial basis, or at the tribal, local or national level. He knew their culture, and he put this knowledge into action in his dealings with them, addressing them through their own core values. He was very closely acquainted with their history, the great figures of their past, the geographical features of the region in which they lived, their daily lives and lifestyles, and even their day-to-day pursuits and occupations. He was well versed in their languages, their accents and dialects, and spoke to them in their own accent and dialect when addressing them. This situation was not lost on his Companions, who from time to time expressed their astonishment at the language he used, and asked him the meaning of his words in order to understand what they heard. For the language that God's Messenger employed in such settings was not only unlike that of the Quraysh, but it was also different to that spoken by surrounding tribes and states. For example, some Yemenite tribes used *am* (*alif* and *mim*) in place of the standard definite article *al* (*alif* and *lam*). When one of them came to God's Messenger and asked him about the propitiousness of fasting while traveling, saying, "*a min am birru am siyamu fi' im safari?*" he used the same dialect in answering him. God's Messenger responded, "It is not a part of righteousness to fast while traveling," in the speaker's own dialect (*laysa min am birri am siyamu fi' im safari*).[430]

We are also able to observe God's Messenger taking new steps to winning over hearts even when setting off for conquest. For instance, when he headed towards the land of the Thaqif for the Ta'if campaign, he saw an unmarked grave whilst scaling the peaks during his advance.

Stopping beside the grave, he said to his Companions:

"This is the grave of Abu Righal, the forebear of the Thaqif. He belonged to the Thamud and was delivered from the destruction that befell his people by virtue of his visit to the Sanctuary. When he left the Sanctuary, the affliction that struck his people seized him in this place, where he was later buried. The sign of this is the golden bough with which he was buried. Were you to open his grave, you would find it there."

Whilst advancing upon the Thaqif, God's Messenger identified the grave of their ancestor Abu Righal, and took a further step towards solving the matter through peaceful means. Indeed, the Companions set about opening the grave at once and before long found the bough that God's Messenger had described. The veracity of yet another disclosure of God's Messenger had thus become manifest.[431]

From time to time, he would ask those who called on him questions about their elders and would speak of their virtuous characteristics. He turned to his audience on one of these occasions and asked whether there were any among them who had seen Quss ibn Sa'ida and heard him speak. When no one else came forward, Abu Bakr stood up and said, "I remember that day like it was yesterday, O Messenger of God." He then recited Quss' famous sermon clearly and very distinctly. The Messenger of God confirmed Abu Bakr's words.[432]

Instrumental to Addas' acceptance of Islam was God's Messenger's saying after having asked him where he came from, "From the town of the righteous man Jonah the son of Matta, my brother!" When reaching out for the grapes he offered to God's Messenger, Addas was startled to hear him recite the words, "Bismi'llahi'r Rahmani'r Rahim" (In the Name of God, the All-Merciful, the All-Compassionate). Hearing the name of Prophet Jonah on top of this stupefied him. His immediate reaction was to exclaim, "How do you know Jonah, the son of Matta? By God, since leaving Nineveh (present-day Mosul situated in the far away Upper Mesopotamia), I have not met ten people who know anything of him. How did you come to know him?" God's Messenger replied, "He is my brother. He was a Prophet, as am I." Immediately, upon this acquaintance, Addas became Muslim.[433]

As can be seen, God's Messenger knew not just of the region in which he lived, but also of the culture and natural resources of distant lands, and he sought to establish a rapport with his audience by sharing this knowledge with them. For instance, in a letter he wrote to the Chief of Hamdan, he made mention of the region's native flora and natural resources, even describing how they drew benefit from these in raising their camels and livestock.[434]

It is reported that he even corrected their mistakes, when necessary. For example, he reminded 'Adi ibn Hatim of a practice that was not permitted according to 'Adi's beliefs, but that he engaged in anyway. God's Messenger thus indicated his knowledge of 'Adi's actual situation, as well as the need for him to reform. 'Adi was astonished at God's Messenger knowing what was not generally known and at his possessing such specific and thorough knowledge about his own beliefs, and so he embraced Islam. He was later to recall this incident, conceding his shame at the attitude he displayed on the day, and added that he was delighted that the Messenger's never mentioned the incident again after that day.[435]

Seeking peace and honoring treaties

Throughout his life, the Messenger of God was always the representative of peace. He concluded agreements with all the diverse groups with which he made contact, and most scrupulously honored these agreements to the end. Hudaybiya generally comes to mind at the mention of peace and was a process characterized by the pursuit of peace. When the life of God's Messenger is examined from a more universal standpoint, it becomes clear that he led it, from beginning to end, as the Prophet of Peace. Even during the Meccan period when a new conflict occurred every day, he was always party to peace, never condoned tension, and he sat and conversed with even the most intractable of people. Even at times where the doors were shut on his face, he bided his time until he could sit down with them in conversation, extended hospitality to them, invited them to meals, organized feasts for them, and called upon them at their homes at the risk of being turned away. And through all this, for every door that was shut, he aimed to open new doors that would allow him to reach them.

With his Migration to Medina, he immediately signed agreements with two different communities with whom he dealt, earned the trust and support of both the Arabs and the Jews despite having come from outside Medina, and established a state on the foundation of peace. This state that was founded on rule of law, embraced and addressed itself to all the subjects, and took it as a duty to ensure that they could all practice their beliefs freely and openly.

God's Messenger's arrival in Medina spelled the end of an ongoing war of 120 years, and a surprise peace was effected between the parties. Even in the conditions of the day, blood feuds that people had thought would never end came to a halt, arbitrary killings were put to an end, and Medina became acquainted with all the seriousness of a state on the path of peace.

Immediately after the establishment of the Medinan State, contact was made with surrounding tribes and towns. While security was ensured via patrols, agreements were made and treaties signed with all the tribes visited, thus expanding the security cordon, until ultimately, a peace that no one could even have imagined was established in the Hijaz. In a region where no one had been able to travel alone between cities, within a very short time a climate of peace formed, where women could travel on their own. And all this was realized with 19 military campaigns and 36 expeditions.

An era when no one trusted the other, those with power acted as they pleased, and the weak had no recourse to any authority if their rights were violated, when perpetrators got off scot-free, and when arbitrary rule was the order of the day[436] was transformed into an extraordinary age centered on justice, and where rule of law defined human affairs.

Reaching this point was, of course, no easy task. There were efforts to undermine this peace with provocations from time to time, but God's Messenger stood behind the promises he made and the agreements he entered into, did not conceal or gloss over wrongdoing, gave those who were wronged their rightful due, and was never the party who broke an agreement. He is, after all, the Prophet of a religion that prioritizes peace and deems keeping agreements the indispensable attribute of a believer. The Qur'an with which he was sent also commands him thus.[437] Declaring, "*How could there be a covenant with those who associate partners with God (and recognize no laws and treaty) on the part of God and His Messenger? —Excepting those with whom you made a treaty in the vicinity of the Sacred Mosque: (as for the latter) so long as they remain true to you, be true to them. Surely God loves the God-revering, pious (who keep their duties to Him)*" (At-Tawbah 9/6), the Qur'an sets out the necessity of granting security to those seeking it. It is also the Qur'an that emphasizes granting protection to people because peace is a positive way for people to recognize the beauties of Islam. And it is the Messenger of God who states, "Whoever kills a person granted permission (visa) to enter your land, temporarily residing therein, or with whom a treaty has been concluded, shall not smell the smell of Paradise,[438] though its smell can be perceived from a distance of forty years,"[439] and "Whoever oppresses a person promised protection (*mu'ahad*)[440] and burdens them beyond their capacity, then I myself will be their accuser on the Day of Judgment."[441] God's Messenger also emphasizes that one who oppresses a person of *dhimmi* status (the non-Muslim subject of the Muslim state) has perpetrated an evil which incurs the curse of God, of His angels and of all humankind, and that such a person will not be regarded favorably in the Hereafter.[442]

This is why the *aman*, or safe conduct granted by any civilian in Muslim society has been viewed as a principle binding on the state as a whole, and which warrants its recognition and endorsement.[443] At a time when women, according to 'A'isha, were often not even treated as human beings, it is evident that the protection granted by any woman held the same status and authority.[444] The best examples of this safe conduct are the protection granted by the Messenger's daughter Zaynab to Abu al-'As,[445] which the Companions did not view favorably at first, and the protection granted by Abu Talib's daughter Umm Hani' to Abu Jahl's brother Harith ibn Hisham,[446] in spite of her own brother 'Ali. In any case, going back on one's words in the eyes of God's Messenger is a sign of downright hypocrisy[447] and wrongdoing that warrants humiliation and disgrace in the Hereafter.[448] Hudhayfah ibn al-Yaman's explanation of why he did not participate in Badr illustrates this:

"Nothing prevented me from participating in the Battle of Badr except for this incident: I came out with my father Husayl to participate in the Battle but we were caught by some Qurayshi unbelievers. Upon seeing us, they said, 'Do you intend to go to Muhammad?' We said, 'We do not intend to go to him, we wish only to go to Medina.' So they allowed us to go in return for our assurance in the name of God that we would turn back to Medina and that we would not undertake or support military action against them. We came to the Messenger of God and related the incident to him. He said, 'Return to Medina. We will honor the agreement made with

them and seek God's help against them.'[449]

As another facet of the pursuit of peace, God's Messenger warmly received envoys from those who saw him as their enemy, and sent them back with gifts as an extension of his kind treatment and reception.[450] His treatment of the envoy from the Quraysh, for instance, is striking. The Quraysh had sent the Copt, Abu Rafi', as their envoy to God's Messenger. When Abu Rafi' entered the Messenger's presence and took in the divinely emanating energy there, his heart softened and he began to look favorably upon Islam. "O Messenger of God," he said, "By God, I will not return to them."

This was, under normal circumstances, a reaction with which God's Messenger would be immensely pleased. But he said, "No. I will not violate the agreement, nor will I be the one to detain an envoy. It is best you go now. Should you find, on reaching Mecca, that your feeling remains unchanged, you can come back."

Abu Rafi' who returned to Mecca at the behest of God's Messenger later came back to Medina and never thought of going back to Mecca again.[451]

Despite all the adversity and provocation, the agreements entered into with diverse communities via the Medina Charter were never violated at all. On the contrary, by renewing these agreements when problems intensified, God's Messenger sought to carry his relations with these communities to a more stable plane.[452]

There are of course a great many examples exemplifying just how careful God's Messenger was on the subject; however, Hudaybiya is the richest example surpassing all others:

God's Messenger set off in the direction of Mecca with peaceful intent, accompanied by around 1500 of his Companions, meaning to circumambulate the Ka'ba and perform the Lesser Pilgrimage that had so embellished his dreams. They were not armed. They had taken along with them their sacrificial camels and, having entered into the state of consecration (*ihram*) and donned pilgrim garb, they came all the way to Hudaybiya despite all the obstacles they faced along the way. The Quraysh, however, allowed them to go no further and hurled death threats at them, though the Ka'ba that was the legacy of Abraham, was not to be monopolized by anyone; all could come and circumambulate it and no one would say a single word. What is more, families would rally for the guests of God coming to visit it, and by means of institutions such as *siqaya*, *hijaba*, *sidana*, and *rifada*, would compete in attending to pilgrims' needs, to facilitate their worship and allow them to observe their rites more comfortably. However, when those who came were believers, the situation changed. Even though it was his homeland, they barred God's Messenger from entering and came between him and the Ka'ba, his "twin."[453] On top of that, they showed no respect or self-control and engaged in provocation.

Despite all the incitement and provocation, God's Messenger's objective was peace with the Quraysh. This is why many envoys shuttled between them, but the peace that he so desired did not seem possible. This nervous wait continued for close to twenty days. At a stage when the bridges had not yet been burnt, the Messenger of God delegated 'Uthman as their last hope and sent him to the Meccans. He was to explain why they had come, and seek a ground for peace by pointing out they had no weapons with them, only their sacrificial animals.

'Uthman went as an envoy, but before long, the news reached Hudaybiya that 'Uthman and ten Companions who had gone to the Ka'ba for worship had been martyred. These reports brought the already escalating tension to a climax. In order to fulfill all the causes, to rule out the possibility of even worse repercussions, God's Messenger called his Companions to take a pledge beneath a tree at Hudaybiya. Waiting for such an invitation until this day, the Companions swore to the death to God's Messenger, to be able to weather this storm that had pushed them to the limits of their patience, and demonstrated through their actions exactly how they would break the hand that encroached on the cause of God. One of the main reasons for making this pledge in the presence of the Qurayshi envoys was to cause the Meccans to step back from the idea of war, and to bring them to a peaceful course of action.

This was what happened. Representatives of the Quraysh, Suhayl ibn 'Amr, Huwaytib ibn 'Abd al-'Uzza, Mikraz ibn Hafs, and other members of the Quraysh present at the time watched developments with heightened attention. In truth, they were perturbed. They knew they could not fight with people who expressed so openly their willingness to go to their death, for this was not a loyalty on the basis of simple blood relations or tribal allegiance. The Companions had as good as begun to compete in demonstrating to the Meccan polytheists, through their own actions, how a leader ought to be respected, just how responsive one could be in carrying out that leader's orders, and precisely what kind of sacrifice could be shown when the situation demanded it. These were virtues that the Quraysh had neither seen nor heard until that day. They were unnerved, and began to believe that they definitely had to find a way to strike an agreement.

The mission had been accomplished and the Meccans saw exactly what kind of impasse their meaningless stance would lead them to, when news arrived that refuted the rumor that 'Uthman and the other ten Companions had been martyred. Hudaybiya, which had been prepared for the worst, now gave a deep sigh of relief.

Suhayl ibn 'Amr and his friends returned to Mecca and began relating the scene that they had witnessed at Hudaybiya, to the Quraysh. They spoke of how every Companion became like a lion when the news of the murder of their friends reached them, and strove to depict the Companions' attitude when God's Messenger summoned them and they took the pledge under the tree. They expressed their concern about the Companions' resolve to fight against all the odds, and emphasized the impossibility of fighting against these death-defying people. Right-minded Qurayshi recognized the difficulty of facing these people, convened, and took the following decision:

"There is nothing better for us than to conclude an agreement with Muhammad on condition that they quit Mecca this year without circumambulating the House. That way, the Arabs and all those who have heard of his coming here will also hear that we have prevented him. They might return next year, enter Mecca, stay therein for three days, then slaughter their sacrificial animals and return. In this way, they will not have made a forcible entry into our city and will reside here for but a few days."

The Quraysh again sent Huwaytib and Mikraz under the leadership of Suhayl ibn 'Amr to God's Messenger. They instructed Suhayl ibn 'Amr, saying, "Go to Muhammad and make peace with him on the understanding that on no account will entry into Mecca be allowed this year. By God, we will not give cause for the Arabs to say that he made a forcible entry."[454]

Suhayl ibn 'Amr and his fellows set off for Hudaybiya once more. When the Messenger of God saw them coming, he said, "The Quraysh

want to make peace seeing that they have sent these men." Reading Suhayl's name, a derivative of the root meaning "to make easy, or facilitate"
as a good omen, God's Messenger remarked upon seeing him, "The matter has been put in order and has become 'easy' (*salaha*)." He presumably
also knew what they had discussed in Mecca and the decision they had
reached. This meant hope was renewed. The Quraysh had registered the
intended message of the Pledge and retreated. This was what the Messenger of God had wanted.

The course of peace had begun at Hudaybiya. Suhayl approached
the Messenger, who was seated on the floor with his legs crossed, and
knelt beside him. 'Abbad ibn Bishr and Salama ibn Aslam ibn Huraysh,
in their armor and helmets, were standing guard by God's Messenger.
The Companions formed a circle around them and followed closely the
next phase of the process.

Deliberations continued at length. Voices were sometimes raised,
and Hudaybiya witnessed a round of vehement negotiations. When Suhayl ibn 'Amr's raised his voice very much at one point, 'Abbad ibn Bishr
said angrily, "Know your place in the presence of God's Messenger and
lower your voice!" 'Abbad had tasted the tranquility of being in the Messenger's presence and enabled the representatives of the Quraysh to recognize this also. As a result of these lengthy deliberations, certain articles
were accepted in principle[455] and they now needed to commit them to
writing.

'Umar's outbursts

The articles and conditions stipulated by the Quraysh deeply offended
the feelings of the believers. Suhayl ibn 'Amr obstinately made no concessions whatsoever, and this stung the believers who saw themselves as
making nothing but concessions to their opponent. Sure enough, their
intent was not reaction to God's Messenger. They merely sought to clar-
ify the matter in all its facets, and still supposed there may be another
way out of the situation. 'Umar, in particular, could not contain himself,
coming to the presence of God's Messenger and saying, "O Messenger of
God, are you not God's Messenger?"

"Indeed," replied God's Messenger, "I am the Messenger of God."

"Do we not stand for truth and they for falsehood?"

"Yes."

"Are not our dead in Paradise and theirs in the Fire?"

"Yes."

"Why then should we make concessions in the matter of our religion and return while God has not yet judged between us and them?"

"I am God's servant and His Messenger. Never will I go against His command, nor will He forsake me, for He is my Helper."

"Was it not you who said that we would visit the House and circumambulate it?"

"Yes, indeed, but did I tell you that you would visit it this year?"

"No."

"Surely, you will go there and you will circumambulate it."

'Umar, who was clearly of a passionate temperament, thought only of that day and, without taking into account exactly what opportunities the absence of war would bring in the future, responded impulsively to these developments, whereas God's Messenger was building the future on the foundation of peace, and acted with the foreknowledge that this process would contribute a lot to both sides.[456]

Despite all the hardships, peace had been established and the time had now come to put the terms of the truce into writing. The Messenger of God summoned 'Ali to set down the text of the agreement and said, "Write, 'In the Name of God, The All-Merciful, The All-Compassionate.'"

Infuriated, Suhayl interjected, "What is the All-Merciful? I neither know, nor recognize the All-Merciful. Write instead, 'In Your Name, O God.'"

For those who had laid their lives on the line in the name of the All-Merciful and the All-Compassionate, this was a suggestion that was enough to make them to lose their heads, and so the words, "By God, we will not write other than 'In the Name of God, The All-Merciful, The All-Compassionate,' swelled to a chorus of protests at Hudaybiya. They refused to accept the absurd request of the Meccans, to whom they had not yielded at Badr, Uhud, and Khandaq. However, seeing what they were as yet unable to see, God's Messenger thought differently. The statement, "In the Name of God, The All-Merciful, The All-Compassionate," written at the top of the document was erased, and in its place was written the customary formula, "In Your Name, O God" as Suhayl had suggested. Clearly, the peace to be gained from the document was more important than the removal of this phrase from its head. After the first complication was overcome, the Messenger of God turned to 'Ali who was writing the treaty and said, "Write, 'This is the agreement concluded between Muhammad, the Messenger of God, and Suhayl ibn 'Amr.'"

He had scarcely finished his words, when Suhayl's objection rose again: "By God," he cried out. "Had I believed you were the Messenger of God, I would neither have prevented your visiting the Sanctuary, nor fought against you and shed blood. Write only your own name and that of your father."

For the Companions who had been subjected to a constant and heavy barrage of provocation for the past twenty days, it seemed this might be the straw that broke the camel's back. The man had the nerve to demand that the expression, "Messenger of God," the Messenger for whose sake many lives had been sacrificed, be removed from the text. Hudaybiya's patience was wearing thin. All eyes were focused on the Messenger, waiting for the smallest sign. But, yet again, the awaited indication did not come. Instead, he said, "By God, I am the Messenger of God, even if you should deny it." Again, he turned to 'Ali and instructed, "Write, this is the agreement concluded between Muhammad, ibn 'Abdu'llah, and Suhayl ibn 'Amr."

This was a command that tore away at 'Ali. He was unable to bring himself to wipe out the divinely certified title of God's Messenger, for whom he had fought for all these years, and was deeply aggrieved. Moreover, this was the view shared by all those at Hudaybiya. Khazraj chief Sa'd ibn 'Ubada and Usayd ibn Hudayr grabbed hold of 'Ali's hand, insisting that the Prophetic title could not be erased, and said, "Either you write 'Messenger of God,' or the matter between us and them will be settled by the sword." 'Ali did not disagree in any event. The 'Ali that had only just removed the statement, "In the Name of God, The All-Merciful, The All-Compassionate," had gone, and in his place was another 'Ali, looking at Suhayl with a piercing gaze, and brandishing his pen against the tyranny of unbelief. He did not want to rub out this blessed title that he deemed his crown, and wished for the words, "Messenger of God" to remain like a seal on the pact. Though this was his desire, he was now face to face with a Prophetic command. He was stuck between contravening the Messenger's order, and removing the title, "Messenger of God." Tension filled the air. Hudaybiya began to buzz like a beehive. Voices were getting louder and louder, and a continuous murmur filled the air. God's Messenger intervened again. He raised his hands and invited his Companions to calm. In his demeanor could be read, "There are many things that while they are not pleasing to you at the beginning, end in all sweetness." Then he turned to his son-in-law, 'Ali, who could not bring himself to carry out this Prophetic command and who was still waiting for a new one, and with dignity and grace, said, "One day you will find yourself in a similar predicament and, on that day, you too will have to make concessions."[457]

For someone like 'Ali, the Prophet's mission was an undeniable part of his very existence; he could not possibly do this. What is more, it was clear that if anyone other than he erased this title, it would inflict a mortal wound on the hearts of the Companions waiting nervously at Hudaybiya. God's Messenger turned to 'Ali once more and said, "Show it to me." 'Ali showed him the line and the Prophet himself erased the phrase "Messenger of God." He asked 'Ali to write "Muhammad ibn 'Abdu'llah" instead, as Suhayl had demanded.

This demand, too, had been met and yet another crisis averted. But Suhayl was about to bring discussions to an end without making mention of the concession that the Meccans had made as he set off for Hudaybiya. Well aware of this, and presumably also aware of discussions in Mecca, God's Messenger reminded him: "Cease coming between us and the Ka'ba so that we too can circumambulate it." It was clear that they thought this a definite commitment and feared that the Arabs and Suhayl, the Meccan delegate, wanted to play ignorant. Suhayl softened seeing the firm stance of the Messenger's Companions, who had witnessed his unnecessary obstinacy and one-sided impositions, and seeing that God's Messenger knew what was happening. He perhaps realized that their sincere requests and wishes need not be opposed completely. This was also the Meccans' view at any rate, and he said that this visit, which he accepted, could only be realized the following year.

Meanwhile, the task of setting down the treaty in writing continued. Suhayl ibn 'Amr said, "If anyone should come to you without the permission of his guardian, you will return him to them, even if he be of your religion." He then stated that they would not return those who returned to Mecca from Medina. It was as though he had singlehandedly composed a statement on behalf of the Quraysh, and was now speaking almost as if he were dictating that statement to God's Messenger. His demeanor and tone of voice infuriated those at Hudaybiya. Shocked cries of "All-Glorified is God" began to rise around him. "How could a person who had come to Medina as a Muslim be returned to the Meccan polytheists!"[458]

On that day, for the sake of putting an end to all hostilities and making peace prevail, God's Messenger accepted all the terms that Suhayl set out, even though the Companions, 'Umar above all, took issue with them. To all appearances, this was a step back; however, this step back was to become a move that would take him perhaps a hundred steps forward in the future. As there would be no fighting for ten years, swords were returned to their sheaths. The anguish they felt at not being able to circumambulate the Ka'ba despite coming so close to Mecca would be soothed by a new journey the following year, and the worship unfulfilled on that day was delayed for a year. The Qur'anic chapter The Victory (Al-Fath) revealed on the return from Hudaybiya put a name to this treaty and referred to this as a "manifest victory." By moving back at the point where tension had reached boiling point, God's Messenger opened a new space to conquer hearts in the future, and affirmed the presence and power of Medina to the Meccans, who until then had not recognized it.

Abu Jandal

With the conclusion of the treaty, a new phase was beginning at Hudaybiya, when suddenly a figure was seen coming from the direction of Mecca, attempting to walk, wearily dragging his iron chains behind him, at the end of what appeared to have been a most arduous journey. All eyes turned to the exhausted man who had fled for dear life and threw himself into Hudaybiya in desperation. Everyone was watching and listening avidly, trying to make out who this person was. Quraysh representative Suhayl ibn 'Amr, in particular, looked the fugitive up and down with piercing eyes to intimidate him, and with the power afforded him by the new truce, calculated exactly how he would get the better of him. The uncertainty did not last long. The young man was none other than the younger son of Suhayl himself. Taking advantage of his father's absence, he had escaped torture and persecution and had come all the way to Hudaybiya to throw himself into the compassionate embrace of the Muslims.

Seeing a second son flee from Mecca to seek sanctuary with the Muslims, after 'Abdu'llah had slipped through his fingers at Badr, Suhayl ibn 'Amr burst into a fit of rage. All his experiences with his brothers Sakran and Salit, son 'Abdu'llah, daughters Sahla and Umm Kulthum, and his sons-in-law Abu Hudhayfa and Abu Sabra ibn Abi Ruhm over many years, flashed through his mind. Only Abu Jandal was left, and now he too was defecting and was trying to throw himself into Hudaybiya's atmosphere of security—and despite his father!

In a rage, Suhayl set upon his son, hurling insults, grabbing him by the neck, and dragging him and knocking him about. He then turned to God's Messenger and said, "And here, Muhammad, we have our first test. You are to give him to me, as the pact between us was concluded before this man came to you. I will not violate the agreement after this point in time, and I swear by God that there will be no treaty, either now or hereafter, unless he is returned."

Every event at Hudaybiya seemed to be detrimental to peace. On the one hand, the Companions had difficulty accepting the process, and on the other there was the pitiable state of the believer who had made it all the way there. On top of this, Suhayl ibn 'Amr, the envoy of the Quraysh and father of Abu Jandal, was threatening to annul the treaty.

This was indeed a heartrending scene. Putting himself on the line, the exemplar of mercy approached Suhayl and petitioned, "Allow him to remain on my account and exempt him from the agreement." But the hardened heart of Suhayl was not inclined to hear this. Instead, he stubbornly reiterated his demands, saying, "I will neither leave him to you, nor exempt him from the agreement," and he threatened to revoke the agreement and cancel everything that had been achieved.

Looking with compassion at Abu Jandal and then his ruthless father Suhayl, God's Messenger repeated, "Indeed, you can do this and you must." But Suhayl ibn 'Amr merely said, "No, I absolutely will not," and nothing else.

Having observed how rigid Suhayl's attitude was and the insistence of God's Messenger, the other two delegates of the Quraysh, Huwaytib and Mikraz, came to reason and supported God's Messenger in his re-

quest to leave Abu Jandal out of the agreement, but even this intervention would not prove enough to convince Suhayl.

Abu Jandal had been following the discussion closely until this
moment, wavering between hope and fear. When he was lifted by both
arms by Huwaytib and Mikraz and carried towards a tent to be returned
to the custody of the Quraysh, he screamed at the top of his voice, his
cries ringing throughout Hudaybiya: "O Muslims, am I to be returned
to the polytheists when you know what they have made me suffer on
account of my religion, when I came to you as a Muslim? You can see
my present state."

Just when he thought he had been saved, Abu Jandal was being
subjected to his father's violence once more, and dragged off to torture.
His cries and screams resounded through Hudaybiya. He was right,
for only he knew all that he had gone through. The thought of what he
would endure after this only exacerbated his cries, and he uttered a long
loud piercing cry as though pleading for mercy. The scene was enough
to overwhelm the onlookers with sorrow and leave them despondent.

Surely Abu Jandal cried out on that day in the helplessness of not
knowing what was in store for him, and he wept because he could not
know of the serenity and peace that God would bestow upon him. Yet
this was a singular cry—one that a few would have to utter so that thousands of people would not cry out in the Hereafter. For who knew at that
point what beauty and acts of goodness could be squeezed into a period of ten years devoid of conflict and clamor, how many hearts in need
could be won over in such a climate, and how a road leading them, too,
to Paradise could be found? Moreover, who knew how much oppression could be prevented in such an atmosphere, and how much bloodshed, which would otherwise have been probable, could be averted?
The Divine revelations conveyed by Archangel Gabriel stated that peace
was the norm, and summoned the community of the Qur'an to exactly
that.[459] In that case, under these circumstances, there was no possibility
of protecting Abu Jandal. Even though it was a decision that scalded the
heart, there appeared no other alternative but to endure it in exchange
for abundant good later.

The Messenger of God, who was the highest, perfect example of
mercy, approached Abu Jandal and in a tone of voice conveying his concern and compassion said, "O Abu Jandal, be patient and compose your-

self, for God will provide relief and a way out of your suffering for you and those of you who are helpless. We have entered into a truce with them and have exchanged a solemn pledge invoking God that none will deal falsely with the other."

'Umar's purpose was for Abu Jandal to take the sword that he had motioned for him to take, and strike his father with it.[460] But Abu Jandal was then in no state to heed 'Umar, and he was to return to the place from which he had fled in the hands of the envoys of the Quraysh.[461]

But there was one notable difference this time: from here on, the winning side in the Hijaz would be the side that was culturally self-assured and skilled in the expression of their views and thoughts, and not those skilled in the use of weapons.

Abu Basir

Abu Jandal's return to Mecca aside, this treaty became a beacon of hope for those who until then had been unable to find a way of migrating to Medina and who continued to be persecuted in Mecca. Abu Basir, who was one such person, also[462] got the chance and escaped to Medina, coming to God's Messenger, with whom he had been yearning to reunite for years. Like Abu Jandal, when he became Muslim he was subjected to imprisonment, torture, and all kinds of insult and injury, and, as soon as he could, he stole away to Medina in the hope of finding sanctuary and freedom from all his worries. His feet were swollen and covered in blisters, as he could make his escape only by running, and had only been able to make it so far by choosing the rough tracks to avoid leaving a trace. When the grueling nature of the journey was added to the years of torture, he was a tragic sight, and an overpowering sorrow engulfed the Messenger's heart, which beat with compassion. However, Abu Basir's flight to Medina in spite of the agreement concluded with the Meccans[463] grieved the Messenger of God even more. He turned to Abu Basir and said the following:

"O Abu Basir, you know the undertaking we have given these people, and it ill becomes us to be the side that is treacherous, for our religion forbids treachery. God will grant deliverance and a way of escape to those who are likewise helpless, so go back to your people."

Distraught, like Abu Jandal, Abu Basir too pleaded, "O Messenger of God, would you have me return to the polytheists who have subjected me to every possible persecution because of my religion?"

While his heart was overcome with unutterable sorrow, God's Messenger repeated, "O Abu Basir, go, for God will grant relief and a way of escape to those helpless like you."[464]

Meanwhile, the Quraysh had convened and taken action to bring back the runaway Abu Basir, to make an example out of him. They sent Khunays ibn Jabir to Medina with a letter written by Akhnas ibn Shariq and Azhar ibn Abd 'Awf. Khunays was to go, remind them of Hudaybiya, demand Abu Basir's return, and take him back with him. With him on this journey was his slave Kawthar. They arrived in Medina three days after Abu Basir, saying, "You well know the terms of the agreement we entered into with you. We agreed in the presence of witnesses that whoever was to come to you from among us would be returned, so turn him over to us."

God's Messenger experienced one of his most trying moments. Protecting a Companion who had come all this way and keeping him by his side in Medina would not solve the problems that would arise in the future, and it would also endanger the current state of peace. In such cases, one sometimes needed to be able to make certain concessions so as to solve the matter at its source in the long-term, and to turn and put one's energy towards building the future with perseverance. Thus, he surrendered Abu Jandal and Abu Basir to the Meccans with his own hands. In spite of the tears trickling down his face while watching them leave, he swallowed yet again the anguish he felt, and took a step back for the general peace that the Hijaz would experience in the future.

Abu Basir was going back to torture, oppression, persecution, and all the associated tribulations and hardships. Before he left, some among the Muslims approached him and reassured him, saying, "O Abu Basir, do not doubt that God will grant you deliverance and relief. For now, try to rejoice in the glad tidings of God's Messenger. Sometimes one man is greater than a thousand men." And they advised him, "You should do such and such."[465]

When the two men who took Abu Basir away reached Dhu al-Hulayfa with him, Abu Basir found a way to kill Khunays, while Kawthar managed to get away. Kawthar fled desperately to Medina, to seek refuge with God's Messenger. God's Messenger was sitting in the mosque with his Companions following the Afternoon Prayer. When he saw the man coming, he said, "This man has seen something frightful." As soon as the man approached, God's Messenger asked him, "What is the matter? What has happened to you?" Gasping for breath, Kawthar stammered, "He has killed him! I swear that your companion has killed my companion! I barely escaped with my life!" In saying these words he sought help from God's Messenger, asking him for protection. Never once turned away any who asked something of him, God's Messenger granted him protection.

Before long, Abu Basir joined them. He had mounted Khunays' camel, and appeared before God's Messenger girt with Khunays' sword, saying, "O Messenger of God, you did what fell on you to do. You have fulfilled your duty under the agreement and God has relieved you of your obligation. You handed me over to my people, as stipulated, while I have defended myself as concerns my religion lest I should be forced into abjuring it and persecuted. I have escaped and am thus here."

Having heard what Abu Basir had to say, God's Messenger first said, "Woe unto you." In his words was condemnation of Abu Basir's actions, as well as the concern he felt about the current situation. Then he added, "Had the men enough with him, this would have meant war."

Abu Basir inferred from these words that God's Messenger would hand him over to the Quraysh once more. Apparently, there was no way of his remaining in Medina with God's Messenger. He was to go and determine his own path himself. And so he left Medina, full of sorrow, bidding farewell to the Messenger with whom he had so longed to be reunited.[466]

In the meantime, the Quraysh who had gotten wind of Khunays' death were raving and could make no sense of all that had happened. Suhayl ibn 'Amr, who had negotiated the agreement, paced back and forth and was at a loss as to what to do in his misery. "This is not what we agreed upon," he kept muttering to himself as he shook his head. He sought a way out, sharing the dilemma that was difficult even in his own mind to sort out. The task of placating him again fell to the Quraysh. "Muhammad has no hand in the matter," they said, defending God's Messenger before Suhayl. "He handed Abu Basir over to your associate. Whatever happened, happened on the return journey to Mecca. Muhammad is blameless in the matter." All the same, these words were not enough to console Suhayl. Leaning his back against the Ka'ba, he said, "By God, I will not remove my back from the Ka'ba until they pay the blood money for this man." In the face of Suhayl's unnecessary insistence, Abu Sufyan said, "By God, this is utter foolishness. No blood money will be paid for him. Why should the Quraysh pay his blood money when it was the Banu Zuhra who sent him?"

Khunays' death had sparked a new dispute between the Meccans. As the killer was a fellow tribesman, Akhnas ibn Shariq also became involved saying, "By God, we will not put up this blood money as we neither killed him, nor commanded his killing. On the contrary, he was killed by a man opposed to us. You had better send news to Muhammad to settle his blood money."

"No," interjected Abu Sufyan once more. "What has Muhammad to do with the matter, that he should pay his blood money? He has no obligation to pay either the blood money, or compensation, for he was in no way involved, and did as was prescribed (by the agreement)."

As can be seen, the Messenger of God executed such a delicate strategy that those who had been vehemently opposed to him until that day now began to defend him. His virtuous stance characterized by principled action, his pursuit of peace, and honoring of any agreement he entered into, caused the adversary, too, to soften, and when others wanted to lay the blame for the situation on God's Messenger, they were the first to come to his defense. In this way, God's Messenger demonstrated to all that he was an authority to which they could turn in any situation. Before long, encouraged by his stance, the Quraysh were to send Abu Sufyan to Medina to inform him that they had voided the article of the Treaty of Hudaybiya in question. This was because after leaving Medina, Abu Basir did not return to Mecca but went instead to al-'Is on the seacoast, where he set up camp.

Every believer in Mecca learned where he was living and every helpless believer (*mustad'af*)[467] came to seek refuge with him. Their numbers reached three hundred and they began to intercept the Meccan trade caravans en route to Syria. How ironic it was that the Quraysh, who had stubbornly forced this article of the treaty upon the Muslims, were now the ones wishing to declare the very same term void. To this end, they appealed in desperation to God's Messenger to take Abu Basir into his community and bring the raids to an end. "Send word to Abu Basir,

Abu Jandal, and those who have joined them," said Abu Sufyan, and he continued as follows:

"Whoever leaves us from this day forth to seek refuge in Medina, keep them there and do not send them back to us. You are no longer liable to do so, for those who have escaped Mecca and have made a place for themselves there have caused us such grief that this situation is no longer tolerable."

The Prophetic stance had yielded fruit once again, and the matter had been solved at its source with patience and prudence. What is more, this was an outcome without any drawbacks, and to which no one would object. As a result of Abu Sufyan's appeal, God's Messenger wrote a letter to Abu Basir who was stationed at al-'Is, inviting him to Medina. As a matter of fact, Abu Basir, who was then stricken with illness, was overjoyed that the letter of the Messenger with whom he yearned to re-unite had reached him, but his heart could not bear it and he died while reading it.[468]

The compensatory pilgrimage

Remaining faithful to the Hudaybiya Treaty, God's Messenger came to Mecca with his Companions for pilgrimage exactly one year later. He was to perform the Lesser Pilgrimage he had been unable to perform a year earlier,[469] and realize for the very first time an act of worship that was in harmony with the spirit of the Ka'ba. In addition, he would conduct a series of meetings and discussions, and would seize the opportunity to win over the hearts of the Meccans.

Even though the essential purpose of this journey was to fulfill an act of worship, God's Messenger erred on the side of caution and on this occasion wanted to carry weapons with him. There was good will because of the point they had reached, but even so, he worried that the Meccans would return to their former ways and, as such, did not rule out the possibility that they might revive their idea to corner and annihilate them. At the same time, carrying arms also gave the message: "Come to your senses, and don't dare resort to force!" For God's Messenger did not want to give rise to any form of tension and wanted to get this message across from the outset to those who let it even cross their minds. To this end, he selected a group of one hundred Companions led by Muhammad ibn Maslama, and sent them as the advance guard on horseback, to reconnoiter the area ahead of the rest of the procession. He also made Bashir ibn Sa'd responsible for weapons such as swords, shields, helmets and spears, and sent them along with Muhammad ibn Maslama and his men. The Companions, too, watched developments with interest. They could not make sense of this altered situation, in comparison to their last experience, and asked, "O Messenger of God, what is it that induces you to proceed armed like this, while they stipulated that upon entry to Mecca we were to have on us only our swords and that these must be in their sheaths?"

"We are not to enter the Sacred Precinct with them," God's Messenger replied. "But it is better that they are close at hand for if they should launch an attack against us, they will be within reach."

Nothing was sacred for the Quraysh. Unlike the believers, they had neither the Qur'an, nor a guide to show them the way. There was merely their fixation on what "the people would say," but a pretext could readily be found when it suited them in any case, and they could do whatever they wished, in complete lawlessness. Hence, the Messenger of God was still not entirely convinced that they would remain true to their word. Perhaps he also sought to demonstrate the importance of precaution to his Companions firsthand.

Muhammad ibn Maslama and the cavalry separated at Dhu al-Hulayfa and went on ahead. When they reached the place called Marr al-Zahran, they came upon a group of men from the Quraysh. This scene naturally disquieted the Meccans. They asked them the reason for this activity. Muhammad ibn Maslama and his companions informed them that the Messenger was following behind. They noticed all the weapons that Bashir ibn Sa'd had with him; their hearts were in their mouths and their faces changed color. They raced back to Mecca and informed the chiefs of the situation. The Quraysh were in a flurry. "How can it be?" they said. "We have done nothing to violate the treaty. We have maintained our part of the truce and are committed to our agreement. Then why are Muhammad and his Companions coming at us armed?"

They supposed what they saw to be at variance with what they knew and could make nothing of these developments, for the Muhammad the Trustworthy that they knew had kept all his promises until that day, and had inspired trust and confidence at every step that he took.

Surely this should be so today also. However, there was a situation that seemed to belie this knowledge, and they sent a delegation headed by Mikraz ibn Hafs to the place known as Ya'jaj, to investigate and verify the reports. Meanwhile, the Messenger himself had also arrived. "By God, Muhammad," they said. "You have never been known to break your word for any reason, whether for something minor or major; while you are now entering the Sacred Precinct with your men bearing arms, even though you agreed to enter only with weapons such as travelers carry, swords in sheaths."

Easing their hearts with every step that he took, God's Messenger said, "I will not bring in weapons against them." Mikraz and his companions gave a deep sigh of relief. Mikraz then commented, "And this is as becomes you. For you are known for your righteousness and trustworthiness." They then hurried back to Mecca to convey to them the news of the Messenger. "There is no need for any concern," they said. "Muhammad is indeed true to the agreement he concluded with you and will not enter Mecca armed."[470]

To all appearances, the Messenger of God was advancing towards the Ka'ba for the purpose of worship. But this advance was of course not one that was limited just to this. He had become, at the same time, an embodiment of the Qur'an, and was entering into the hearts of the Meccans. This was, above all, a journey that inspired trust. All the singular beauties of Islam had become embodied in human form and were walking towards Mecca in rendition.

It was the fourth day of the month Dhu al-Hijja. With the first rays of the morning sun, God's Messenger set off from Marr al-Zahran and headed in the direction of Mecca. After many years, the Ka'ba was to be reunited with its "twin" for the very first time. That troublesome city to which he had bid farewell seven years before, he was now entering, ready to address and solve all troubles. He had all the animals driven ahead, and followed on, heading towards the Ka'ba. When they reached Dhu Tuwa, proclamations of God's greatness could be heard and they continued to call out, "At Your service, O Lord! At Your beckoning and call!" They were to learn the meaning of reverence to the Ka'ba for the very first time, from the Messenger of God. 'Abdu'llah ibn Rawaha took the reins of the Messenger's camel Qaswa' and recited lines of poetry expressing the present state of things and how they came to be. Finding this strange, 'Umar called out to him, questioning whether it was appropriate, and was answered by none other than God's Messenger, who said, "Indeed I can hear, O 'Umar! Leave him be. For his words are more forceful (for the Quraysh) than the showering of arrows."[471]

God's Messenger then turned to 'Abdu'llah and instructed him to recite upon entry to Mecca: "There is no deity but God, Who has fulfilled His promise, supported His servant, and Who alone defeated the troops." From that point on, 'Abdu'llah ibn Rawaha repeated the words that he had just learned from the Messenger and the Companions began reciting them also. Mecca, for years in mourning, took on a festive air for the first time. The joy of the Migrants, in particular, was ineffable, because for them a memory was hidden in every corner of Mecca. Notably, the innocent children of the Banu Hashim formed a circle around God's Messenger in a great demonstration of affection.

They then reached the Ka'ba. The Messenger of God and the Ka'ba met again at the same point—the *mihrab* and *minbar* once again stood side by side. As a precaution against any harm to the Messenger, the Companions formed a "human wall" around him. As in the agreement, they would remain there for three days, which would be filled with turning to and seeking refuge in their Lord, and devoted servanthood.

Devotion was complete and servitude to God at its highest point. The circumambulation of the Ka'ba was about to begin, and before hailing the Black Stone, God's Messenger gathered one end of his pilgrim garb under his right arm, exposing his right shoulder, and trailed the other end over his left shoulder. He prayed for his Companions with the words, "May God have mercy on one who today has shown them their full strength," and also recommended them to do their best to appear strong enough to deter the Quraysh. His aim was to show the polytheists, who saw them as weak and who spread rumors to this effect, the dignity and might of the believer. To that end, he instructed his Companions to perform the first three rounds of circumambulation vigorously and briskly, with head high and chest up, and he set this example. What the Meccans, who had taken to the hills, witnessed was truly a spectacle—over two thousand people, with sonorous voices and strong steps but tears in their eyes. Sounds of glorification (*takbir*) and the pilgrims' call (*talbiya*), which defied description, reverberated from the mountains of Paran surrounding Mecca and echoed in the Valley of Becca.

The time for the Noon Prayer arrived, and God's Messenger told Bilal to recite the Call to Prayer. Causing the sound of "One, One!" to resound through the Paran Mountains, Bilal cried out God's name at the Ka'ba for the first time, to his heart's content and without reserve. For the Meccans, however, this illustrated vividly how much an Abyssinian slave that they had snubbed and despised had been elevated. Everything they saw and heard pointed to a new era by Divine design, unique in every way.

The Meccans watched those circumambulating the Ka'ba from Mount Qu'ayq'an overlooking the *hijr* enclosure. They shuddered at the sound of the Call to Prayer as they heard it for the first time, and talked amongst themselves as they watched in wonderment and stupefaction. Abu Jahl's son 'Ikrima emphasized that his father would not have been able to endure this scene. He said, "Indeed God has been most generous to Abu al-Hakam, for he will not hear this slave say what he says today!" Safwan ibn Umayya joined him. Like 'Ikrima, he too said, "Praise be to God Who took away my father before he saw this!" Khalid ibn Asyad joined the chorus: "Praise be to God Who caused the death of my father before he could witness the day when Bilal stands bellowing above the Ka'ba!" Suhayl ibn 'Amr and the men with him covered their faces when they heard this, for they could not bear even the very mention of God's name.[472]

But the agenda of Mecca that had thought of nothing but hatred and animosity was changing. They began to look with admiration and envy at the angel-like demeanor of people that until recently they had not been able to bear. While their tongue could not venture to utter it, they watched the actions of these people, equal only to the circumambulation of the angels, with feelings of admiration and awe.

They had begun to trust what they saw in place of what they had heard. Until just yesterday they had heard nothing but bad things about these people, and heard they were run down from exhaustion. So everything they had heard was a lie. "Are these people weak from fever?" they asked themselves. And they questioned themselves: "These people are stronger than so and so and such and such. Look at them, they are not satisfied with walking, but race around like gazelles!"

At one point, the Messenger of God sent word to them of his desire to enter the Ka'ba. It is quite probable that he was seeking an opportunity to make contact with them in addition to deepening his worship. They, however, were infuriated, and turned him down saying, "There was no such stipulation in the agreement!" So, there was not the slightest point to which they could raise objection, for everything was coming to pass exactly as prescribed in the undertaking the year before.

Finally, the Messenger of God offered the Prayer for circumambulation and headed for the hillocks of Safa and Marwa. Here, he strided between them seven times until he stopped at Marwa and sacrificed his offering. It was then time to come out of the state of consecration, and he called Khirash ibn Umayya, and asked him to shave his head for him. The Compensatory Pilgrimage was thus complete.[473]

Time of parting

The three days came to an end. There was now, however, one major change: 'Abbas proposed that the Messenger of God take his sister-in-law Barra in marriage, pressing home her loneliness, and the hardship and suffering she had endured. One of eight sisters, Barra (Maymuna)[474] was closely related to many of the leading actors of the day, such as Khalid ibn al-Walid.[475] The Messenger of God agreed, and as he was in the ritual state of *ihram*, left the process for his impending marriage to Maymuna.

Also at the end of the three days, Suhayl ibn 'Amr and Huwaytib ibn 'Abd al-'Uzza came to the Messenger's tent at Abtah and said, "The time stipulated in the treaty for your stay in Mecca has expired, so leave us." God's Messenger then said, "Can you not give us time so that I might hold the wedding feast here in Mecca for you to join us?"[476] "We stand in no need of your food," was their response.[477] "Leave us at once. The three days prescribed in our agreement are over and you have no other option but to leave our land immediately."

Seeing their incivility about this most innocent invitation, the Khazraj chief Sa'd ibn 'Ubada exclaimed angrily, "May you leave without your mother! This is neither your land nor that of your forefathers! By God, we do not depart from it except as the treaty specifies and indeed not coerced by you!"

Sa'd's outburst made the Messenger smile. This was perhaps the sensitivity their leader deserved, but the delicacy of the situation did not allow it, and God's Messenger clearly wanted to charm them with his kindness. So he turned to Sa'd and said, "O Sa'd, do not harm a people who visit us during our stay."

'Ali had also arrived in the meantime and reminded them that the stipulated period of three days had elapsed. God's Messenger acknowledged this, saying, "Yes, prepare for departure immediately and inform the people."[478]

God's Messenger then called Abu Rafi', giving him instructions as to his departure from Mecca. By returning to Medina, God's Messenger unarguably indicated the true place of return, and he departed having won over the hearts of the Meccans. Now, at the Ka'ba, the call for Abu Rafi' to quit Mecca rang out:

"Let there be no Muslim remaining here by evening!"

This was indeed what happened. By the evening of that day, none of the Companions were left in Mecca, as they had all set off for Medina alongside God's Messenger. The reassurance this gave was more powerful than the most eloquent of sermons. It reached deep into the people's hearts, like a key that could unlock many a seemingly impenetrable door.

Violation of the treaty

Despite the imposed conditions and all the provocation, the Messenger of God maintained peace to the end, and did not in the slightest way break the terms agreed. Regrettably, the same did not hold true for the Meccans. The truce had hardly been in force for two years[479] when a group of the Quraysh took advantage of Abu Sufyan's having gone to Damascus for trade.[480] For no apparent reason and in the depths of night they attacked the Khuza'a tribe, who had formed an alliance with God's Messenger at Hudaybiya, and they killed them indiscriminately—men and women, old and young. They even pursued those who fled for their lives to the Ka'ba to seek sanctuary, and killed them wherever they found them.

This was a flagrant breach of the Treaty of Hudaybiya, and it unsettled and disturbed everyone. From now on, the Meccans would be on a knife-edge; they well knew that as soon as God's Messenger, who always strove to eliminate oppression and injustice, and his Companions learned of this breach of the treaty, they would make the Meccans pay the price for their wrongdoing and murder.

Indeed, before long, a delegation came to Medina, seeking help from God's Messenger. These were members of the Khuza'a tribe, who had allied with the Messenger on the day the treaty was concluded at Hudaybiya. They spoke of how the Quraysh, who sided with the Banu Bakr and Banu Nufatha, surprised them in a night raid at their watering place in Watir, massacred twenty-three people—the majority of whom were women and children—and how they left many more for dead. On top of that, they added that leading Meccans such as Safwan ibn Umayya, 'Ikrima ibn Abi Jahl, Huwaytib ibn 'Abd al-'Uzza, Shayba ibn 'Uthman, and Mikraz ibn Hafs had also been present at the attack, and they pleaded for justice from God's Messenger.[481]

While these events were taking place in Medina, Abu Sufyan who returned from Damascus expressed his unease at what had happened in his absence and against his wish. He condemned the Meccans for becoming embroiled in the incident that he had warned against beforehand, and made it very clear that there would be dire consequences. When morning came and the gravity of what had happened became clear, the Quraysh bitterly regretted what they had done. They knew that God's Messenger would not remain silent, and that he would assuredly call them to account. "Muhammad will surely attack us," they said in their deliberations, discussing possible options, and which of these they would accept. They were very sorry, but it was too late—the die had been cast. They began to discuss making incredible offers to save their skins or justify their actions. After lengthy discussions of all the alternatives, Meccan chief Abu Sufyan finally took the floor. Rejecting all the suggestions, he said, "The only option is to deny Quraysh complicity in violating the agreement and cutting short the fixed period. There can be no blame upon us if the people acted without our consent and consultation."

This might have been so from Abu Sufyan's perspective, for he had not known about or taken part in the night raid. However, this was not true at all for the others; in spite of this, they unanimously accepted Abu Sufyan's proposal, saying, "This is the right decision. There is no other decision save to deny all that happened." In fact, from another standpoint, this meant the increasing isolation and marginalization of the Meccan opposition.

Even though they had agreed to a formula that would, on the face of it, save them, they could not overcome their inward unease. Abu Jahl's brothers, Harith ibn Hisham and 'Abdu'llah Abi Rabi'a, approached Abu Sufyan to voice their concerns. They said, "This matter must be rectified. For if this affair is not corrected and peace re-established, surely Muhammad and his Companions will come here and ruin you."

Abu Sufyan heard them and thought deeply about what they said. He remembered the dream that his wife Hind had seen. Hind, the daughter of 'Utba, who was killed at Badr, related that she saw a river of blood flow forth from Hajun, north of Mecca, towards Mecca, until it stopped at Khandama, remained for a while, and then disappeared. When she awoke in terror and explained the dream to her husband Abu Sufyan, he recoiled from the meanings that her dream contained, and began fearing its evil import for the fate of the Meccans. He faced a great dilemma. He first explained this dream to those who came to him and then said, "By God, this is an affair that I was not involved in, but which I cannot remain out of."

By this point, the other Meccan leaders had joined them. Abu Sufyan was facing one of the most crucial moments of his leadership. With the weight of helplessness upon him, he turned to the Meccans and began to reproach them:

"This is not a responsibility that can be laid upon my shoulders only. No, by God, neither was I consulted, nor did I approve when news of it reached me. By God, if my instincts are right, Muhammad will surely attack us. Alas, my intuition never fails me. I see no other option but to go to Muhammad and ask him to extend the period of the truce and renew the agreement before the affair reaches him."

A wave of regret engulfed the council. The people who until only yesterday saw no option other than mounting a challenge, now drew back as the dire implications of the affair dawned upon them, and they began to agree with Abu Sufyan. "By God, you speak the truth," they said to him. They then resolved to send Abu Sufyan to the Messenger of God in Medina, to persuade him to extend the length of the truce and reaffirm the peace agreement. Shortly after this, Abu Sufyan was on the road to Medina, accompanied by his slave.[482]

Meanwhile, the Messenger of God turned to his Companions and said, "You can expect to see Abu Sufyan come to you soon to renew the treaty and extend its duration." However, he did not omit to add the outcome: "But he returns empty-handed and displeased."

Yet, God's Messenger did not immediately advance upon them with his forces as they had assumed. Again, he preferred to solve the matter through discussion and deliberation. Sending his Companion named Damra to Mecca, he urged those unrestrained by law to abide by the rule of law and presented them with three alternatives in view of their indefensible action and killings:

1. To pay the blood money for those killed from the Khuza'a.
2. To revoke their pact with the Banu Nufatha.
3. To accept and openly declare their violation of the Treaty of Hudaybiya.

But the Quraysh, who supposedly sought a solution, once again began to throw their weight around, and refused to accept any of the three alternatives put before them. They became caught up in trivialities. Accepting the first alternative would mean their humiliation, and this was one of the most important considerations for a community of the Age of Ignorance. Dissociating themselves from the Banu Nufatha amounted to abandoning their own pact, and becoming a mere spectator to their annihilation before Medina. This they saw as a disgrace that would be spoken of for centuries. Only one alternative remained: to declare the Treaty of Hudaybiya null and void. But this did not suit their interests either. For this meant war all over again and they no longer entertained any hope of defeating the Muslims in such an encounter. Neither could they put away their pride. Despite everything, the decision was made, and it was final: "We will not pay the blood money of the Khuza'a, nor will we forgo our pact and give up our allies." This was a pronounced expression of their readiness to face whatever consequences would follow, including a resumption of hostilities. So Damra, the Messenger's envoy, returned to Medina with their definitive response.[483]

Meanwhile, Abu Sufyan had arrived in Medina, going from door to door in his attempt to resolve the matter. For this, he first wanted to use his ties of kinship. He visited his daughter, Umm Habiba, and pleaded for her intercession, though he had disowned her until just recently. However, this was in vain, for he was not even given a cushion to sit on.

Seeing that her door was shut to him, he decided to go to God's Messenger himself. He was in the mosque, and Abu Sufyan called out to him saying, "Muhammad, as I was not present at Hudaybiya, the pact will have to be renewed and extended."

When Abu Sufyan raised the issue of re-establishing the Treaty of Hudaybiya and extending it as though nothing had happened, God's Messenger called out to him, "O Abu Sufyan, is this really what you have come for?"

"Yes," he replied. But this was not at all convincing. So God's Messenger asked, "Or has there been an incident on your side?" Abu Sufyan just exclaimed, "God forbid! We are still true to the agreement we signed at Hudaybiya. We will neither alter our stance, nor abandon it."

He was just stalling, and he said nothing more. He seemed not to be the same Abu Sufyan who had heard the anguish of the Khuza'a, sat with his associates in Mecca and assessed the situation, spoken his final words and sent the Messenger's envoy back to Medina, later voiced his concern regarding the violation of the treaty, and who had come to Medina purely for the sake of consolidating it. God's Messenger turned to him and declared, "It is we who are true to the Treaty of Hudaybiya, and we have neither altered it, nor violated it."

God's Messenger was presumably disturbed by the prevarication of Abu Sufyan who merely kept repeating the same things and refused to get to the point. Even if he himself was not complicit, those who had perpetrated this crime were subject to his authority and there was no way that he could extricate himself from the situation. Yet now, here he was, speaking of the truce but he would not come to the issue of the breach. There was no point in continuing the conversation and so as not to waste any more time, God's Messenger preferred to go back into the mosque.[484]

Doors were now being shut on Mecca's formidable leader. Nonetheless, he attempted to force open other doors and the first to which he went was that of Abu Bakr. He repeated similar things to him and asked Abu Bakr to persuade the Messenger of God on his behalf. But he found this door closed also. On that day Abu Sufyan went to all the leading members of the Migrants and Medinan natives one by one, including 'Umar, 'Uthman, 'Ali, and Sa'd ibn 'Ubada, but to no avail.[485] He went to 'Ali one last time and said, "O Abu Hasan, I see that I am in a most hapless situation. Can you not advise me?"

"By God, I do not know what will help you in your present circumstances," 'Ali began. "Are you not the chief of Banu Kinana?" "Indeed, I am," Abu Sufyan replied. 'Ali then advised him, "Why do you not declare publicly that you have granted protection to the Banu Kinana, then return home?"[486]

"Do you suppose this might do me some good?" Abu Sufyan had no hope, but he had no other choice. He was desperate. 'Ali was well aware of this, and he replied, "No, but I do not think that there is anything else that you can do."

The Abu Sufyan who had thrown down the gauntlet at Uhud, sought to meet in battle again at Badr, hired an assassin in the hope of killing God's Messenger, and who had gathered the mob at Khandaq to attack the Messenger, had collapsed. He came to the mosque again in one last hope and, making one final effort, called out to the people, "O people, I have provided protection for them to make truce between people. By God, I do not think that there is anyone who will contravene my word in this matter."

He then came to the Messenger of God one last time. "O Muhammad," he said. "I have guaranteed protection between our men."

He still failed to admit the horrendous crime and thinking only of the Quraysh, wanted to be certain of their fate. But there was still the blood of twenty-three people that had not been avenged. For a long time now, there had been too many chiefs in Mecca. Thus God's Messenger turned to him and said, "Only you say so, Abu Hanzala!" This was his final word.

The Meccans' plan had not succeeded. From this point on, there was nothing Abu Sufyan could do but return to Mecca bent beneath the burden of what might happen, and so he mounted his camel and headed for Mecca.[487]

The journey to hope

The Meccans had turned down the demands of God's Messenger and obtained no result from the diplomatic moves on which they had pinned their hopes, so they were left with no other option than to wait. Each passing day for them meant added anxiety, for they had no knowledge of developments in Medina and could not predict what was in store for them. They supposed that they would be called to account for what they had done, but had no indication as to how and when this would happen. Being unable to get news from Medina, in particular, was very troubling to them. They eventually resolved to dispatch Abu Sufyan and Hakim ibn Hizam in the direction of Medina to gather intelligence. This way, they would at the very least be able to warn the Meccans of developments beforehand. In sending him off, they asked Abu Sufyan repeatedly, "Should you meet Muhammad, obtain protection for us from him." This, in one sense, came to mean a journey to a new hope at a point where all hope had been lost.

On the way, Budayl ibn Warqa joined them and Abu Sufyan headed off towards Medina once more in a delegation of three. When night fell as they reached Marr al-Zahran, the scene they met indicated a new era for Mecca, as Marr al-Zahran was full of joy and merriment by the light of ten thousand fires.

The Marr al-Zahran strategy

After the Quraysh's attack on the Khuza'a, who were allied with God's Messenger, the killing of twenty-three people, and the Messenger's envoy being sent back empty-handed, the Messenger of God began preparations for the conquest of Mecca, and set off with ten thousand men from Medina, where he had first arrived with only two people. This was of course only the outward face of events. In actual fact, God's Messenger had set off on the journey for the sake of the Meccans who had rejected him down while he invited them constantly and strove with all the resources at his disposal to win them over. He was now going to them personally, to be able to take them by the hand and lead them to Paradise. In the prevailing conditions if ten thousand mere ants had marched, this would have been noticed; so what kind of strategy had he implemented that not even a single soul from Mecca noticed until he came all the way to Marr al-Zahran, that was but a stop away? For he did not want even a single person to be harmed and desired that Mecca's conquest be realized without bloodshed.

It worked. On the evening of their arrival at Marr al-Zahran, God's Messenger instructed all his Companions to light a fire each.[488] At the time, each fire usually meant a tent in which between five and ten people were staying. Travelers made stops on journeys that continued for many months and five to ten people would rest in each of the tents that was pitched. A fire would be lit in front of every tent for the purpose of preparing food, keeping warm on cold nights, or to obtain enough light. That is to say, every fire meant at least five and up to ten people. So, this was another of the strategies of God's Messenger. By instructing his Companions to light a fire for every person, he made it look as if the strength of his Companions was at least five times greater than it was, and to prevent the Quraysh, who he had thus unsettled, from resorting to the use of arms. In other words, this was an awe-inspiring scene that demonstrated how many people God's Messenger had reached until that day, and how many people he could stir into action with him. Well-versed in the culture and certain that he knew the Meccans very well also, the Messenger of God sent a silent but forceful message in order to prevent bloodshed, showing his strength as tenfold.

Abu Sufyan and his associates were completely overwhelmed at this scene. They multiplied the estimated number of fires by at least five and began to believe that an army of at least fifty thousand men was facing them. What is more, their opponents' numbers might even exceed a hundred thousand. Whilst Mecca had been slumbering unawares, Medina had mobilized, and the Messenger of God had come all the way to Mecca with an unseen army.

God's Messenger informed his Companions of the exact location of Abu Sufyan and his friends, who were watching them, and instructed them to bring them to him. The Companions went to the place specified by God's Messenger, apprehended the three Meccans, and brought them back to where the army was encamped. Naturally, their first contact was with 'Umar who was in charge of the night guard. "We have captured some Meccans and brought them to you," they said. 'Umar was unaware of the details of developments. "By God, if you have not brought Abu Sufyan, then tell me not that you have brought a man," he teased.[489] Upon scanning the new arrivals more closely, his manner changed entirely. "O enemy of God," he exclaimed when he saw Abu Sufyan. "Praise be to God Who has enabled us to capture you without any pact or agreement!"[490]

When saying this, 'Umar was thinking of all the blows they had suffered from Mecca for all these years and reacting to the leader who was its representative. But he could not deal with this on his own, so he hastened to God's Messenger to inform him of this critical development.

At the same time, 'Abbas who had just joined God's Messenger a few days earlier[491] also learned of the situation, and showed his delight at the arrival of his old friend Abu Sufyan.[492] On top of this, he offered protection to his close friend Abu Sufyan and his companion Hakim ibn Hizam. He wholeheartedly desired that they should be honored with Islam and strove to do everything in his power to facilitate this. He became anxious, however, at 'Umar's manner of departure and hurried off behind him. He had guessed what might happen and wanted to prevent a potential mistake.

They entered the Messenger's presence in succession. "O Messenger of God," said 'Umar, and swiftly proposed to punish Abu Sufyan.

His friend of many years, 'Abbas, realized just how justified he was in rushing after him;[493] he immediately interrupted and said, "O Messenger of God, I have given him my protection."

When 'Umar continued to remonstrate 'Abbas turned to him and said, "Gently, 'Umar! Had he been one of the Banu 'Adi ibn Ka'b, you would not have said this; but you know that he is one of the Banu 'Abd Manaf."

'Umar was of a vigorous temperament, but he was a man who always gave credit where credit was due. Such a man could not engage in partisan-like behavior and discriminate in favor of his near kin. "Gently, yourself, 'Abbas!" he immediate retorted. "By God, your accepting Islam the day you did was dearer to me than if al-Khattab, my father, had been the one to do so. As I well know that your accepting Islam was dearer to the Messenger of God than my father's would have been."[494]

Even though 'Umar was speaking the truth, there was nothing more that he could do, for where protection had been granted all he could do was to re-sheathe his sword and stand aside. From then on, nobody could lay a hand on Abu Sufyan. But 'Abbas did not want to risk it, so he moved closer to God's Messenger. Placing his hand on Abu Sufyan's head, he entreated, "By God, none shall be alone with him on this night without my being present."

It was completely clear from his behavior that he wanted to take the closest interest in his long-time friend. 'Abbas would prepare him for belief as much as he possibly could, and who knows what he would be able to relate to him, that had not been possible until now. For from this moment on, 'Abbas became transformed into a merciful fountain of words openly telling the Meccan leader about Islam.

Abu Sufyan reborn

The Call to Prayer began as soon as the time for the Morning Prayer set in, and the Companions were repeating the call. Abu Sufyan, however, had woken to the day with the sound of the Call to Prayer for the very first time. These sounds, which came from all directions, and the people rushing back and forth to perform the ritual ablutions did not escape his notice. He could make no sense of all this stir at such an early hour of the morning and became rather unsettled. It is quite likely that he feared for his life, in spite of the protection that he was granted. He called out to 'Abbas, wanting to understand what all the fuss was about. "O Abu Fadl," he said. "What is the matter with everyone? What are they doing? Or do they mean to kill me?"

His friend would again put his mind at ease. "No," replied 'Abbas, "they have risen for the Prayer." Relieved, to some degree, Abu Sufyan was now curious. "And how often do they pray?" he asked. "Five times in all, night and day," 'Abbas replied.[495]

After this, they too began to move towards God's Messenger. There was something else that drew Abu Sufyan's notice at this point. As the Messenger of God performed his ablution, the Companions next to him could not bear for even a single drop of his ablution water to fall to the ground and, seeking the spiritual blessings in it, scrambled for every drop, to wipe them over their faces or skin. Abu Sufyan witnessed a reverence he had never seen in the court of any ruler.

The people then lined up in rows for prayer, standing behind God's Messenger when the muezzin pronounced the second call to the Prayer (*iqama*) indicating that the congregational prayer was about to begin and then the Noble Prophet commenced the Prayer with a proclamation of God's greatness (opening *takbir*). The Companions followed. When he began reciting the Qur'an, everyone remained silent. When God's Messenger knelt, they knelt, all in complete synchrony. For Abu Sufyan, everything was so novel, so fresh. In addition to what he had seen before, he now witnessed their manner of standing before their Lord, and saw with admiration the point which the Meccans of yesterday had reached. This state was enough to melt Abu Sufyan's heart, and when they all placed their foreheads on the ground in unison, the sight completely overwhelmed him. He seemed to feel the heads placed on the ground being brushed with spiritual favors coming from beyond the firmaments, and he said of this, "By God, in my life I never saw the submissiveness I have seen today, of a people coming from here and there—not even in the case of the Persians who deem themselves noble, or the Greeks who pride themselves on their superiority." He then turned to 'Abbas and said, "O Abu Fadl, By God, your brother's son is greater than kings!"

Abu Sufyan had slowly begun to open the door, but he was yet not ready to enter. "This is not kingdom, but Prophethood," 'Abbas said, correcting him. This statement also served to demonstrate the difference between the two worlds. In response to 'Abbas' words, Abu Sufyan made do with saying, "Perhaps it is something like that."[496]

Then, they approached God's Messenger. God's Messenger turned to Abu Sufyan in great compassion and said, "O Abu Sufyan, has not the time come for you to recognize that there is no deity but God?"

This was a response that Abu Sufyan had not at all expected. The lips from which he expected reproof, anger, and bitterness were pouring forth mercy, compassion, and affection. There were so many questions that had previously plagued his mind. There was nothing to be concerned about. Muhammad the Trustworthy was a leader who could forgive when he held power. He did not strike at the first chance, and even at a point where his opponents faced loss, he invited them once more to triumph, and to absolute triumph at that. Abu Sufyan took a deep breath. He felt as though every word that came from the Messenger's blessed mouth warmed his heart, and he wanted to let himself go into the embrace of the Prophetic mercy that he had long striven to resist. So he began with, "By my mother and father!" Nothing remained of his former severe stance. He spoke with his head bowed and a genuine sense of surrender. As a person in his right mind and one who knew full well what he was saying, he said, "How great are your mercy, your compassion, and your forgiveness! Had there been another deity besides God, he would have surely availed me by now. For both you and I constantly sought help from our deities, but it was always you who received it. By God, had not yours but my deities been true instead, would things have ended this way?"

The Messenger of God responded to him once more, saying, "Woe upon you, O Abu Sufyan! Has not the time come for you to recognize that I am the Messenger of God?"

He had come to the last part of a long and difficult journey but Abu Sufyan could not bring himself to take the final step and proclaim, "Yes!" "By my mother and father," he repeated to God's Messenger. "How merciful, elevated in compassion, and pardoning you truly are! But, as to that, by God, I still have my doubts."

'Abbas, too, who had done nothing but show Abu Sufyan the way and granted him protection, ran out of patience. He did not want his fellow to turn around and go back just because of a little doubt, after he had come so far. In a serious tone, he warned him about the severe danger he was facing.

He looked carefully at his friend, 'Abbas, who spoke in a language that he could clearly understand. He was right in what he said, but cutting off the past with complete disregard was not that easy. But his heart could not remain indifferent to this heartfelt invitation and he was spent. After standing quietly for a moment, he said, "I bear witness that there is no deity but God, and I also bear witness that Muhammad is His servant and His Messenger."[497]

With his acceptance of Islam, Abu Sufyan's companions, Hakim ibn Hizam and Budayl ibn Warqa, to whom 'Abbas had also granted protection, also embraced Islam.[498] These were undoubtedly the first fruits of conquest. They had been freed of the burden of polytheism, and had released themselves to the boundlessness of belief.

Now that they had made their position clear, they spoke much more comfortably. What they wondered now was where and how this journey would come to an end. The Messenger of God recounted one by one all the schemes at the Ka'ba, the designs against God and His Messenger, and the murder of twenty-three innocent people in a night raid in complete disregard and defiance of the Treaty of Hudaybiya, and stated that the time had now come to devote the Ka'ba, the Sacred House, exclusively to God. With heads bowed, they confirmed everything he said. They had indeed saved themselves, but lying before them was a phase whose outcome was still unclear. So they said, "O Messenger of God, grant protection to the people."

'Abbas had already stepped in and suggested to God's Messenger that as Abu Sufyan was by nature a proud man, it would mean a lot to grant him an honorable position. Abu Bakr supported Abbas' view. So the Messenger of God declared, "Whoever enters the house of Abu Sufyan is safe."[499]

The treatment that he had expected as a leader had come, but it was not enough for him. He perhaps recognized that boundless mercy and wished for more. So he called out, "And how many will my house hold?" Naturally, he regarded it as insufficient as he could almost see the Meccans flooding to his house en masse. "Whoever enters the house of Hakim ibn Hizam is safe," God's Messenger declared, in this way also honoring the cousin of his beloved wife Khadija.[500] However, the Meccan envoys were still waiting for more. Seeing this, God's Messenger expanded the sphere of sanctuary as far as possible and said, "Whoever enters the Ka'ba is safe." The Meccan envoys wanted more and asked, "How many people can the Ka'ba hold?" It was as though these people who had until just a few hours ago represented Mecca had gone, and people who had dedicated themselves to winning over the Meccans had come in their place. And so came the final and most comprehensive decree:

"Whoever closes their door is safe."[501]

This was, in any event, the winning decree—the one which would conquer Mecca—and there could not have been a decree greater in scope.

Meanwhile, everything that had happened in Mecca over the past twenty years flashed though Abu Sufyan's mind, everything they had aspired to, struggled for, and what they were now doing! Was what they did in the past right, or the point to which they had come today? He recalled everything from the moment they had come to Marr al-Zahran until now, and thought that he had no other choice but to accept all this, since he faced a force that was impossible to resist. He could not solve the dilemma he found himself in, and could not put out of his mind the reaction he would face from the people whose leader he was when he returned to Mecca in this state. He could not free himself from the Meccans' reactions that would soon come on this path where he would become a target for them, and he was thus extremely distressed. He was the chief of the Meccans and he possessed the power to mobilize the surrounding tribes whenever he wished. Just when he came face to face with his carnal self, there came Satan, who began whispering his evil to him; at one point, the thought of going to the surrounding tribes and amassing a large army one last time passed through his mind. It could be possible. He could survive today only to face the Messenger of God tomorrow, even mightier, and could exact his revenge for today. But while he was still entertaining such fancies, a hand touched his shoulder from behind, and said, "Then God would put you to shame and we would be victorious once again." Startled, he looked round at the owner of that hand and saw that it was none other than God's Messenger. He was deeply ashamed. Before him stood a person who knew even what he kept hidden in the most innermost recesses of his heart and mind, and in all sincerity he exclaimed, "I bear witness that you are the Messenger of God!" He then added, "I turn to God and seek His forgiveness for what I have said. Until now, I had some doubts concerning your being a Messenger of God and so kept telling myself, but these thoughts have all vanished. By God, it was none other than the whims of my carnal soul that drove me to entertain such a thought."[502]

Now he too had decided on his course and, conceding the error of his ways so far, opted for the path of peace and security. The seventy-year-old Meccan leader who had led the way in unbelief for twenty-one years was now being reborn. No doubt this rebirth would not be limited to him, and would serve to ease the birth pangs of the Mecca he represented, for he would go to Mecca as a vanguard and invite its people to peace and amity in a language that was becoming to him as its leader.

The day of mercy

Abu Sufyan's longtime close friend 'Abbas viewed his going with concern.[503] He came to God's Messenger and said, "O Messenger of God, I am not certain whether Abu Sufyan will remain committed. Can you not keep them with you a while longer so that they may watch the army pass and better grasp the situation?"

Abu Bakr shared this view. God's Messenger sent 'Abbas after Abu Sufyan and his travel companion Hakim ibn Hizam, who had already set off in the direction of Mecca, to call them back. Seeing him approach with speed, Abu Sufyan, suspecting bad intentions, remarked, "What is it, O Banu Hashim? Or is this treachery?" Understanding his friend's apprehension, 'Abbas was quick to allay his fears, and said very directly, "Those who stand behind God's Messenger are not treacherous. I just have a request for you. I only ask that you wait here until morning, observe the armies of God march by and behold what God has in store for the idolaters."[504]

It was a reasonable suggestion. At the return of the Meccan envoys, Messenger's herald at Marr al-Zahran announced loudly, "Let every tribe immediately begin preparations for travel, gather with their leader beneath their own standard, with their weapons and munitions loaded upon their mounts." All the troops were thus mobilized, in formation.

It did not take long. Soon, every tribe had lined up in rows with their leader and commander, beneath their banners, ready, waiting for the Prophetic command.

The time had now come to show to Abu Sufyan the march of the forces that had bedazzled in the dark of night, now in daylight. The forces set out in divisions in the direction of the nearer end of the valley where Abu Sufyan waited. It was as though the earth merged with the sky, and was advancing towards Abu Sufyan in an awesome harmony. Marr al-Zahran was witness to a celestial march. The forces moved in the direction of Mecca, twenty divisions led by their commanders, with their standards held aloft.

This was a scene that left Abu Sufyan awe-struck. Marr al-Zahran had been all but readied as a ceremonial ground for Abu Sufyan's eyes. For every approaching division, Abu Sufyan asked his close friend 'Abbas who they were. 'Abbas informed him of their identity and told him how they had become Muslim, relating the dynamics which led to their total transformation. They passed by Abu Sufyan in all their magnificence in groups of two hundred, three hundred, four hundred, five hundred, eight hundred, nine hundred, and a thousand, with their standards rippling above them, with proclamations of God's greatness.[505]

'Abbas, with trembling heart, watched Meccan chief Abu Sufyan closely. As the army marched before them division by division, he strove to dispel the doubts that arose in his mind, and spoke feelingly of the dynamism of Islam. Abu Sufyan asked question after question, and 'Abbas related to him the truth in a way he could readily understand and as one who for years shared the same thoughts and sentiments. Abu Sufyan finally asked him questions concerning the Kinana, who were then approaching, and 'Abbas replied that they were the "Banu Layth, Banu Damra and the Banu Sa'd ibn Bakr." "Yes!" Abu Sufyan exclaimed. "The people of ill omen! It is because of them that Muhammad now attacks us!" It was time to make the point and 'Abbas immediately struck home with his words: "God has destined good in this, Muhammad's offensive.

For it is by virtue of this that today you have attained peace and security, and are now all entering the fold of Islam."[506]

Just at that point, the Khazraj tribe headed by Sa'd ibn 'Ubada approached. They numbered one thousand. As a matter of course, Abu Sufyan inquired about them and 'Abbas responded to him with the same equanimity. The Messenger of God, about whom Abu Sufyan kept on inquiring, was also in that division. 'Umar's booming voice was immediately recognizable in the army that proceeded majestically. He urged the troops to march in order and proper formation. The Helpers and Migrants put on a multicolored display with their distinctive flags. They were fully equipped. Abu Sufyan could not help but exclaim at one point, "Who can withstand all these forces!"

Passing by at the very same moment, Sa'd ibn 'Ubada called out in a deep voice to Meccan leader and new Muslim, Abu Sufyan, who had caused them so much grief until that day, "Today is the day to make history. Today, the sacredness of the Sanctuary shall be lifted. Today is the day that God will humiliate the Quraysh!"[507]

These words sent a chill right through Abu Sufyan. He was sweltering in the heat of July[508] to be sure, but Sa'd's words froze him on the inside. They pierced his mind and left him utterly dejected. Behind his words was an anger that he had not heard until this point, and that had not been visible to him in what he was witnessing. What is more, the one uttering these words was no ordinary person. He was the leader of one of the two biggest tribes in Medina, the chief of the Khazraj, Sa'd ibn 'Ubada. Abu Sufyan sought to alleviate his fears and exclaimed, "O 'Abbas, how excellent a day for you to protect me!"

Just then, the Messenger of God, the embodiment of mercy, approached on his mount, Qaswa'. To his right was Abu Bakr and to his left was Usayd ibn Hudayr. "Look, God's Messenger!" 'Abbas exclaimed with great excitement. Abu Sufyan said, "The sovereignty of your brother's son has today grown mighty indeed." 'Abbas was again left to correct him: "O Abu Sufyan," he said. "This is not sovereignty, but Prophethood!"[509]

But Abu Sufyan could not get Sa'd ibn 'Ubada's words out of his mind. They had really hit home. He looked at God's Messenger at length—there was not a single sign of violence or aggression. Far from it, he advanced with compassion and was bent in humility. In the tumult and upheaval in his imagination, he tried to reconcile his disposition with the Sa'd he had just heard, but could not do so. He finally understood that God's Messenger and violence just could not be reconciled. He, too, turned to the haven in whom all sought refuge, and to make certain that there was no mistake, he called out, "O Messenger of God, did you command the killing of your people? Look at what Sa'd ibn 'Ubada is saying!"

God's Messenger was, of course, not aware of this, but he knew something was wrong because Abu Sufyan was so perturbed. "What has he said?" he asked with great sensitivity. Abu Sufyan repeated verbatim Sa'd's words. "While you," he then said, "are the best of people, the most merciful of people, and the best of people to their kin, in God's name, I ask that you are benevolent to your people."

The Messenger of God was uneasy also, for Abu Sufyan was not just one man. The disquiet he felt on that day could affect the Meccans exponentially. And Sa'd's words, in his inability to discern the Messenger's intention and in succumbing to the force of his emotion, were utterances that did not in fact reflect what was to happen after this point. On top of that, what he had said was categorically opposed to the general strategy being scrupulously followed. In fact, the Messenger had never had any notion of retaliating for the harm done to him up until now. What mattered was that the people perceive and understand the truth, and set out on the path of their deliverance, and that he would make further gestures even to those who wished to deprive him of the right to live. In any event, the pain and anguish of the past was about to give way to the joy of reunion. Sa'd had lost control of his emotions and had made an isolated outburst, but neither his position, nor the context and the timing would allow what he said to happen. So God's Messenger called out, "Sa'd is mistaken, O Abu Sufyan." He wished to express that his fears were groundless. In the clear, velvet tone of voice that set Abu Sufyan's heart at ease, he then said, "Today is the day of mercy! Today, God shall raise the honor of the Ka'ba! Today, the Ka'ba will be spread with a covering and adorned. Today will be the day when God will honor the Quraysh."

In fact, these words of God's Messenger would have sufficed to relieve both Abu Sufyan and all the Meccans. However, God's Messenger did not stop there, and he dismissed Sa'd ibn 'Ubada, whose opinion he frequently sought and whom he loved dearly, from his post as commander.[510] Sa'd was the leader of the Khazraj, and his fellow tribesmen viewed him as a compassionate father figure who protected them and saw to their welfare, so removing him from his position at such a time was not easily accepted. At the same time, he was leading his men in the greatest of all conquests. Despite the fact that conditions were anything but conducive to his dismissal, God's Messenger addressed the incident head-on and did not leave it unresolved. Even though it was a commander who had uttered these words, he stripped him of his title and appointed Sa'd's son, Qays, in his place.[511]

In this way, he demonstrated to members of his community in positions of leadership that removing an individual or commander from office when necessary was also part of the Prophetic methodology. But this was not a Prophetic practice that could be implemented anywhere and at anytime, and only those walking on the Prophetic path could do so.[512]

Attitude of the Meccans

Abu Sufyan was reborn at Marr al-Zahran, and he now returned to Mecca with a brand new identity. Seeing his arrival from afar, his wife Hind went into a rage. She noticed almost at once that her husband, whom they had sent to inspect the surrounds, had returned a changed man. This she read from his manner of walking. She called out to the Meccans, pointing to her husband, "Kill this traitor!" When he came up to her, she seized him by the throat, screaming insults at him while pulling at his beard. "Kill this old coward! What a rotten protector and disgraceful leader of the people," she screamed, kicking her husband, the chief of Mecca, for all the Meccans to see.

An argument between husband and wife was getting far out of hand. Hind possessed a spirited and dominant temperament; she knew how to make herself heard in assemblies and drew people's attention with her flair for language and literature. But times had changed, and it was a new era. Even the sun rose over Mecca in a different way that day. Worried by his wife's evil intent, Abu Sufyan felt that there was no need to be foolish and he invited the Meccans to common sense. Indicating his wife Hind with one hand, he scolded the Meccans saying, "O people of the Quraysh, shame on you! Let not this woman deceive you. Here is

Muhammad in full march upon us with an army that you cannot possibly resist. And he is right on our doorstep."

All their worst fears were coming true. Their leader, Abu Sufyan, had brought the news they had so dreaded. All hope was lost and the Quraysh could see no future; they were done for. They looked at one another, trying to make sense of what Abu Sufyan was saying. He was in dead earnest. Medina had truly come all the way to their door in the tens of thousands, while the Meccans had remained unaware. What could they possibly have done at this point against an army that was but a short distance away? At a loss, they wondered what to do. The best suggestion came again from Abu Sufyan: "O people, embrace Islam and you shall be safe."[513]

This was a second shock to them. They had already suspected as much, but thought they might be mistaken. Now, however, the situation was completely different and at a time they least expected it, Abu Sufyan was himself saying that he had become Muslim. What is more, he invited them to do the same, wanting them to accept the religion that they had resisted for twenty-one years, and he was suggesting them to leave all their reservations behind.

They were in complete despair. Until that day, where God and His Messenger were concerned, they had spoken nothing but hatred and hostility in Mecca and had constantly thought of evil. Even though they could not entirely ignore their consciences, or the objections they raised from time to time, they always managed to crush them under the plans for chaos that came out of the Dar al-Nadwa, and thus blocked the Prophetic mercy that was struggling for their sake despite everything they had done. The despair they now faced brought these barriers to mercy to their notice and they tried now to see the matter through the eyes of their leader. This was not all that he had to say to them, in any case, and he began to tell them of the amnesty from God's Messenger: "Whoever enters the house of Abu Sufyan is safe," he had barely managed to get out, when someone in the crowd shouted, "May God denounce you! What good will Abu Sufyan's house be for all of us?"

He had reacted in exactly the same way at Marr al-Zahran and made a similar objection. Looking at the interjector as if to say, "Just wait. Do not rush!" Abu Sufyan continued, "Whoever closes their door is safe! Whoever enters the Ka'ba is safe."

Like it or not, there was nothing to be done. It appeared that the Quraysh had no other choice but to give in. The truth of the matter was, however, that the Eternal Power Who years earlier foretold the entry into Mecca in peace and security, now bestowed the equitable leader, Abu Sufyan, with insight, and he was now playing out his fate in the surrender of Mecca.

Self-effacement and humility

The self-effacement and humility that God's Messenger showed in realizing the conquest of Mecca was important to his winning over the hearts of the people. This behavior of God's Messenger was not particular to just that day, or exhibited temporarily and only to the Meccans. He was always the epitome of self-effacement and humility. God's Messenger, the humblest servant of the All-Merciful to walk the earth, is the perfected human being who represents God's will in this to the utmost degree [514] and who prescribed [515] the same to his Companions. For humility is the most important criterion of greatness. Bowing in humility is the hallmark of those of elevated stature.

Hence, at the conquest of Mecca, the pinnacle of his twenty-one year endeavor, we see God's Messenger at the peak of humility also:

On the thirteenth of Ramadan, a Friday, he set off from Marr al-Zahran with his Companions and traveled to Dhu Tuwa. He was finally to advance from here on the homeland that he had been forced to leave eight years earlier, the blessed city of Mecca, hosting the Sacred House within its walls. Everyone wanted to set off with him on this historic journey, and like stars haloing around the moon, they flowed towards the Valley of Becca in anticipation of certain victory. He had wrapped a long turban around his head, letting the end trail down over his shoulder. [516]

Behind him, [517] rode Usama, the son of the freed slave whom God's Messenger had promoted to the rank of commander. Clinging on to him from behind on such a historic journey, with arms that carried the potential to rule the future, was not the child of one of his leading Companions, or even one of his grandchildren Hasan and Husayn, whom he described as "two sweet basils," but the son of the slave who nobody thought anything of until he was taken by the hand in Islam. [518] In this, as always, the Messenger of God showed in his own behavior how all human beings, no matter their origin or status are equal before God.

He was bent double in humility on the back of his blessed camel, so much so that his beard was almost touching the saddle of his camel, Qaswa.[519] "My Lord," he said. "The true life is the life of the Hereafter."[520]

In this way, he reminded the people that it is not the conquest of lands that is difficult; the true conquest is when people use their willpower to rule over their own inner world in spite of all the forces of their emotions and faculties. He thus exhorted those around him to avoid making the errors that would leave them in trouble in the Hereafter. At the same time, for the Meccans this humble posture was laden with messages concerning how they would be treated, despite their knowing no bounds in their hostility for the past twenty years. No one would be looked down on, no one would be omitted, feelings of revenge would not be acted out, nothing unfavorable from the past would be brought up, nobody's wrong would be held against them, and not a single person would be harmed. For the Messenger of God came to Mecca with the ideal of letting live. This is why he exhorted his Companions constantly: if resistance was mounted, they were only allowed to fight against those who fought against them. His every step was an expression of yet another unique example for the believers, and the Messenger's Conquest would be realized in a manner and context that befit him. He divided his Companions into four columns and ordered them enter the city from four different directions.

He himself entered from the upper Ma'la quarter. These were places that bore the traces of three years' exile. These were places where Yasir and Sumayya were martyred, where Bilal's cries of pain echoed in the Paran Mountain ranges, and whose streets bore the trace of many a bitter memory, of Khadija, the foremost model of faithfulness, stoicism, and patience.

Meanwhile, the Meccan women displayed their jubilation by brushing the necks of the steeds with the kerchiefs they held in their hands. Far from meeting any resistance, as the Messenger of God entered Mecca, both doors and hearts opened wide for him. A conquest accompanied by the Meccans' songs of festivity was taking place. Upon entry into the city, slight resistance was encountered only at one of the points of entry, where Khalid ibn al-Walid entered from the lower end of the city. Those mounting this resistance were Khalid ibn al-Walid's former friends. Suhayl ibn 'Amr, Safwan ibn Umayya, and 'Ikrima led the small band, and when they realized that they could not contend with the Khalid ibn al-Walid they knew so well, they scurried away and fled. This demonstrated clearly that the true conquest had been accomplished earlier, and that those who had trouble stomaching it were a small, local faction. Hearts had been conquered and the only thing that remained to do was to enter the city and "put a seal" upon it. As this seal was being put on the city, Mecca was preparing to host its true owner. When God's Messenger saw the state of the women, he called out to Abu Bakr saying, "What was it that Hasan had said?" Abu Bakr, of great discernment, grasped his meaning and began to recite a poem that depicted the scene before him. This was, of course, the very same poem that Hasan ibn Thabit had recited prior to Mecca's conquest and in which he had portrayed the women brushing the necks of the horses with their kerchiefs in jubilation upon the troops' entry into Mecca by way of Kada', precisely as was the case now. The Messenger of God commanded his own division to "Enter from the direction indicated by Hasan."[521]

He also summoned Zubayr, whom he referred to as his "disciple," and ordered him to fix the banner he carried with him at Hajun and wait for his arrival there. Hajun was another source of sorrow for the Messenger, for it was to this land that, after a three-year boycott, he had entrusted his beloved wife of twenty-three years Khadija, who had supported him in the most difficult days in Mecca. He would soon go and stand beside her grave and pray for her at length. Even when on the road to the Conquest, God's Messenger changed his route and, in profound loyalty to her, prayed beside Khadija's grave for a considerable period.[522]

When he passed Adhakhir and saw the Meccan houses, he stopped and began praising God in deep gratitude and thankfulness. Again, he had turned to God and was beseeching Him. He then said, "O Jabir, this is where we will pitch our tent. This is also the place where the Quraysh swore an oath of loyalty to unbelief and where they once resolved to destroy us."[523]

This no doubt meant, "From this day forth, it is not they who will set the agenda in Mecca, but us." This was an outcome that demonstrated the greatness of Divine Power. The site that would bear witness to the judgment that the Meccans made on that day against God's Messenger and his Companions and the one that would attest to the judgment that

God's Messenger would today give in regard to them, was one and the same. The sole difference was that everyone had now begun to realize the difference between the two.

As he rode on, he recited the Qur'anic chapters *Al-Fath* (The Victory) and *An-Nasr* (Help) and declared, "This is what God has promised me." On that day, there were those who approached him and asked, "O Messenger of God, where will you stay tomorrow?" They presumably wished to learn whether he would go to the house that he was forced to leave years earlier, so that they could go and prepare it for his arrival. This would mean the other Migrants could also go to their former homes. But God's Messenger said, "Has 'Aqil left us any house to lodge in?" Abu Talib's eldest son 'Aqil had taken possession of everything that God's Messenger had left behind, his house included, and had later sold them to others. Those who heard this offered other houses for God's Messenger to stay in, but he did not take up any of these offers, instead indicating the direction of Hajun, where Zubayr had planted his standard. While God's most beloved servant was conquering this most venerable city in His eyes, he did not expect nor desire applause or show, and would stay in a tent pitched at Hajun. That was where he would remain up until his departure for Medina.[524]

There is another detail worthy of note: on conquering Mecca—the land where he was born and raised, where he had so many memories, bitter and sweet, and where he was honored with the mission of Prophethood—and was reunited with his twin,[525] God's Messenger shortened his Prayers.[526] This was a clear sign that he planned to stay in Mecca for no more than fifteen days. That is to say, contrary to the misrepresentation aimed at instilling fear in the people, he had not come to occupy the city. He had set off from Medina with the intention of returning there after taking on board his ship the Meccans who had not been able to understand the language of his call from afar.

Suhayl ibn 'Amr

Suhayl ibn 'Amr was one of the small band of Meccans who tried to resist Mecca's conquest, but who fled when they realized that they did not have the power to do so. He was one of those who read the situation early on. For there was not the slightest sign of hate or enmity in this advent, and God's Messenger was coming to acquaint God's servants with God. As soon as he realized this, he summoned his grandchildren to his hiding place and sent them with a message to his son, 'Abdu'llah. He had stopped at nothing to make life a living hell for his son and subjected him to years of torment, but he now appealed to him. He had one wish: he wanted his son to secure amnesty from Muhammad the Trustworthy for him too. Even though the general state of affairs caused him to be hopeful, he was nonetheless afraid for his life. Putting himself in the place of God's Messenger, he thought about what he would do if he were to be given such an opportunity; he recalled all that he had done and he thus issued in his mind his own death warrant. After all, what would the Quraysh not have done in this situation?

When 'Abdu'llah received his father's message, it made him forget all the years of hardship and sorrow. In great joy, he ran to God's Messenger, who was then walking towards the Ka'ba. He was certain that God's Messenger too would be overjoyed at this news. "O Messenger of God," he said. "My father... Will you grant my father Suhayl protection?"

The heart of God's Messenger was big enough to hold everyone, and his eyes filled with tears of happiness. How could they not? For here was a message from the eloquent orator of the Quraysh, who until that day had financed the army of hatred and animosity, and knew no bounds in his vituperation. He had brought down his wall of hate and had now begun to see boundless mercy. Thus, as soon as he heard these words, he replied, "Yes, he too is protected, and he has the protection of God, so let him come out now."

But he did not stop there as Suhayl ibn 'Amr had hurt so many and had done evil to all those around God's Messenger. One of these people might be unable to control himself and say hurtful things to Suhayl on his way here, and might make his coming to God's Messenger difficult. God's Messenger needed to ensure Suhayl's safety along the way so as to prevent such a mistake from being made, and he said to those who were around him:

"*Let whoever meets Suhayl not stare at him. Let him now come out from hiding. For, by my life, Suhayl is a possessor of intelligence and honor. And a person like Suhayl cannot possibly remain indifferent to Islam. Surely, he has realized that where he stood until now could not avail him.*"[527]

These were words that could confer great honor and dignity upon Suhayl, right at the point when he thought he was done for. Hearing them from God's Messenger, 'Abdu'llah rushed to the place where his father was in hiding, excited to share with him this news. When he reached him and informed him of God's Messenger's words, it felt as though his heart might burst. Even though he strove to suppress his elation, it was not possible, and he wept in the enthusiasm of knowing that he would henceforth see his father, who made life unbearable for him, in the same rank.

Suhayl was overjoyed at the news his son relayed to him, and deeply moved at having once again received mercy from the one that he had so vehemently opposed. Just when he thought himself finished, he had a new lease of life. He looked at 'Abdu'llah, for whom he had until yesterday been filled with hatred and contempt, and for the first time in years felt a warmth in his heart. His face that had had been pale with anxiety until that moment now glowed, and his knees that had been weak with distress gained strength. He rose and paced back and forth, trying to process all these gestures. In an attempt to express his appreciation of God's Messenger, he declared, "By God, he was righteous in his youth as he is now, while he is in possession of such power!" Suhayl had entered a vast garden of love. He lost himself in the tears of happiness that flowed down his son's face, and he began to feel deep remorse for all that he had done to his pure heart. The happiness of his son only added to his own. These feelings were uniting a father holding onto life anew and his son who had longed for his coming. Two hearts that had been estranged were reunited, and were clinging onto each other, never again to be separated.

He could not remain indifferent to such a clear and unmistakable message and he immediately set out with his son 'Abdu'llah. The place where he would find God's Messenger was obvious. The influential orator of the Quraysh, Suhayl ibn 'Amr, was going to the Ka'ba.

It was as though a carpet had been rolled out beneath his feet in welcome. He neither heard an ill word from anyone, nor caught sight of a hateful glance. Far from it, everyone who saw him coming gave way to him, as if they could see the difference in his step and were doing everything possible to avoid causing any delay to his reunion with God's Messenger. And so, in the city of Mecca with a population of ten thousand, where even more than that number had just arrived, Suhayl went all the way to the Ka'ba without experiencing even the slightest disturbance, obstacle or hindrance.

Divine approval

The "*minbar*" of Medina had reunited with the "*mihrab*" of Mecca, and the Messenger of God was at the Ka'ba. He first greeted it from afar with the staff he had in his hand and then began to recite proclamations of God's greatness. Everyone who heard him started repeating his proclamations at the top of their lungs, until it seemed as though the city shook. God's Messenger then motioned for the people to be silent. For it was now time for circumambulation. After hailing the Black Stone from a distance, God's Messenger began to circumambulate the House, with Muhammad ibn Maslama holding the reins of his camel.

On that day there were three hundred idols around the Ka'ba, each of them coated with lead. The city's inhabitants would slaughter their sacrificial animals here and voice their needs kneeling before them. Since the Ka'ba had now become a united whole with Islam, it had to be purged of the wide array of idols, with names such as Hubal, Isaf and Na'ila. As God's Messenger passed by each of them, he pointed at it with the staff he held in his hand, and the idol at which he pointed fell face first to the ground. While doing this, he recited the verse from the Qur'an that means, "*The truth has come, and falsehood has vanished. Surely falsehood is ever bound to vanish by its very nature*" (Al-Isra 17:81).

At the completion of his circumambulation, after each circuit[528] of which he hailed the Black Stone, he dismounted his camel and immediately headed for the Station of Abraham, where Prophet Abraham had stood for Prayer. At this point, he was still wearing his armor and helmet, and the turban he wore fell down over his shoulders. He offered two units of Prayer at the Station of Abraham and then approached the well of Zamzam, where he said, "I would have drawn a bucket of water from the well if I didn't know the sons of 'Abd al-Muttalib would prevail over me in this matter."[529] 'Abbas immediately grasped the meaning of God's Messenger's words, drew a bucket of water from the well and offered it to God's Messenger. The Messenger of God drank from it and then performed his ablution with it. In the meantime, the Companions had gathered around him, racing to catch whatever water they could from his ablution water, wiping it all over their face and hands to obtain its spiritual blessing.

In every step of God's Messenger was the exhilaration of worship. He was dispelling all the rumors, fears and concerns, and was demonstrating in person that his sole objective was God's good pleasure and approval.

General amnesty

God's Messenger went inside the Ka'ba with Usama ibn Zayd and Bilal al-Habashi, and offered Prayer between its pillars. He then stepped out on to its entrance, looked out at the curious eyes gathered around him, and said, "What do you expect of me and what do you think about the treatment that I am to accord you?" He asked the question to be sure, but the Quraysh who had no strength left to speak were enveloped in a deathly silence. For they heard these words from one whom they had banished from his homeland for no good reason, whose life in the city they had turned into a living nightmare by waylaying him at every corner, and whom they had made repeated attempts to kill. Had it been anyone else in the same situation, he would have put everyone to the sword, or would have reduced them to the degradation of slavery from which they could not free themselves for generations. They were face to face with a greatness they could not even dream of; he did not domineer despite the fact that he held domination over everything, and he did not stoop to opportunism despite the fact that he had every opportunity. All kinds of things had been said in Mecca about him, including, "He's going to kill us," "He's going to take revenge," "He's going to interfere with our way of life," "He's going to meddle with what we wear," and "He's going to intrude into our night life," and they had slandered him greatly. Mecca had, until that day, been completely engrossed in lies and falsehood, and they had done the most righteous servant of God great injustice.

They could not find anything to say. Heads lowered, nobody said a single word. Finally, a voice rose from the crowd, breaking the silence, "We say what is good, and expect nothing but goodness from you. For you are a noble brother and the son of a noble brother."

Naturally, all eyes turned in the direction of the voice, and before them stood yesterday's implacable enemy Suhayl ibn 'Amr. He had come to join those who followed this path directed wholly by worship with no other objective than to earn God's good pleasure and approval. He now rushed to the aid of the silent masses, and told God's Beloved, who sought any excuse to forgive, that he hoped for forgiveness for yesterday's ingrates. What did God not have power and disposal over? If Suhayl had submitted, who could not? They were experiencing a day so contracted that it seemed as though years had been squeezed into minutes. Before they could even recover from one shock, another followed, and in the light of the flashes of lightning coming one after another, they seemed to see the illumination of their horizon.

God's Messenger too had seen the speaker. He who was the master of the spoken word well understood the implication of Suhayl's words. Suhayl was asking God's Messenger for the treatment that Joseph afforded his brothers after everything had been revealed—his brothers who had made plan after plan to kill him, thrown him into a well and left him for dead, robbed him of his life by making him suffer in one dungeon after another. Or Suhayl had inferred this from the Noble Prophet's general manner and was informing others of what he was going to do.

The Messenger, whose countenance shone like the full moon, beamed and in a tone of voice that pierced their souls he declared, "Go, for you are all free!"[530] This was truly as magnanimous as Prophet Joseph's call to his brothers. As opposed to what they expected, they met no censure or even the slightest insult. This chivalry was enough to melt even the hardest of hearts. The heads that had been wrapped in a deathly silence shortly before now lifted and they were looking at each other in utter stupefaction. They had attained favors they could not have dreamt of and had been received with humanity beyond their comprehension.

From this day on, the proclamation of faith resounded from the Sacred House. Suhayl ibn 'Amr[531] at the forefront, the masses flocked in hosts, lining up to dive into the sea of mercy that they had only just begun to recognize despite its having cascaded around them for twenty-one years, and they let themselves go within Islam's boundless mercy in order to be purified in it.

All of a sudden, Mecca had become transformed into a place of festivity and rejoicing. The masses that had been all but finished were beginning to be reborn. When those who had discovered the wealth of belief that they had been late in acquiring put all their prejudices aside, they began to see what they had not been able to see before, and began to realize that there were also sounds their ears had been stranger to. Those who had been slaves to an empty obstinacy, a blind envy and a futile hatred until this day, were swept up in remorse for having living in complete ignorance of the most magnanimous people the world had ever seen, and made pledge after pledge in the presence of God's Messenger to have their past wrongs forgiven. They interrupted their joy with praise and thanks to God and experienced the jubilation of being acquainted with God's Messenger before departing from this world as some of their friends had. Even if it was late, they had found him and what did anything else matter? Although they had been reborn and purified with the choice they made,[532] those who could not forgive themselves would pursue their quest for expiation with great exertion and endeavor. For instance, Suhayl stated as follows:

"*By God, however hard I have exerted myself alongside the polytheists, I will exert myself at least to the same degree in the cause of Islam. Whatever wealth I spent while with the polytheists, I will put forth at least an equal measure in charity. Perhaps in this way, I can hope to atone for all the wrong I have done.*"[533]

Living for others

In Mecca, which had until only yesterday been hell-bent on killing, a life oriented to living for others had begun. Those who saved themselves went in pursuit of another to save them too, and strove to allow those who could not see this Sun of Mercy to open their eyes to him. This reflected the Messenger's attitude. There were many who had indeed come to him, but those who broke away risked eternal loss. This was one of the key matters for him while he was living in Mecca. His eyes sought them out, he inquired after them to their relatives, and he sent people to see them. To those for whom he had waited thirteen years, about whom he concerned himself for another eight years in Medina, and to whom he finally came in all humility as a result of their inability to understand his call, he did not take the approach, "I have done what I needed to do. What else can I do? They shouldn't have gone!" He viewed no one as "casualties of their upbringing." Indeed, he had all the Meccans in his sights. He wanted to reach those who ran away as a result of the influence of their past experiences, he wanted to sit and speak with them and, at the very least, to free them of their emotionality so as to allow them to exercise their preference on the basis of their own free will.

Abu Lahab's sons 'Utba and Mu'attib

After the Conquest, God's Messenger called his uncle and asked, "O 'Abbas, where are your nephews 'Utba and Mu'attib? I do not see them." His manner in inquiring after them was imbued with mercy and compassion, although 'Utba and Mu'attib were the two sons of Abu Lahab, who was lost for all eternity and whose destruction was confirmed in the Qur'an. In addition, one of them had fallen for the empty promises of the Quraysh years earlier and had divorced one of the daughters of God's Messenger, thus abandoning her. "O Messenger of God," 'Abbas replied, "they have disappeared from sight, together with some other Meccan polytheists." The Messenger of God said in the same tone, "Go and bring them to me."

At the behest of God's Messenger, 'Abbas inquired, until he eventually found Abu Lahab's two sons in the valley of 'Urana. He sat and spoke with them at length. He described the air of festivity in Mecca and called them to the warm climate of the Prophet, the Sun of Mercy, saying, "The Messenger of God invites you." Before long, 'Utba and Mu'attib returned with him to Mecca.

Filled with delight at the arrival of Abu Lahab's sons, the Messenger of God stood up, took their hands, gave each of them his arm, and led them to the Ka'ba. He stood with them for a long time at Multazam, the area between the door of the Ka'ba and the Black Stone. 'Abbas too had come and was following God's Messenger. At one point, he said, "O Messenger of God, may God make you forever joyful! I see joy in your face."

"Yes," God's Messenger replied in complete contentedness. "I asked God for these cousins of mine, and He gave them to me."

In spite of their father Abu Lahab, 'Utba and Mu'attib, whom the Prophetic mercy had embraced, began to proclaim wholeheartedly, "There is no deity but God, and Muhammad is His Messenger!" The two brothers were to make such progress from the moment they took their place amidst the halos around this sun, that they would be two of the approximately eighty people present and standing their ground at the fiercest stage of Hunayn, which was experienced just days later.[534]

Harith ibn Hisham

Abu Jahl's brother Harith ibn Hisham was also among those who fled on the day of Conquest. Abu Talib's daughter, Umm Hani', had rushed after and caught up to him, granting him protection and so rescuing him from the hands of her brother 'Ali. She then came to the presence of God's Messenger, wanting to secure the protection that she had granted to Harith, who had breathed hatred for the past twenty-one years. When God's Messenger saw that she was exerting herself with the same sensitivity as his, he said, "We give protection to those to whom you give protection and we give security to those to whom you give security."[535] Even an iceberg melted away in the presence of the Sun of Mercy. This vanishing was only in relation to hatred and animosity to be sure; on the contrary, the autumn of his life had turned into spring, and Harith ibn Hisham, who was near death, was being reborn too.

He was Abu Jahl's full brother and undoubtedly the staunchest of his brothers in unbelief. He was such an important and eminent figure for Abu Jahl that he even had poems composed in his praise. His tribe held him high esteem and their respect for him never failed. He had fought against Islam at such places as Badr, Uhud, and Khandaq, and was present wherever his brother Abu Jahl held the post of flag bearer. He served as Abu Jahl's partner, so to speak, in the torture and persecution of his brothers Salama and 'Ayyash, and was the one who accompanied Abu Jahl all the way to Quba' (near Medina) to take their brother 'Ayyash back to Mecca, where they continued to persecute him. When the time came for Mecca's conquest, he too wanted to offer resistance, but seeing that all efforts were in vain, went into hiding instead.

Now, Harith was experiencing a true conquest in relation to his inner world. Whatever reservations and habits remained from Abu Jahl, he left them all behind, drew a thick curtain over his past, and set foot in a brand new world. He was henceforth to live a most careful and pure life.[536]

Harith was one of those who thrust himself onto the battlefront at Hunayn straight after the Conquest. Whilst fighting against the Hawazin, he was at the same time wielding his sword against the dark world of twenty-one years in which his brother Abu Jahl served as standard-bearer. He was ultimately to join the forces at Yarmuk along with his other brother 'Ayyash ibn Abi Rabi'a and his nephew 'Ikrima ibn Abi Jahl, where he was martyred. He was one of the four fallen soldiers who were not to have even single drop of water after the battle, in the famous story of self-sacrifice and preferring others over oneself.[537]

Wahshi

Another of those who fled on the day of Mecca's conquest was the black slave Wahshi, who had killed the Messenger's uncle and milk-brother Hamza in return for the guarantee of his emancipation. When he learned of God's Messenger's conquest of Mecca, he feared for his life and took flight. In actual fact, he did not know precisely what darkness this flight entailed, and because he wanted to escape, turned down the chance that had come knocking on his door. Fortunately for him, however, there was a compassion that held by the hand one who falls, and God's Messenger sent some of his Companions to him too. He sent them with a letter containing, by way of invitation, the following Qur'anic verse (which means):

Except he who gives up his way in repentance and believes (without associating partners with God), and does good, righteous deeds—such are those whose (past) evil deeds God will efface and record virtuous deeds in their place (and whose faculties which enabled the evil deeds He will change into enablers of virtuous deeds). God is All-Forgiving, All-Compassionate. (al-Furqan 25:70)

While Wahshi felt a pang pierce through his heart upon receiving the Messenger's letter of invitation, he wanted complete assurance of this invitation, and replied saying, "O Messenger of God, I have committed an offense well-nigh equivalent to unbelief. Will God turn my evil deeds into virtuous deeds?" Grieved and at the same time hoping for a good response from Wahshi, God's Messenger sent a second letter to his uncle's killer. This time he sent the following verse (which means):

Indeed God does not forgive that partners be associated with Him; less than that He forgives to whomever He wills (whomever He has guided to repentance and righteousness as a result of his choosing repentance and righteousness by his free will). Whoever associates partners with God has indeed strayed far away (from the Straight Path). (an-Nisa 4:116)

Moved by this second call and his heart softened even further, Wahshi sought an even more specific guarantee, with his reply this time being to the effect of "O Messenger of God, God has made the forgiveness mentioned in the verse contingent upon His Will. What will I do if He does not will so for me?" Upon this, God's Messenger sent a third letter that would give Wahshi even more hope, stating the following verse:

O My servants who have been wasteful (of their God-given opportunities and faculties) against (the good of) their own souls! Do not despair of God's Mercy. Surely God forgives all sins. He is indeed the All-Forgiving, the All-Compassionate. (az-Zumar 39:53)

It was as though God's Messenger was saying:

O one who has led his life in waste and vain, who brought Badr, Uhud, and Khandaq to ruin for the sake of his own interests, and who fought against the Muslims even at Mecca's conquest, you must not despair of God's infinite mercy. No matter their gravity or greatness, the sins of the wrongdoers are even more trifling than the floating foam on the ocean, when compared with God's boundless mercy.[538]

Soon after the three successive letters of invitation, Wahshi came to Mecca once more and attained peace and tranquility in the presence of God's Messenger. Henceforward, there was to be a new Wahshi, one who fought to bring those who rebelled against God's cause to their knees. Indeed, he was to drive his lance right through the chest of the false prophet Musaylima the Liar. By defeating a man who was the 'father of lies' with the very same spear he had used in his days of unbelief to martyr one of the best of men, Hamza, his expiation was complete.[539]

Safwan ibn Umayya

Although in a panic he exclaimed, "Never shall we allow Muhammad to enter Mecca,"[540] when Safwan ibn Umayya encountered his old friend Khalid ibn al-Walid at Khandama as he entered the city during the Conquest, he soon realized that they could not resist and fled. He decided to flee to Abyssinia, and so he traveled to Jeddah, where he waited for a ship on which he could set sail to Yemen.

Meanwhile, 'Umayr ibn Wahb had come to God's Messenger and said, "O Messenger of God, Safwan ibn Umayya is the lord of his people, but he is fleeing from you for a land beyond the sea. Will you give him a promise of safety?"[541] The man who uttered these words was a man whom Safwan ibn Umayya had hired and sent to Medina to assassinate God's Messenger. Convening after the Battle of Badr, they resolved that the only thing that would put them at ease was to have God's Messenger killed. Safwan ibn Umayya then offered to discharge all his debt and take care of his family, and send the son of his paternal uncle 'Umayr to Medina for the task. So much confidence did Safwan have in him that he consoled the grief-stricken Meccans, who had stopped eating and drinking in their sorrow, telling them that very soon news would arrive from the direction of Medina to give them solace.[542] However, before long, he was devastated at the news that his uncle's son who had gone to Medina to kill had instead defected. He had been disappointed yet again.

Everyone had a wish, but it was always God's will that prevailed. All that Mecca's erstwhile leaders could hope to do now was to escape, and 'Umayr was now doing his utmost to find Safwan and reach out to him to offer him something better. This endeavor suited the wishes of God's Messenger and with great happiness he stated, "The son of your uncle shall be safe."

'Umayr was full of joy, and he immediately set off to Jeddah—three days' travel—with news of the amnesty from God's Messenger. What is more, he was going there for Safwan ibn Umayya who had severed all connection with him from the day that he had embraced Islam. Accompanying him on the journey was his son Wahb, who had been taken prisoner at Badr and later released.

When they reached Jeddah, Safwan was about to board the vessel, when he was intercepted by 'Umayr ibn Wahb. Seeing his cousin 'Umayr from a distance made Safwan uneasy. "Alas!" he exclaimed. "Do you see who has come?" He pressed his slave to hurry so that they could get out of sight as soon as possible. His slave was more discerning. "It is 'Umayr ibn Wahb who comes," he said, as if to indicate there was no need for any concern. "What is 'Umayr ibn Wahb to me?" he said.

"By God, his sole concern was to kill me, and now he comes to do just that! He has already supported Muhammad against me before," said Safwan.

A person was enemy to what they did not know, and Safwan was still influenced by his prejudices, and spoke as the victim of his groundless fears. Meanwhile, 'Umayr approached. Unaffectedly, he called out, "O Abu Wahb!" 'Umayr was extremely careful not to further startle an already frightened Safwan. "May I be your ransom," he exclaimed. "I come to you just now from the best of people, the most righteous, the most forbearing and the most excellent in honoring the ties of kinship. May my father and mother be your ransom! Fear God and whatever you do, do not destroy yourself. Look, I have brought you an assurance of protection from God's Messenger."

"Woe be to you," Safwan retorted. "Be off with you, and be gone from my sight!"

On one side was an affectionate heart rushing from place to place for weeks on end with the ideal of letting others live, while on the other, was a hardened heart rejecting the opportunity that came his way. But 'Umayr was not one to give up easily, and he said with the same delicacy, "O Safwan, may my mother and father be your ransom! I come to you from the best of people, the most righteous, the most forbearing and the son of your paternal uncle. His strength is your strength, his honor your honor, and his dominion your dominion."

Safwan took a deep breath at such a sincere invitation, and finally said what he had been unable to say until now: "I fear that I will be killed."

Ignorance was precisely so. There was no light in the world of a bat that saw the dark of night as its shelter, even though, with the sunrise, the darkness had retreated to its own cloister, leaving a crystal clear and luminous world. Nevertheless, seizing the opportunity, 'Umayr assured him that there was no reason to fear, saying, "He is too forbearing and generous for that!"[543] But Safwan could not overcome his doubts and the exchange between them dragged on. Finally, he said, "I will not return until you bring me a sign that I can recognize."[544]

If nothing else, 'Umayr's efforts allowed him to leave the door open. True friendship was revealed at times like these. Anyone could be there during the good times, but true friendship was shown at times when people were left alone to face their demons. The human being, whom God created as a noble creature, was worth all the effort in the world. Despite the distance of three days' travel,[545] he would fulfill his cousin's request. Saying, "Don't go anywhere until I bring you what you ask for," 'Umayr left Jeddah for Mecca.

With bated breath he came into the presence of God's Messenger. "O Messenger of God," he said, "I reached Safwan and informed him of your protection, but he hesitated without seeing a sign from you, and refused to come."

This was 'Umayr's way of requesting a token from God's Messenger so that he could go back with it. Seeing 'Umayr, who had put aside his own personal spiritual advancement for the sake of saving another person at the edge of the abyss, God's Messenger removed the turban he had been wearing when he conquered Mecca,[546] and gave it to him. The faithful friend was as happy as if it had been bestowed upon him, and taking the Messenger's turban, made for Jeddah once more, to see Safwan.

'Umayr ibn Wahb traveled for approximately another eighty kilometers to Jeddah with the turban of God's Messenger. He went immediately to Safwan ibn Umayya and handed the turban to him. Safwan again enumerated his fears, one by one. He had, however, softened with all the earnestness and effort that he saw from his friend, as well as the turban that he had brought. He could no longer remain indifferent to 'Umayr's invitation, after he had put everything on the line for him. He changed his course and they all went back to Mecca together.

When they reached the Ka'ba the Messenger of God was leading the Afternoon Prayer, and they stood waiting. What an extraordinary sight this was—more persuasive than the most eloquent rhetorician's sincere and perfect composition. To the chaotic Mecca he had deserted had come a complete regularity and order. Safwan stood and watched, and as soon as the Messenger of God completed his Prayer, Safwan shouted, "O Messenger of God, 'Umayr ibn Wahb came to me with your turban and asserted that you invited me here. If this is a matter with which you are satisfied, grant me two months."

He was still afraid. This was probably the reason he did not get down from his mount. He would escape at the first sign of trouble and save himself. Reading his concerns, God's Messenger said, "Dismount, Abu Wahb." The Sun of Mercy was calling an ice-cold, unfeeling heart to his warm and accepting atmosphere that was capable of melting even icebergs. But Safwan said, "No," to this call also. "By God, not until you make this matter clear to me." Thereupon, God's Messenger said, "Rather, you will have four months."[547]

Safwan, who had trembled with fear until that moment at the

thought that all of this might be a ploy to capture him, was now calm. He gave a deep sigh of relief. Instead of embarking upon a venture in Abyssinia in which he did not know what he would face, he received safe conduct and the permission to stay in Mecca for four months, and would spend this time without fear, to make up his own mind and come to a final decision. There was no need for him to fear, for he was now safe. As a first sign of this trust he dismounted and approached God's Messenger.[548] Now Safwan, too, had entered the warm and soothing climate of God's Messenger and had begun letting himself go to its gravitational attraction.

From this day forth, Safwan traveled as he pleased through Mecca. During this time, his wife Fakhita also embraced Islam and wanted her husband too to become acquainted with its beauty as soon as possible. She took an eager interest in her husband and tried her utmost to persuade him. She even insisted and put pressure on him, but this troubled Safwan, as he was not a man to be pressured. He became irritated by his wife's excessive urging and, referring to God's Messenger, said, "What is it to you? Are you more benevolent than him? I said, 'Grant me two months,' and he gave me four months' time instead!"[549]

Hind

Hind, one of the leading players of Uhud, withdrew into her shell in the face of the developments in Mecca and locked herself in her house, as, despite everything that had happened in the past, her sons and daughters, and now her husband Abu Sufyan, had changed sides. On top of that, even the people with whom she came together and planned and took up arms and went to the front line had changed, and she was left all alone. With the Conquest, as well as the hatred and animosity she already harbored, Hind was boiling with anger and had become all but explosive in the wake of events over which she had completely lost control. Each new report she heard was enough to send her mad, for the journey to the Sun continued at full speed. Even Ramla, the daughter of her uncle Shayba who was killed at Badr, and Fatima, the daughter of her brother Walid who was also killed at Badr, had also become Muslim, and this she could not stomach. She protested in verse:

> "Whilst God has poured forth such misfortune upon us, one after the other, in Mecca and from around Hajun,

How is it that you share the same religion with those who killed your
father,
And still sit with them?
Or has the news of your father's death not yet reached you?"[550]

She had realized that these struggles were in vain, as she was face to face with an unstoppable wave. When she realized that she could not bear any more, she locked herself up in her house. At the same time, this meant Hind's withdrawing into herself—the Hind who possessed a "poetic spirit" and was famous for this in gatherings and assemblies. She was now in the throes of despondency and despair.

All the while, God's Messenger was following Hind closely, wanting to reach out to and deliver her from her current predicament, in which she was spiraling towards the Fire. But it was not possible to reach a woman who had withdrawn into her house and was nurturing her grief. The only alternative was to reach someone who could reach her and this is exactly what the Messenger of God did.

Only a few days had passed since Conquest. Calling Abu Sufyan, whom he saw during circumambulation, the Messenger of God said, "You said to Hind, 'Do you think that this is from God?' 'Yes,' she replied, 'This is from God.'" While continuing to circumambulate the House, he related the particulars of their conversation the night before.

This was indeed what had happened. When the proclamations of God's greatness had continued until morning, Abu Sufyan had leaned over and whispered into Hind's ear, "Do you think that this is from God?" He was of course referring to the Conquest, but Hind, whose mouth was sealed, could only say, "Yes." She just could not bring herself to accept this. She had also presumably said unpleasant things, things that embarrassed Abu Sufyan.

Abu Sufyan was shell-shocked. God's Messenger related to him one by one things that none but his wife Hind had heard. Given that he had not spoken of this to anyone else, Hind must have gone and recounted all this to another person and this in turn must have reached God's Messenger. "No, none other but Hind could have divulged this. I'll show her!" he was just thinking to himself when God's Messenger again started with the words, "O Abu Sufyan!" He had either guessed what would be running through Abu Sufyan's mind, or read it from his manner. To be more precise, God's Messenger was calling out to Abu Sufyan who had not grasped his meaning, was still preoccupied with the idea of a "secret" that he assumed his wife had disclosed, and whom he was making plans to interrogate. God's Messenger then said, "Your wife Hind is blameless in the matter, for she has not made your secret known. Rather, it was God Who informed me of it."[551]

On another day, the Messenger of God saw Abu Sufyan looking pensive and sad. He and his wife had probably argued once again. He needed to be with them on such a day when their relationship was on a knife-edge, and God's Messenger called out to him once again, "You said to Hind, 'Do you think this is from God?' She replied, 'Yes, this is truly from God.'"

This was exactly what had happened. This was the main topic on the agenda in Mecca at the time and this was what Abu Sufyan constantly discussed with his wife. But only Hind and Abu Sufyan knew this. Dazed, Abu Sufyan exclaimed, "I bear witness that you are God's servant and Messenger!" He then said, "By Him Who is invoked in oaths, no one but I alone heard Hind saying this."[552]

Collecting himself with this special attention of the Messenger of God and casting off his distressed state, Abu Sufyan was impatient to relate this incident to his wife. The truth of the matter was, a new invitation was going to Hind via her husband, Abu Sufyan.

In the meantime, Hind had been having dreams and she related them to her husband.[553] The pessimism and waking nightmare she was experiencing in her inner world appears to have been projected onto her spiritual world. On a night when she again fell asleep after discussing with her husband everything that they had experienced, she saw herself in pitch darkness and was unable to see anything; however, before long, everywhere became suddenly illuminated, as though the sun had risen. But at the center of this radiance was Muhammad the Trustworthy who was inviting her to belief.[554]

The following night was no different. The Messenger of God, whom she met while walking, called her to the same source of light saying, "Come to the soundest of paths." Strangely enough, Hubal and Isaf, two of the idols she worshipped all her life, warned her of the wrong path she was following. The next night had been a complete nightmare for her. She was right on the edge of Hellfire and the Angels of the Fire were about to cast her in. Meanwhile, pointing at Hind, Hubal kept screaming, "Throw her into the Fire!"

At the most critical point, when she was drenched in sweat and exclaimed, "I am done for!" someone appeared behind her, and holding her by her dress, compassionately rescued her from the clutches of the Angels of the Fire. Just as she clung onto life anew, she wondered who had saved her from the Fire. She turned around only to see Muhammad the Trustworthy standing before her. The Rose who transformed every place to a garden of Paradise had delivered her from the Fire.

"What is all this supposed to mean?" she asked herself upon waking up. She then went to the idol in her house and began to strike it with the cloth in her hand, saying, "How we were deceived by you!"[555]

Hind was intelligent enough to know well the meaning of the messages in her dreams when combined with those with which her husband came. The Sun of Mercy was inviting to his boundless world even the woman who had mutilated the body of his uncle Hamza, who had chewed on his liver, and who spat it out onto the foothills of Uhud when she could not swallow it.

That which captivated her, however, was a different scene that she had been watching with awe for days. The Ka'ba in the clutches of the idols had gone and in its place there seemed to be an entirely different building. A throng of people now circled it. What is more, this throng increased with every passing minute and was as harmonious as it was exuberant in its movement. This universal language produced by those who spoke with their actions had softened even Hind's hardened heart of hearts.

Even though her feelings still wanted to take her back to the past, there was no going back for Hind. She too had opened the door to the new and was on the verge of leaving aside blind obstinacy. She finally approached her husband Abu Sufyan and indicating the Messenger of God, said, "Take me to your friend, I too wish to pledge my allegiance to him."

Abu Sufyan was overjoyed to be sure, but he could not help but ask, "What is it that brings you to such a point about that which you denied until just yesterday? What has changed?" Hind, who until that day had stopped at nothing in her evil, gave an extraordinary reply: "By God, I have never before seen such servanthood to God as I have seen in the worship performed in this mosque over the past few days. They spend the entire night in prayer."[556]

The language of action struck Hind more than words. As she stated, the Ka'ba had never before been witness to such servitude, such worship. This presence which entertained no other expectation than Divine approval, made a mark on Hind's heart, like an elixir that dissolves even the toughest of rust. The thick walls built up over twenty-one years had thus been removed and a journey to the Sun had begun for her also.

For Abu Sufyan, this was the most important matter that he needed to share at once; however, he hesitated upon remembering Uhud. This was because even he was disturbed by the scene he saw that day, as commander of the army that displayed that brutality. One of the leading actors in it was no doubt his own wife Hind. And what about what she had done to Hamza? Uhud had caused God's Messenger to weep bitterly. And what about those for whom death warrants were issued?[557] This was a frightening prospect; what if he reminded them of Uhud or Hamza?

Abu Sufyan's happiness was short-lived and was replaced by a strange sense of sorrow. He could not overcome his concern and lead her to God's Messenger. He turned to her and said in so many words that she needed to resolve her issue on her own. This was his way of saying, "Don't get me involved!"[558]

She was on her own. One of the rare women at the time who was present in the public arena, Hind was again to stand on her own two feet. Taking nine other Meccan women with her, including 'Ikrima's wife, Umm Hakim, Safwan ibn Umayya's wife, Fakhita bint al-Walid, and Abu Jahl's daughter, Juwayriya, she went to 'Uthman and said, "We too wish to pledge allegiance to God's Messenger. Will you help us?"[559]

A kind and gentle man, 'Uthman did not turn away those who came to his door, and he accompanied them to God's Messenger, who was at Mount Safa, accepting pledges of allegiance. Hind feared being a target of harassment on her way and veiled her face to avoid being recognized.

When the men finished pledging their allegiance, God's Messenger accepted the women's pledges. The women too lined up to attain spiritual purity. At this stage, 'Umar was seated by God's Messenger, conveying to him the words of the women pledging their allegiance.

It was now time for Hind and her associates to make their pledge. The Messenger of God enumerated the various conditions and they confirmed their acceptance of these. At one point, Hind said to the Messenger of God, "By God, you ask of us something that you have not asked of the men!"

These were the last words that ought to be said to the Messenger of God, of all people. But Hind was still so new as to be unaware of such sensitivities. It is interesting that this was not the only comment that Hind made on that day. When God's Messenger stated, "And you must not commit adultery," Hind said, "O Messenger of God, does a free woman commit adultery?" This was a display of her temperament. The Messenger of God continued, "And you shall not kill your children." The most interesting response came again from Hind: "We raised them from infancy, and you killed them on the day of Badr when they grew up, so you are the one to know about them!"[560] She was referring to her two brothers and her stepson, Hanzala, who were killed at Uhud. Contrary to popular belief, her reply caused the Messenger of God and 'Umar to look at one another and smile.

"And you shall not steal," was the next Prophetic stipulation, to which Hind remarked, "By God, I used to take a little of Abu Sufyan's money and I do not know whether that is lawful for us or not." Abu Sufyan, who was watching them, heard this and shouted so that God's Messenger too could hear, "You are absolved for whatever you took in the past!" This exchange caused all those present to smile.

The Messenger of God continued with the announcement of the next stipulation: "You shall not invent slanderous tales." Hind was rather pleased with this condition, for she had been the subject of precisely such slander years ago by her first husband, and her marriage had broken down as a result. As one who knew best what such slanderous accusations meant, she said, "By God, slander is a disgraceful act, but it is sometimes better to overlook it."

The Messenger of God issued the final condition: "You shall be obedient." Held in high esteem until that day, Hind again called out, "Only in the matters of enjoining the good!" The Messenger of God then said to 'Umar, "Accept their pledge. May God forgive them, for God is forgiving and merciful."[561]

Their pledge was complete and Hind had become Muslim along with her companions. None of what she expected to happen, however, did happen. No mention was made of Uhud, nor of what she had done to Hamza. No old scores were settled, as her husband had feared. Far from it, there was not even any reaction to Hind's interruptions and retorts. This could mean two things: either God's Messenger had treated her as any ordinary woman due to his not have recognized her, or there was truly a profound clemency in his presence. Hind said, "O Messenger of God, praise be to God Who has made manifest the religion which He has chosen for Himself. I entreat you by our shared lineage, that I too can be favored with it. O Muhammad, now I too am indeed a woman who believes in God and attests to His Messenger."

She was still hesitant, and the waves in her inner world swelled. Had God's Messenger known that the person standing before him was Hind? She could have no relief until she freed herself from this doubt. Mustering all her courage when they were yet stupefied from being imbued with the spiritual hues of his presence, Hind removed the veil over her face and, as though appealing for his intercession before God, said, "It is I, Hind, O Messenger of God, Hind bint 'Utba."

Was it possible that God's Messenger, the most excellent judge of character, had not recognized her? But even though everything was as clear as day to him, he could not have revealed it to anyone. Notwithstanding the deep pangs of anguish he felt in his heart, he never made this clear, and the same was true today. This was also a characteristic attribute of the Divine. In such situations, God forgave all evil and wrongdoing besides the association of partners with Him, and accepted them into His presence as pure as the day that they were born. His most beloved servant on earth would do the same. The Prophet of Mercy turned to Hind and with a most courteous tone of voice, said, "Greetings to you."[562]

What greatness was this! His demeanor was unchanged. That is to say, he had known from the very beginning. What warmth was this, despite all the coldness of the past! All her fears and concerns disappeared. How could they not, as the Messenger of God did not hold anything that she had done against her, did not remind her of yesterday, and did not mention the name, "Hamza"? She ought not have remained insensible to this unequalled boundlessness. And she could no longer contain the storms that broke within her one after the other. She had at this moment realized the difference between the thick walls of unbelief, which blinded the human being, and belief. She lifted her head that she had bowed in apprehension until just a moment ago and exclaimed as follows:

"O Messenger of God, by God, what was most desirable to me until today was the humiliation of you and the people of your tent, but today I woke up, and there is no one on earth for whom I wish more glory and prosperity than you and your household."

Hind had been freed of all the blame and burden of the years, and had become as light as a butterfly. What a great gift was freedom from servitude to servants and attaining the presence of God, the One and Only Being worthy of worship. The load she felt on her shoulders on the way to Safa was completely lifted and she went home with a light heart.

Soon after, a person was seen to arrive at the Messenger's tent at Abtah, and enter with a suitable modesty. Whilst passing the tray in her hand to God's Messenger, she said, "O Messenger of God, indeed, my mistress Hind sends you this gift, and asks your pardon."[563] From that day forth, notwithstanding God's forgiveness, she continued to seek atonement for the past that she just could not erase from her consciousness; what is more, her sons and daughters were with her in her struggle.[564]

'Ikrima

One of the women who accompanied Hind to Safa to pledge allegiance to God's Messenger, was the wife of Abu Jahl's son 'Ikrima, Umm Hakim.[565] Until that day, she breathed the air of hatred and hostility that pervaded the house of Abu Jahl—the locus of unbelief—and was party to a violent opposition to the Muslims. However, on the day when flowing mercy found its course, she joined her sister-in-law, Juwayriya[566] to go to God's Messenger and profess her acceptance of Islam. But she had one problem: there was a death warrant for her husband, 'Ikrima, who had killed and persecuted many people.[567] When 'Ikrima[568] realized that he could not withstand the force of the current, he gave up, abandoned the thought of resistance,[569] and escaped to Yemen to save himself.[570]

Umm Hakim, however, who had experienced the ineffable atmosphere in the presence of God's Messenger, and who had saved herself after all these years, was now gripped by a new panic: was there no way of saving her husband too? The atmosphere she experienced in the presence of God's Messenger had encouraged her. Within the short space of time that she remained at Mount Safa, she realized that everything she had heard until that time was a great lie, and was filled with a sudden fear for her husband, who had fled as the victim of this same lie. In any event, those who saved themselves on that day dedicated themselves to saving another and, setting an example of great loyalty and faithfulness, she did the same. She seized this opportunity to help her husband with whom she had shared her life, and said, "O Messenger of God, 'Ikrima, the son of my paternal uncle, fled from you to Yemen, for he feared that you will kill him. Will you grant him protection?"

It was clear from her manner that she wanted God's Messenger to take him too aboard his ship, so that they could make the journey to eternal life together. Had she said instead, "He shouldn't have killed so many people," "He shouldn't have fled," "What can I do for him as a woman on my own?", nobody would have condemned her. For a woman at the time to leave her home amounted to putting herself in great danger. Making a long journey was inconceivable. Even men could not travel on their own for fear of falling prey to bandits. However, this woman had risked everything and was now seeking amnesty for her fugitive husband from God's Messenger.

What had she learned about Islam? Which Qur'anic verse or Prophetic Tradition had she become acquainted with? How many minutes in duration was her dialog with God's Messenger? She possessed no knowledge about Islam. She had not even seen a page of the Qur'an, let alone read it. What she had witnessed was only that before them stood the Sun of Mercy who embraced everyone, including Abu Jahl's daughter-in-law and Harith ibn Hisham's daughter, and Abu Jahl's son. He did not condemn anyone to everlasting perdition, but instead condemned perdition itself to perdition.

Umm Hakim perceived the warmth of this atmosphere, and realized that there was room enough in this heart for her husband too, who had set sail towards eternal ruin. She thus sought immunity from God's Messenger for 'Ikrima also. The Messenger of God who was already seeking any excuse to forgive, turned to Umm Hakim and, in response to her sincere appeal, said, "He is protected."

It was just as she hoped, and she was, in an instant, filled with joy. Now, she was eager to acquaint her husband with this Mercy, and she set off without a moment's delay. Accompanying her was a slave from Rum, whom she took with her to protect her on the extremely arduous journey to Yemen, to bring back her fugitive husband. However, she saw the greatest treachery from this slave, for he harassed her and made advances towards her. She knew that she would not be able to protect herself, and realized that she had to be clever to avoid any harm. So she played for time until she found some people along the way from whom she could appeal for help. When they met a clan of 'Akka, she sought their help against him. They caught the slave and tied him up with rope. The accounts also say that 'Ikrima killed this slave on the way back from Yemen, after his wife told him everything that had happened.[571]

Yet, while she endured many trials along the way and although her feet became swollen from walking and she grew weary, she remained determined and made it all the way to the coast of Tihama, in search of her husband. It did not take long for her to realize that the person she saw from afar was her husband 'Ikrima. She called out to him and began waving to catch his attention.

One bolt of lightning followed another in 'Ikrima's dark world: what was this woman doing here? Moreover, how and with whom had she come here? And for what reason had she come? Could she have escaped too? Tempests raged in his inner world where he wavered between fear and panic. So many questions gnawed at his mind that he could not find answers to any of them and could not make any sense of his wife's arrival from afar. He first stared at her blankly from a distance, as if to say, "What are you doing here?" Affectionately, she exclaimed, "O cousin!" She then continued, "I come to you from the most magnanimous of people, the most righteous of people, and the best of people. Do not destroy yourself!"

His wife was saying strange things he was not at all accustomed to. Whilst he looked at her puzzled, she turned to him most compassionately and said, "I have asked God's Messenger to grant you protection. This he has granted, and he has forgiven you."

'Ikrima was lost for words. Given that she said, "Messenger of God," she too must have become Muslim. Anyway, no woman in her right mind would come here, or indeed could come here otherwise. What greatness, what nobleness was this! In spite of all the wickedness that his father had marshaled from the very outset, and the unspeakable evil that he himself perpetrated, had God's Messenger now said that he forgave those who did all this and was prepared to embrace them also?

Who else could have shown such magnanimity?

So he must have forgiven him! His self-interrogation on the boat came to his mind at one point. The boat he had embarked upon to cross the sea was caught in a storm and almost sank. Between Mecca and Yemen, the mountain-like waves were about to engulf the boat. He had fled for his life, and was instead facing death. When he took refuge in Lat and 'Uzza, the captain had said angrily, "Turn to God sincerely, for your gods will do you no good here!" He asked the boat's master, "Then what should I say?" and the captain replied, "Say 'There is no deity but God.'"

"I did not flee except from this," 'Ikrima bridled.

Yet, on that day, when the boat he had embarked upon was on the verge of sinking, Muhammad the Trustworthy,[572] from whose mercy he sought succor, had found the son of Abu Jahl and the new leader of the Banu Makhzum in Yemen and was inviting him into his atmosphere of mercy.

Since the day he fled, everything seemed to be calling him to the same point and every call caused storms to rage within him; a transformation had thus begun in his inner world. The self-sacrifice of his wife was the powerful touch that most tugged at his heartstrings. He felt himself weaken. The 'Ikrima who had fled for his life, from "conquest," was experiencing a conquest within his innermost self.

He looked at his wife, who had made a sacrifice that no other could possibly endure. "This is true happiness," his gaze said as he kept his eyes fixed on Umm Hakim. He could not understand why his wife would come all the way here and asked her, "Have you really done this?"

"Yes," she said, resolutely. "Indeed I spoke to him and asked him to grant you protection."

During times of success and prosperity everyone is close by and does their utmost to help, but the truly chivalrous souls reveal themselves only at such critical times as these. They do not hesitate to take the necessary steps, and even face a great many dangers to help. How could he remain indifferent to such a sincere heart?

Umm Hakim related to him everything that happened in Mecca. She spoke of the movement of the people to the Ka'ba like moths to the light, the breezes of profound forbearance and mercy becoming manifest in Mecca, the return of even those who, like himself, had fled wanting to disappear without a trace, and of the great honor they received upon their return. She implored her husband to return to Mecca with her. After all, there was the assurance given by Muhammad the Trustworthy who did not remind anyone of their past mistakes or put them to shame, and who pardoned even those who had made attempts on his life, holding them in high esteem: no harm would come to him.

'Ikrima's journey to the Sun was about to begin. He turned his face towards the Ka'ba to return in great hope to the Mecca from which he had only just fled in great fear.[573]

Meanwhile, the Messenger of God who was sitting with his Companions at the Ka'ba looked towards the horizon and said, "Ikrima ibn Abi Jahl comes to you as a believer and a Migrant." There was also a word of caution to his Companions: "But do not insult his father. Indeed, insulting the dead causes grief to the living and does not reach the dead."[574]

So the Messenger of God was expecting Abu Jahl's son. What is more, with these words, God's Messenger was doing the groundwork for 'Ikrima's arrival and reminding his Companions of a Qur'anic method. For God prohibits the reviling of those things cherished by others and warns that this type of behavior is an invitation to others to do the same to what the believers themselves hold dear.[575] The Prophetic enjoinder: "Do not revile your mother and father," was also a warning in this regard.[576] Even if the addressee was Abu Jahl, a believer ought not to push them towards the Fire.

'Ikrima and his wife finally reached Mecca. They came straight to the Ka'ba. God's Messenger was seated in conversation with his Companions. As soon as he saw them approach, he jumped up, as yet another person had come with whom he was preoccupied even in his dreams.[577] Opening his arms wide, he walked towards 'Ikrima. The Companions were astounded. It was as though they were witnessing the surprise reunion of two old friends who had not seen each other in years. The Messenger of God had not even noticed his cloak had fallen off. "Welcome, O migrant rider," he said. Yet another iceberg was melting before this wholehearted greeting of the Sun of Mercy, and began rising to join the clouds after dissolving in the sea of mercy.

The general scene confirmed his wife's words, but 'Ikrima nevertheless indicated his wife, who was veiled and stood waiting to one side, and said, "O Muhammad, this woman has informed me that you granted me protection." The one who had just embraced him so warmheartedly said in a most affectionate tone of voice, "She spoke the truth, you are protected." And this was final. 'Ikrima reached out to this friend, dearer to him than his own soul.

In the shame he felt before the Messenger, who pardoned him despite the fact that he was deserving of punishment many times over, he said, "This state is indeed the state of submission, for had you killed me, you would have killed an evildoer and one embroiled in wrongdoing. By pardoning, you hold by the hand one of your kin and restore him back to life." It was as though he declared, "I accept your invitation," and he asked, "So what do you ask of me, O Muhammad! What is it that you call me to?"

God's Messenger replied, "I call you to bear witness that there is no deity but God and that I am His Messenger, that you will rise for Prayer, that you will give the prescribed alms," and he continued until he had enumerated all the injunctions of Islam. He invited 'Ikrima, whom he had taken into his warm and welcoming atmosphere, to fulfill the key obligations of Islam. In response, 'Ikrima made the declaration that served as recognition of the value and magnitude of God's Messenger in his eyes: "By God, you do not invite except to the truth, to goodness, and to that which is best. You were, by God, among us before you invited to what you invite, and you were the most truthful of us in speech and the best of us towards people. I bear witness that there is no deity but God and that Muhammad is His servant and His Messenger."[578]

Yet another lifeless heart had become acquainted with Islam, and there was no one on earth who could be happier than God's Messenger. Sharing his joy with 'Ikrima, God's Messenger said, "Ask of me anything as the people have asked of me and I will grant it to you." But 'Ikrima cared not for worldly wealth. He bowed his head in shame, and said the following:

"*I shall not ask you for worldly possessions, as I am one of the richest among the Quraysh, but I ask that you beseech God's forgiveness for me, for every hostility I directed against you, every step I took on the path of evil, and every word of insult I expressed to you directly or in your absence.*"

'Ikrima had allowed the language of his heart to speak. God's Messenger raised his hands and supplicated for him:

"O Lord, forgive him all the hostility that he directed against me, every step he took in pursuit of extinguishing Your Light, forgive him whatever he has said in my presence or in my absence."

'Ikrima was being favored with mercy the magnitude of mountains when he was only beginning to open the door. Feeling to his core the joy of being honored with such a profound supplication at the door of the All-Merciful from His most beloved servant, 'Ikrima exclaimed, "I am satisfied, O Messenger of God!"

'Ikrima, who was ascending at great speed towards his own summit, did not stop there. Like the others, he was ashamed of his past. Notwithstanding the fact that he was forgiven, he could not forgive himself. He turned to the Messenger of God and said the following:

"O Messenger of God, I swear by God, before you, that from this day forth I will spare no expense in spending in the way of God, and will spend twice that which I used to spend to turn others away from the path of God. Whatever efforts I made in fighting against those on God's path, I shall double in the way of God. I will dedicate myself to the path of God, and strive to atone for my actions for as long as I shall live."[579]

God, Who brings forth the living from the dead, raised a hero the likes of 'Ikrima from among the descendants of Abu Jahl, the possessor of a hardened heart that was worse than lifeless and who earned notoriety as "the Pharaoh of the community." The person who had constantly caused problems for the past twenty-one years had gone, and in his place was a person who was so devoted that he willingly risked his all in God's cause.

God's Messenger, with endless mercy, would monitor 'Ikrima's safety and security, warn those who caused him any offense on account of his father, and in so doing, protect 'Ikrima from new trials and tribulations. This was because some individuals who were as yet unfamiliar with the essence and indeed gravity of the matter, would speak ill of his father, and hurt him by saying to him directly, "What do you expect, he is the son of Abu Jahl, the enemy of God!" Indeed, what they said was correct: his father had been an unmitigated enemy of God, but even though he knew the truth of these words, he could not conceal his hurt at hearing them, and took offense at their dredging up his past and being so scathing about his family. After all, he was the son of his father. This was a matter that was beyond his control, and when all this became too much for 'Ikrima to bear, he came to Umm Salama, the wife of God's Messenger, in great embarrassment, and said, "The way things stand, I will not be able to stay here for much longer and will have to return to Mecca."[580]

Sharing his concern, Umm Salama informed God's Messenger of the situation and he was deeply grieved at what he heard. After leading the Prayer, he addressed the congregation and warned those who offended 'Ikrima against displaying such behavior ever again:

"*Human beings are like raw materials. Those who were best during the Age of Ignorance are best in Islam, when they attain understanding. So let not a Muslim be injured on account of any unbeliever. Do not injure the living on account of the dead.*"[581]

Not content with just this, God's Messenger also forbade calling him "ibn Abi Jahl," or "son of Abu Jahl."[582] These words of caution left a mark and from that day on, the Companions never uttered similar words in reference to 'Ikrima, or indeed to any other, and wholeheartedly embraced everyone who came to the Prophet's Mosque as a believer, irrespective of the wrongs of their past.[583]

In spite of all this, however, 'Ikrima still felt embarrassment upon remembering his past and diverted his gaze in shame. The day of Badr, on which his father died, in particular, he never forgot. He would more often than not begin his words with, "Praise be to God who saved me from death at Badr," and would express his gratitude for being Muslim and for God's having allowed him to see these days.[584] The new 'Ikrima was someone whose worship left an indelible impression, and whose capacity for self-criticism people admired.[585] He would place against his face the Qur'an that he had opposed for years on end and spoken ill of, saying in between his tears, "The Word of my Lord!"[586] In short, 'Ikrima henceforth lived as a man of his word,[587] and this was how he died. One of the two men who went out for single combat[588] (*mubaraza*) against the Byzantine Roman forces, 'Ikrima received mortal wounds in the battle following great deeds of heroism, and subsequently died as a martyr. Prior to his death, he asked his fellow men, "Who will take an oath to fight to the death?" His childhood friend and commander of the forces, Khalid ibn al-Walid, understood his meaning and pressed, "Do not do this, 'Ikrima, for your death will be a severe blow to the Muslims." But he had made up his mind long before and saw Yarmuk as his one chance of reunion with the Rose of his Heart. Making his preparations with great resolve, 'Ikrima said to Khalid, "Make way, O Khalid! You enjoyed the privilege, in the past, of being with the Messenger of God, while my father and I were but his bitterest enemies. Leave me now to make up for all that I have done."

He then disappeared from sight. When the battlefield was inspected after sunset, 'Ikrima was found fatally wounded. There were seventy arrow, lance, and sword wounds in his body. Seeing him in such a state, Khalid sighed and said to himself, "So you go before me, do you?" and praised God for taking 'Ikrima to Him in the purest possible state.

By his side on this journey was his only son, 'Amr.[589] When his faithful wife, Umm Hakim, received the news of his injury, she rushed to his side. When he saw her shedding tears, he said, "Do not weep, for I will not die until I behold victory."

He thus demonstrated that he was a man of such quality that even in his dying hour, he was preoccupied with the honor of Islam. His uncle and father-in-law, Harith ibn Hisham, had also been brought to the same place. He too was critically wounded. In their manner was such an air of gaiety that one would think they were making preparations for a celebration. Harith ibn Hisham's eyes were beaming with joy. He turned to his son-in-law and saw he was breathing his last and said, "Rejoice, for God has bestowed upon us yet another victory!"

'Ikrima received the good news that he had been waiting for. He tried to stand up, and sought help from those around him. As though standing in the presence of God's Messenger, he kept his eyes fixed on a certain point and said, "O Messenger of God, have I kept my promise? Has your "Migrant rider" (*Rakib al-muhajir*) fulfilled his pledge to you?"

He was thus alluding to the Noble Prophet's greeting him as such on his return from Yemen and the promise he made to God's Messenger that day. As he proceeded to the Divine presence, in his demeanor was visible a manner resembling that of Prophet Joseph, who said, "*My Lord, take my soul to You as a Muslim, and join me with the righteous*" (Yusuf 12:101).

As he was slipping to the other side of the thin veil separating the world from the Hereafter, he asked for a sip of water. His father-in-law, who was about to drink from the water skin held to his mouth, motioned for the water to be given to his son-in-law instead. 'Ikrima was just about to take a sip when the cries of another could be heard, calling out for water. Out of the corner of his eye, he saw that the voice belonged to 'Ayyash ibn Abi Rabi'a. His lips were parched with thirst, so he had great difficulty speaking, but when they leaned over, they could make out that 'Ikrima too refused to take the water and was saying, "Take the water to him." But it was too late, for 'Ayyash had breathed his last and took flight without a single drop of water. When they went to the others who had previously wanted water, to 'Ikrima and his father-in-law Harith, their situation was the same. The heroes of Yarmuk had left an abiding lesson in self-sacrifice even at their dying moments, and had departed.[590]

These were the fruits of the twenty-one-year effort of the Sun of Mercy. He had transformed coal into diamond, and extracted individuals who were as pure gold from the slurry.

Loan request

Mecca had indeed been conquered, but there were still those who did not embrace Islam or who were not yet firm in their convictions. The Messenger of God wished to meet with them and take them aboard his ship also. To this end, he sought different channels of establishing rapport with and making contact with them.

As will be remembered, the Khuda'a tribe who acted on the basis of feelings of revenge throughout the Conquest, shed blood in retaliation for their twenty-three fellow tribesmen who had been slain, and killed two Meccans.[591] God's Messenger was angry with the Khuda'a for causing new tension as he strove to conquer the hearts of the Meccans. Without making the twenty-three people the Meccans had killed a matter of negotiation, he sought to defuse the situation by taking upon himself the payment of blood money for all those who were slain. If he had said here, "You killed twenty-three people, and they have killed two of your people. As it stands, you are required to pay the blood money for twenty-one people," he would have been more than justified. However, God's Messenger did not want to push his audience away and constantly gave of himself, so he did not do this. He raised the issue of reparations only for the Meccans whom the Khuda'a had killed.

More than that, he saw paying the reparations himself as a means to sit and talk with the Meccans. This allowed him to meet some of those

Meccans who remained aloof from him, who preferred to watch from a distance, or within whom, despite their having stepped into the luminous world of Islam, belief had not completely settled. He thus appealed to Safwan ibn Umayya, whom he had given four months to make a decision, Abu Jahl's brother 'Abdu'llah ibn Abi Rabi'a, and Huwaytib ibn 'Abd al-'Uzza, for a loan.[592]

They gave God's Messenger a total of one hundred and thirty thousand dirhams in loans. Fifty thousand dirhams was from Safwan ibn Umayya,[593] and forty thousand each from 'Abdu'llah ibn Abi Rabi'a[594] and Huwaytib ibn 'Abd al-'Uzza.[595]

This was in spite of the fact that in the company of God's Messenger at the time were such affluent individuals as Abu Bakr, 'Uthman, and Talha, who would have given not just their wealth, but their lives should he have asked for them. It can thus be seen that the objective was not just to borrow money: God's Messenger was to come together with these people who had not yet been able to overcome their unease, and follow them closely so as to facilitate their joining him or, for some of them, ensure that the belief with which they had only just become acquainted, became firmly established in their hearts.

The Messenger of God made a similar request during the unexpected Hunayn development that took place nineteen days after the Conquest. As the Messenger of God went to stave off the Hawazin attacks, he sent word to Safwan ibn Umayya: "O Abu Umayya, lend us these weapons of yours so that we may fight our enemy tomorrow."[596]

Concerned by these successive demands and not yet knowing the Messenger of God as the prophet that he was, Safwan ibn Umayya asked, "Are you demanding them by force?" He was justified in asking such a question, as this was common practice at the time. On top of that, the Messenger of God had made a new request, without having paid off the earlier loan. So Safwan's apprehension was only to be expected. However, his addressee now was a Messenger without equal, and the latter replied, "No. On the contrary, as a loan for a length of time."

Had God's Messenger given no guarantee of return, there would have been nothing that Safwan ibn Umayya could have done. He could have even viewed this as justifiable, as these weapons were to be used in defense of the city. Safwan was an inhabitant of the city and there was nothing more natural than for him to give the weapons demanded during mobilization. What is more, the individual demanding them was the conquering commander of this city. The situation, however, was quite extraordinary again. This Commander requested these weapons as a loan to be repaid. This was a stance that defied all of Safwan's prior knowledge and, in wonder at God's Messenger's words, he managed to get out the words, "In that case there is no objection."[597]

There was one shock after another in his inner world. The past flashed before him and he had now begun to think how right people were in calling him Muhammad the Trustworthy. Indeed, if he was the one giving his word, then he would most certainly fulfill it. So Safwan went and brought back with him four hundred coats of mail[598] and weapons such as swords and shields, which he entrusted to God's Messenger without any doubt about their return.[599]

Hundreds of Meccans who were treated with this degree of warmth and affinity, such as Safwan ibn Umayya, Hakim ibn Hizam, Harith ibn Hisham, 'Abdu'llah ibn Abi Rabi'a, 'Abbas ibn Mirdas, Aqra' ibn Habis, 'Uyayna ibn Hisn, Huwaytib ibn 'Abd al-'Uzza, joined the Messenger's forces while they were yet polytheists, and went to Hunayn to fight with him on the same side.[600]

This was the first time they stood with the Messenger, against whom they had repeatedly fought and raised armies for twenty-one years. Even though they were as yet unable to accept his invitation, they had entered his gravitational field, and were correcting their former knowledge with every gesture and act of chivalry they saw and heard.

However, at only the beginning of Hunayn, the forces faced catastrophe and their line broke in the face of an ambush, and the panicked soldiers began fleeing in all directions. Most of them were the Meccans who had joined the forces saying, "Let's just wait and see. If he is victorious at Hunayn also, we will make our decision then and become Muslim." They had also hoped to gain war spoils. They were now running for their lives after being ambushed while advancing at the front of the army. The Muslim army was thus in total disarray and confusion. At this point, some of them even cried out, "Surely sorcery is vain today."[601] These were no doubt the words of those who, while they were in close proximity to God's Messenger, did not yet know him, for those who made the smallest effort to get close to him, to better acquaint themselves with who he was, were not as impulsive. For instance, Safwan ibn Umayya from whom

God's Messenger borrowed money, as a result of which Safwan had the opportunity to sit down and converse with the Messenger, did not share their view. Moreover, to his half-brother Kalada ibn al-Hanbal, who shouted, "Muhammad and his Companions will not recover from it," he called out in anger, "Shut up! May God close your mouth! I would rather be ruled by a lord of the Quraysh than a lord of the Hawazin!"[602]

Safwan ibn Umayya, who had sent a paid assassin to Medina after Badr to kill God's Messenger and who had been ready to give away fortunes for this purpose, now could not accept the defeat of God's Messenger and was furious. This report could not be true! He summoned one of his slaves and instructed, "Go and find out what the battle cry is on the battlefield," with a demeanor that seemed to say, "Go and bring me news of the triumph of Muhammad the Trustworthy." When the slave relayed upon his return that he had heard, "O Bani 'Abdu'r Rahman, O Bani 'Ubaydu'llah, O Bani 'Abdu'llah," Safwan was reassured. For these were the words of Muhammad the Trustworthy. He heaved a deep sigh of relief, and said, "Muhammad is victorious, as these were the battle cries of the Muslims during battle."[603]

Hearts to be reconciled

After Hunayn, the Messenger of God, the Prophet of Mercy, also dealt with the Ta'if situation, and then returned to Ji'rana. A completely new chapter of history was being written for all the world to see. Muhammad the Trustworthy found any excuse, so to speak, to forgive people and on the smallest pretext took steps that would please those he addressed. Preferring forgiveness when he possessed the power to punish was not a feature of any ordinary man. They had never before seen this, and had never heard of such chivalry from their forebears. Even at Ta'if, when it was said, "The fortresses have fallen," he abandoned the siege and let the people be. Furthermore, he did not oblige those who asked him to curse the people of Ta'if for causing them so much strife without provocation, and instead entreated God for them saying, "O God, guide the Thaqif and bring them to Islam."[604] He did not pursue the Hawazin, who suffered a crushing defeat, and even returned to them the spoils that fell to his share. This was not all, however. The overarching justice and mercy of his Prophetic nature persisted.

After the Battle of Hunayn at Ji'rana, the Hawazin left behind more than forty thousand sheep and twenty-four thousand camels. In addition to this they left four thousand *'uqiyya* of silver and other property and goods of unknown quantities.[605]

Needless to say, those who had fulfilled their obligations on the battlefield expected remuneration for their efforts. Some of them were very forceful in their demands, saying, "O Messenger of God, divide our spoil of camel and herds among us." So insistent were they that they literally forced him back against a tree so his mantle was torn off, and he was forced to dismount there. Upon this, he called out to them, "O people!" He was clearly angered. "Give me back my mantle. For, by Him in Whose hands is my life, had I camels as numerous as the acacia trees of Tihama, I would have divided them among you, and you would not have found me to be a miser, a coward, or a liar."[606]

Then he took a hair from the hump of his camel and held it between his fingers, high up for the people to see, saying, "O people,[607] by God, no part of your spoils shall come to me that exceeds by as much as this hair my rightful share of a fifth,[608] and that fifth I return to you; and so return whatever you have from the spoils, down to the needle or thread, and do not claim anything as your own. For this will be a grave disgrace and ignominy to a person on the Day of Judgment."[609]

Through these words, God's Messenger signaled exactly how he would use the fifth of the spoils that God had put at his disposal. Hearing these words, the Companions recalled similar warnings he gave on the way to Ta'if. For that matter, most of those who had been with him since Medina had heard similar words of caution during the distribution of the Khaybar spoils[610] and from that day on preferred writhing with hunger to appropriating public property, however small.

Shortly after the Messenger's warning, one of the Companions approached with a ball of twine. His face was drained of color, and he was too ashamed to look God's Messenger in the face. "O Messenger of God," he said, "I had taken this ball to sew a pack saddle for my camel that has a sore back."

These episodes show how the Messenger did not neglect any segment of society. While the doors had been opened wide for those whose arrival was still awaited, those at the center were shown the way to their own summit of perfection, and were advancing on the path from which there was no return. Seeing the sensitivity of his Companion, God's Messenger answered, "As for my rightful share of it, it is yours!" But this Companion was determined to avoid such dire consequences, and he handed the ball of twine to the official in charge of the spoils.[611]

When the time came for the distribution of the spoils, everyone waited eagerly to see who would get what share. Before beginning the division, one-fifth was set aside to be allocated by the Messenger. Contrary to what people were accustomed to, the Messenger of God unexpectedly prioritized the Meccans, who had hitherto led the people in hostility and enmity, and treated them in a way that they could not even imagine. He would now soften with his benevolence, the hearts of those whose progress he was ensuring inch by inch, and he would introduce the warmth of the light of mercy into their darkened worlds.

Those who were present at the distribution of the spoils observed the Messenger giving certain people a greater share, that is, to those people who had been, for the most part, eager to kill God's Messenger if they could find the opportunity. They were only going along with the prevailing circumstances and planning to change tactics whenever it suited to obtain what they had been unable to gain thus far. Yet now, they were beginning to experience a completely new process. God bestowed a fortune upon the Messenger by means of the Hawazin, and he was giving this fortune to the Meccans so that they too could come to know the Bestower of this fortune Himself. This was a horizon to which they had been oblivious until this time.

Virtually everyone saw that he gave without the smallest fear of poverty, for God's Messenger gave a fortune to each of these people who would henceforth be known as *mu'allafa al-qulub*, those whose hearts to be reconciled. For example, he gave one hundred camels to Abu Sufyan, who had become Muslim immediately before Conquest. This was a great fortune, and the Messenger of God gave without asking for any return. What is more, this was not all he gave. Among the spoils Abu Sufyan received on the day were also forty *'uqiyya* of silver.[612] In addition, God's Messenger made similar gestures to Abu Sufyan's sons, Yazid and Mu'awiya. Abu Sufyan's family all at once came into possession of an enormous fortune of three hundred camels and one hundred and twenty *'uqiyya* of gold.[613] God's Messenger, who had until this day taken them by the hand for the sake of their Hereafter, was now taking them by the hand for their life in the world, conferring upon Abu Sufyan a favor that would not cause him to pine for his lost rank of leadership. Abu Sufyan was embarrassed by this grand gesture. "May my mother and father be your ransom," he said. "How generous you truly are! Surely, I fought you until now, but you were generous and the best of the people in war no less than you are generous and the best of the people in peace. May God reward you abundantly!"[614]

The Messenger of God kept a keen eye on developments, closely observing individuals. He had his eye, in particular, on those who had not yet made up their minds about their acceptance of Islam and who stood at a crucial point. Among them was Safwan ibn Umayya, who could not help looking at the sheep and camels out to pasture in Ji'rana's passes. God's Messenger approached Safwan and said, "Do you like what you see in this pass?" This was a sincere voice, one that came from the heart. The very same voice he heard when the Messenger said, "I have given you four months." One could not tell the possessor of such a voice, which warmed one's heart, anything but the truth. "Yes," he said, nodding. God's Messenger, who had brought Safwan to this point, painstakingly, inch by inch, said, "It is yours with everything in it."[615]

Safwan was utterly dumbfounded. A human being could not be this generous. The Prophetic mercy had become a waterfall, and was gushing into the hearts of the Meccans. For in the place he was referring to when he said, "It is yours," were one hundred red dromedaries. On top of that, these were not in repayment for the loans he had given, but a fortune that was granted without any expectation or obligation.

The time had now come for Safwan, and he proclaimed, "I bear witness that there is no God but Allah and that you are His Messenger!"[616] Then, as if to emphasize the final step that convinced him, he said, "For only a Messenger can give with such generosity."[617]

Safwan ibn Umayya, who had been given four months to think in return for the two months he requested, had given way. Close attention, constant contact, repeated acts of benevolence, and finally gestures with worldly wealth and possessions, completely softened Safwan's feelings, and he joined ranks with the Messenger, whom he had viewed for years on end as his "enemy." In describing his inward state at the time, Safwan was later to say, "The Messenger of God gave to me from the spoils of Hunayn while he was the most hateful person on earth to me; he kept giving without expecting anything in return until he became the dearest person on earth to me."[618]

To Suhayl ibn 'Amr[619] and Huwaytib ibn 'Abd al-'Uzza, from whom God's Messenger had also borrowed money, God's Messenger gave one hundred camels each.[620]

The family of Abu Jahl was not forgotten in the chivalrous display. Abu Jahl's brother Harith ibn Hisham was given one hundred camels,[621] while 'Ikrima, who had sought forgiveness from God's Messenger in lieu of worldly wealth and possessions when he embraced Islam, received fifty camels.[622] Abu Jahl's other brother, Khalid ibn Hisham, was also among those who received benevolent treatment from God's Messenger on the day. Hisham ibn al-Walid, brother of Abu Jahl's first cousin Khalid ibn al-Walid, was also among them.

Hakim ibn Hizam,[623] Harith ibn al-Harith, 'Ala' ibn Jariya,[624] Asid ibn Jariya, 'Abbas ibn Mirdas,[625] Qays ibn 'Adi, Nudayr ibn al-Harith,[626] Asid ibn Haritha,[627] 'Uyayna ibn Hisn, and Aqra' ibn Habis were each given one hundred camels. Many others were given between fifty to hundred camels each.

It is interesting to note that God's Messenger gave the chief architect of Hunayn and the reason for all this trouble, Malik ibn 'Awf, one hundred camels. God's Messenger restored Malik's family and possessions also, and when Malik returned to his homeland, he returned with a hundred camels accompanying him as though nothing had happened. According to the customs of the day, however, he would have been taken captive, as the leader of the losing side in battle, and lived the remainder of his life as a slave to his captor, or to those to whom this master sold him at the slave market.

Even more intriguing is the fact that God's Messenger also extended this gesture to Shayba ibn 'Uthman. The latter had burned with feelings of revenge from Uhud, pursued God's Messenger on the battlefield at Hunayn to avenge the death of his father, come all the way up to God's Messenger on the battlefield, and finally raised his sword against him with murderous intent.[628]

However, after giving these people such an enormous amount of wealth and possessions as "those whose hearts were reconciled," God's Messenger only gave his own Companions between four and forty camels each. For cavalry, this figure was twelve camels or one hundred and twenty sheep. This is to say that to the Meccans, whose hearts he wanted to win over with material possessions, God's Messenger gave perhaps twenty or even fifty times that which he gave to Abu Bakr, 'Umar, 'Uthman, and 'Ali.

While hearts were being conquered with such magnanimity on the one hand, on the other hand, Sa'd ibn Abi Waqqas said, "O Messenger of God, you have given 'Uyayna ibn Hisn and Aqra' ibn Habis a hundred camels each and have left out Ju'ayl ibn Suraqa."

When he heard Sa'd's words, the Messenger of God explained why he gave to those who had just become Muslim or whom he hoped would become Muslim, or to those against whose harm he wanted to be assured:

"By Him in whose hand is my soul, if the world were filled with the likes of 'Uyayna ibn Hisn and Aqra' ibn Habis, Ju'ayl ibn Suraqa would be better than them all. I treated them with such generosity that they may warm to Islam. As for Ju'ayl ibn Suraqa, I have entrusted him and those like him to their Islam and to the lofty rewards that have been prepared for them in the Hereafter."[629]

This put at ease the hearts of all those who were apportioned less. In fact, God's Messenger said, "Would it not please you that while they take away sheep and camels, you will return to your homes with the Messenger of God?" to the great happiness of all those who heard it.[630]

'Abbas ibn Mirdas regarded the share that fell to his lot as insufficient and expressed his dissatisfaction and petulance in a poem, not hesitating to say explicitly that he also wanted a hundred camels, like those given to Aqra' ibn Habis and 'Uyayna ibn Hisn whom he saw as his equals. In this way, he claimed that his horse's share in the spoils was parceled out between Aqra' ibn Habis and 'Uyayna ibn Hisn, and that his legitimate right had been usurped. However, that given to Aqra' ibn Habis and 'Uyayna ibn Hisn was not the outcome of merit, nor was that given to those other than the *mu'allafa al-qulub* an injustice. Everyone needed to be content with what fell to their share and not compare themselves with anyone else, as the Messenger of God did not act except by Divine ordinance. However, those who knew were not the same as those who did not know, and as soon as God's Messenger became aware of 'Abbas' dissatisfaction, he sent for him. Reminding him of his poem, he asked, "Was it you who just said, 'My spoils and those of my horse 'Ubayd are shared by 'Uyayna and Aqra'"?[631]

He had uttered these words. Abu Bakr was witness to this, and 'Abbas did not deny it. The Messenger of God then told Bilal, "O Bilal, take him and cut off his tongue. And give him something to wear." Abbas did not realize this was a metaphor and became very anxious. Bilal exclaimed, "Be silent! Your tongue will not be cut off as you suppose. He ordered me to give to you until you were satisfied." So Bilal supplied 'Abbas ibn Mirdas with as much clothing as he would need and then gave him a hundred camels, like 'Uyayna ibn Hisn and Aqra' ibn Habis.[632]

The call to prayer at Ji'rana

Abu Mahdhura was one of those who came to Hunayn although he was not yet Muslim. Yet these people could not swallow recent developments and were still filled with hate for God's Messenger who had conquered their city. They were going to see how events unfolded and determine where they stood accordingly.

Although it did not start well for them, the battle of Hunayn resulted in victory for the Muslims, and God's Messenger was about to make his return to Medina. But the time for Prayer had come and, as a matter of course, the Prayer was to be observed first. Bilal began reciting the Call to Prayer. When Abu Mahdhura and his friends heard this sound reverberating throughout Ji'rana, they began making fun of it, repeating the words they heard in a loud voice and laughing in mockery. Abu Mahdhura's voice was unmistakably the loudest and at the end of the Call to Prayer, God's Messenger indicated for his Companions to bring the youths to him.

Abu Mahdhura came forward with his friends. They supposed that they would be disciplined by the triumphant commander and would be made to answer for their actions. Contrary to expectation, the Messenger of God looked affectionately at the youths standing before him, and said, "Continue the Call to Prayer that you have been repeating." He then had each of them recite the Call to Prayer one by one. God's Messenger also asked, "Which of you raised your voice the most?" Naturally, all eyes focused on Abu Mahdhura and their words confirmed it. The Messenger of God asked Abu Mahdhura to recite the same Call, after which he remarked, "How beautiful is the voice that I have heard. Now get up and recite the Call to Prayer." God's Messenger dismissed his friends, and

Abu Mahdhura was the only one left. Albeit reluctantly, Abu Mahdhura complied and recited what he knew of the Call to Prayer.[633] God's Messenger placed his hand upon Abu Mahdhura's forehead and taught him the Call to Prayer one line at a time:

"*Allahu Akbar! Allahu Akbar! . . . La ilaha illallah!*"[634]

God's Messenger also instructed Abu Mahdhura to raise his voice when saying, "*Allahu Akbar*" and "*La ilaha illallah*," and to lower his voice slightly when saying, "*Ashhadu anna Muhammadu'r Rasulullah*." Upon completion of his recital, God's Messenger wiped his hand over Abu Mahdhura's face and back, then prayed for him saying, "May God treat you with goodness and bless you." He then gave him a bundle in which there was some silver. All the hatred and enmity within the heart of Abu Mahdhura, who was only moments ago ridiculing the Call to Prayer with his friends, had gone and he had all at once become the Caller to Prayer (*mu'azzin*) of the Messenger of God. He now felt an indescribable affection for God's Messenger. "O Messenger of God," he exclaimed. "Will you command me to recite the Call to Prayer in Mecca?"

God's Messenger replied, "I declare you to be Mecca's Caller to Prayer. Go forth and recite the Call for the Meccans." He then added, "Go and say to 'Attab ibn Asid, 'The Messenger of God has commanded me to recite the Call to Prayer for the Meccans.'"[635]

Settlement of debts

With the Hawazin situation averted, the Messenger of God returned to Mecca once again with his Companions. As soon as he arrived, he sought to repay the outstanding debts to Safwan ibn Umayya, Suhayl ibn 'Amr, 'Abdu'llah ibn Abi Rabi'a, and Huwaytib ibn 'Abd al-'Uzza, to each of whom he had already given a large fortune. This was presumably his way of keeping his finger on the pulse of these people who had only just become Muslim. The Messenger of God did not content himself with merely settling his debt, but also thanked them, wished blessing and prosperity for them, and included them in his prayers.[636] For instance, for the brother of Abu Jahl, 'Abdu'llah ibn Abi Rabi'a, from whom he had borrowed forty thousand dirhams after Mecca's conquest, he prayed: "May God bless your family and your property. Surely the reward for a loan is full repayment and acknowledgment."[637]

Imparting a new message with every statement, every act, and every step, God's Messenger, the Master of Mercy, embraced everyone with each of these steps and encompassed them within his warm and welcoming atmosphere. In the eyes of those who had glared at him with bitter hatred until just recently, were now looks of mercy and compassion. What is more, they felt deep shame for all that they had done. Although God's Messenger forgave them when they came to him, in their newfound realization they could not forgive themselves, and exerted themselves to an extreme degree to make up for what they had done. In the warmth of mercy, God's Messenger brought out into the open the precious metals that lay latent in them, and was now building a brand new civilization with them.

CHAPTER 3

THE END OF HATRED AND ENMITY

The End of Hatred and Enmity

So what, then, was the outcome of all this hostility and hatred? If we take the conquest of Mecca as a basis, who were the winners or losers of this twenty-one year struggle? Whose efforts yielded positive results and whose efforts were in vain? Let us take a look:

Family of Abu Jahl

Without a doubt, the most important figure leading the opposition of the Quraysh in hatred and hostility was Abu Jahl. His ambition made him think that the ends justified any and every means. It was he who dragged the people into the Badr undertaking and who was responsible for the downfall and ruin of himself and all those he dragged along with him as the victims of his unbridled ambition. With a strong hold on his brothers, 'Uthman ibn Hisham,[638] al-'As ibn Hisham,[639] 'Umar ibn Hisham,[640] and 'Umara ibn al-Walid, he turned them into inveterate enemies of the Messenger as well. For this reason, his brothers did not deviate from Abu Jahl's path and died before seeing the conquest of Mecca. His other brothers, however, Salama ibn Hisham, [641] 'Ayyash ibn Abi Rabi'a,[642] Harith ibn Hisham,[643] Khalid ibn Hisham,[644] 'Abdu'llah ibn Abi Rabi'a,[645] his son[646] 'Ikrima,[647] and his daughters[648] Jamila[649] and Hunfa[650] chose not the path of their brother and father, but that of his archenemy, God's Messenger. Among those choosing this path was also Asma' bint Mukharriba,[651] mother of Abu Jahl. From the perspective of Badr, the sole loser of this fifteen-year struggle was Abu Jahl. 'Ayyash ibn Ani Rabi'a and Salama ibn Hisham joined the caravan early on, while 'Abdu'llah ibn Abi Rabi'a, Harith ibn Hisham, and Khalid ibn Hisham held out until the Conquest, living a life parallel to that of Abu Jahl as the chiefs of Meccan hostility and opposition. But the road leading to Conquest softened their hearts too, and from that day on they became the most important representatives of the cause that they had hitherto fought against. The following words of Harith ibn Hisham, whom the Meccans held in high esteem, to the masses at Badha' who followed him out of Mecca to prevent him from going to the front line, are enlightening. In tears, he said:

"O people, I am leaving Mecca, not because I do not hold you dear to me, nor because I seek a more auspicious place than this one. The matter

is more serious than that. How many chivalrous souls went out on this path, while they were neither older than nor nobler than us. We, however, have just woken up. By God, had the mountains of Mecca turned into gold and we spent it in the cause of God, we would not have been able to attain even a day's worth of what they have done. By God, they are ahead of us in this world and have moved on, while we shall try to catch up to them in the Hereafter. This is why I am leaving. Do not suppose that we leave our homes today for another, or that we go to another neighbor for every neighbor we leave behind. And in doing this, we expect nothing in return, nor acclaim. The matter is much greater than this. We go to struggle in the way of God!"[652]

The identity of the four famous people who died on the battlefield at Yarmuk without being able to take a single mouthful of water is also of paramount importance in indicating the subsequent progress of the family of Abu Jahl. Three of the four individuals who demonstrated the self-sacrifice of preferring others to themselves by sending to another the water they needed so much were from Abu Jahl's household. Two of them were his brothers 'Ayyash ibn Abi Rabi'a and Harith ibn Hisham, while the third was his son 'Ikrima.[653] The people that had until only just recently derived pleasure from killing had disappeared, and in their place were brand new personalities who dispersed about the earth with the ideal of enabling others to live. God's Messenger transformed even those figures who had made it their life's mission to kill into heroes of letting live, and demonstrated in practice that even the most difficult and intractable people could advance in that way.

Abu Jahl's descendants were also very different. For instance, his grandson 'Ikrima ibn Khalid was an important scholar who was a student of such leading Companions as 'Abdu'llah ibn 'Umar, and 'Abdu'llah ibn 'Abbas. He also gained recognition as *thiqa* (fully qualified) in hadith transmission and such great scholars from the generation of the Successors as 'Amr ibn Dinar transmitted Traditions from him.[654]

Family of Abu Lahab

Despite being his uncle, Abu Lahab was unarguably one of those most vehemently and implacably opposed the Messenger of God. He stood shoulder to shoulder with the merchants of malice, and together with his wife, Umm Jamil, perpetrated every possible evil against his nephew. Although they gave their two sons in marriage to two of the daughters of God's Messenger prior to his Prophethood, they revoked their agreement, wanting to deal another blow to God's Messenger.[655] The Qur'anic chapter entitled Tabbat was revealed because they committed the most evil in spite of being close kin. In it, the torment they will face in the Hereafter in punishment for all of these evils is declared until the end of time.[656]

What was Abu Lahab's fate?

When he learned of the crushing blow they received at Badr, his sister-in-law brought him crashing to the ground with a mighty blow to his head with a tent pole. His son 'Utayba fell prey to a lion, dying between the beast's jaws on one of his journeys to Syria.

What of the other family members?

God's Messenger sent his uncle 'Abbas in pursuit of 'Utba and Mu'attib, who fled after Mecca's conquest, and had him bring them back to Mecca. So elated was God's Messenger upon their return that he took both of them in his arms and walked with them to the Ka'ba. He stood with them at the area between the door of the Ka'ba and the Black Stone, where he proclaimed all prayers were answered, and offered lengthy supplication. When 'Abbas, looking on in awe, saw the smile on the face of God's Messenger, he inquired as to the reason. "I see joy in your face!" he exclaimed. The Prophet of Mercy turned to his uncle and said, "I asked God for these cousins of mine, and He gave them to me."[657]

After 'Utba and Mu'attib, Abu Lahab's daughters Durra,[658] 'Azza,[659] and Khalida[660] also accepted Islam. Durra, who had married Dihya al-Kalbi after embracing Islam and migrating to Medina, once came to the Messenger of God and asked, "O Messenger of God, am I the only child of a polytheist in this city?" This was because some threw in her face the punishment her parents were to receive in the Hereafter and deeply offended her. There were even those who claimed that her emigration would not be valid. She endured all these comments patiently until she could no longer endure this relentless ordeal and went to God's Messenger. After consoling her, he asked her to remain seated and wait for him. He then led the Noon Prayer in the mosque and addressed the congregation as follows:

"O people, what is wrong with people that they injure me through my family? Whoever injures any member of my family has injured me, and whoever injures me will assuredly have incurred the wrath of God. By God, my intercession on the Day of Judgment will be for my family first. Why do you hurt the living on account of the dead? Do I not have a family as you do? Durra is my uncle's daughter. Let not any, henceforth, speak anything but good with respect to her."[661]

The others

The fate of the others was no different. The sons of the infamous enemy of religion, Walid ibn al-Mughira—who died in Mecca in the year of the Migration of a wound he received from a poisoned arrow—Walid,[662] Khalid,[663] and Hisham,[664] his wife Lubaba[665] and daughters Fakhita,[666] Fatima,[667] and 'Atika, as well as his sister Umm Habib,[668] chose not his path, but that of God's Messenger.[669]

'Uqba ibn Abi Mu'ayt had thrown the waste of a slaughtered camel upon God's Messenger, and was described by him as the most wretched of his tribe. He was executed on the return from Badr. His wife Arwa bint Kurayz,[670] sister Busra,[671] sons Walid,[672] Khalid,[673] and 'Ammara,[674] and daughters Umm Kulthum,[675] Zaynab, and Hind, embraced Islam.[676]

What follows is a lengthy list of all those who came to God's Messenger and accepted Islam:

Fatima,[677] wife of 'Utba, who was killed at Badr after having been forcibly taken there by Abu Jahl, and his sons Abu Hudhayfa,[678] Abu Hashim,[679] and Walid,[680] and his daughters Fatima,[681] Umm Khalid,[682] Umm Aban,[683] and Hind;[684]

Ramla[685] and Fatima, the daughters of Shayba, who was also coerced into fighting at Badr where he too was slain;[686]

the sons of Abu al-Bakhtari, Aswad,[687] and Muttalib,[688] and his daughter Umm 'Abdu'llah[689] (Abu al-Bakhtari, whom God's Messenger had granted protection by virtue of all that he had done to protect him, died because of his inability to overcome societal pressures);

Fakhita,[690] wife of Umayya ibn Khalaf, who was another one of those killed at Badr, and his sons Ayhah,[691] 'Abdu'r Rahman,[692] Rabi'a,[693] and Safwan,[694] and his daughters Taw'ama[695] and Fatima;

Wahba[696] and 'Abdu'llah,[697] the sons of 'Umayya's brother, Ubayy ibn Khalaf—who came to Uhud to kill God's Messenger but who was wounded and later died in the surrounds of Mecca—and his daughter Hind;[698]

'Ata,[699] Firas,[700] and Nadir,[701] the sons of Nadr ibn al-Harith—who followed God's Messenger wherever he went to insult him publicly and dissuade all those with whom he made contact from listening to him, and who faced the death penalty after Badr—and his daughter Qutayla[702] and brother Nudayr;[703]

Sufyan,[704] the brother of Aswad ibn 'Abd Yaghuth who died before the Migration, his sons Wahb,[705] Miqdad,[706] and 'Abdu'r Rahman,[707] and his daughter Khalida;[708]

Habbar,[709] the brother of Zam'a ibn Aswad who was slain at Badr, who was forgiven despite the fact that a death warrant was issued for him, his sons, Yazid,[710] Wahb,[711] and 'Abdu'llah,[712] and his daughter Sawda;[713]

Hind[714] and Rayta[715]—the daughters of Munabbih ibn al-Hajjaj, who died at Badr along with his brother and son—and Umm 'Abdu'llah, the daughter of his brother Nubayh;[716]

Aswad, son of Nawfal ibn Khuwaylid, who was killed at Badr;[717]

the sons of Harith ibn Qays (also known as Ibn al-Ghaytala), Tamim,[718] Bishr,[719] Sa'id,[720] Abu Qays,[721] 'Abdu'llah,[722] Sa'ib,[723] and Ma'mar;[724]

Harith,[725] and Hajjaj;[726]

the sons of Sa'id ibn al-'As ibn Umayya, who died from illness in Mecca, Khalid,[727] 'Amr,[728] Aban,[729] Sa'id,[730] and 'Abdu'llah;[731][732]

Fatima, daughter of Aswad ibn 'Abd al-Asad, who was killed at Badr; and[733]

Hisham[734] and 'Amr[735], the sons of al-'As ibn Wa'il, who referred to God's Messenger as *abtar*,[736] meaning "devoid of progeny," as well as his daughter Hajar.

Those who witnessed firsthand the conquest of Mecca, such as Abu Sufyan,[737] Suhayl ibn 'Amr, and Hakim ibn Hizam,[738] embraced Islam as a family, put aside their past, and became the representatives of the cause of God's Messenger. In fact, there was almost no one who saw the Conquest and did not change sides, and who did not become acquainted with the system of thought they had fought against for twenty-one years without embracing Islam. The few who were indecisive within this time stepped into this new world until there was no one remaining in Mecca who had not become Muslim in the lead up to the Farewell Pilgrimage. The meaning of this is obvious: the denial of those who called God's Messenger *abtar*, itself became *abtar* or barren, and it was not adopted or espoused even by their own descendants. That is to say, their opposition was a fool's errand, a waste of all their time and effort. Even glaciers melted before the Prophetic Sun, with not a single sliver of the icebergs of unbelief remaining. In concentrating on this happy ending and examining those who embraced Islam at this time, we can say unequivocally that had the Abu Jahls of the time who engaged in a fruitless undertaking seen the days of conquest, they too would have become willing members of this luminous world.[739] For the likes of Harith ibn Hisham, 'Ikrima, Suhayl ibn 'Amr, and Safwan ibn Umayya were no different to them. They looked from the dark worlds they established with hate and enmity through the windows of their preconceptions, and were therefore unable to see the Prophet of Mercy. Even when they advanced upon him to kill him, they could not see that he was tormenting himself with grief for them. A conquest needed to be accomplished for them to understand this; the conquest of Mecca meant the dawn of a new era in which they would be able to see in all clarity the Messenger of God, whom they constantly suspected and doubted from behind their heavy walls. On that day, he brought to naught all the prejudices in their minds, and just at a point when they thought it was all over, he afforded them most honorable treatment. With one gesture and kindness after another, those heavy walls came crashing down, and the tattered curtains they had drawn in between were annihilated one by one. This annihilation was for them the beginning of a new existence. Now, before them stood the Sun of Mercy that was so radiant that no one could close their eyes to it, a Supreme Compassion so manifest that it could not be concealed with lies and slander, and an embodiment of Mercy that pursued even those who fled or withdrew into their own shell, rushing to embrace them, in spite of everything.

Hence, when this entire series of events is considered as a whole, it as though we can almost hear God's Messenger saying to us:

If you have no hesitations concerning the path on which you tread, then there is no need for you to fear the censure of the censurer. For if the path on which you tread is a "Prophetic" one, this will be your precise destination, as it is not possible for aimless crowds to establish themselves where there are those who are well aware of every step they take and who take these steps in cognizance of the era in which they live. It is self-evident that those who remain outside their respective era cannot make a positive contribution to their age.

A tried and tested methodology

The Sun that rose over the skies of Mecca eight years later melted all the masses of ice in their entirety and, transforming them each into a cascade that would give life to other places, set off once again for Medina. He did not give up in the face of resistance and sought ways of coming together even with those who were furthest away. He made contact with everybody, shutting the door on no one, shed tears for those being led towards the Fire and exerted himself to the utmost to hold them back. The fabric he had begun to weave thread by thread, he completed with one on one follow-up. He did not lose sight of the whole by aiming for large-scale results. Far from it, he won over all the Meccans with active patience, and all his listeners had now become servants of the All-Merciful. Having planted seeds for twenty years, closely nurtured their young shoots, seen to their maintenance and care, tended the soil and given them water, he was now returning to Medina after gathering their fruits and reaping their harvest. He did not sit on Mecca's throne; instead he established himself on the throne of people's hearts.

He was able to accomplish this transformation in a period of only twenty years. So how did the Messenger of God take a city that was so tough, so bloodthirsty, and so driven by preconception and prejudice and free it of all the habits and practices of its past and transform one hundred percent of its inhabitants?

Behind this transformation were such virtues as patience to all the suffering and persecution they were exposed to, fortitude, compassion, forbearance, mercy, and humility, in addition to great precision and indescribable effort. Above all, he had aimed to convey all aboard this ship to the shores of salvation. He did not leave a single person whose hand he had not held, and there was not a sole individual on the path to the Fire that he did not intercept, and try to deflect their course to Paradise. In this way, he demonstrated firsthand to all those to come, that this was a path that could readily be trodden. At the same time, this was a clear indication of which methods and procedures were necessary on which particular paths and trajectories, to reach the shores of salvation. For this:

– He knew his audience very well, and accurately read their expectations, concerns for the future, and their specific circumstances and conditions;

– He valued his audience, listened to them to the end, patiently endured the release of all the aversion they had built up inside, did not respond in anger to their manner which was more often than not invective, and thus did not sever his connections;

– Dialog with the people was one of his primary methods, so much so that it could even be said that his whole life, from beginning to end, was comprised of such dialog;

– At times when doors were shut on him, he formulated new means of opening new and different doors that no one could have even thought of;

– Although he was subjected to evil, he never turned to it himself;

– He always did what behooved him;

– He hurt no one in aggression; when defending himself he sought to minimize harm to everyone;

– He always responded with the utmost sensitivity to a situation;

– He never resorted to brute force to end conflicts;

– He taught those who sought to counter the aggression that he faced so that they too adopted his ways;

– He did not shut the door on anyone;

– On the contrary, he left no person on whose door he had not knocked;

– He advocated and displayed universal human values;

– He did not base his judgment on the rubble of other value systems;

– He targeted negative attributes, not individuals, when correcting them;

– He extended hospitality, giving to others while depriving himself, and gave away everything he had, first of all to those who deemed themselves his greatest enemies;

– He was mild in manner, preferring silence even at times when he might have made himself heard, and did not turn people away by showing a harsh attitude;

– Just as he quarreled with no one, he did not become party to an existing quarrel;

– He was by no means harsh and severe, but always assumed a soft and gentle manner;

– He never took a reactionary stance: every step he took was directed at initiating a new phase;

– He never thought of returning evil for evil. Far from it, always responding with goodness to those who harmed him was his most salient characteristic;

– He did not discriminate. Justice was his supreme mark, even to those who opposed him;

– He did not favor his kin and demonstrated personally and to the end of his life that all are equal in the eyes of the law;

– The way he exemplified through his life the ideals and truths revealed to him was extraordinary. He trained his Companions as individuals adopting the same course, transforming them into perfect representatives, in their action and behavior, of the language of the heart;

– Even when he was attacked and assaulted, he preferred to step back to ease the tension and, in this way, obviated those problems that had the potential to carry over into future situations;

– He was very saddened when he learned of the forces that advanced upon him. By no means did he desire a scenario that would destroy the climate of peace that he had built inch by inch;

– He never saw war as a means to solve any problem. All such painful memories as Badr, Uhud, Khandaq, and Hunayn, were destructive intervals of time that were the work of others. However, he sought to extract good even from these, and ultimately won over the hearts of all those who fought against him;

– He sent envoys to the enemy forces that were close to attack and took every possible step to dissuade them from fighting. Even when they were at his door with their swords, he did not allow fighting without first having done everything possible in the name of diplomacy, and without first exhausting all local remedies;

– He approached even those who came to kill him, with kindness and, granting free pardon to some of them, declared their immunity and took their lives into his own protection;

– Where he was forced to fight, he brought distinct and delicate rules to war, taking such groups of noncombatants as women, children, the elderly, and the clergy into protection. Included in this were even trees and plant life. What is more, he followed these rules meticulously in practice and did not refrain from punishing those who violated them;

– So meticulous was he in this regard that despite the presence of women and children in the armies that attacked him to put an end to his life, no woman or child was ever touched or hurt where he himself was present;

– To rebuild the positive climate that war had destroyed, he set to work immediately. He reached out to everyone anew, completely over-looking all the evil perpetrated against him, opening a brand-new page for those with a dark past;

– He saw, but turned a blind eye, he heard, but pretended not to hear, and did not hold anyone's bad deeds against them;

– Who knows what anguish he suffered, but he saw none of it as a reason for complaint. His inner world bubbled like magma, but he extinguished whatever lava there was around him, within his own bosom;

– Even if his emotional world was crushed, he did not act on the basis of anger and fear, but always preferred sound thought and reason;

– He saw his adversaries as the Companions of the future and treated them accordingly, taking into account that even if they were different then, they would understand the truth when the time came;

– He did not allow cursing and damnation, and did not join others in invoking maledictions;

– He did not regard anyone as inconsequential, or believe that nothing good would come of them;

– Peace was one of his most distinctive attributes. He always aimed at reaching an agreement, and was never the side to violate it;

– He never revealed the faults of others and always concealed them, even when they were quite overt or blatant;

– He strove to affect those individuals and families that withdrew into themselves by means of new ties of kinship, and even at times when all doors were shut on him one by one, he opened new doors that would never shut. He became a relation to those who saw him as a rival;

– He was always extremely hospitable and invited people to his meals and celebrations;

– Another facet of his methodology was exchanging gifts with people, even if they did evil;

– He reached out to those who deemed him their archenemy, even when they were at their weakest point. He prayed for and inquired after them, and sent them aid and assistance to alleviate their difficulty;

– He made gesture after gesture, did kindness after kindness, and when the Meccans experienced trouble with another nation, he intervened and solved their most critical problems;

– He gave the Meccans the right to travel freely to Damascus en route to Medina;

– He sent repeated invitations to them from Medina, and to those who did not understand the language of these invitations, he went in person.

– He did not shame anyone for what they did in the past, and did not reopen old wounds. On the contrary, he treated honorably every single person he addressed, attracting their awe and admiration;

– He neither spoke ill of anyone, nor allowed others to do so;

– He sent messengers after those who fled, knocked on the doors of those who withdrew to their homes, and ultimately transformed the leading foes of yesterday into tomorrow's heroes of love;

– He did not rush and seek to make sweeping gains. He worked away at the monotonous task, thread by thread, until he eventually won over his addressees in their entirety;

– He demonstrated time and again that a person could become a righteous Companion even if of his archenemy Abu Jahl's temperament. All that was necessary was to know how to sit with people and the correct way of approaching them. This showed that there was no human being on earth whose heart could not be won over, and that there was no problem that could not be solved.

In short, who knows what many other steps God's Messenger took, conquering the whole of Mecca as a result of a chain of activities and endeavors left unrecorded in history. Considering the outcome from this perspective reveals that behind the healing of such deep wounds in such a short space of time, the permanent solutions brought to seemingly unresolvable deep-seated problems, and the transformation of individuals thought impossible, there must have been many other initiatives. So, despite his life being the most minutely recorded throughout human history, all of the actions, strategies, and words of God's Messenger have not been transmitted to our day.

On the basis of all that has been relayed to us over the generations it can be said that God's Messenger focused on the human being, addressed the human being, and invested in the human being at the level of the individual, and brought the individual to a level of responsiveness where they could take to heart whatever they had heard. This is, in any case, the method that the Qur'an exhibits in its principle of gradualism. Up until the time it turned its addressees into human beings of such a stature, it constantly reinforced belief, and almost all of the thirteen-year Meccan period was spent on persuading people. The words of 'A'isha indicate which methods were used to solve the problems of the day while taking human nature into consideration:

"The first to be revealed of the Qur'an was a chapter of the Mufassal (the latter portion of the Qur'an) in which Paradise and the Fire is mentioned. When many people joined Islam, and they gradually became more inclined to putting it into practice, the lawful and the unlawful were revealed. Had the first thing to be revealed been, 'Do not drink wine,' people would have said, 'We will never give up wine.' Had it had been revealed, 'Do not fornicate,' they would have said, 'We will never give up fornication.'"[740]

The period of which 'A'isha speaks—of the people's internalizing Islam and becoming more disposed to translating it into action—presents a phase beginning with belief in God, and continuing all the way to believing in life after death and the reckoning to be given for this life. In examining the legislative history of Islam from this standpoint, it becomes clear that other than the prescribed Prayer—which came to the fore in the last years of the Meccan period—no legal judgment gained prominence in the thirteen-year Meccan period. Conversely, it is apparent that the core values were repeatedly reinforced with the Qur'anic revelations during this period.[741] The meaning of this is axiomatic: Problems cannot be solved without first solving the human factor. Where the human factor is solved, a greater part of the problems will solve themselves. If we look at the Age of Happiness from this perspective, we can see that from the lives of the Companions, which were enriched with the core values so that they tended immediately to put into practice everything they learned, all the problems remaining from the Age of Ignorance began to disappear one by one. From the moment the last word was said on an issue, not even the slightest trace of doubt about it remained.

People were sensitized by constantly referring to such issues as belief in all its facets, truth and justice, reckoning and being called to account, the sensitivity of the balance in the Hereafter, and the notion that no good or evil done to any living being will go unrewarded or unpunished, and the tendency to evil began to disappear from society.

One course people did not take during the Age of Happiness was to ignore existing problems or solve them in part by offering daily, temporary solutions, or to make the problems of tomorrow unsolvable by the way they dealt with existing ones. Far from it, by aiming at the whole, they tackled problems from the root. As a case in point, the maxim we see in use during the Age of Ignorance, "Help your brother, whether he is inflicting wrong or is wronged,"[742] was developed and enriched by God's Messenger. Freeing it from the meaning, "Help your own, whether they are right or wrong," the statement is instead invested with the meaning, "Help your brother, whether he is inflicting wrong or is wronged." A matter that deserves separate attention is the Messenger's use of the term "brother" to refer to the one inflicting wrong also. This identifies an objective that would, in turn, eradicate the oppression of the oppressor. The wording at the beginning of the Prophetic Tradition is the most cogent demonstration of this. For the Companions who heard these words from God's Messenger said, "O Messenger of God, we can help him if he is wronged, but how we can help him if he is inflicting wrong?" God's Messenger replied, "You can hold him by the hand [to prevent him from inflicting wrong.]"[743] Again, the meaning is clear: the aim is to ensure that all elements that are potential problems cease to be problems at all. This is the general policy that we see God's Messenger implemented throughout his twenty-three-year Prophethood.

When we look at the Age of Happiness from this vantage point, we see that the people being addressed are raised to a level at which they can take to heart every matter that is discussed and act accordingly, and at which they possess the sensitivity to be able to overcome problems of any nature. Within this context, the sensitivity that the Companions exhibited when the verses at the end of the Qur'anic chapter al-Baqarah were revealed, is telling. Archangel Gabriel conveyed the ordinance: "*To God belongs all that is in the heavens and the earth,*" after which he brought the verse below:

Whether you reveal what is within yourselves (of intentions, plans) or keep it secret, God will call you to account for it. He forgives whom He wills (either from His grace, or His grace responding to the repentance of the sinful), and He punishes whom He wills (as a requirement of His justice). God has full power over everything. (Al-Baqarah 2:284)

As with every new decree that came, this message billowed across the Medinan skies and brought about a new flurry amongst the Companions. What they felt this time, however, was different: those who heard it were drained of color and went weak at the knees. For in this verse, God was making known that He would call to account not only for those actions projected outward, but also for intentions and plans.

Before long, the people flooded the Prophet's Mosque. All who came lost themselves in silent contemplation. These people, who had turned pale and whose knees had given way, then said:

"*O Messenger of God, we were charged with such deeds as the prescribed Prayer, fasting, struggling in the way of God, and charity, which were within our power to perform, but now, such a verse has been revealed to you that it lies beyond our capacity.*"

Needless to say, this was not an objection to the newly revealed verse. On the contrary, it was their way of seeking refuge in Divine compassion anew, for fear that they would not be able to fulfill a Divine commandment, and in the trepidation that they would not be able to maintain the conduct required by the gravity of this verse. The one and only master of that compassion, the Messenger of God, knew the inner worlds of these people whom he himself had raised; however, his audience was not only those who flocked to the Prophet's Mosque in his own time, but every believer who would transform the entire globe into a place of worship in the universal sense. This is why, addressing his Companions at the first instance, he stated as follows:

Do you intend to say what the People of the Book said before you: "We hear and disobey"? Rather, say, "*We have heard and we obey. Our Lord, we seek Your forgiveness, and to You is our final return.*"

They did not think any differently. They were merely concerned that they would not be able to control their hearts and feared that they might not be able to carry out the Divine command. With these words of God's Messenger, the Prophet's Mosque shook with the reverberation of voices rising from all sides and declaring, "We have heard and we obey!"

Carrying his audience to such a degree of sensitivity, God's Messenger turned each of them into a part of the solution. Even if it took time initially, he ultimately raised them to be the masters of winning over people's hearts.

The Farewell and the duty entrusted

These efforts of God's Messenger were clearly not limited to the city of Mecca, and were valid for all the people he addressed in his day, in Medina first and foremost.

When the day of separation was approaching and sunset was close, God's Messenger increased the number of Companions he sent to neighboring tribes and states, and received a new delegation in Medina almost every day. Considering the fact that the population of Mecca and Medina at the time was ten thousand, the massive crowds that gathered at 'Arafat during the Farewell Pilgrimage are the clear fruits of a great endeavor in such a short time.

Now, we see God's Messenger in the process of leave taking. He would sit and talk at length with the delegations sent by neighboring tribes and states, would accompany them to the outskirts of the city, and when the time came for separation, would send after them asking their pardon. When sending Mu'adh—one of those of whom he makes special mention saying, "Learn to recite the Qur'an from four,"[744] and whom he describes as the most knowledgeable of the community in matters of the lawful and unlawful—to Yemen, they set off together and God's Messenger accompanied him right to the city's outskirts.[745] As they traveled, God's Messenger asked him, "You are going to a nation of the People of the Book; according to what will you judge?"

"According to the Book of God," Mu'adh replied.

"And if you cannot find it therein?"

"According to the Practice of the Messenger of God."

"And if you cannot find it therein?"

"Then I will exercise independent reasoning (*ijtihad*) to form my own judgment."[746]

When Mu'adh, as a Companion who had internalized the Qur'an and the Prophetic Practice, said that he would render an independent ruling based on the intellectual repertoire he acquired from these two sources, God's Messenger expressed his approval and the time for departure had come. Taking his leave from God's Messenger, Mu'adh set off on his journey, and when God's Messenger called out him, "O Mu'adh," he turned to him.

"You will not find me in Medina upon your return," God's Messenger said. "You shall find only my Mosque and my grave."

These words shook Mu'adh. As he was leaving, the Messenger of God was speaking to him of yet another separation, and was seeking his pardon.[747] The journey that every human being is destined to travel was now before God's Messenger, and the Most Beloved of God was preparing for Union.

We also see him, during this time, increasing his visits to those Companions he had already entrusted to the earth, and making more frequent visits to the Jannat al-Baqi cemetery in Medina, as well as to Uhud. Just as he exchanged pardons with his Companions who were still living, he conversed and exchanged pardons with those in the grave, bidding farewell to the world and everything in it.

Taking leave after leave, he traveled all the way to Mecca once more, and would fulfill his Major Pilgrimage obligation for the very first time. He went to Hajun before proceeding to 'Arafat. He stood by the grave of his wife Khadija, with whom he shared twenty-five years, and prayed for her, too, at length. For God's Messenger, Hajun was the site where his two sons were also buried. Perhaps in catching sight of their graves, he said inwardly, "There is not long to go now, soon we will be reunited."

The yield of twenty-three years had been gathered at 'Arafat. Ten thousand Companions stood before him, to carry as a trust each of the words that would fall from his lips, and they were paying the utmost attention. "O people," he began his sermon, *"I know not whether after this year, I shall ever be amongst you again."* In his every manner, in the rise and fall of his voice, and in his facial expressions and gestures could be read the signs of separation. From time to time he asked them whether he had fulfilled his duty and held those present at 'Arafat as witnesses, after which he proclaimed, "Be my witness, O Lord, that I have conveyed Your message to Your people." Such statements as, "All those who listen to me shall pass on my words to others and those to others again," expressed another dimension of this parting.

It was a Friday. As the sun was setting, the Angel of Revelation, the

Truthful Gabriel delivered the final trust of the Qur'an. God declared:

This day, those who disbelieve have lost all hope of (preventing the establishment of) your Religion, so do not hold them in awe, but be in awe of Me. This day I have perfected for you your Religion (with all its rules, commandments and universality), completed My favor upon you, and have been pleased to assign for you Islam as religion (Al-Ma'idah 5:3).[748]

This seemed to be the final fruit of the period that began with the dominion of Hira. There were those who stepped aside and wept as soon as they heard these words. This did not escape the Messenger's notice and approaching 'Umar, he asked him, "What is it that makes you cry?" He turned to the Messenger in awe and admiration and said, "I cry because until now we experienced a constant heightening in our religion. While now it has attained perfection. Anything that has attained perfection is destined to fade away from what it is."

'Umar was keenly discerning and before him there was situation that could be concealed no longer, and the Messenger of God said, "You have spoken the truth."

Of course, God's Messenger spoke the truth also. However, there was another truth that had to be told here. This cause conveyed by God's Messenger would not remain confined to Mecca and Medina, and would reach all corners of the world. When once describing this truth, the dreams of which had become etched in his consciousness, he said, "God gathered up the earth for me so that I saw its east and its west; and indeed the dominion of my community will reach those parts of the earth which have been shown to me."[749] The time had now come to entrust the same truth to everyone.

Joy and sorrow had become intertwined, and a heavenliness that defied description had pervaded 'Arafat. God's Messenger had bid farewell and the time had come for departure. He turned once more to his Companions, all of whom he convened with for the first time here, and stated the following:

"My duty is only to convey the message. Indeed, it is God Who grants guidance. O people, there is no Prophet or Messenger to come after me and no new community to be formed. Indeed, this Religion, or this affair[750] *will reach wherever the night and day has reached. God will not leave a single mud brick house, nor any tent from animal hair or hide, but that He will allow this Religion to reach it, with it raising and honoring some, while*

humbling and lowering others. He will raise and honor Islam, while hum-bling and lowering unbelief.[751]

There was added import to God's Messenger's making these declarations at 'Arafat,[752] where he bid farewell to everyone. In this way, he showed the yield of twenty-three years kneaded with great anguish and suffering, and gave the following message for his universal cause to attain its objective:

This affair is not theory, but practice. This shows that this is possible. The way in which this affair was realized is self-evident, and its method manifest. The rest, then, is entrusted to you. Be those who will take this cause and carry it to every corner of the globe, until there is no house or tent left on earth to which you have not conveyed it.

His Companions, who fully grasped his meaning, scattered to all parts of the world from that day forth, even going all the way to China, until there were very few who remained in the Hijaz.[753] Wherever there is a stir and dynamism in his name today, it is without a doubt by virtue of the blessing of the Companions who went thus far in their day.

Passed on from one to another, akin to a relay, the banner has come all the way to our day. Toiling in our time to realize his aim is a duty and obligation incumbent upon every person who sees the Messenger of God as their guide.

This path is the path of the Prophet and his Companions;

It is the trust of the Sun of Mercy who warms even the hardest of hearts!

Its aim is to reach every heart;

Only through such a path is possible the conquest of hearts!

It is he who shows how it is trodden;

It is tried and tested!

But it requires patience, forbearance, self-sacrifice, altruism, and resolve!

It is the path trodden by the Prophets;

Its fruit is the Mercy of the All-Merciful and Paradise;

Its sustenance is talk of the Beloved;

Its consequence is the approbation of the jinn and humankind!

Thousands of greetings to the travelers of this path!

APPENDIX

ENDNOTES

AN OVERVIEW OF CONFRONTATIONS DURING THE TIME OF THE PROPHET

Endnotes

1   The Prophetic statement is: "There is no Prophet or Messenger to come after me and no new community to be formed. Indeed, this Religion will reach wherever the night and day has reached. God will not leave a single mud brick house, nor any tent from animal hair or hide, but that He will allow this Religion to reach it, with it raising and honoring some, while humbling and lowering others. He will raise and honor Islam, while humbling and lowering unbelief." Six Companions narrate it. Four of these Companions state that they heard these words from God's Messenger during the Farewell Pilgrimage. Ibn Hanbal, *Al-Musnad*, 4/103 (16998); 6/4 (23865); Hakim, *Mustadraq*, 4/476 (8324), 477 (8326); Al-Bayhaqi, *Al-Kubra*, 9/181 (18399, 18400); Haythami, *Majmau"z-Zawaid*, 4/15; 6/7 (9807); 6/14; 8/262, 263; At-Tabarani, *Al-Kabir*, 2/58 (1280); *Musnadu'sh-Shamiyyin*, 2/79 (951); Ibn Munda, *Iman*, 2/982 (1085); Ibn Hibban, 15/91 (6699); Al-Hindi, *Kanzu'l-Ummal*, 1/469 (1345).

2   Qusayy ibn Kilab is also known as the progenitor of the Quraysh tribe.

3   As the Khuda'a is said to have covered and hidden the well of Zamzam before leaving Mecca, water became the most difficult commodity to obtain. The tribe charged with the difficult task of providing people with water would construct reservoirs where rainwater would be collected. In the season of Pilgrimage, they would transport the water and offer it to pilgrims who came for the purpose of worship.

4   It is the privilege of providing the visiting pilgrims with food and water.

5   These tribes and their representatives during the pre-Prophethood period can be summarized as follows:

- Abu Jahl was responsible for carrying the war banner known as *uqab*, as well as *qiyada*, or the command of troops in war.

- The Messenger's uncle 'Abbas ibn 'Abd al-Muttalib was the possessor of the *siqaya, or providing water for the pilgrims in the name of the Banu Hashim.*

- Harith ibn 'Amr undertook *rifada*, the administration of the poor tax collected from affluent Meccans and employed to provide food for the poor pilgrims, whether itinerant or resident.

- 'Uthman ibn Talha from the Banu 'Abd al-Dar was the custodian of the standard, or *liwa'*, which was the symbol of Meccan power. He also oversaw the *sidana*, or possession of the keys of the Ka'ba. The office of *hijaba*, relating to the covering of the Ka'ba, and the functioning of the Nadwa Council where the Meccan chiefs took all decisions, was held by the same individual.

- Yazid ibn Zama'a coordinated the consultative mechanism known as the *mashwara* when decisions were to be taken in the name of the Meccans.

- Abu Bakr, the sage of the Banu Taym, known for his command of the genealogy and family history of the Quraysh, was recognized as the authority of appeal in what was called *ashnaq*, denoting affairs relating to blood money, penalties and compensation.

- Fellow tribesman of Abu Jahl, Khalid ibn al-Walid was in charge of *qubba*, collecting individual contributions for equipping the forces that were to set off on a campaign, in conjunction with the office of *a'inna*, or command of the Quraysh's cavalry corps. The ambitious Abu Jahl attached special importance to the offices of these posts and held Khalid ibn al-Walid in high esteem. For the sake of these two institutions that he would make the foundation of his future mission, he protected Khalid ibn al-Walid.

- 'Umar from the Banu 'Adi held the office of *sifara*, or ambassadorship, being the plenipotentiary authorized to act on the State's behalf.

- To Safwan ibn Umayya from the Banu Jumah belonged the presidency of *aysar*, or divination by arrows.

- Harith ibn Qays from the Banu Sahm was responsible for *amwal al-muhajjara*, the offerings to the Sanctuary, protecting these on behalf of the State.

God's Messenger was to abolish these offices after his return to Mecca, leaving only those of *siqaya*, belonging to 'Abbas, and *sidana*, held by 'Uthman ibn Talha. See Abu Dawud, *Diyat*, 17, 24; Ibn Hanbal, *Al-Musnad*, 2/36; 3/410; 5/411; *and* Daraqutni, *As-Sunan*, 3/105.

6   *Munafara*, is essentially a form of contest in which two individuals dispute their claims to honor and nobility before a judge or arbitrator.

7   Mu'awiya, who appointed Umayya's grandson as governor here years later, skillfully used the credit of his grandfather who lived amongst them years earlier as a Qurayshi who served the Ka'ba, and gained great influence in Damascus.

8   It could even be said that this incident forms the basis of the disputes and disagreements of the Andalusian Umayyads to continue to the very end. Ibn Sa'd, *At-Tabaqat*, 1/76; At-Tabari, *Tarikh*, 1/504, 505.

9   In almost all Qur'anic exegetical works scholars propound the view that the individual referred to in the following Qur'anic verses is Walid ibn al-Mughira:

Leave Me (to deal) with him whom I created alone, And I enabled for him abundant wealth, And children around him as means of power; And I have granted him all means and status for a comfortable life. And yet, he desires that I should give more. By no means! Surely he has been in obstinate opposition to Our Revelations. I will oblige him to a strenuous climb. He pondered and he calculated (how he could disprove the Qur'an in people's sight). Be away from God's mercy, how he calculated! Yea, be away from God's mercy! How he calculated! Then he looked around (in the manner of one who will decide on a matter about which he is asked). Then he frowned and scowled. Then he turned his back and (despite inwardly acknowledging the Qur'an's Divine origin), grew in arrogance, And he said: 'This is nothing but sorcery (of a sort transmitted from sorcerers) from old times. This is nothing but the word of a mortal.' I will make him enter a pit of Hell. What enables you to perceive what that pit is? It leaves none (but entirely burns everyone of those thrown into it), nor does it spare anyone (so that they might die and escape). It scorches up the skin. Over it there are nineteen keepers. (Al-Muddathir 74:11–30)

10   Al-Bayhaqi, *Ad-Dalail*, 2/208; Ibn Kathir, *Al-Bidaya*, 3/70.

11   Ibn Hisham, *Sirah*, 1/200-201; Al-Bayhaqi, *Ad-Dalail*, 2/207–208; Ibn Kathir, *Al-Bidaya*, 3/69–70. Relevant narrations have been combined.

12   Derived from the root *saba'a*, which signifies the act of leaving one religion and entering another. The term *sabi'* is one that is used in reference to worshipers of angels or heavenly bodies. While believing in a sole Creator of the universe, they say that the overseeing of the world and human beings was left to the charge of heavenly bodies. The Qur'an makes mention of them in one of its verses in juxtaposition with the believers (Al-Baqarah 2:62). Prophet Abraham was sent to guide them (See Surah al-An'am 6:75). Belief in astrology and the power of stars in our day are remnants of Sabean belief. By using this term in relation to the Messenger of God, the Meccans no doubt sought to break his influence over the people and thus discredit him.

13   Ibn Hanbal, *Al-Musnad*, 27/148 (16603); As-Salihi, *Subulu'l-Huda*, 2/452

14   By means of this phrase, the narrator presumably ascribes this attribute to himself due to his having still not shed the ways of the Age of Ignorance, and it is clear that the implication here is the early days of Islam.

15   Al-Bukhari, *Tarikh*, 8/14; Tabarani, *Al-Kabir*, 20/342 (805)

16   Ibn Hanbal, *Al-Musnad*, 31/342 (19004); Al-Hakim, *Mustadraq*, 1/61 (39); 2/668 (4219); Daraqutni, *As-Sunan*, 3/462 (2976); Al-Bayhaqi, *Al-Kubra*, 1/123 (358);

6/34 (11096); Tabarani, *Al-Kabir,* 5/61 (4582); 8/314 (8175); 20/343 (806); Ibn Abi Shayba, *Al-Musnad,* 2/322 (822); *Musannaf,* 7/332 (36565); Ibn Huzayma, *As-Sahih,* 1/82 (159); Ibn Hibban, *As-Sahih,* 14/517 (6562)

17   A similar situation can be seen in his promptings while beside his uncle who was on his deathbed. At a point when the Meccans too prevailed upon him, God's Messenger said, "O Uncle, say, 'There is no god but Allah,' and I will bear witness before God of your having said it." Al-Bukhari, *Janaiz,* 80 (1360); Muslim, *Iman,* 9 (24); Ibn Hanbal, *Al-Musnad,* 39/78 (23674).

18   An-Nur 24:54; Ar-Ra'd 13:40; Al-Ghashiyah 88:21

19   Al-Ghashiyah 88:22

20   Al-Kahf 18:6; Ash-Shu'ara 26:3

21   As in: *"(Even so, O Messenger) adopt the way of forbearance and tolerance, and enjoin what is good and right, and withdraw from the ignorant ones* (do not care what they say and do)" (7:199); "They spend (out of what God has provided for them,) both in ease and hardship, ever restraining their rage (even when provoked and able to retaliate), and pardoning people (their offenses). God loves (such) people who are devoted to doing good, aware that God is seeing them" (3:134); "Call to the way of your Lord with wisdom and fair exhortation, and argue with them in the best way possible" (16:25); and, "O you who believe! Come in full submission to God, all of you, (without allowing any discord among you due to worldly reasons), and do not follow in the footsteps of Satan, for indeed he is a manifest enemy to you (seeking to seduce you to rebel against God, with glittering promises)" (Al-Baqara 2:208). See also al-Mumtahana 60:8; al-Waqi'a 56:25-26; al-Furqan 25:63; al-Qasas 28:55; az-Zukhruf 43:89; an-Nisa 4:90; al-Anfal 8:61; Muhammad 47:35; Mu'minun 23:96; and al-Ma'ida 5:13

22   Al-Anbiya' 21:107; Muslim, *Birr,* 24 (2599); Abu Dawud, *Sunnah,* 11 (4659)

23   Al-Kahf 18:6; ash-Shu'ara 26:3; al-Fatir 35:8

24   God's Messenger expresses this in the following way: "There is no harm nor return of harm." Ibn Majah, *Ahqam* 17 (2340); Malik, *Muwatta'* 4/1078 (2758).

25   For instance, he once advised Abu Dharr, "Fear God wherever you are, and follow up a bad deed with a good one so that it wipes it out, and behave well towards people." At-Tirmidhi, *Birr,* 55 (1987). On another occasion, he said to 'Ali: "There will come the time where you will see disputes after me, so if you have a way of ending them in peace, then do so." Ibn Hanbal, *Al-Musnad,* 2/106 (695). On another occasion, he addressed Salama ibn Akwa', who had recovered the possessions that the Ghatafan had seized and wanted to respond to the thieves with even greater

severity, saying, "O son of al-Akwaʾ, you have been given power, so be kind." Al-Bukhari, *Maghazi*, 37 (4194); Muslim, *Jihad*, 45 (1806); Ibn Hanbal, *Al-Musnad*, 27/42 (16513).

26   At-Tirmidhi, *Birr*, 55 (1987)

27   Ibn Kathir, *Bidaya* 3/32; Ibn Asakir, *Tarikh*, 30/46

28   Ibn Kathir, *Bidaya*, 3/33; Ibn Asakir, *Tarikh*, 30/53

29   At-Tirmidhi, *Birr*, 71 (2018)

30   Muslim, *Birr*, 23 (2594)

31   An-Nasai, *Jihad*, 1 (4279); Al-Hakim, *Mustadraq*, 2/382 (2424); Al-Bayhaqi, *Al-Kubra*, 9/19 (17741)

32   At-Tabari, *Tafsir*, 9/165; Ibn Kathir, *Tafsir*, 3/531

33   At-Tabari, *Tafsir*, 17/183

34   When he was once offering prayer with friends in one of the city's outer neighborhoods, a band of Meccan polytheists attacked and in the ensuing altercation, Saʿd ibn Abi Waqqas struck the head of one of them with the jawbone of a camel and wounded him. This was the first blood to be shed in Islam. Ibn Hisham, *Sirah*, 1/171. In the early days, God's Messenger offered his prayers with his wife Khadija and ʿAli in Mina, which was a considerable distance from Mecca. Ay-Bukhari, *Tarikh*, 7/74–75; Ibn Hanbal, *Al-Musnad*, 3/306 (1787); Ibn Hisham, *Sirah*, 1/171; Ibn Abdilbarr, *Istiab*, 2/204; Al-Bayhaqi, *Ad-Dalail*, 2/162–163.

35   He made this statement upon setting off to visit the Kaʾba and being prevented from doing so by the Meccans. Al-Bukhari, *Shurut*, 15 (2731–2732); Abu Dawud, *Jihad*, 3/75 (2765); Ibn Hanbal, *Al-Musnad*, 31/213 (18910).

36   The Messenger's most inveterate enemies were his next-door neighbors. The closest to him in kin was Abu Lahab, whose house adjoined his. Though his other neighbors with adjoining houses, separated only by a wall, were no different to Abu Lahab. Hakam ibn Abi al-ʾAs ibn Umayya, ʿUqba ibn Abi Muʾayt, ʿAdi ibn al-Hamraʾ, and Ibn al-Asdaʾ al-Hudhali took their enmity as far as Abu Lahab, doing whatever they possibly could to cause him grief at any opportunity. Those closest in proximity, Abu Lahab and ʿUqba ibn Abi Muʾayt, excelled in antagonism and estrangement. Abu Jahl's house was not considered far either. They were this close to God's Beloved, yet stood so far from him. They were complicit in unremitting evil. On one day, they would throw sheep filth on top of him, and on another day, they pour that filth into the jug containing the Messenger's ablution water. To prevent further harm from them, God's Messenger constructed a wall between

them, but they confronted him with a new scheme every day, and relentlessly repeated their acts of ignominy for thirteen years.

37   There are a great number of examples in latter sections of this work.

38   For the Qur'anic verses revealed expressly state that one is permitted to defend oneself and respond in like manner when wronged or facing persecution; nonetheless, patience is advised, with the route of pardon again being shown as the right path. See Al-Baqarah 2:194; ash-Shura 42:39–43; an-Nahl 16:126; and al-Ma'ida 5:45.

39   The maledictions that God's Messenger invoked upon them in one or two cases, as an exception, need to be considered within precisely such a context; just as these men personally confronted and opposed God's Messenger, they also came between him and the Meccans, and through the pressure they exerted on the people and the walls they put up, they prevented any chance of the people's seeing reality for what it was. Many a right-minded person remained in Mecca as a result of these incomprehensible attitudes and left this world without ever having the chance to become acquainted with the truth. Otherwise, when left to their own devices, there were a significant number of people who appear to have been of two minds; had their paths crossed with God's Messenger in one way or another, they too might have come to Islam, like the others whose paths did cross, and they might have thus secured both their world and their Hereafter.

40   This member of the family is mentioned in some transmissions as being his daughter Zaynab (Tabarani, *Al-Kabir* 3/268; Ibnu'l Athir, *Usdu'l Ghaba*, 5/124; Ibn Abdilbarr, *İstîâb* 1/170), while Fatima in other sources (Al-Bukhari, *Wudu'* 69 (240); Muslim, *Jihad*, 39).

41   Tabarani, *Al-Kabir* 3/268; Ibnu'l Athir, *Usdu'l Ghaba*, 5/124; Ibn Abdilbarr, *Istiab* 1/170

42   While the narration names Walid ibn 'Uqba, this individual is said to have been Walid ibn 'Utba. Al-Bukhari, *Wudu'* 69 (240); An-Nawawi, *Sharhu'l Muslim*, 12/152.

43   Al-Bukhari, *Wudu'* 69 (240); Muslim, Jihad, 39; An-Nasai, *Sunan*, 1/188 (292). Witnessing this incident on the day, 'Abdu'llah ibn Mas'ud explicitly states that he himself saw that these individuals (the seventh whose name he did not remember and thus could not cite) whom God's Messenger left to God, were killed at Badr without exception. Al-Bukhari, *Wudu'* 69 (240), *Al-Maghazi*, 7 (3960); Muslim, *Jihad*, 39; An-Nasai, *Sunan*, 1/188 (292).

44   When God's Messenger, who was experiencing one of the most difficult days of his life, left the Ka'ba to return to his home, he chanced upon Abu al-Bakhtari on the way. Abu al-Bakhtari was a fair man. When he saw God's Messenger grieved and sorrowful, he asked him, "What is the matter?" God's Messenger's heart was so pained that he could not even bring himself to speak. He merely wished to be left to continue on his way and this is what he requested of Abu al-Bakhtari. But Abu al-Bakhtari would not give up. He was, after all, an understanding man and the manner of God's Messenger showed that something very serious had indeed happened to him. Hence, he said, "God knows that I will not leave you until you tell me what has happened, for it is clear that something has happened." Seeing that Abu al-Bakhtari would not let up, God's Messenger began to relate everything that had happened to him. Abu al-Bakhtari was infuriated at what he heard and he exclaimed, "Come on, we're going to the Sanctuary!" And so they came back to the Ka'ba together. Meanwhile, Abu Jahl and his cohorts were as happy as could be, laughing away without the slightest care in the world. It could even be said that they were laughing so uncontrollably that they had to lean on one another to avoid falling. Abu al-Bakhtari went straight to Abu Jahl, the ringleader. "O Abu al-Hakam," he boomed, "was it you who instructed camel entrails to be thrown onto Muhammad? For this is how cruelly he has been treated!" With an air of utter indifference, he seemed to say, "What of it?" No sooner did his admission come out of his mouth than Abu al-Bakhtari raised his whip and smote Abu Jahl with it on the head. Clearly, this inhumanity perpetrated against all these innocent people had stirred the fair-minded into action. Everyone stood aghast at one of the rare moments where life in Mecca came to a standstill. Once their astonishment passed, they reacted against Abu al-Bakhtari. The matter was about to get out of hand and Abu Jahl's first words were directed at them: "Shame on you!" he shouted. "Can't you see, Muhammad wants to set us against one another so that he can quietly slip away?" He then thrust his filthy hands towards God's most beloved servant and, as if wanting to hold the pulse of the people in his hand, he said, "Go easy on him." In saying this, of course, he had some other, ulterior motive. For right after, he pointed to Abu al-Bakhtari and said, "Otherwise, we're going to lose our close friends!" Tabarani, *Al-Awsat*, 1/232–233 (762); Al-Bazzar, *Musnad*, 5/240 (1853); As-Salihi, *Subulu'l-Huda*, 2/437.

45   When 'A'isha asked, "Have you ever experienced a worse day than the day of Uhud?" God's Messenger replied, "I experienced much harm from your people," and related this incident. Al-Bukhari, *Bad'u'l-Khalq*, 7 (3231); Muslim, *Jihad*, 39.

46   Ibn Hisham, *Sirah*, 2/268; Ibn Abi Shayba, *Musannaf*, 6/68 (29528)

47   Al-Bukhari, *Badu'l Khalq*, 7 (3231); Muslim, *Jihad*, 39 (1795)

48   Halabi, *Sirah*, 2/57, 58

49   Abu 'Ubayda broke two teeth to remove the two pieces of metal from the shattered helmet that pierced the face of God's Messenger.

50   At-Tabari, *At-Tafsir*, 7/194; Ibn Kathir, *At-Tafsir*, 2/114

51   Muslim, *Jihad*, 37; Ibn Majah, *Fitan*, 23 (4025); Al-Bayhaqi, *Dalail*, 3/215. In the face of such magnanimity, such individuals who came forth in anger exclaimed, "May my mother and father be your ransom, O Messenger of God, while Noah invoked God's wrath upon his people saying, *'My Lord! Do not leave on the earth any from among the unbelievers dwelling therein!'* you, bent double, face stained with blood, and your teeth even broken, still pray for them and say, 'My Lord, forgive my people for they do not know!' Whereas had you entreated God thus also, surely we would have all been destroyed, never again to be redeemed!" Al-Ghazali, *Ihyau'l Ulumi'd-Din*, 1/273.

52   The only Companion whose limbs had not been severed and body mutilated was the very young, recently married Hanzala. When his father Abu 'Amir, who had come to Uhud with fifty of his men, saw that his son had been martyred, he approached him and, nudging him for some time with the tip of his foot, said, "This would not have happened had you listened to me!" He then turned to the Meccan women who were mutilating the martyred and asked them not to touch him, saying, "This is my son!" Waqidi, *Al-Maghazi*, 229.

53   Al-Bukhari, *Al-Maghazi*, 17 (4043); Waqidi, *Al-Maghazi*, 229; Ibn Hisham, *Sirah*, 2/61; Al-Bayhaqi, *Dalail*, 3/214

54   Hakim, *Mustadraq*, 4/202 (4946); Al-Bazzar, *Musnad*, 17/21 (9530); Tabarani, *Al-Kabir* 3/143 (2937)

55   An-Nahl 16:126; Ibn Hisham, *Sirah* 2/63; Hakim, *Mustadraq*, 4/202 (4946); Al-Bazzar, *Musnad*, 17/21 (9530); Tabarani, *Al-Kabir* 3/143 (2937). It is stated that the Qur'anic verse in question was revealed in response to the Companions' voicing their feelings of vengeance against the Meccans after the atrocity at Uhud, and that when they had the opportunity at Mecca's conquest, God's Messenger did not permit this. At-Tirmidhi, *At-Tafsir*, 17 (3128); Ibn Hanbal, *Al-Musnad*, 3/152 (21267); An-Nasai, *Al-Kubra*, 10/145 (11215).

56   Such mutilation was generally performed by cutting off the ears and noses and the hacking of limbs. The Messenger of God forbade this act of savagery unequiv-

ocally and never allowed his Companions to engage in this, even when they had the chance. Al-Bukhari, *Mazalim*, 30 (2474); Abu Dawud, *Jihad*, 120 (2666); Ibn Hisham, *Sirah*, 2/63.

57   Reciting the words, *"Surely we belong to God (as His creatures and servants)*, and surely *to Him we are bound to return,"* upon receiving news of someone's death, is referred to as istirja'. *The transliteration of this is: Inna lillahi wa inna ilayhi raji'un.*

58   As-Salihi, *Subulu'l Huda*, 4/224

59   The Prophet declared amnesty after the conquest of Mecca and accepted those who asked for forgiveness. However, four Meccans received capital punishment – Miqyas ibn Subaba, Huwayrith ibn Nuqaydh, 'Abdu'llah ibn Hilal al-Khatal, and Fartana – who persisted in their animosity and posed serious threat to the public order (At-Tirmidhi, *At-Tafsir*, 17 (3128)).

60   While there are those who assert that this verse was revealed on the day of Conquest, (At-Tirmidhi, *At-Tafsir*, 17 (3128); Ibn Hanbal, *Al-Musnad*, 3/152 (21267); An-Nasai, *Al-Kubra*, 10/145 (11215) it is more plausible that it was revealed at Uhud. Ibn Hisham, *Sirah*, 2/63; Hakim, *Mustadraq*, 4/202 (4946); Al-Bazzar, *Al-Musnad*, 17/21 (9530); Tabarani, *Al-Kabir* 3/143 (2937).

61   The Qur'anic verse, *"Competing in increase of worldly goods (seeking and then boasting of the acquisition of things, wealth, pedigree, and posterity) distracts you (from the proper purpose of life), Until you come to the graves,"* points to this issue.

62   An examination of the early works in the History of Islam demonstrates that almost ninety percent of them either focused on battles *per se*, or were studies that were centered on the issue of battles.

- Aban ibn Uthman (100–5/718–24): Kitabu'l-*Maghazi*,

- Amir ash-Sa'bi (103/721): *Al-Maghazi*,

- Wahb ibn Munabbih (104–110–4/722-3-4–8): *Kitabu'l-Maghazi*,

- Ibn Abi Ayyash: *Kitabu'l- Maghazi*,

- Asim Ibn Umar ibn Katada (119–20–1/737–8): *Kitabu'l-Maghazi*,

- Shurahbil ibn Sa'd ibn Ubada (123/740--1): *Kitabu'l-Maghazi*,

- Ibn Shihab az-Zuhri (124/742): *Kitabu'l--Maghazi*,

- Amr ibn Abdillah as-Sabii al-Hamadanai (127/745): *Al-Maghazi* wa Futuh,

- Yazid ibn Ruman al-Asadi (130/747–8): *Kitabu'l-Maghazi*,

- Abdullah ibn Abi Bakr ibn Muhammad (130–135/747–752-3): *Kitabu'l-Maghazi*,

- Muhammad ibn Abdirrahman al-Madani (131/748-9): *Kitabu'l-Maghazi,*

- Dawud ibn Husayn al-Amawi (135/752–3): *Kitabu'l-Maghazi,*

- Musa ibn Ukba (141/758): *Kitabu'l- Maghazi,*

- Sulayman ibn Tarhan at-Taymi (143/760): *Kitabu'l-Maghazi,*

- Ibn Ishaq (150–1/767–8): *Kitabu'l- Maghazi,*

- Muhammad ibn Ishaq (151): *Kitabu's-Sirah wa'l-Mubtada' wa'l-Maghazi,*

- Ma'mar ibn Rashid (152–3–4/769–770–1): *Kitabu'l-Maghazi,*

- Abu Ma'shar as-Sindi, Abdurrahman ibn Walid (170/787): *Kitabu'l-Maghazi,*

- Waqidi (207/822): *Kitabu'l-Maghazi,*

As can be seen, almost all of these works focus on battles and have titles whose main theme is battle.

63   The Prophethood of the Messenger of God began in the month of Ramadan, of the year 610, and he passed away on the twelfth of Rabi' al-Awwal, in the year 632. Under normal circumstances, the time between these two dates is 7,960 days. However, due to the habitual tendency, particularly during the Meccan period and until the Farewell Pilgrimage, to tamper with the number of months, there is no way of providing an exact figure. When the desire to go to battle clashed with the "sacred months" during which fighting was prohibited, the Arabs at the time intercalated a month and, as such, prevented people saying of them that they, "fought during the sacred months." This practice, which the Qur'an refers to as *nasi,* was abolished by God's Messenger and by raising the issue during the Farewell Pilgrimage, he declared, "Surely time has completed its cycle and is as it was on the day that God created the heavens and the earth." Waqidi, *Al-Maghazi,* 730; Ibn Hisham, *Sirah,* 2/379.

64   Some sources indicated that this was a Monday which coincided with the eighth day of the month of Ramadan. Ibn Hisham, *Sirah,* 1/361. However, according Ibn Hisham's assessment here, Badr should have taken place on the nineteenth of Ramadan and the same author also states that Badr took place on a Friday. In saying this, he presumably refers to the date on which God's Messenger set off in pursuit of the Meccan caravan.

65   After a discussion of Badr having taken place on the seventeenth of Ramadan, Ibn al-Athir also mentions the possibility of its coinciding with the Friday that was the nineteenth of Ramadan. Ibn al-Athir, Al-Kamil, 2/12.

66   Bayhaqi, *Dalail,* 3/202; Ibn al-Kathir, *Al-Bidaya,* 4/11

67 Although there were isolated encounters from time to time, these can hardly be referred to as battles.

68 The forces coming all the way to Khandaq have been referred to as the Ahzab, or Confederate forces, as nearly all those tribes outside Medina combined to form a coalition against the Muslims.

69 Ibn al-Kathir, *Al-Bidaya*, 4/113. Some sources state that God's Messenger was away from Medina during the Khandaq campaign for fifteen nights. Ibn Sa'd, *At-Tabaqat*, 2/54.

70 The Second Badr is the encounter that Commander of the Meccan forces Abu Sufyan announced when leaving Uhud, saying, "You were victorious at Badr, while today at Uhud, we have defeated you. The matter thus remains undecided. We shall meet again at Badr next year, where the victor will be determined in a decisive battle." However, despite the fact that he was the one to make the call, Abu Sufyan did not turn up, and God's Messenger returned to Medina after a sojourn of ten days.

71 Ibn Hisham, *Sirah*, 2/157, 158. The number of martyrs is cited as three in some sources. Ibn al-Athir, *Al-Kamil*, 2/72.

72 Ibn Hisham, *Sirah,* 2/213. The number of Companions martyred at Khaybar is reported to be 15, 20, or 21. The woman who poisoned a Companion is included in this figure. Waqidi, *Al-Maghazi*, 481; Az-Zahabi, *Tarikh*, 2/246, 247; Ibn al-Kathir, *Al-Bidaya,* 4/232, 233.

73 Waqidi, *Al-Maghazi,* 481.

74 A closer examination of the unfolding of these two events, which appear on the surface to be banishment, indicates that their expulsion from the city at a point where they expected execution due to the severity of their crimes, was a great grace. When examined from yet another perspective, and taking into account the historical and cultural context, it can readily be said that for a people who rose against their own State and who took this uprising all the way to an armed resistance, this banishment could have even constituted a form of protecting them against the reaction that the city's other inhabitants would have shown to them, and to prevent any potential aggression that such a reaction could have triggered.

75 Al-Bukhari, *Buyu'*, 14; *Rahin,* 2, 5; *Istikhraz,* 2; Muslim, *Musaqat.* 124; At-Tirmidhi, *Buyu'* 20; An-Nasai, *Buyu',* 83. Abu Rafi', one of the Companions, relates, "A guest once came to the Messenger of God. He sent me to a Jew in Medina to ask to buy some foodstuffs to be paid for later, so that he could attend to his guest. I went.

The man said, 'I won't give anything without security.' When I returned to inform God's Messenger, he said, 'By God, I am recognized as trustworthy in the heavens and trustworthy on earth. Even so, take my coat of mail to him as security.'" (At-Tabari, *At-Tafsir*, 16/235) And so, on the day of his demise, his coat of mail was in pledge to a Jewish merchant for thirty *sa'a* of barley. This incident is illustrative and cogent proof of a very natural and unaffected life shared with all the various segments making up the social fabric. The transaction was made with a Jew who lived in Medina, and was a neighbor to God's Messenger, while retaining his Jewish identity. For the same term was not used for Jews who had become Muslim, such as 'Abdu'llah ibn Salam; they were henceforth referred to by their actual name or with their honorific. There is no possibility of this man's concealing his identity due to societal pressures, as he turned down the Messenger's request and made a demand showing lack of trust in God's Messenger, who was known for his trustworthiness. The more significant aspect of the matter is that the Messenger of God, who was Head of State, did not request what he needed from Companions who had devoted all to his cause, such as Abu Bakr, 'Umar, 'Uthman, but from a Jewish merchant and citizen of the state. What is more, he left his armor with him as collateral. From yet another perspective, when the Messenger sent Abu Rafi' to the same Jewish man despite the fact the latter made his distrust clear and did not show even basic courtesy, it demonstrated the will and resolve of God's Messenger to continue such a relationship. Moreover, it is also a given that what he requested was foodstuff to serve God's Messenger's guest who had come to him wanting to learn about Islam. The fact that God's Messenger did not meet this need from the state treasury or from his leading Companions, but firstly and insistently from his Jewish neighbor, requires separate discussion of interactions between the members of Medinan society. When all this is taken into consideration, the meaning of God's Messenger's preference is significant indeed. This transaction being made with a Jewish merchant living in Medina demonstrates that what was experienced in the past was left in the past. Mutual visits between neighbors, transactions that were the natural result of sharing the same space, society–state relations, and interfamilial communications continued along their natural course.

76 Ibn Hisham, *Sirah*, 2/121; al-Halabi, *Sirah*, 2/359. Some sources suggest that it lasted for fifteen days. Waqidi, *Al-Maghazi*, 279; At-Tabari, *Tarikh*, 3/90.

77 Badr, Uhud, Khandaq, the Second Badr, Hunayn, Ta'if, and Tabuk are implied.

78 Due to their different statuses, this figure does not include Hudaybiya, the Compensatory Pilgrimage, the Conquest of Mecca, Banu Qaynuqa, Banu Nadir, Banu

Qurayza, Wadi al-Qura, Fadak, Tayma', Bi'r al-Ma'una, and Raji'.

79   On a day when the Meccans subjected him to severe torture, Khabbab came to God's Messenger in a wretched state and voiced his complaint saying, "O Messenger of God, will you not ask for help for us? Will you not pray to God for us?" God's Messenger who had been using his cloak as a cushion in the shade of the Ka'ba, straightened up, and with disapproval visible on his face, said, "Among those who came before were such people that they would be placed in a ditch which was dug for them in the earth. Then a saw would be brought and smote on their head and they would be cut in half, but that would not deter them from their religion. They would be raked with iron combs which would remove their flesh from their bones or sinews, but that would not deter them from their religion. By God, God will complete (perfect) this affair (His Religion) so that a traveler will be able to go from San'a' to Hadramawt fearing only God, and where none will fear the wolf for their sheep, but you are trying to hasten things." Al-Bukhari, *Manaqib*, 29 (3852); Abu Dawud, *Jihad* 107 (2649).

80   The most striking example of this is transmitted by 'Adi ibn Hatim when he relates his experiences upon first meeting God's Messenger. After saying that God's Messenger told him all about his own self, those things that were not generally known by others, and describing his embarrassment before God's Messenger as a result, he explained, "'Now 'Adi,' he said. 'It may well be that the poverty you see among its followers prevents you from joining this religion. Or perhaps you suppose that the Arabs have abandoned them.' He then looked at me and said, 'O 'Adi, do you know of Hira (a city near Kufa, in Iraq, that was the seat of the Persian ruler)?' 'I have not seen it, but have heard of it.' God's Messenger said, 'By the One Who holds my soul in His Hand, this affair will not be complete, until a woman travels from Hira on her own fearing none but God, and will perform the circumambulation of the Ka'ba, and the treasures of Chosroes, the son of Hormuz, will be laid open before the Muslims!' 'The treasures of Chosroes, the son of Hormuz?' I asked incredulously. 'Yes, the treasures of Chosroes, the son of Hormuz,' he said. He then said, 'By God, wealth will flow so copiously among them that there will not be the people to take it.'" Having heard all this from God's Messenger on that day, 'Adi ibn Hatim was to remark years later, "A woman now travels unafraid from Hira to the Ka'ba, to circumambulate it. And I was one of those who opened the treasures of Chosroes. By God, the third will come to pass. Wealth will be so abundant that you will go out looking for a person to accept it, only to find none to accept it from you. For this is what God's Messenger has said." Ibn Hisham, *Sirah*, 2/364

81 At Mu'ta, where the Muslims met the Byzantine Romans, Khalid ibn al-Walid was responsible for an extraordinarily successful campaign where, with his army of 3,000 men up against the Byzantine Roman army of of about 200,000 men, he withdrew with only 12 losses, with some sources putting this figure at 8 or 9.

82 As there is no information available concerning the time some teams set off, how long they remained stationed at their destination, and the date of their return to Medina, there is no way of assessing the precise duration.

83 The 70 Companions martyred at Bi'r al-Ma'una and Raji' have been excluded from these figures, as their aim was to teach the people about Islam in the lands to which they went and they were ambushed and killed on the way.

84 Due the different circumstances, these figures do not include the 14 people and the 400 members of the Banu Qurayza sentenced to death at different times for their war crimes and treason. The nature of the Banu Qurayza incident will be discussed later.

85 Some sources put the figures for the members of the Banu Qurayza killed at 600, 700, 800, or 900, making it clear that rule of thumb was applied due to a resentment felt towards the Jews, with the figures being rounded off. A critical indicator is the sources recounting that these people were gathered in the house of Zayd ibn Haritha. It is inconceivable for the house of a person who came from a background of slavery and who led a very simple existence with very limited means, and which was parallel with the lives of those closest to God's Messenger, to fit such a number of people. Another reason for these high figures was the presence of those who sought to turn this into a smear campaign. Moreover, all of those killed on the day were not from the Banu Qurayza. Among them were also members of other tribes who cooperated treasonably from the outside. Nonetheless, we have taken the number of people killed from the Banu Qurayza to be 400. In spite of all this, we can still see different examples of the Prophet's largesse. God's Messenger gave them the right to choose the judge who would render the verdict. He even turned a blind eye to their efforts to influence the justice mechanism right up until the time judgment was to be delivered. It is for this reason that they did not object to the verdict and were resigned to it. Not even the slightest objection was raised, during this decision-making process or during its execution, neither by the Jews at that time, nor by their allied tribes and clans, on the basis of any wrong or injustice being done to them.

86 It can be said that this number was a maximum of 1,500 with the inclusion of those who were not recorded, or who were taken or buried by the enemy.

87   Regrettably, human history has seen many great massacres in certain major periods. See Oral Sander, *Siyasi Tarih*, İmge Kitabevi: Istanbul, 2000, Vol. 1, p. 351; William Woodruff, *Modern Dünya Tarihi*, Pozitif Yayınları: Istanbul, 2006, pp. 458, 468; Clive Ponting, *World History*, Pimlico: London, 2001, pp. 769–770, 781–782, 855; John B. Harrison, Richard E. Sullivan, and Dennis Sherman, *A Short History of Western Civilization*, 7th Edition, McGraw-Hill Publishing Company, pp. 672, 694, 719, 750; Matthew White, *The Great Book of Horrible Things*; Robin. W. Winks, *A History of Civilization*, ninth edition, Prentice-Hall, 1996, p. 555.

88   Ibn Hisham, *Sirah*, 2/515

89   For instance, until the time God's Messenger addressed this inequality, the Banu Qurayza were regarded by the other Jewish tribes as of a lower class, were treated as inferior, and were snubbed and slighted. While relatives were only given 50 camels in blood money when a member of their tribe was killed, for example, they needed to pay 100 camels to the family of those they killed.

90   Ibn Hisham, *Sirah*, 2/139

91   Hakim ibn Hizam was to act with the Meccans until the conquest of Mecca and was to embrace Islam after Conquest. Said to have been 60 years of age at the time, Hakim lived for another 60 years and died aged 120. Ibn Abdilbarr, *Istiab*, 1/184.

92   He wanted to turn back at least a couple of times before reaching Badr, but was prevented from doing so by Abu Jahl's intervention. It becomes apparent that 'Utba had a constant fear, from the very beginning, of the error of what they were doing. Ibn Hisham, *Sirah*, 1/368.

93   "Ibn al-Hanzaliyya" was an epithet others used for Abu Jahl and referred to his mother's tribe. A pejorative, it was used to express his disagreeable temperament when he did what he wanted to do without care for the opinion of others.

94   He asked 'Ali and Hamza immediately afterwards the identity of the man who wanted to stop the people from going to battle. As-Salihi, *Subulu'l Huda*, 4/31.

95   Reference here is to 'Utba's son Abu Hudhayfa.

96   Waqidi, *Al-Maghazi*, 78; As-Salihi, *Subulu'l Huda*, 4/33

97   Possessing the strength to deter the enemy from resorting to violence is a Qur'anic injunction. God declares: "*(Believers:) make ready against them whatever you can of force and horses assigned (for war), that thereby you may dismay the enemies of God and your enemies and others besides them, of whom (and the nature of whose enmity) you may be unaware. God is aware of them (and of the nature of their enmity). Whatever you spend in God's cause will be repaid to you in full, and you will*

not be wronged" (al-Anfal 8:60). The Prophetic statements referring to strength and power must be understood as statements uttered with this deterrent effect in mind.

98   Al-Bukhari, *Jihad,* 97 (2930); Muslim, *Jihad,* 28 (1776); Ibn Hisham, *Sirah,* 1/370

99   Al-Bukhari, *Jihad,* 78 (2899)

100   After setting off for battle, God's Messenger concealed his destination and headed towards the actual destination only after covering a considerable distance. This tactic was employed in almost all his campaigns with the exception of Tabuk. Al-Bukhari, *Jihad,* 103 (2947); Muslim, *Tawba,* 9 (2769).

101   Gülen, M. Fethullah, *The Sacred Trusts,* p. 2, Tughra Books: NJ.

102   Ibid.

103   These five universals, or rights, are the preservation of belief, life, the mind, property, and honor/progeny. While alcohol and drugs are prohibited due to their impairing the mind's function, fornication has been forbidden due to its giving rise to confusion of lineage. Ghazali, *Mustasfa,* 1/174.

104   Muslim, *Iman,* 62 (226); At-Tirmidhi, *Diyat,* 22 (1418–1421); Abu Dawud, *Sunnah,* 32 (4771– 4772); An-Nasai, *Al-Kubra,* 3/455 (3544); Ibn Majah, *Hudud,* 21 (2580–2582)

105   In the early years of the Meccan period, when he joined the next-door neighbors of God's Messenger in assaulting him from all sides, Ubayy too made repeated threats to kill him. So unyielding and excessive was he in doing so that God's Messenger was once forced to say to him, "And perhaps I, you," as if to say, "What makes you so certain?" (Waqidi, *Al-Maghazi,* 200; Ibn Hisham, *Sirah,* 2/55). As can be seen, God's Messenger did not even utter the word death, but as this was Ubayy's entire preoccupation, this was what he understood. Ubayy never forgot these words that had shot through him, and at the moment he felt the lance, he realized that his end was near and lamented loudly.

106   Close to Tan'im, and approximately ten kilometers from Mecca. This is also where the grave of the Mother of the Believers Maymuna is located, the very place where she had spent her wedding night with God's Messenger. Ibnu'l Athir, *Usdu'l Ghaba,* 7/263.

107   Waqidi, *Al-Maghazi,* 200–201; Ibn Hisham, *Sirah,* 2/55

108   While one narration states that the lance struck him in the thigh, the situation remains the same. As-Salihi, *Subulu'l Huda,* 4/208.

109   Ibn Hisham, *Sirah*, 1/371. Abu al-Bakhtari was among the slain at Badr in spite of this. Ibn Hisham, *Sirah*, 1/372

110   Ibn Hisham, *Sirah*, 1/371; Ibn Kathir, *Al-Bidaya*, 3/284; Al-Bayhaqi, *Dalail*, 3/140

111   Ibn Hisham, *Sirah*, 1/372

112   The words of God's Messenger to 'Ali, when sending him to conquest on the day of Khaybar, can be recalled here: "Proceed without looking back until you alight in their quarter and then invite them to Islam and tell them what is incumbent on them regarding the rights of God. By God, it is better for one man to be guided by you than for you to possess the most valuable red camels." Al-Bukhari, *Fadail*, 9 (3701); *Jihad*, 102 (2942); Muslim, *Fadail*, 4.

113   Waqidi, *Al-Maghazi*, 515

114   The Prophet's Companion Burayda relates a similar saying. Muslim, *Jihad*, 3 (1731); At-Tirmidhi, *Seerah*, 48 (1617); *Diyat*, 14 (1408); Abu Dawud, *Jihad*, 90 (2612, 2613); Ibn Hibban, *Hudud*, (4473).

115   Abu Dawud, *Jihad*, 85 3/37 (2614)

116   Al-Bayhaqi, *Al-Kubra*, 9/90

117   Khirash ibn Umayya, also known by the honorific Abu Nadla, accompanied God's Messenger at such critical points as the Muraysi expedition, the conquest of Khaybar, and Hudaybiya. On the day of Hudaybiya, God's Messenger sent him to the Quraysh in Mecca to inform them that they had with them their offerings, and that they merely wanted to circumambulate the Ka'ba and then turn back. He would cut the hair of God's Messenger from time to time and was the one who shaved his hair at Hudaybiya, to leave the ritual state of *ihram*. God's Messenger was very grieved at his killing Junaydib on the second day of Conquest. He rebuked Khirash as mentioned above and made Khirash's tribe, the Khuda'a, pay his blood money. He died during Mu'awiya's caliphate. Waqidi, *Al-Maghazi*, 422, 567–568; Ibn Hisham, *Sirah*, 2/259–260; Ibnu'l Athir, *Usdu'l Ghaba*, 2/161; Ibn Hajar, *Isabah*, 1/480.

118   On this day, God's Messenger took the payment of compensation of one hundred camels upon himself, despite his having no involvement in the killing which had angered him so much. What is more, in order to pay it he borrowed from the Meccans.

119   He once saw some people crowded around something and sent someone to see the reason for this. When he learned that a woman had been killed he said, "They were not to be killed! He then sent word to Khalid commanding him not to kill

any woman or child. Abu Dawud, *Jihad*, 121 (2669); Ibn Hisham, *Sirah*, 2/286

120 Al-Bukhari, *Al-Maghazi*, 58 (4339). The sources make mention of three similar incidents involving Khalid. The first of these is at Adhakhir, during Conquest, the second immediately after Conquest in the raid to Banu Jadhima, and the third at Hunayn. During the Banu Jadhima raid, a disagreement arose between Khalid and the Companions under his command, and they disobeyed Khalid's order to kill the captives. When they returned to Medina and the incident was relayed to God's Messenger, he was extremely angered by what he had heard and thrice declared that he was innocent of what Khalid had done. Waqidi, *Al-Maghazi*, 585–591; Ibn Sa'd, *At-Tabaqat*, 2/148; Ibn Hisham, *Sirah*, 2/270; At-Tabari, *Tarikh*, 3/67, 68. When he learned of Khalid's having killed a woman at Hunayn, he sent one of his Companions to tell him, "The Messenger of God forbids the killing of women or children!" Ibn Hisham, *Sirah*, 2/286.

121 In this verse, God declares: "*No soul, as bearer of burden, is made to bear the burden of another. We would never punish (a person or community for the wrong they have done) until We have sent a Messenger (to give counsel and warning)*" (Al-Isra 17:15). For related verses, refer to Al-An'am 6:164; Fatir 35:18; Az-Zumar 39:7.

122 Waqidi, *Al-Maghazi*, 603, 604; Al-Bukhari, *Janaiz*, 92 (1385); 79 (1358, 1359); Muslim, *Qadar*, 6 (2658); Abu Dawud, *Sunnah*, 17; At-Tirmidhi, *Qadar*, 5 (2138)

123 It is quite apparent that the incidents under discussion took place soon after Khalid ibn al-Walid's acceptance of Islam, when he was yet unaware of the Prophet's sensitivity on this point.

124 Nubata, who was killed during the Banu Qurayza affair, was killed in reprisal for the Companion that she had killed; *Qisas*, or retribution, was also exacted in the case of Zaynab bint Harith, whose attempted poisoning of God's Messenger at Khaybar resulted in the killing of another Companion; and Fartana, again, was killed for a former crime.

125 We see this stance at Uhud also. Taking the sword that God's Messenger had given him and rushing onto the battlefield, Abu Dujana cleaved through the lines until he raised his sword above the head of someone who jumped in front of him. A shriek—a woman's voice—rose above the battlefield. He saw that it was Hind, the wife of the Meccan commander Abu Sufyan. "I hated the idea of striking a woman with the sword of the Messenger of God," he said, and returned to his ranks. Waqidi, *Al-Maghazi*, 206. Another person given such a chance would have jumped at killing the wife of the enemy commander.

126   Waqidi, *Al-Maghazi*, 370

127   For relevant warnings, see Al-Bukhari, *Jihad* 148 (3015); Muslim, *Jihad*, 8 (1744); Abu Dawud, *Jihad*, 121 (2668); At-Tirmidhi, *Seerah*, 19 (1569); An-Nasai, *Seerah*, 31 (8564)

128   Waqidi, *Al-Maghazi*, 370. Things turned out just as Hakam had anticipated. When she was being sought for murder, Nubata came to 'A'isha's chamber. Upon hearing her name being called out outside, she said, "My husband killed me." 'A'isha was baffled. This woman who had been laughing hysterically did not look to be a woman that was to be killed. When she related everything that happened to her, the matter came to light and she paid the price of her crime with her life. The only woman killed from the Banu Qurayza that day was Nubata. Waqidi, *Al-Maghazi*, 370.

129   It is well known that the Messenger of God entreated God, saying, "O Lord, here come the Quraysh with all their conceit and and pomp to challenge You and make a liar of Your Messenger. O Lord, I beseech You to grant us the help which You have promised. O Lord, drive them to the ground the morning of this day!" Waqidi, *Al-Maghazi*, 77; As-Salihi, *Subulu'l Huda*, 4/31.

130   Muslim, *Jihad*, 18 (1763); At-Tirmidhi, *At-Tafsir*, 9 (3081); Ibn Hanbal, *Al-Musnad*, 1/32; Said ibn Mansur, *As-Sunan*, 2872

131   To see all the narrations in their entirety, see As-Salihi, *Subulu'l Huda*, 4/36.

132   Bayhaqi, *Ad-Dalail*, 2/336; 3/54

133   In a verse depicting the day, God Almighty was to describe the scene: "*When you were imploring your Lord for help (as a special mercy), and He responded to you: 'I will help you with a thousand angels, coming host after host'*" (Al-Anfal 8:9). Muslim, *Jihad*, 18 (1763); At-Tirmidhi, *Tafsir*, 9 (3081); Ibn Hanbal, *Al-Musnad*, 1/30.

134   As-Salihi, *Subulu'l Huda*, 4/38

135   As-Salihi, *Subulu'l Huda*, 4/43-44

136   Jabir shares the following account: "On the day of Badr, we were observing the prayer with God's Messenger. At one point, he smiled. At the completion of the prayer, we asked, 'O Messenger of God, we saw you smile during the prayer.' He said, 'Mika'il passed by me, with dust on his wings, having just returned from pursuing the people (on the battlefield). When he smiled at me, I smiled back.'" Abu Ya'la, *Al-Musnad*, 4/49; Haythami, *Majmau'z-Zawaid*, 6/283.

137   Al-Anfal 8:44

138   Muslim, *Jihad*, 30 (1779); Ibn Hanbal, *Al-Musnad*, 21/22 (13296)

139   Ibn Hisham, *Sirah*, 1/371

140   This without a doubt vividly illustrates just how necessary is belief for a believer who is subjected to similar ordeals, and how indispensable is "conversation with the Beloved."

141   Al-Bukhari, *Riqaq*, 38 (6502)

142   Suhayl ibn 'Amr, who was taken captive at Badr and was to return to Mecca after paying his ransom, describes extraordinary visions at Badr.

143   At the end of the fighting, Gabriel came to the Messenger of God and said, "O Muhammad, my Lord has sent me to you and He commanded me not to leave you until you are satisfied. Are you satisfied?" The Messenger of God replied, "Yes." He then told God's Messenger that he could now leave Badr. Waqidi, *Al-Maghazi*, 111.

144   Al-Bukhari, *Salah*, 109; Muslim, *Jihad*, 107

145   This topic is examined in further detail under the heading "The Inevitable End of Hatred and Hostility." Just to give an idea, there was not a single Meccan who witnessed the conquest of Mecca and did not eventually side with God's Messenger.

146   The underlying factor was of course not limited to this incident alone. Behind this was, no doubt, who knows how many more efforts and initiatives, which are discussed under the heading, "A Tried and Tested Methodology."

147   Ibn Hisham, *Sirah*, 1/378; Ibnu'l Athir, *Usdu'l Ghaba*, 6/69

148   Al-Bukhari, *Al-Maghazi*, 8 (3976); Muslim, *Janaiz*, 9 (932); Ibn Hanbal, *Al-Musnad*, 21/22 (13296); An-Nasai, *Janaiz*, 117 (2213–2214); Haythami, *Majmau'z-Zawaid*, 6/90

149   For instance, on that day, the Messenger of God buried his uncle and milk brother Hamza and the son of his paternal aunt 'Abdu'llah ibn Jahsh together in one grave, 'Abdu'llah ibn 'Amr and 'Amr ibn Jamuh in another grave, Kharija ibn Zayd and Sa'd ibn Rabi' in one grave, and Nu'man ibn Malik and 'Ubada ibn al-Hashas in yet another.

150   This incident coincided with the last days of Rajab. This is why the issue of intervention was perceived in different ways among the Companions; however, as they were approaching the bounds of the Sacred the affair ended in intervention. For fighting during the sacred months was prohibited during the Age of Ignorance also. As mentioned earlier, when the Quraysh were forced to fight, they could only

do so after tampering with dates and announcing their intercalation. Through this tactic, that the Qur'an terms *nasi*, they were supposedly not doing anything unlawful, and were brazenly deceiving themselves. At-Tawbah, 9:37; Ibn Kathir, *At-Tafsir*, 2/358; Ibn Hisham, *Sirah*, 1/161. Ibn Hisham, *Sirah*, 1/356; At-Tabari, *Tarikh*, 3/15.

151   At-Tabari, *Tarikh*, 3/15. Gabriel came during this time to reveal the following verse of the Qur'an (which means): *"They ask you about the Sacred Month and fighting in it. Say: 'Fighting in it is a grave sin; but barring people from the way of God, unbelief in Him, and denying entry into the Sacred Mosque, and expelling its inmates from it are far graver and more sinful in the sight of God; disorder (rooted in rebellion to God and recognizing no laws) is far graver and more sinful than killing'"* (Al-Baqarah 2:217).

152   Waqidi, *Al-Maghazi*, 47; Ibn Sa'd, *At-Tabaqat*, 4/102. Hakam ibn Qaysan was to continue his life as a fine Muslim, make important progress with respect to his learning, and was to pass away to the eternal realm after attaining martyrdom during the Bi'r al-Ma'una incident. Waqidi, *Al-Maghazi*, 47; At-Tabari, *Tarikh*, 3/15; Ibn Sa'd, *At-Tabaqat*, 4/102; Ibnu'l Athir, *Usdu'l Ghaba*, 2/54.

153   At one point that day, when seated with his Companions, God's Messenger turned in the direction of Mecca and said, "And peace be upon you!" After which he was overcome with great sorrow. Those watching him in astonishment and wonder asked, "O Messenger of God, to whose greetings of peace do you respond?" God's Messenger then said, "The greetings of Khubayb. The Quraysh have killed him." These greetings of peace were to be Khubayb's last words in Mecca. He was the first Muslim to be killed at the stake in the way of God. Upon receiving news of his martyrdom, God's Messenger sent 'Amr ibn Umayya and Salama ibn Aslam to Mecca and, after facing a great many ordeals themselves, they rescued Khubayb's body from the polytheists. Ibn Hisham, *Sirah*, 4/126,127; At-Tabari, *Tarikh*, 2/79, 80.

154   Waqidi, *Al-Maghazi*, 115; Ibn Hisham, *Sirah*, 1/380; At-Tabari, *Tarikh*, 3/40; Halabi, *Sirah*, 2/257; Ibnu'l Athir, *Al-Kamil*, 2/25 (131); Ibn Kathir, *Al-Bidaya*, 3/322; Tabarani, *Al-Kabir*, 22/393; As-Salihi, *Subulu'l Huda*, 4/66

155   Al-Bukhari, *Jihad*, 142 (3008); Al-Baghawi, *At-Tafsir*, 2/377 (1103). This reflects the general manner of God's Messenger: after Hunayn, he sent his Companion Busr ibn Sufyan to Mecca, to purchase new clothing for all of the captives, most of whom were women and children. His command was carried out and this was a crucial factor in the decision of these people who would soon afterwards embrace Islam. Waqidi, *Al-Maghazi*, 627.

156 One of the *mu'allafa al-qulub*. Ibn Hajar, *Isabah*, 2/250; Ibnu'l Athir, *Usdu'l Ghaba*, 2/139.

157 Waqidi, *Al-Maghazi*, 114

158 Waqidi, *Al-Maghazi*, 114, 115

159 Ibn Hanbal, *Al-Musnad*, 33/364 (20201); Waqidi, *Al-Maghazi*, 106

160 'Umayr ibn Abi Waqqas, the brother of Sa'd who was martyred at Badr, was the youngest of those fighting at Badr. God's Messenger, who under normal circumstances turned away children who wanted to enlist for battle, had given permission to him due to his great insistence. He came to Badr on the day with the sword that his brother Sa'd had girt around his waist dragging along the ground. Ibn Hisham, *Sirah*, 1/414; Waqidi, *Al-Maghazi*, 106.

161 Waqidi, *Al-Maghazi*, 106. When the number of Companions at Badr and the fact that they remained there for three days is taken into account, it appears that these words of caution were expressed either as the battle raged, or as soon as it had finished. For it is difficult to imagine that Sa'd ibn Abi Waqqas was not told of his brother 'Umayr's martyrdom later. This means that God's Messenger's view was unchanged from the beginning and he thus took the necessary precaution.

162 Waqidi, *Al-Maghazi*, 106, 107; Ibn Hisham, *Sirah*, 1/380

163 Among the people who approached God's Messenger after the battle was 'Amr ibn al-Rabi', brother of Abu al-'As ibn al-Rabi'. He gave the purse in his hand for the release of his brother saying, "I have here the ransom that Zaynab has sent for her captive." God's Messenger first opened the purse. In his hands was the cherished keepsake of his his beloved wife Khadija. It was the necklace that she had taken off and placed on the neck of her daughter Zaynab herself. This treasured piece took God's Messenger back, and he was overwhelmed with the emotion brought on by the memories that came flooding back. The paragon of faithfulness, the Messenger of God turned to his Companions and said, "If you deem it appropriate to release Zaynab's prisoner for her and return to her that which belongs to her, then do so." The Qur'anic verses revealed at this time referred the releasing of captives, either on ransom or gratuitously, to the discretion of the believers. (Muhammad 48:4). Needless to say, the Companions replied in unison, "Yes, O Messenger of God!" However, God's Messenger had one condition. He summoned Abu al-'As and whispered something in his ear. Those waiting anxiously observed Abu al-'As nodding his head in acknowledgment, as his father-in-law had requested that he send Zaynab back as soon as he returned.

164   Waqidi, *Al-Maghazi*, 115; At-Tabari, *Tarikh*, 3/40

165   Ibn Hisham, *Sirah*, 1/381; Ibnu'l Athir, *Usdu'l Ghaba* 6/209; At-Tabari, *Tarikh*, 2/460; Ibn Kathir, *Bidaya*, 3/322; As-Salihi, *Subulu'l Huda*, 4/66

166   Walid ibn al-Walid was the son of Walid ibn al-Mughira, one of the ringleaders of unbelief from before the Messenger's Prophethood and one who had incited the Meccans against the Banu Hashim at every opportunity. After Badr, Khalid ibn al-Walid arrived with his other brothers and, paying the ransom, wanted to take him back with them to Mecca. Walid, however, had at this point chosen to embrace Islam. When they reached Dhu al-Hulayfa, he escaped, rushed back to God's Messenger, and professed his acceptance of Islam. When his brothers came at him with great violence saying, "Why did you not become a Muslim before you were ransomed?" he replied, "Had I become Muslim then, it would have been supposed that I did so to be released." Despite this he was forced back to Mecca, incarcerated, and subjected to all sorts of torture. He is one of those people whom God's Messenger included in his special *qunut* invocation. He found a way to escape during the Compensatory Pilgrimage and reunited with God's Messenger. Waqidi, *Al-Maghazi*, 129; As-Salihi, *Subulu'l Huda*, 4/79.

167   Waqidi, *Al-Maghazi*, 115; Ibn Hisham, *Sirah*, 1/645

168   Those who died were 'Amr ibn Hisham (Abu Jahl), 'Umar ibn Hisham, and al-'Asi ibn Hisham. Abu Jahl was also chief of his tribe, the Banu Makhzum. Ibn Hisham, *Sirah*, 1/417.

169   The name of his uncle, who was also taken captive on that day, was Khalid ibn Hisham. Ibn Hisham, *Sirah*, 2/5.

170   Waqidi, *Al-Maghazi*, 116, 118

171   Ibn Sa'd, *At-Tabaqat*, 4/9; Ibnu'l Athir, *Usdu'l Ghaba*, 3/164; Ibn Abdilbarr, *Istiab*, 2/240

172   Hakim, *Mustadraq*, 3/318; Ibn Hisham, *Sirah*, 3/200; At-Tabari, *Tarikh*, 3/42; Ibn Hajar, *Isabah*, 3/213

173   At the same time, God's Messenger did not contemplate subjecting anyone to torture, even if a prisoner of war, and forbade it vehemently. For he was the awaited Prophet of the End of Time. The day would come when Suhayl too would surrender, and do such things that would please the likes of 'Umar also. The day that God's Messenger bade farewell to the world and those in it, he would address the Meccans and prevent those people, in whose hearts belief had not yet become firmly established, from reverting to unbelief. Waqidi, *Al-Maghazi*, 1/107; Ibn

Hisham, *Sirah*, 3/200, 6/89; At-Tabari, *Tarikh*, 3/42.

174   Seeing the hesitation experienced in Mecca on the day of God's Messenger's demise, Suhayl stood at the door of the Ka'ba, and with the tremendous speech that he gave, he rallied the people once again around the Ka'ba. When Suhayl's words reached 'Umar in Medina, he broke out in sobs and said to those around him, "Had I done what I said I would do on that day, I would not have heard these words from Suhayl today." Weeping bitterly, he continued, "So this is what God's Messenger meant when he said, "Leave him, O 'Umar!"

175   That Gabriel came to God's Messenger in the meantime, and informed him that he was free to do as he wished in relation to the captives, is also referred to in narrations. Waqidi, *Al-Maghazi*, 107; Ibn Sa'd, *At-Tabaqat*, 2/22; Abdu'r-Razzaq, *Musannaf*, 5/209; An-Nasai, *Al-Kubra*, 5/200; As-Salihi, *Subulu'l Huda*, 4/61.

176   On that day, Abu Bakr said to God's Messenger, "They are your people and your family, some your cousins, some fellow tribesmen, and some brothers. Release them on ransom and this will empower the Muslims against unbelief. And it may well be that God will bring their hearts to you." Muslim, *Jihad*, 18; Waqidi, *Al-Maghazi*, 108; At-Tabari, *At-Tafsir*, 10/46; *Tarikh*, 3/47; Al-Bayhaqi, *Dalail*, 3/137; As-Salihi, *Subulu'l Huda*, 4/60.

177   'Umar said on the day, "These are the people who have called you a liar, driven you out, and fought you. I do not share Abu Bakr's opinion. I am of the opinion that you should hand so-and-so to me that I may strike his neck. Hand 'Aqil over to 'Ali so that he may strike his neck, and to Hamza leave so-and-so, so that he may strike his neck! Let us make known to God that we have no mercy in our hearts for the polytheists. They are the leaders of the Quraysh and guides of the false." Muslim, *Jihad*, 18; Waqidi, *Al-Maghazi*, 107; At-Tabari, *At-Tafsir*, 10/46; *Tarikh*, 3/48; Al-Bayhaqi, *Dalail*, 3/137; As-Salihi, *Subulu'l Huda*, 4/60.

178   'Abdu'llah ibn Rawaha said, "O Messenger of God, look for a valley with a lot of firewood in it, put them in it and set fire to it around them." At-Tabari, *Tarikh*, 3/48; Ibn Kathir, Al-Bidaya, 3/312; Al-Bayhaqi, *Dalail*, 3/138; Ibn Abi Shayba, *Al-Maghazi*, 195; As-Salihi, *Subulu'l Huda*, 4/60.

179   Yunus 10:88; Ibn Hanbal, *Al-Musnad*, 6/138, 139; At-Tabari, *At-Tafsir*, 10/46; *Tarikh*, 3/48; Ibn Kathir, *Al-Bidaya*, 3/312; As-Salihi, *Subulu'l Huda*, 4/61

180   As-Salihi, *Subulu'l Huda*, 4/61

181   There are accounts to the effect of Suhayl ibn Bayda' having embraced Islam while in Mecca, that he concealed this from people, and that he was forcibly brought

to Badr. 'Abdu'llah ibn Mas'ud even states that he saw him offering the prayer in Mecca. Ibn Hanbal, *Al-Musnad*, 6/140; At-Tabari, *Tarikh*, 10/46; Al-Baghawi, *Mu'jamu's-Sahaba*, 3/104 (1013).

182   Ibn Hanbal, *Al-Musnad*, 6/140; Tabari, *At-Tafsir*, 10/46

183   Ibn Hanbal, *Al-Musnad*, 6/140; Tabari, *At-Tafsir*, 10/46; *Tarikh*, 3/48; Ibn Kathir, *Al-Bidaya*, 3/312; Al-Bayhaqi, *Ad-Dalail*, 3/139; Ibn Abi Shayba, *Al-Maghazi*, 196

184   Waqidi, *Al-Maghazi*, 107; Ibn Sa'd, *At-Tabaqat*, 2/16; Ibn Sayyidi'n-Nas, *Uyunu'l-Athar*, 1/333

185   See for examples: An-Nahl 16:125; Al-Baqarah 2:109; Al-Jathiyah 45:14; Fussilat 41:34

186   The Quraysh sent only fourteen or fifteen of their men to Medina three days after Muttalib arrived with his father's ransom, and they were forced to pay the amount of ransom fixed by him. Waqidi, *Al-Maghazi*, 1/129.

187   The *'uqiyya* is an ancient metric unit of mass; 1 *'uqiyya* is equivalent to 1283 grams.

188   God's Messenger said of Abu Wada'a, "He has an affluent and prosperous son in Mecca who will surely exceed his ransom." The Meccans were not at all impressed when he was the first to go to Medina and remit this amount. When they learned he had slipped away from Mecca despite their warnings, they looked on him as "young and opinionated." Waqidi, *Al-Maghazi*, 122; Ibn Hisham, *Sirah*, 1/382; At-Tabari, *Tarikh*, 3/42; Haythami, *Majmau'z-Zawaid*, 6/91; Ibn Athir, *Usdu'l Ghaba*, 1/614.

189   Ibn Hisham, *Sirah*, 1/389; Waqidi, *Al-Maghazi*, 121; As-Salihi, *Subulu'l Huda*, 4/69

190   Prior to the emergence of Islam, the inhabitants of Mecca were ahead of the Medinans in literacy. Ibn Sa'd, *At-Tabaqat*, 2/22; Al-Bayhaqi, *Sunan*, 6/322; Ibn Sayyidi'n-Nas, *Uyunu'l-Athar*, 1/373; As-Salihi, *Subulu'l Huda*, 4/69.

191   Waqidi, *Al-Maghazi*, 130; Ibn Hisham, *Sirah*, 1/389; Al-Halabi, *Sirah*, 2/296

192   Waqidi, *Al-Maghazi*, 128, 130

193   In a verse revealed one day later, God Almighty seemed to foretell the encounter which would take place in a year's time at Uhud:

It is not for a Prophet to have captives until he has widely exhausted the enemies in the land. You (O believers) seek the fleeting gains of the present, worldly life, but God wills that the Hereafter will be yours. God is All-Glorious with irresistible might, All-

Wise. Had there not been a previous decree from God (that gains of war are lawful and captives can be released in return for ransom), a tremendous punishment would surely have touched you because of what you took (the gains of war, and the captives taken in expectation of ransom, before the enemies' power in the land had been sufficiently suppressed and exhausted). (But since such a decree has already come) now enjoy as lawful and pure and wholesome of what you have obtained (as gains of war and ransom); and keep from disobedience to God in all your actions. Surely God is All-Forgiving, All-Compassionate (especially toward His believing, pious servants). (Al-Anfal 8:67-69)

As such, He was to convey to them that the release of the prisoners on such a day, when they had not become powerful enough, was not right strategically, but that this was the decree on this matter nonetheless. As a result of this, God's Messenger would weep at length with his two Companions. Muslim, *Jihad*, 18; As-Salihi, *Subulu'l Huda*, 4/61.

194   *Sa'd ibn al-Nu'man, one of the notables of the 'Amr ibn 'Awf,* had come to Mecca on the presumption that those who came for worship would be safe, and in consideration of all his service to the Meccans. The Quraysh had decreed that any coming to Mecca with the aim of worship could not be touched. In spite of this, Abu Sufyan cornered and took Sa'd prisoner as he circumambulated the Ka'ba, in flagrant disregard of their pledge and all their traditions. There was neither war nor confrontation, but with one of his sons killed at Badr and the other captured, Abu Sufyan wanted to save his son 'Amr without paying any price and without effort. He was on the lookout for that opportunity. To those who asked him why he did not attempt to pay his son's ransom, he replied, "Am I to lose both my blood and my wealth?" This was his way of reminding them of his son Hanzala who was slain at Badr. Now, his chance had come. Ignoring this blackmail, God's Messenger handed Abu Sufyan's son 'Amr to the 'Amr ibn 'Awf and sent to him to Mecca in exchange for Sa'd. Ibn Hisham, *Sirah*, 1/384; At-Tabari, *Tarikh*, 3/43; Ibn Kathir, *Al-Bidaya*, 3/311; Al-Halabi, *Sirah*, 2/451, 452.

195   Al-Bukhari, *Al-Maghazi*, 12 (2970); Waqidi, *Al-Maghazi*, 109; Ibn Hajar, *Isabah*, 1/259

196   Waqidi, *Al-Maghazi*, 109; Ibn Hisham, *Sirah*, 1/234

197   Ibn Hisham, *Sirah*, 1/234; Ibnu'l Athir, *Usdu'l Ghaba*, 2/569

198   Ibnu'l Athir, *Usdu'l Ghaba* 1/516

199   Al-Bukhari, *Al-Maghazi*, 12; Waqidi, *Al-Maghazi*, 121; Ibn Hajar, *Isabah*, 1/259.

Some sources indicate that he became Muslim either before or during the Conquest. Ibn Hajar, *Isabah*, 1/259.

200 Waqidi, *Al-Maghazi*, 121; Ibn Hajar, *Isabah*, 1/259

201 Ibn Hisham, *Sirah*, 1/383; At-Tabari, *Tarikh*, 3/42.

202 Another narration reads: "Had I heard her poem before this, I would not have had him killed." Ibnu'l Athir, *Usdu'l Ghaba*, 7/235; Ibn Abdilbarr, *Istiab*, 3/253; Al-Halabi, *Sirah*, 2/255; As-Salihi, *Subulu'l Huda*, 4/73

203 Waqidi, *Al-Maghazi*, 109

204 Nawfal ibn al-Harith was the son of the Messenger's paternal uncle. The stance of God's Messenger on the day and his uncle 'Abbas' paying his ransom was enough to soften his heart and he accepted the Islam that he had fought against for fifteen years and for which reason he had come to Badr. Ibn Sa'd, *At-Tabaqat*, 4/34; Ibnu'l Athir, *Usdu'l Ghaba*, 5/347; Suhayli, *Rawdu'l-Unf* 3/127. There are also accounts that the Messenger's knowing of the wealth and possessions he had hidden in Jeddah, of which no one else had knowledge, contributed to his acceptance of Islam on this day. Hakim, *Mustadraq*, 4/270 (5123); Al-Bayhaqi, *Dalail*, 3/144; Ibnu'l Athir, *Usdu'l Ghaba*, 5/347; As-Salihi, *Subulu'l Huda*, 4/69.

205 Waqidi, *Al-Maghazi*, 129; As-Salihi, *Subulu'l Huda*, 4/79

206 Sa'ib ibn 'Ubayd who was among those captured on the day of Badr had also softened and began to show signs of changing sides. However, he kept this concealed until the payment of his ransom, after which he proclaimed his acceptance of Islam. When asked why he did not profess this earlier, he said, "I did not like to deprive the believers of such an opportunity." Ibnu'l Athir, *Usdu'l Ghaba*, 2/396; Ibn Sayyidu'n-Nas, *Uyunu'l-Athar*, 1/333.

207 Ibn Hajar, *Isabah*, 3/1845; Ibnu'l Athir, *Usdu'l Ghaba* 5/182; Ibn Abdilbarr, *Istiab*, 2/374; Suhayli, *Rawdu'l-Unuf,* 3/127

208 Ibnu'l Athir, *Usdu'l Ghaba* 1/693; Ibn Hajar, *Isaba*, 1/355

209 Waqidi, *Al-Maghazi,* 131; Ibn Hajar, *Isabah*, 2/1189

210 Ibnu'l Athir, *Usdu'l Ghaba* 5/147; Ibn Hajar, *Isabah*, 3/1821; Ibn Abdilbarr, *Istiab* 2/406

211 Al-Halabi, *Sirah*, 2/209

212 Ibnu'l Athir, *Usdu'l Ghaba*, 1/349, Ibn Hajar, *Isabah*, 2/988

213 Ibnu'l Athir, *Usdu'l Ghaba*, 1/195, 349. Even though two brothers of 'A'idh b. al-Sa'ib and Bijad ibn al-Sa'ib, by the names of Hajib and 'Uwaymir, had been killed at Badr on that day. Ibn Hisham, *Sirah*, 1/417.

214   He plotted with Safwan ibn Umayya after Badr and came all the way to Medina on the pretext of saving his son Wahb ibn 'Umayr. He came, however, with murderous intent, wanting to kill the Messenger of God and exact his revenge. 'Umar was suspicious and waited with his hand on the hilt of his sword. When God's Messenger asked him what had brought him to Medina, he said that it was for his prisoner. After informing him that his son would be released, God's Messenger inquired about his sword that he held so tight in his grasp. He said that he had forgotten all about it. However, he completely relented in the presence of God's Messenger, who informed him of his knowledge of his true intention and his schemes. He, in turn, surrendered in the presence of God's Messenger, leaving behind whatever there was in the name of animosity, in the past. For God's Messenger described to him in detail his conversation and all his designs with Safwan ibn Umayya and revealed a secret that none but he and Safwan knew. On that day, 'Umar said, "Surely, I preferred swine to him when he appeared, but in this hour he is more agreeable to me than my own children." Waqidi, *Al-Maghazi*, 119,120; Ibn Hisham, *Sirah*, 1/390; At-Tabari, *Tarikh*, 3/47; Al-Bayhaqi, *Dalail*, 3/148; Ibnu'l Athir, *Usdu'l Ghaba*, 4/288; *Al-Kamil*, 2/28.

215   After his father 'Umayr ibn Wahb, who had come to kill God's Messenger, became Muslim, God's Messenger said to his Companions, "Teach your brother the Qur'an and release his prisoner." He had thus been set free. He too became Muslim on that day, by means of his father, 'Umayr, who contributed to the embracing of Islam of a great number of people after his return to Mecca. Waqidi, *Al-Maghazi*, 130; Al-Bayhaqi, *Dalail*, 3/149; Ibn Abdilbarr, *Istiab*, 3/43; Ibnu'l Athir, *Usdu'l Ghaba*,4/288, 289; 5/430; Suhayli, *Rawdu'l-Unf*, 3/127.

216   The new leader of the Meccans, Abu Sufyan, who breathed hate and enmity as a result of the crushing defeat at Badr, sent this Bedouin to Medina to kill God's Messenger, in return for a handsome fortune. Making a stealthy entry into the city, he came all the way to the presence of God's Messenger, asking which of the people he was. When God's Messenger saw him, he said to his Companions, "This man intends some treachery, but, by God, God will foil his artful scheme." The Bedouin approached as though wanting to confide a secret to him. Quick in sensing his design and, on the basis of the Messenger's words earlier, 'Usayd ibn Hudayr pulled him away, saying, "Keep away from God's Messenger!" He pulled on his garment so violently that the dagger the man hid in his loincloth was revealed. "O Messenger of God," 'Usayd cried, "this is the very man with treacherous intent!" When everything became clear, the Companions, 'Usayd foremost, seized

him and he cried, "My blood, take my blood!" The Messenger of God said to him, "Speak the truth; who are you and why have you come? If you speak the truth, your honesty will serve you well, but if you lie, I will come to know what you hide."

"Then, will I be free?" the young Bedouin asked. "Will I be safe?" Having received the security he sought, he began relating everything from the very beginning. The matter was now clear. In spite of this, 'Usayd ibn Hudayr received this youth as a guest in his own home that same night. When they returned to the Prophet's Mosque the following morning, God's Messenger said to him, "I have already given you assurance of safety, so you are now free to go wherever you want, or you may wish to prefer something better than that." The warmth in his expression and the affection in his tone of voice reassured the young man. "What would that be?" he asked. "That you bear witness that there is no god but God, and that I am His Messenger," God's Messenger answered. Seeing now the difference between Mecca and Medina and overcome by saturation of the spiritual effusion and serenity of his presence, the Bedouin said, "I bear witness that there is no god but God, and I also bear witness that you are His Messenger." He then said, "By God, O Muhammad, what a benevolent person you are! I was never so afraid of any man until I saw you, when all my strength left me. Then you perceived my intention, when no rider could have reached you before me to inform you of it. And no one was informed of my intention besides. It was then that I realized that you are protected against all evil that you are Truth and the party of Abu Sufyan is that of Satan." Ibn Sa'd, *At-Tabaqat*, 2/72.

217   Waqidi, *Al-Maghazi*, 120; Ibn Hisham, *Sirah*, 1/391; Ibnu'l Athir, *Usdu'l Ghaba*, 4/288, 289; 5/430

218   Waqidi, *Al-Maghazi*, 140; Ibn Hisham, Sirah, 1/391; Ibn Sa'd, *At-Tabaqat*, 3/310; Ibn Kathir, *Al-Bidaya*, 3/97

219   Ibn Hisham, *Sirah*, 1/403. His name is also mentioned as being 'Amr.

220   'Abdu'llah is reported to have been among the first believers and the first to migrate to Abyssinia. After returning to Mecca following his three-month stay in Abyssinia, he is said to have been held captive and tortured by his father Suhayl ibn 'Amr, which continued until he was forced to utter professions of unbelief, like 'Ammar ibn Yasir, and he was then forcibly brought to Badr to fight against God's Messenger. A Companion with wounded heart, he came and joined the Muslims when the battle started, also bringing with him 'Umayr ibn 'Awf. (Ibn Hisham, *Sirah*, 1/403).

221   Ibnu'l Athir, *Usdu'l Ghaba*, 2/579; Ibn Hajar, *Isabah*, 1/785, 786; Ibn Abdilbarr, *Istiab*, 1/365

222 Ibn Hajar, *Isabah*, 2/1276; Suhayli, Rawdu'l-Unf 3/127; Ibn Abdilbarr, *Istiab*, 2/274

223 Abu al-'As returned to Mecca after Badr and fulfilled his promise to God's Messenger, against all the opposition he faced from the Meccans, sending his daughter Zaynab back to Medina. In the ensuing altercation, Zaynab fell from her camel and miscarried. (Hakim, *Mustadraq*, 4/48; Ibn Abdilbarr, *Istiab*, 4/1854; Al-Halabi, *Sirah*, 2/453). Captured six years later when his caravan was intercepted at al-'Is by the *mustad'afin* who had set up camp there, he was later released when Zaynab learned of the incident and granted him protection. He subsequently returned to Mecca, returned the goods in the caravan to their rightful owners, and returned to Medina where he embraced Islam. God's Messenger renewed his daughter's marriage to Abu al-'As. Ibn Hisham, *Sirah*, 3/204, 205; At-Tabari, *Tarikh*, 2/43.

224 Ibnu'l Athir, *Usdu'l Ghaba*, 2/144; Ibn Abdilbarr, *Istiab*, 1/235; Ibn Hajar, *Isabah*, 1/469; Suhayli, *Rawdu'l-Unf*, 3/126

225 Ibnu'l Athir, *Usdu'l Ghaba*, 2/114; Ibn Hajar, *Isabah*, 1/455; Ibn Abdilbarr, *Istiab*, 1/235

226 Ibn Hajar, *Isabah*, 2/1246; Ibnu'l Athir, *Usdu'l Ghaba*, 4/17; As-Salihi, *Subulu'l Huda*, 4/79 .

227 Ibnu'l Athir, *Usdu'l Ghaba*, 1/614; 6/321; Ibn Hajar, *Isabah*, 4/2400; Ibn Abdilbarr, *Istiab*, 3/178; Suhayli, *Rawdu'l-Unuf*, 3/126

228 Ibnu'l Athir, *Usdu'l Ghaba* 3/170; Ibn Hajar, *Isabah*, 2/1002; Ibn Abdilbarr, *Istiab*, 2/37; Suhayli, *Rawdu'l-Unuf*, 3/127

229 Ibn Hajar, *Isabah*, 1/682; Ibnu'l Athir, *Usdu'l Ghaba*, 2/389; Ibn Abdilbarr, *Istiab*, 1/361; Suhayli, *Rawdu'l-Unuf*, 3/126

230 As-Salihi, *Subulu'l Huda*, 4/79; Suhayli, *Rawdu'l-Unuf*, 3/127; Ibn Sayyidin-Nas, *Uyunu'l-Athar*, 1/333

231 Ibnu'l Athir, *Usdu'l Ghaba*, 3/510; Ibn Hajar, *Isabah*, 2/1203; Suhayli, *Rawdu'l-Unuf*, 3/127

232 Ibn Hajar, Isabah, 3/1633-1634; Ibnu'l Athir, *Usdu'l Ghaba*, 4/402; Ibn Abdilbarr, *Istiab*, 2/295; Suhayli, *Rawdu'l-Unuf*, 3/127

233 Ibn Hajar, *Isabah*, 4/2302; Ibn Abdilbarr, *Istiab*, 3/146; Ibnu'l Athir, *Usdu'l Ghaba*, 6/209

234 According to Muhammad Hamidullah, 186 people became Muslim and migrated to Medina in the twenty-one-year Meccan period (Hamidullah, İslâm Peygamberi, 1/181). Accordingly, $(186 \div 21 = 8.86)$ 8.8 people embraced Islam per year in

Mecca. If we take this figure to be 300—assuming that Hamidullah did not mention those believers that we could not possibly know, or who were not documented—then (300÷21=14.29) 14 people became Muslim each year. So, the number of people reached in a period of approximately ten days was around the number of people won over in two years. Taking into account the second probability, more people were reached in ten days than were reached in a single year.

235 Sources relate that he contributed to the guidance of many people, but provide no figures. Waqidi, *Al-Maghazi*, 120; Ibn Hisham, *Sirah*, 1/391; At-Tabari, *Tarikh*, 3/47. It must not be forgotten that the minimum figure for many in Arabic, is three.

236 For instance, God's Messenger released the captive by the name of Yasar, from the Banu Sulaym who were readying an attack against Medina, without demanding anything in return. Ibn Sa'd, *At-Tabaqat*, 2/31; Ibn Sayyidi'n-Nas, *Uyunu'l-Athar*, 1/391. Similarly, he released the captive taken at Dumat al-Jandal (Waqidi, *Al-Maghazi*, 298) and the individual engaging in espionage for the Jews at Khaybar. Waqidi, *Al-Maghazi*, 446. Interestingly, both individuals who received this favor from God's Messenger embraced Islam. Waqidi, *Al-Maghazi*, 298, 446.

237 The fourth verse of the Qur'anic chapter Al-Hujuraat was to be revealed within this context. At-Tabari, *Al-Jamiu'l-Bayan*, 26/122; Ibn Hanbal, *Al-Musnad*, 3/488; Ibn Sa'd, *At-Tabaqat*, 2/161; Wahidi, *Asbabu Nuzuli'l-Qur'an*, 1/259.

238 Ibn Hisham, *Sirah*, 2/355. It is also reported that Juwayriya's name was Barra and that God's Messenger named her Juwayriya. Muslim, *Sahih*, 3/1687 (2140); Abu Dawud, *Sunan*, 2/81 (1503); Ibn Hanbal, *Al-Musnad*, 1/258 (2334); 1/316 (2902); 6/429 (27461).

239 Waqidi, *Al-Maghazi*, 303, 304

240 Ibn Asakir, *At-Tahzib*, 1/307; Ibnu'l Athir, *Usdu'l Ghaba*, 1/617

241 Among those Abu al-Shahm freed for fifty dinars were two devout Jewish women who each had three children with them. Waqidi, *Al-Maghazi*, 1/523; Salihi, *Subulu'l-Huda wa'r-Rashad*, 5/16.

242 Waqidi, *Al-Maghazi*, 368

243 Waqidi, *Al-Maghazi*, 374

244 At-Tirmidhi, *Seerah*, 17 (1566). 'Ali purchased two slaves, brothers, and employed them in two separate places. When God's Messenger learned of this, he summoned 'Ali to bring those two brothers and instructed him not to separate them. Ibn Hanbal, *Al-Musnad*, 2/155 (760). This is why Muslim scholars have em-

phatically stressed that not only mother and child, but father and child, as well as siblings should not be separated. Some would even take entire families and would keep them in the same place as a result of this Prophetic admonition. Ibn Majah, *Tijarah*, 46 2/755 (2248); Ibn Qayyim, *Zadu'l Maad*, 3/114.

245   Waqidi, *Al-Maghazi*, 372; At-Tabari, *Tarikh*, 3/111; Ibn Hajar, *Isabah*, 4/2512

246   Ibn Hisham, *Sirah*, 2/363

247   In saying this, he meant, "You would have killed one whose kindred, in a blood feud, would seek to avenge his death."

248   Al-Bukhari, *Al-Maghazi*, 70 (4372); Ibnu'l Athir, *Usdu'l Ghaba*, 1/477–478. Meanwhile, Thumama had asked God's Messenger, "The cavalry captured me while I was on my way to make the Lesser Pilgrimage. What do you think I should do now?" The Messenger of God told him to proceed.

249   An-Nisa' 4:24

250   Waqidi, *Al-Maghazi*, 627

251   Ibn Sa'd, *At-Tabaqat*, 1/237

252   Waqidi, *Al-Maghazi*, 627

253   Rejecting all offers made to him one by one, 'Uyayna was to take an old woman from among the captives thinking that she was of a noble status in her tribe and that her ransom would therefore be high. He, however, was to fall prey to his own ambition, and was not able to receive a penny from this prisoner, nor in ransom, and was forced to return empty-handed. As-Salihi, *Subulu'l Huda*, 5/393-394.

254   Waqidi, *Al-Maghazi*, 631–637; Ibnu'l Athir, *Al-Kamil*, 2/139; At-Tabari, *Tarikh*, 3/188–189

255   Just as there would have been among them such people as Abu Dharr whose temperaments did not yet allow them to endure such circumstances, it is also quite likely that there were those that God's Messenger appointed himself. For God's Messenger advised Abu Dharr, who had learned of this and come to Mecca in the early days of Islam, "Conceal this matter and speak of it to no one. Return to your land. When it reaches you that we have been victorious, then you can return" (Al-Bukhari, *Badu'l Khalq*, 4 [3199]). This demonstrates that God's Messenger did not want to increase the tension and that he advised his Companions to avoid situations that would provoke their audience.

256   When this verse was revealed and until Mecca's conquest, migration to Medina was incumbent upon the believers. This was due to the difficulty of the believers' pre-

serving their belief among the Meccan polytheists, in the midst of their mocking, ridicule, and casting doubt in their hearts and minds. On the other hand, it was important for the believers to share the lived experience of Islam's beauty and be receiving the proper learning and training. Moreover, the believers needed to unite and establish their own forces where they could defend their own rights and not leave the granting of these rights to the mercy of the unbelievers. In these verses, those who did not migrate to Medina and instead remained within the polytheist community of Mecca are referred to as those, "*in the state of wronging themselves.*" Some among them preferred their comfort, habits, families, property and possessions, and other interests, to their religion. This is why the excuse, "*We were under such oppression in this land that we could not find a way to faith,*" was not accepted from them. They were thus threatened with an unspeakable end, with punishment in the Fire. However, the grounds of the elderly, the men without means, and the women and children who were truly unable to migrate were accepted in the next verse. The obligation to migrate to Medina during the Age of Happiness ended with the conquest of Mecca, but the verse indicates that where the same conditions as those in the Meccan period exist, migration may still be required. At-Tabari, *Tafsir,* 5/199, 273.

257   At-Tabari, *Tafsir,* 5/273; Tabarani, *Al-Kabir,* 11/272 (11708)

258   At-Tabari, *Tafsir,* 5/273

259   Al-Bukhari, *Adhan,* 128 (804); *Abab,* 110 (6200); *Daawad,* 58 (6393); *Ikrah,* 6940; Muslim, *Masajid,* 54 (675); Ibn Hanbal, *Al-Musnad,* 12/202 (7260)

260   Al-Bukhari, *Shurut,* 15 (2731–2732); Abu Dawud, *Jihad,* 168 (2765); Ibn Hanbal, *Al-Musnad,* 31/213 (18910)

261   Ibn Asakir, *Tarikh,* 39/77, 79; *Sirah,*Al-Halabi, *Sirah,* 3/23; Ibn Qayyim, *Zadu'l Maad,* 3/258; As-Salihi, *Subulu'l-Huda,* 5/46

262   Ibn Asakir, *Tarikh,* 39/77, 79; Bayhaqi, *Dalail,* 4/133; Ibn Qayyim, *Zadu'l Maad,* 3/258; Az-Zahabi, *Tarikh,* 2/219. Due to 'Uthman's not disclosing the Messenger's secret to anyone, we have no information concerning the identity of these individuals. Although the names of such individuals as 'Abbas, his wife Umm al-Fadl, her servant Abu Rafi', and Suhayl ibn Bayda' are enumerated, then it is clear that the numbers were not limited solely to them. It is quite likely that the Companions who came to Badr not of their own accord but forced by the Meccans, the individuals to whom God's Messenger granted immunity, as well as those who migrated to Medina immediately after Conquest, are those who fulfilled this responsibility. It was a necessity of being a believer to desire an unobstructed reunion after twen-

ty-one years of trial, suffering, adversity, longing, and separation.

263   One may think they would not have faced such a predicament had they sat at home and not left their houses. However, it should not be forgotten that they would be giving themselves away to the Meccans in this case. Especially since they were coerced to go to Badr, it quickly becomes apparent that they could not possibly remain in their own homes when war raged outside.

264   Ibn Sa'd, *At-Tabaqat*, 4/98; Al-Balazuri, *Ansab*, 1/210. In Mecca at the direction of God's Messenger, Walid saw a woman carrying food, and suspecting that she knew where 'Ayyash and Salama were imprisoned, asked her where she was going. When she replied indeed that she was taking food to two men who were locked up, Walid followed her, helped them escape, and took them with him to Medina without a single soul finding out. Ibn Sa'd, *At-Tabaqat*, 4/98–99.

265   Ibn Kathir, *Tafsir*, 7/319

266   Ibn Kathir, *Tafsir*, 7/319; Tabarani, *Al-Kabir*, 2/290

267   Some sources identify this individual as Himas. Waqidi, *Al-Maghazi*, 557; Ibn Hisham, *Sirah*, 2/255; Ibn Athir, *Al-Kamil*, 2/247.

268   Ibn Hisham, *Sirah*, 5/67; Ibn Kathir, *Al-Bidaya*, 4/296

269   Although there were individuals whom the Companions suspected of being Muslim, this cannot be said for certain. For instance, it is stated that Suahyl ibn Bayda' was Muslim while in Mecca, that he hid this from the people, and that he was forced to go to Badr. 'Abdu'llah ibn Mas'ud had reported seeing him observing the prayer in Mecca. However, a great many sources state that he embraced Islam after Badr. Ibn Hanbal, *Al-Musnad*, 6/140; At-Tabari, *Tarikh*, 10/46; Al-Baghawi, *Mu'jamu's Sahaba*, 3/104 (1013).

270   While some sources indicate that he became Muslim in later years, after Badr, Khaybar, or the Conquest (Ibn Abdilbarr, *Istiab*, 2/240; Abdu'l Ghani, *Mu'jam*, 11/4050), *this is due to the concealment of his Muslim identity by virtue of his position and the mission he undertook.*

271   Ibn Asakir, *Tarikh*, 26/284; Abdu'l Ghani, *Mu'jam*, 11/4050

272   Hakim, *Mustadraq*, 4/384 (5454); Ibn Asakir, *Tarikh*, 26/286; Ibn Hajar, *Tazhib*, 5/122; Ibn Athir, *Usdu'l Ghaba*, 6/102; Az-Zahabi, *Siyar*, 2/78; Abdu'l Ghani, *Mu'jam*, 11/4050

273   Ibnu'l Athir, *Usdu'l Ghaba*, 7/246; Ibn Abdilbarr, *Istiab*, 2/563. Sources that refer to his acceptance of Islam on the eve of Badr have documented what they could discern from the outside, and propounded this view because it later became ap-

parent that he had become Muslim.

274   Abu Rafi' was 'Abbas' servant in any case. He had presented him as a gift to his nephew God's Messenger. The fact that his master was a Muslim also signified for him a path leading to freedom. Ibn Sa'd, *At-Tabaqat*, 4/73, 74; Ibn Asakir, *Tarikh*, 26/295.

275   Ibn Hanbal, *Al-Musnad*, 3/306 (1787); Ibn Sa'd, *At-Tabaqat*, 8/18 Ibn Abdilbarr, *Istiab*, 2/204. 'Afif ibn Qays, who had not embraced Islam on this day but later on, was later to say in great sorrow, "How I should have wanted to have been a Muslim on that day and to have been the fourth of them!" Hakim, *Mustadraq*, 3/201 (4842).

276   This is how Arabs used to address Medinans at the time, implying the Aws tribe also. Ash-Shimrani, *Akhlaqiyyatu'l Harb*, 61.

277   Ibn Hisham, *Sirah*, 1/266

278   Ibn Hisham, *Sirah*, 1/266

279   Ibn Sa'd, *At-Tabaqat*, 4/23; Ibn Abdilbarr, *Istiab*, 2/240; Ibn Hajar, *Tazhib*, 5/214; Hamidullah, *Wasaiq*, 70; Ibn Athir, *Usdu'l Ghaba*, 3/164; Ibn Asakir, *Tarikh*, 26/286; Abdu'l Ghani, *Mu'jam*, 11/4050

280   Ibnu'l Athir, *Usdu'l Ghaba*, 3/164

281   Ibnu'l Athir, *Usdu'l Ghaba*, 3/164 Ibn Asakir, *Tarikh*, 26/296, 297

282   Ibn Asakir, *Tarikh*, 26/287. The Abu Jahls of the era had established such a climate during the entire Badr process that rejecting or opposing the idea of battle at the time amounted to direct opposition to them.

283   Ibn Kathir, *Al-Bidaya*, 3/323; Tabarani, *Al-Kabir*, 1/308. It has also been suggested that underlying his reluctance to participate in this battle was the dream seen by 'Atika bint 'Abd al-Muttalib. After this, he was afraid and did not dare to go to battle. Waqidi, *Al-Maghazi*, 59; At-Tabari, *Tarikh*, 3/40.

284   Ibn Kathir, *Al-Bidaya*, 3/272

285   Events transpired exactly as Abu Hudhayfa feared. The first person to be killed at Badr was his father. His uncle and brother were also among the slain.

286   This pleased 'Umar greatly, as this was the first time that the Messenger of God had addressed him with this honorific. Ibn Hisham, *Sirah*, 1/371; Ibn Sa'd, *At-Tabaqat*, 4/7; *Sirah*, Al-Halabi, *Sirah*, 2/231; As-Salihi, *Subulu'l Huda*, 4/49

287   Ibn Abi ShaybaIbn Abi Shayba, *Musannaf*, 7/481 (37390); Tabarani, *Al-Kabir*,

3/165

288   Ibn Hisham, *Sirah,* 3/177; Ibn Sa'd, *At-Tabaqat,* 4/7; At-Tabari, *Tarikh,* 2/34; Bay-
       haqi, *Dalail,* 3/141; Ibnu'l Athir, *Al-Kamil,* 2/22; Ibn Hibban, *Sirah,* 1/173; *Si-
       rah,*Al-Halabi, *Sirah,* 2/231; Ibnu'l Athir, *Al-Kamil,* 2/22; As-Salihi, *Subulu'l Huda,*
       4/49

289   The Prophet's uncle 'Abbas was taken captive by a Companion of slight build by the
       name of Abu al-Yasar, while 'Abbas was strongly built. Later, God's Messenger was
       to say to Abu al-Yasar, "O Abu al-Yasar, how did you manage to capture 'Abbas?"
       Overcome with embarrassment, Abu al-Yasar replied, "O Messenger of God, a man
       such as I have never seen either before or afterwards helped me." "A noble angel
       helped you," remarked God's Messenger. Ibn Hanbal, *Al-Musnad,* 5/334 (3310); Ibn
       Sa'd, *At-Tabaqat,* 4/8; At-Tabari, *Tarikh,* 3/41; Ibn Asakir, *Tarikh,* 26/288.

290   Ibn Sa'd, *At-Tabaqat,* 4/9; Ibn Abdilbarr, *Istiab,* 2/240

291   Ibn Hanbal, *Al-Musnad,* 5/141 (3001); Ibn Sa'd, *At-Tabaqat,* 2/16; Ibn Kathir, *Bi-
       daya,* 3/310; Ibn Asakir, *Tarikh,* 26/291-292; Az-Zahabi, *Siyar,* 2/83; Ibn Abi Shay-
       ba, *Al-Maghazi,* 203

292   At-Tirmidhi, *Tafsir,* 9 (3080)

293   Sources indicate that this verse was revealed by Gabriel, who came to inform
       God's Messenger that the Meccan forces were on their way. At-Tabari, *Tafsir,*
       9/199; Tabarani, *Al-Kabir,* 4/174 (4056).

294   Ibn Kathir, *Bidaya,* 3/312; Bayhaqi, *Dalail,* 3/138; Ibn Abi Shayba, *Al-Maghazi,*
       195; As-Salihi, *Subulu'l Huda,* 4/60

295   Bayhaqi, *Dalail,* 3/138; Ibn Abi Shayba, *Al-Maghazi,* 195; As-Salihi, *Subulu'l
       Huda,* 4/60

296   Al-Bukhari, *Itq* 11 (2537); *Al-Maghazi,* 12 (4018); Ibn Sa'd, *At-Tabaqat,* 4/10; Ibn
       Asakir, *Tarikh,* 26/292; Ibn Kathir, *Bidaya,* 3/315

297   In some traditions this expression reads, "I was a Muslim, but the people forced
       me (to fight) against my will." The Messenger responded, "God knows best con-
       cerning your situation. If what you say is true, God will reward you for it. How-
       ever, to all appearances, they were against us; so ransom yourself." Ibn Sa'd, *At-Ta-
       baqat,* 4/10; Bayhaqi, *Dalail,* 3/142; At-Tabari, *Tarikh,* 3/43; Ibn Hibban, *Sirah,*
       1/184; Ibn Asakir, *Tarikh,* 26/288; Hargushi, *Sharafu'l-Mustafa,* 3/14.

298   At-Tabari, *Tarikh,* 3/43; Ibn Asakir, *Tarikh,* 26/288

299   Ibn Sa'd, *At-Tabaqat,* 4/10; At-Tabari, *Tarikh,* 3/43; Bayhaqi, *Dalail,* 3/142, 143;

Ibn Kathir, *Al-Bidaya,* 3/314; Ibn Hibban, *Sirah,* 1/184; Ibn Asakir, *Tarikh,* 26/289; As-Salihi, *Subulu'l Huda,* 4/69; As-Salihi, *Subulu'l Huda,* 4/69

300   Ibn Hanbal, *Al-Musnad,* 5/335 (3310); At-Tabari, *Tarikh,* 3/43; Bayhaqi, *Dalail,* 3/143; Ibnu'l Athir, *Al-Kamil,* 2/26

301   Bayhaqi, *Sunan,* 6/322; *Dalail,* 3/150

302   Hakim, *Mustadraq,* 4/385–386 (5457–5458); Ibn Hisham, *Sirah,* 1/381, 382; At-Tabari, *Tarikh,* 3/41; Bayhaqi, *Dalail,* 3/146; Ibn Kathir, *Al-Bidaya,* 3/324; *Sirah,* Al-Halabi, *Sirah,* 2/258; As-Salihi, *Subulu'l Huda,* 4/67

303   The letter in which 'Abbas informed God's Messenger of the state of affairs and said, "So do what you must when they come to you," reached God's Messenger when he was in Quba'. He had Ubayy ibn Ka'b read the letter to him and concealed its contents until his return to Medina. Al-Balazuri, *Ansab,* 1/313; Ya'qubi, *Tarikh,* 2/31; Hamidullah, *Wasaiq,* 68; As-Salihi, *Subulu'l Huda,* 4/182

304   Waqidi, *Al-Maghazi,* 170

305   Al-Balazuri, *Ansab,* 1/313; Ya'qubi, *Tarikh,* 2/47; As-Salihi, *Subulu'l Huda,* 4/69

306   Waqidi, *Al-Maghazi,* 170

307   Ibn Sa'd, *At-Tabaqat,* 4/12

308   Ibn Athir, *Al-Kamil,* 2/118; *Sirah,* Al-Halabi, *Sirah,* 3/112; Ibn Asakir, *Tarikh,* 26/296, 297

309   Ibn Athir, *Al-Kamil,* 2/118; Al-Halabi, *Sirah,* 3/112

310   When considering the strategies of God's Messenger in the lead up to Mecca's conquest, it is self-evident that the second is Abu Sufyan.

311   Ibn Abdilbarr, *Istiab,* 3/1430

312   Ibn Hajar, *Isaba,* 8/47

313   Umm Hakim was the daughter of Khalid ibn al-Walid's sister Fatima bint al-Walid. She was among the women who came to Uhud with the Meccan forces. After her husband 'Ikrima's martyrdom at Yarmuk, she was to marry Khalid ibn al-Sa'id, and with the post of the tent she had pulled out, killed seven enemy soldiers after the martyrdom of her own husband, on her wedding day. The bridge on which they pitched their tent is today known as the Bridge of Umm Hakim. Mizzî, *Tazhibu'l-Kamal,* 17/40; Ibn Hibban, *Sikat,* 1/221; Ibn Sa'd, *At-Tabaqat,* 4/99; Ibn Abdilbarr, *Istiab,* 4/1933.

314   Ibnu'l Athir, *Usdu'l Ghaba,* 7/226; Ibn Hajar, *Isaba,* 4/2606

315 Ibn Hajar, *Isaba,* 8/193; Ibn Hayyat, *Tabaqat,* 1/299

316 Ibn Asakir, *Tarikh al-Madinati Dimashq,* 69/149

317 Ibn Asakir, *Tarikh al-Madinati Dimashq,* 69/149

318 Al-Imran 3:103; Al-Anfal 8:63; Ibn Hanbal, *Al-Musnad,* 3/57, 76, 77; 3/104, 105, 253; 4/42

319 Abu Sufyan was absent from Badr, as he had gone to Damascus with the Meccan trade caravan. His two sons Hanzala and 'Amr, however, were present, the first of whom was killed and the second taken prisoner. When the entire Meccan leadership was killed at Badr, Abu Jahl most particularly, he remained the undisputed leader in the Mecca of the post-Badr era. The task of representing the spite and vengefulness of the Meccans who were in mourning, henceforth lay on his shoulders. In fact, Abu Sufyan had a more level-headed bearing until the Migration, became rather anxious after it due to economic concerns, but after Badr became a complete "hawk." The first thing he did on the day was to send a hired assassin to Medina to kill the Messenger of God.

320 This is a verse from the Qur'an that we, too, read today and which offers us the same glad tidings—of course for those who take the Prophetic way as their guide and thus aspire to reach all people.

321 On the basis of the expression and style employed in the verse, many exegetes purport that implied in the love and friendship mentioned is this kinship that God's Messenger was to establish with Abu Sufyan. Wahidi, *Tafsir,* 2/1089; Ibn Kathir, *Tafsir,* 4/349, 350; Qurtubi, *Jami',* 18/58; Suyuti, *Durru'l Mansur,* 8/130.

322 Ibn Asakir, *Tarikh,* 3/207; 69/148, 149

323 As with his predecessor, this Negus too embraced Islam and indicated in the letter he wrote to the Messenger of God that should he so wish, he was prepared to renounce the throne, leaving everything behind to come to him in Medina. The Messenger's letter of reply advised him to remain in Abyssinia. Hamidullah, *Wasaiq,* 118–120.

324 The letter includes the Prophet's request for the Negus to send back those of his Companions who had migrated there. Ibnu'l Athir, *Usdu'l Ghaba,* 4/182.

325 Umm Habiba's husband was 'Ubaydu'llah ibn Jahsh, son of the Prophet's paternal aunt. He was also brother to Uhud martyr 'Abdu'llah ibn Jahsh and Zaynab, the wife of God's Messenger, whose marriage was ordained in the heavens. Hamna bint Jahsh, who was married to Mus'ab ibn 'Umayr, was another one of his siblings. He was among the first to profess belief in Islam. Had he been

able to preserve this privileged position, we would have seen his name among those held up by the Qur'an as *Sabiqun al-Awwalun* (the First and Foremost to embrace Islam and excel others in virtue). He was also a person of good standing in his community. This is precisely why Abu Sufyan, one of the two individuals who had their sights set on governing the Mecca of the future, gave his own daughter in marriage to him. But although he was Abu Sufyan's son-in-law, becoming Muslim in Mecca at the time was a nightmare. Like many of his friends, he too migrated to Abyssinia with his family to practice his religion more freely there. However, the migration to Abyssinia was not a migration of three to five days, but lasted for exactly sixteen years. During this time, 'Ubaydu'llah ibn Jahsh's two weaknesses surfaced. To begin with, he severed all contact with Mecca, closed himself off to any news from there, retreated into his own little world, and broke away from the most dynamic sources of spiritual sustenance—the Qur'an and the Messenger of God. Subsequently, he broke off his ties with his friends in Abyssinia and began a solitary existence. According to the statements of God's Messenger, Satan is the associate of one alone, and this loneliness handed him over to his carnal self and Satan. As estrangement happens gradually, he could not see what was happening, until he eventually stumbled into the abyss. The cultural surroundings in which he found himself in the Abyssinia to which he had migrated sixteen years prior, so as to freely practice his faith, began to have greater appeal. Rather, with the emptiness of spiritual nourishment, there came other things to fill the void, and 'Ubaydu'llah ibn Jahsh washed onto different shores. His wife, Umm Habiba, also put pressure on him. But she was a woman who knew how to stand firm; her nourishment was complete and her bearing amongst her friends was as it always had been. Unfortunately, in the end, 'Ubaydu'llah ibn Jahsh died a Christian in the lands to which he went to live freely as a Muslim. Ibn Sa'd, *At-Tabaqat*, 8/77; Ibnu'l Athir, *Usdu'l Ghaba*, 7/116.

326   Known more by her honorific than by her own name, Umm Habiba's actual name was Ramla bint Abi Sufyan. Ibn Sa'd, *At-Tabaqat*, 8/76; Ibn Hajar, *Isaba*, 4/2508; Ibnu'l Athir, *Usdu'l Ghaba*, 7/116; Az-Zahabi, *Siyarul A'lami'n-Nubala*, 1/441.

327   The Negus granted both requests. Firstly, he sent a messenger from among the women to Umm Habiba. A date was set for a wedding feast, with a bridal due being determined for the bride, and a marriage ceremony taking place by proxy in Abyssinia. The Messenger of God was in Medina at the time. See Ibn Sa'd, *At-Tab-aqat*, 8/77; Ibn Hajar, *Isaba*, 4/2508; Ibnu'l Athir, *Usdu'l Ghaba*, 7/117, 4/182.

328   Umm Habiba had seen her husband in a dream before all these events erupted

and clearly understood, on the basis of her interpretation, that things would not go well. Ibn Sa'd, *At-Tabaqat*, 8/77; Ibn Hajar, *Isaba*, 4/2508; Az-Zahabi, *Siyaru'l A'lami'n-Nubala*, 2/221.

329   Underlying Abu Sufyan's joy was without a doubt his son-in-law's conversion to Christianity, as much as expectation of his daughter's return to Mecca.

330   At the same time, Umm Habiba was more closely related to God's Messenger, prior to her marriage, than any of his other wives, and there are a great many examples of cases where this affinity gives rise to others. This is one of the reasons her father, Abu Sufyan, assumed a more amenable stance towards the Prophet until Badr. A notable case is the occasion where Abu Sufyan was seated with Abu Jahl when the Messenger of God passed by. As soon as Abu Jahl saw God's Messenger approach, he turned to Abu Sufyan and said, mockingly, "O Banu 'Abdu'l Shams, look, here comes your Prophet." In spite of their being on the same side (in opposition to God's Messenger), Abu Sufyan said in reply, "Why does it surprise you that that one of us should be a Prophet?" Abu Jahl continued, "While that Prophet arose from those among us who are fewer in number and lower in status, what surprises me is that such a young man should be a Prophet when there are instead all these elders and nobles of seniority and status." The Messenger of God overheard their discussions. He approached and said, addressing them directly, "As for you, Abu Sufyan, it is not that you care for God and His Messenger that you objected, but you did so purely for the sake of your lineage. But you, Abu al-Hakam, you are going to laugh little and weep much." Realizing that he had blundered yet again, Abu Jahl hid his chagrin and attempted to justify his actions, saying scornfully, "O son of my brother, how you have frightened me with your tidings!" Ibn Kathir, *Bidaya*, 3/65; Suyuti, *Hathaisu'l Kubra*, 1/241. When Abu Sufyan learned, on another occasion, that Abu Jahl hurled insults at the Prophet's daughter Fatima and slapped her face, he took Fatima with him, stating that he could not remain silent in the face of such injustice. So affected was God's Messenger by Abu Sufyan's way of dealing with this situation, that he praised him. Qazwini, *Tadwin*, 1/201. There are also narrations that refer to Abu Sufyan's coming to the Messenger of God, at around the same time, and asking him to make the prayer for rain. (Al-Bukhari, *Istisqa*, 2, 13; *Tafsir Surah (30), (44) 5*; Muslim, *Sifatu'l Munafiqin* 39; At-Tirmidhi, *Tafsir Surah (44)* 1. See also Hamidullah, 1/99, 100. On another occasion, their paths crossed and Abu Sufyan, who was traveling with his family, asked his son Mu'awiya to get down from his mount and asked God's Messenger to mount it instead. Seeing this as an auspicious opportunity, God's

Messenger related the beauties of Islam to him throughout the journey and invited him to accept Islam. But this was something that Abu Sufyan was not yet ready for. When the time came to part, God's Messenger went on his own way. Hind, *who witnessed all this, could contain herself no longer and complained, saying, "Did you have my son get off his mount in order to listen to all this!" Abu Sufyan's reply was:* "Do not speak such words, for his is a noble spirit." Ibn Abi Shayba, *Musannaf,* 1/458; Tabarani, *Mu'jamu'l Awsat,* 6/361; Haythami, *Majmau'z Zawaid,* 6/20.

331   Due to the camel's being one of the limited subjects of Arabic literature at the time, their idioms appear to exhibit parallels with this concern. Hakim, *Mustadraq,* 4/24; Ibn Sa'd, *At-Tabaqat,* 8/99.

332   Ibnu'l Athir, *Usdu'l Ghaba,* 7/397

333   Examining the end results of this letter for both Mecca and Abyssinia, it is certainly significant for international relations and should be examined further for its contribution to solving the problems of our day.

334   Abu Sufyan's statement can also be translated as "Terrible things have happened to you since you left me."

335   Waqidi, *Al-Maghazi,* 1/321; Ibn Sa'd, *At-Tabaqat,* 8/99, 100; Ibn Kathir, *Al-Bidaya,* 4/280; *Sirah,*Al-Halabi, *Sirah,* 3/7; Ibn Asakir, *Tarikh,* 69/150, 151

336   Her name is also recorded as being *Hasana, Hamna,* or *'Azza.* Ibnu'l Athir, *Usdu'l Ghaba,* 7/102; Ibn Hajar, *Isaba,* 4/2497

337   An-Nisa 4:23; Al-Bukhari, *Nikah* 20, 25, 26, *Nafaqat* 16; Muslim, *Rada',* 15; Tabarani, *Al-Kabir,* 23/224; Ibn Hajar, *Isaba,* 7/586, 633

338   Due to this independence, some scholars have asserted that Abu Sufyan lost his former power and gave this dissenting group a free hand in the administration of Mecca. Al-Halabi, *Sirah,* 2/653.

339   Safiyya's original name was Zaynab. The name Safiyya, meaning "distinguished," was given to her after Khaybar because the Prophet chose her as his wife. Ibn Hajar, *Fathu'l-Bari,* 7/480.

340   Waqidi, *Al-Maghazi,* 321; Ibn Hisham, *Sirah,* 2/135; Bayhaqi, *Dalail,* 3/408; Al-Halabi, *Sirah,* 2/415

341   Waqidi, *Al-Maghazi,* 329–331; Bayhaqi, *Dalail,* 3/428–429

342   Relations with the Jews can be delineated in four distinct phases: 1. The preparatory process before the Migration, from the beginning of the Messenger's Prophethood in Mecca, 2. The first two years of Migration in which no problems were

experienced, 3. The problematic years until Khaybar, 4. The three and a half years of peace from Khaybar until the Prophet's demise. Unfortunately in our day, the period of peace in which the Messenger of God solved all existing problems is not considered, while Khaybar, where tension had reached a peak, is made the focus. If people today seek a solution and are sincere in their desire, they should focus on the last three and a half years of the Prophet's coexistence with the Jews, in which he resolved every manner of difficulty and dilemma.

343   Khaybar here refers to the course of events beginning with the expedition from Medina in the last days of the month of Muharram, including the siege which continued until the end of Rabi' al-Awwal, and which ended with ultimate victory in the month of Safar. See Waqidi, *Al-Maghazi*, 441; Ibn Hisham, *Sirah*, 2/202; Al-Halabi, *Sirah*, 3/45; At-Tabari, *Tarikh*, 3/144.

344   We cannot possibly understand the greatness of the Messenger's preference on that day without first asking ourselves the question, "What kind of reaction would we, as today's Muslims, have if one of our leaders married a Jewish woman?" One who took such a step today would risk complete rejection in the Muslim world, whoever they may be, and even if they were to accomplish the impossible, that leader would never be favored again. In fact, if, for the sake of argument, God's Messenger were living today and he made the same preference today as he did on that day, then today's Muslims would raise objections. The reason for this is obvious: from the very establishment of the State of Israel, the first news item on the agenda in the Muslim world has been its leader, while the second has always been the issue of Palestine. To be more precise, an overt hostility toward Jews has been shown on the basis of Palestine. This has perpetually been presented as material for domestic politics, and for 65 years the minds of Muslims have been shaped by this enmity. The Muslim world today is at a dead end in this regard and has come to the point where it will not be able to think clearly until the matter of Palestine is resolved. However, upon examination of the interactions that God's Messenger had with the Jews and his practices in this regard, it quickly becomes apparent that problems of any nature can be resolved.

345   Her father Huyayy ibn Akhtab was killed as a war criminal alongside the Banu Qurayza. Waqidi, *Al-Maghazi*, 368; At-Tabari, *Tarikh*, 3/110; Az-Zahabi, *Tarikh*, 2/180.

346   Al-Bukhari, *Salah*, 12 (371); Muslim, *Nikah*, 14; Ibnu'l Athir, *Usdu'l Ghaba*, 7/168; Ibn Kathir, *Al-Bidaya*, 4/214

347   There were bruises on Safiyya's face, around her eye, the day she was brought

to God's Messenger; she had been beaten by her husband for fear that her dream would come true. For when God's Messenger had come all the way to their door during Khaybar, she understood that the dream she saw on her wedding night would be fulfilled and also told her husband so. On the night of her marriage to Kinana ibn Abi'l-Huqayq, she saw a full moon coming from the direction of Medina and falling into her lap. When she related her dream to Kinana the following morning, he immediately understood its meaning and in a fit of rage, exploded, "What is this dream but that you seek the new king of the Hijaz, Muhammad, for a husband!" And more than mere reaction, he gave her such a blow in the face that he blackened her eye. Waqidi, *Al-Maghazi*, 1/674; Ibn Kathir, *Sirah*, 3/374; Ibn Qayyim, *Zadu'l Maad*, 3/290.

348   Waqidi, *Al-Maghazi*, 465; Ibn Hisham, *Sirah*, 2/209; At-Tabari, *Tarikh*, 3/147; Bayhaqi, *Dalail*, 4/232; Ibn Hajar, *Isaba*, 4/2558; Ibnu'l Athir, *Usdu'l Ghaba*, 7/169; Ibn Kathir, *Al-Bidaya*, 4/214

349   Waqidi, *Al-Maghazi*, 465

350   As expressed earlier, Safiyya's former name was Zaynab.

351   This place is referred to as Sadd al-Sahba' or Sadd al-Rawha' in the sources.

352   Safiyya avoided the wedding banquet. When God's Messenger brought it up some six miles distance from Khaybar and inquired as to the reason for her reluctance, Safiyya replied, "Since we were then in close proximity to the Jews, I feared that they might harm you." Ibn Hajar, *Isaba*, 4/2558.

353   Al-Bukhari, *Buyu'*, 111 (2235)

354   Ibn Hisham, *Sirah*, 2/211; Hakim, *Mustadraq*, 5/37 (6865); Bayhaqi, *Dalail*, 4/233; Ibn Sa'd, *At-Tabaqat*, 8/99; Az-Zahabi, *Siyar*, 2/408

355   Ibn Hisham, *Sirah*, 2/211; Ibn Kathir, *Al-Bidaya*, 4/230

356   Ibn Hajar, *Isaba*, 4/2558; Ibn Athir, *Usdu'l Ghaba*, 7/169. Hurt by all these incidents which seemed to come one after the after, Safiyya was on another occasion sitting downheartedly on her own, when God's Messenger noticed she was dispirited. When he asked the reason, he uttered similar words to her on that day too: "You ought to have responded to them by saying, 'My husband is Muhammad, my father is Aaron and my uncle, Moses!'" Waqidi, *Al-Maghazi*, 466; Ibn Sa'd, *At-Tabaqat*, 8/127; Qurtubi, *Al-Jami' li Ahqami'l-Qur'an*, 16/326; Ibn Hajar, *Isaba*, 8/101; Ibn Athir, *Usdu'l Ghaba*, 3/375. It is quite probable that these were perceived to be separate events as a natural outcome of their being transmitted by different narrators.

357 There are accounts to the effect of this wife being Zaynab bint Jahsh. Safiyya is reported to have been deeply grieved by the remark she made on this day. Ibn Hajar, *Isaba*, 4/2558.

358 Ibn Hajar, *Isaba*, 4/2558; Ibn Athir, *Usdu'l Ghaba*, 7/169

359 Ibn Hajar, *Isaba*, 4/2558

360 During the Caliphate of 'Umar, Safiyya's maidservant went to the Caliph and complained that Safiyya sanctified Saturdays, and that she maintained her ties with the Jews. 'Umar asked her about what he had heard. She replied: "I have not loved Saturday ever since God has replaced it with Friday, and I only maintain ties with those Jews with whom I am related through kinship." Safiyya then asked her maidservant what made her say such a thing and she replied, "It was Satan." To this truthful confession, Safiyya responded, "Go, you are free," and thus emancipated her. Ibn Hajar, *Isaba*, 4/2559.

361 At the time, there was a group of eight or ten people who held sway over the Medinan Jews. As a result of the pressures exerted by this group, those members of the community whose hearts inclined to Islam were unable to express their true identities, else they became sitting targets and were immediately ostracized. For instance, while it is evident that Safiyya's brother was Muslim, no mention of his name is made in the canonical hadith collections. Abu Dawud, *Ayman*, 18. When all the narrations concerning the Jews are taken into account, two categories of traditions emerge: in the first one those Jews who came to God's Messenger are named one by one; the second category contains such expressions as, "A group from among the Jews," "Some Jewish scholars," or "A group of Jews." The content of the discussions with those in the first category are negative, tense and unsettling in tone. The atmosphere of the gathering where the second group of people was present, however, is characterized by warmth, friendliness, and the desire to learn. Taking into consideration the pressures from the overbearing faction in question, it becomes clear that the Companions transmitting the conversations did not name the Jews in the second category so as not to reveal the identities of these people who were forced to hide.

362 From another standpoint, it can also be argued God's Messenger experienced various associations in connection with the persons of Umm Habiba and Safiyya. A sensitive, feeling soul such as himself, and the possessor of such a strong memory, whose memories of the past were as fresh and vivid in his mind then as they were when he lived them firsthand, naturally remembered the plots and conspiracies that Abu Sufyan and Huyayy ibn Akhtab formed against him.

However, God's Messenger, who also represented the epitome in respect to his willpower, never made such sentiment felt, by no manner of means projected it to his wives, and not in the least were these associations ever externalized. This goes to show that what matters most in problem resolution is to be able to endure trials and hardship patiently, to hide the distress one suffers from others, and to be able to take lasting steps in the name of sacrifice, even if a bitter pill to swallow.

363   Such contractual agreements are termed *mukatab* in Islamic legal theory. One could manumit the slave or concubine in one's possession by stipulating a certain sum of money to be paid within a specified time. That this was encouraged is also clear. It was considered a gracious gesture toward a slave. Indeed, it is understood that Juwayriya, who was on the receiving end of such a gesture on this day, and witnessed who knows what other scenes during these discussions and deliberations, became Muslim in spite of her father.

364   Ibn Hisham, *Sirah,* 2/183; Az-Zahabi, *Tarikh,* 2/145

365   At the time, the triumphant commander's marrying the wife or daughter of the commander of the vanquished forces was taken to be testament to his victory.

366   Abu Dawud, *Sunan,* 4/22 (3931); Ibn Hanbal, *Al-Musnad,* 6/277 (26408); Hakim, *Mustadraq,* 4/28 (6781); Al-Bayhaqi, *Sunan,* 9/74. The rest of the captives were to gain their freedom through an amount of ransom being paid by fellow members of their tribe, and thus all the captives from the Banu Mustaliq tribe were to be set free.

367   Abu Dawud, *Itk,* 2 (3931); Ibn Hanbal, *Al-Musnad,* 6/277 (26408); Ibn Hisham, *Sirah,* 2/183

368   Ibn Hisham, *Sirah,* 2/184

369   Through the Messenger's marriage with Sawda, who joined the felicitous household following the death of Khadija, a softening began in the attitude of her blood relations and after a certain period of time, this marriage too began to bear fruit. For instance, her brother 'Abd ibn Zama'a himself provides an account of how he tore his hair out on the day that the Messenger of God married Sawda, how he arrived from pilgrimage his hair covered with dirt, and how he thought of this when he came to perceive the truth later, saying in embarrassment, "What a fool I was! The day the Messenger of God married Sawda, I covered my head with dirt!" Ibnu'l Athir, *Usdu'l Ghaba,* 3/510; Ibn Hajar, *Isaba,* 2/1203.

370   Ibnu'l Athir, *Usdu'l Ghaba,* 2/14; Ibn Hajar, *Isaba,* 3/412; Ibn Abdilbarr, *Istiab,*

3/255; Mizzi, *Tazhibu'l Kamal*, 13/119

371 Ibn Hajar, *Isaba*, 8/95

372 These were Lubaba Sughra who was married to Walid ibn al-Mughira, 'Abbas's wife Lubaba al-Kubra, *'Isma' who was married to Ubayy ibn Khalaf, the wife of Ziyad ibn 'Abdu'llah 'Izza, Huzayla who was married to an unnamed Bedouin, Asma who was married to Ja'far, Hamza's wife Salma, Salama the wife of 'Abdu'llah ibn Ka'b, and Zaynab bint al-Khuzayma who was married to 'Abdu'llah ibn Jahsh.*

373 Ibnu'l Athir, *Usdu'l Ghaba*, 2/140.

374 As mentioned earlier, Walid ibn al-Walid had embraced Islam after Badr. After this day, God's Messenger made a special prayer from Medina for Walid, who was subjected to much torture from his brothers including Khalid ibn al-Walid, reciting the *qunut* in his prayers. After he found an opportunity to escape to Medina, he never returned to Mecca. As-Salihi, *Subulu'l Huda*, 4/79.

375 Compiled from different sources and put in order. Even though not in precise chronological order, their content and essence remain unchanged. Ibnu'l Athir, *Usdu'l Ghaba*, 5/423, 424; Bayhaqi, *Dalail*, 4/350; Ibn Kathir, *Al-Bidaya*, 4/258.

376 Ibnu'l Athir, *Usdu'l Ghaba*, 5/423, 424; Bayhaqi, *Dalail*, 4/350; Ibn Kathir, *Bidaya*, 4/258; Suyuti, *Hasais* 1/412; Hamidullah, *Wasaiq*, 85, 86

377 Safwan ibn Umayya was married to Khalid ibn al-Walid's sister Fakhita.

378 Suyuti, *Hasais*, 1/247

379 Az-Zahabi, *Siyaru'l A'lami'n-Nubala*, 2/202

380 Ibnu'l Athir, *Usdu'l Ghaba*, 5/423; Az-Zahabi, *Siyaru'l A'lami'n Nubala*, 2/202

381 Az-Zahabi, *Siyaru'l A'lami'n-Nubala*, 2/202. Similarly, Sawda was from the tribe of Suhayl ibn 'Amr and was married to one of his brothers before she married God's Messenger. At the same time, she was the sister of Hakim ibn Hizam. Zaynab bint Khuzayma, who remained married to God's Messenger for a few months due to her early death, was a member of the Hawazin tribe who took virtually everything that moved with them in their advance against God's Messenger at Hunayn. Ibn Asakir, *Tarikh*, 3/206.

382 Ibnu'l Athir, *Usdu'l Ghaba*, 3/246; 5/427; Ibn Abdilbarr, *Istiab*, 2/61

383 Al-Mumtahana 60:8

384 Waqidi, *Al-Maghazi*, 288; Ibn Hisham, *Sirah*, 2/132; Ibn Sa'd, *At-Tabaqat*, 2/47; At-Tabari, *Tarikh*, 3/93; Ibn Kathir, *Al.Bidaya*, 4/96; Bayhaqi, *Dalail*, 3/386; Az-Zahabi, *Tarikh*, 2/139

385   It rained so much that the Companions came and requested God's Messenger to pray for it to stop. He then raised his hands and said, "O Lord, around us and not upon us!" Al-Bukhari, *Istisqa*, 13 (1020); Ibn Kathir, *Bidaya*, 3/115.

386   It is said that verses 10–16 of the Qur'anic chapter Ad-Dukhan were revealed within this context, or that it describes their attitude. Badr is also identified as the result of this attitude of ingratitude. Al-Bukhari, *Istisqa*, 13 (1020); Ibn Kathir, *Bidaya*, 3/115.

387   The Khaybarites were a worldly-wise people. What is more, they possessed a collective coffer comprising pots filled with gold accumulated over the years. From this they would give loans only to replace the amount taken with the interest they charged on repayment. Following the Conquest, they refused to reveal these treasures and upon the Prophet's urging retrieved them. Waqidi, *Al-Maghazi*, 464; Bayhaqi, *Dalail*, 4/233; Al-Halabi, *Sirah*, 3/62; Az-Zahabi, *Tarikh*, 2/243.

388   Sarahsi, *Mabsut*, 10/92

389   At-Tabari, *Tarikh*, 2/452; Ya'qubi, *Tarikh*, 2/37

390   Ya'qubi, *Tarikh*, 2/37

391   Ibn Asakir, *Tarikh*, 23/441–442; Hamidullah, *Wasaiq*, 76

392   Al-Bukhari, *Istisqa*, 13 (1020); Ibn Kathir, *Bidaya*, 3/115

393   Thumama was captured on his way to make the Lesser Pilgrimage. Pilgrimage was a form of worship observed by certain individuals as a remnant from the time of Abraham, albeit in an altered and even eviscerated form. When he embraced Islam upon his liberation, he referred the matter to God's Messenger, consulting him as to what he needed to do in this situation. The answer he received led him to Mecca.

394   For relevant transmissions, see Al-Bukhari, *Al-Maghazi*, 70; Muslim, *Jihad*, 58; Ibn Hanbal, *Al-Musnad*, 2/452; Ibn Hisham, *Sirah*, 4/285; Ibn Sa'd, *At-Tabaqat*, 5/550; Ibnu'l Athir, *Usdu'l Ghaba*, 1/294, 295; Ibn Abdilbarr, *Istiab*, 1/214, 215; Bayhaqi, *Dalail*, 4/81; Ibn Hajar, *Isaba*, 1/411

395   Ibn Hanbal, *Al-Musnad*, 19/106 (12050)

396   Muslim, *Fadail*, 14 (2312); Ibn Hanbal, *Al-Musnad*, 19/107 (12051)

397   Ibn Sa'd, *At-Tabaqat*, 1/227, 240; Ibn Kathir, *Bidaya*, 5/56, 94. The Hanifa delegation is said to have numbered 19. Ibn Sa'd, *At-Tabaqat*, 1/240.

398   Ibn Sa'd, *At-Tabaqat*, 1/227; Ibn Kathir, *Bidaya*, 5/93

399   Ibn Sa'd, *At-Tabaqat*, 1/238, 239

400   Ibn Sa'd, *At-Tabaqat*, 1/230; Ibn Kathir, *Bidaya*, 5/95

401 Ibn Sa'd, *At-Tabaqat*, 1/234

402 Ibn Sa'd, *At-Tabaqat*, 1/231; Ibn Kathir, *Bidaya*, 5/95

403 Ibn Sa'd, *At-Tabaqat*, 1/228; Ibn Kathir, *Bidaya*, 5/94

404 Gathering that the Negus would pass away, he said to Umm Safiyya, "I have sent gifts of perfume to be presented to the Negus, but I believe that he will pass away before these reach him. If this is indeed the case and these gifts are returned, I will present them to you." Bayhaqi, *Ma'rifatu's Sunan*, 8/200 (11640).

405 Namely, more detailed information as concerned the letter he had written to him, if he would mention "night" upon reading his letter of reply, and whether he noticed anything of interest on his back, between his shoulder blades. Indicating that he saw all three of these things in the presence of God's Messenger, the envoy related that he made a note of each of these. Ibn Hanbal, *Al-Musnad*, 24/418, 419 (15655).

406 In his letter, Heraclius asked, "O Muhammad, in your letter you invite me to a Paradise as wide as the heavens and the earth. Where, then, is the Fire?" Upon reading this, the Messenger of God exclaimed, "Glory be to God! Where is the night when morning comes?"

407 The Messenger of God also invited the aforementioned envoy to Islam, saying, "What about embracing Islam, the pure religion, the religion of your forefather Abraham?" The envoy, however, replied, "I am a messenger from a people, and am on their religion. I would not abandon this religion until I return to them." God's Messenger then recited the verse from the Qur'an: "You cannot guide to truth whomever you like but God guides whomever He wills. He knows best who are guided (and amenable to guidance)." Ibn Hanbal, *Al-Musnad*, 24/418, 419 (15655).

408 Ibn Hanbal, *Al-Musnad*, 24/418, 419 (15655); Ibn Asakir, *Tarikh*, 2/40, 41; Ibn Kathir, *Bidaya*, 5/31

409 Al-Bukhari, *Jihad*, 176 (3053)

410 Ibn Sa'd, *At-Tabaqat*, 1/228; Ibn Kathir, *Bidaya*, 5/94

411 Ibn Sa'd, *At-Tabaqat*, 1/236

412 Ibn Sa'd, *At-Tabaqat*, 1/238, 239; Ibn Kathir, *Bidaya*, 5/50-51; Bayhaqi, *Dalail*, 5/326. God's Messenger saw them off with gifts as they departed from Medina.

413 Ibn Sa'd, *At-Tabaqat*, 1/226; Ibn Kathir, *Bidaya*, 5/93

414 Ibn Hisham, *Sirah*, 2/363; At-Tabari, *Tarikh*, 3/203–204; Ibn Kathir, *Bidaya*, 5/69

415   Al-Bukhari, *Jihad,* 100 (2937); Muslim, *Fadail,* 47 (2524)

416   Ibn Hajar, *Fath* 6/108

417   Ibn Sa'd, *At-Tabaqat,* 3/203; Bayhaqi, *Dalail,* 2/219; Ibn Asakir, *Tarikh,* 44/25

418   Ibn Kathir, *Bidaya,* 5/31

419   Waqidi, *Al-Maghazi,* 640

420   Mughira ibn Shu'ba, who is acknowledged as one of the four geniuses of the Arabs, became Muslim during the battle of the Trench. Ibnu'l Athir, *Usdu'l Ghaba,* 5/238.

421   Ibn Qayyim, *Zadu'l-Maad,* 3/31

422   At-Tirmidhi, *Tafsir,* 20; At-Tabari, *Tafsir,* 16/77, 78; Ibn Kathir, *Bidaya,* 5/53; Hamidullah, *Wasaiq,* 174

423   Ibn Hisham, *Sirah,* 2/507; Ibn Sa'd, *At-Tabaqat,* 1/357; Hamidullah, *Wasaiq,* 174. As result of these meetings God's Messenger granted concessions to all the adherents of this faith by means of the Najran Christians; indeed, these are as important as the Charter of Medina. Al-Bukhari, *Al-Maghazi,* 68; Ibn Kathir, *Tafsir,* 1/369; Hamidullah, *Wasaiq,* 124–126; *Islam Peygamberi,* 1/621.

424   While signs began to appear in earlier periods, the emergence of the hypocrites in the general sense was before Uhud. At a point where the Muslims went to counter the Meccan forces that had come to avenge the defeat at Badr, nearly a third of the army splintered and gave themselves away collectively for the very first time.

425   Ibn Hisham, *Sirah,* 2/172; Waqidi, *Al-Maghazi,* 307

426   Ibn Hisham, *Sirah,* 2/172; Waqidi, *Al-Maghazi,* 309

427   Al-Bukhari, *Tahajjud* 36 (1186); Muslim, *Masajid,* 47 (263)

428   Bayhaqi, *Dalail,* 5/257; Ibn Kathir, *Bidaya,* 5/21

429   Al-Bukhari, *Janaiz,* 85; *Tafsir,al-Baraa,* 12; Muslim, *Fadailu's-Sahaba,* 25

430   Al-Bukhari, *Sawm,* 36 (1946); Muslim, *Sawm,* 92 (1115); Abu Dawud, *Sawm,* 44 (2407); At-Tirmidhi, *Sawm,* 18 (710); Tabarani, *Al-Kabir,* 11/187; Ibnu'l-Arabi, *Ahkamu'l-Qur'an,* 2/361; Tawalisi, *Al-Musnad,* 2/679

431   Bayhaqi, *Dalail,* 6/297; Ibn Kathir, *Mu'jizatu'n-Nabi,* 1/244; Makrizi, *Imta',* 14/105–106; Suyuti, *Hasais,* 1/452

432   An excerpt of Quss ibn Sai'da's sermon: "O people, gather, listen and take note. All who live die and all who die are lost forever. There are many signs in the heavens and lessons on earth from which to draw lesson. The earth is a ground laid out, the

heavens a roof raised up. The stars come and go, seas do not dry out. Dark night, and the sky are divided into constellations. Quss swears a true oath by God that there is a religion that is more pleasing to Him and better than the religion in which you believe. The time of His Messenger's advent is near. His shadow hovers above your heads. How is it that I see people go but not return? Were they content to remain in the place to which they went and did so? Or were they abandoned and now are sleeping? Assuredly, time will reach completion and the written decree, as sharp as a surgeon's knife and as accurate as a precise scale, will be fulfilled." Al-Halabi, *Sirah*, 1/319.

433 Ibn Hisham, *Sirah*, 2/268, 269; Bayhaqi, *Dalail*, 2/415

434 Qadi Iyad, *Shifa*, 1/71

435 Ibn Hisham, *Sirah*, 2/363

436 Placing emphasis on human rights, the Qur'an explicitly pronounces the necessity of administering criminal sanctions in the event of the killing of any individual, whoever they may be. (See an-Nisa' 4:92)

437 See for examples: al-Ma'idah 5/1; at-Tawbah 9/4, 7; an-Nahl 16/95; al-Isra 17/34

438 The term *mu'ahad* employed in the Tradition clearly includes anyone who has been promised protection. Ibn Hajar, *Fathu'l Bari*, 12/259.

439 Al-Bukhari, *Jizya*, 5 (3166); Ibn Hanbal, *Al-Musnad*, 11/356 (6745)

440 Abu Dawud, *Kharaj*, 33 (3052)

441 For other relevant Prophetic Traditions, see Abu Dawud, *Jihad*, 152 (2759); At-Tirmidhi, *Siyar*, 27 (1580); Ibn Hanbal, *Al-Musnad*, 32/182 (19436)

442 Al-Bukhari, *Jizya*, 10 (3172); Muslim, *Hajj*, 85 (1370); Ibn Hanbal, *Al-Musnad*, 15/91 (9173)

443 Just as immunity is a given for a person who is granted safety (*aman*)—in conformity with Islam's clearly delineated criteria in the matter—a Muslim's complicity in crimes committed against such a person has also been deemed unlawful. See Al-Anfal 8:72.

444 Abu Dawud, *Jihad*, 167 (2764)

445 Ibn Hisham, *Sirah*, 1/388

446 On the day of Mecca's conquest, Umm Hani' came to God's Messenger at forenoon. God's Messenger was performing the major ablution, while his daughter Fatima screened him with his garment. When she gave the greeting of peace to God's Messenger, he asked who had arrived. "It is me, Umm Hani'," she replied,

and he welcomed her. After his ablution, he wrapped himself in the garment and offered eight units of Prayer. Umm Hani' then said, "O Messenger of God, the son of my mother, 'Ali, says that he is determined to kill so and so, son of Hubayra, a man whom I have placed under my protection." The Messenger of God said, "We give protection to whoever you have given protection to, Umm Hani." Muslim, *Salatu'l-Musafirin*, 13 (336); Ibn Hisham, *Sirah*, 2/257-258; Ibn Sa'd, *At-Tabaqat*, 2/110; Bayhaqi, *Dalail*, 5/80–81.

447   Al-Bukhari, *Jizya*, 17 (3178)

448   Al-Bukhari, *Jizya*, 22 (3187); *Adab*, 99 (6177); Muslim, *Jihad*, 9 (1735-1738)

449   Muslim, *Jihad*, 35 (1787)

450   Among these delegates were also the men of the false prophet Musaylima the Liar. Abu Dawud, *Jihad*, 166 (166, 2761); Hakim, *Mustadraq*, 2/155. As stated by 'Abdu'llah ibn Mas'ud, the principle of not killing envoys existed at that time also. Bayhaqi, *Kubra*, 9/212.

451   Abu Dawud, *Jihad,* 163 (2758); Ibn Hanbal, *Al-Musnad,* 39/282 (23857); An-Nasai, *Kubra,* 8/52 (8621); Ibn Hibban, *Sahih,* 11/233 (4877); Tabarani, *Al-Kabir,* 1/323 (963); Hakim, *Mustadraq,* 3/691 (6538); Bayhaqi, *Kubra,* 9/244 (18428)

452   The best example of this is the Messenger's reaffirmation of the agreements he made with the Banu Qurayza Jews, in the face of the treachery of some Jewish tribes despite their joint establishment of the State of Medina and their being party to the Medina Charter. Ibn Hisham, *Sirah*, 2/515.

453   By virtue of the Messenger of God being the "first Light" created, and the Ka'ba's status as the first place of worship on earth, they have been deemed "twins." For further reference, see Gülen, *Reflections on the Qur'an, Commentaries on the Selected Verses of the Qur'an*, Tughra Books: NJ, 2012.

454   Ibn Hisham, *Sirah*, 2/196; Bayhaqi, *Kubra*, 9/371 (18809)

455   The terms agreed upon were as follows: 1. There would be no conflict for ten years. 2. Each party would be secure against any threat or injury. 3. God's Messenger and his Companions were to withdraw from Mecca this year to return the following year, where they would be able to visit the Ka'ba. During this visit, they would be able to stay for three nights, bringing in no other weapons than those of a traveler, the swords remaining in their sheaths. 4. If anyone were to come Muhammad without the permission of his guardian, he would be sent back, even if he had accepted Islam; however, if those with Muhammad were to go to the Quraysh, they would not be returned. 5. There would be no bad faith or antagonism between the

parties, with honesty and honor prevailing between them. 6. Anyone wishing to enter into a pact or agreement with either party would be able do so. As soon as the last article was accepted, the Khuza'a promptly announced, "We have concluded a pact and agreement with Muhammad," and thus made clear their side. Ibn Hanbal, *Al-Musnad*, 31/218 (18910); Waqidi, *Al-Maghazi*, 429; Ibn Hisham, *Sirah*, 2/196; Ibn Sa'd, *At-Tabaqat*, 2/74.

456   So highly strung was 'Umar that he approached Abu Bakr telling him similar things. Abu Bakr, the paragon of fidelity, responded to each of his questions with great self-possession, with each of his responses paralleling those of God's Messenger. Abu Bakr then said to 'Umar, "O Ibn al-Khattab, follow what he says, for I bear witness that he is the Messenger of God, and he is not to against His command." "I, too, bear witness that he is the Messenger of God," 'Umar replied. Abu Bakr continued: "God is his helper, and God will never neglect him, so do not depart one inch from his path. By God, he is forever upon the path of truth." It was clear that God was showing the Community of Muhammad, in the person of 'Umar, exactly what kind of attitude needed to be adopted in similar situations. Through this incident, God was demonstrating, in praxis, the importance of not reacting purely on the basis of the concerns of the day, but taking into account all outcomes, and the equanimity that is therefore required. Years later, 'Umar was to bitterly regret all his actions and words on the day, and was to say: "I continued to fast, give in alms, observe supererogatory prayer, and free slaves, for fear of the words I had spoken, until I hoped it would be set right." Abu 'Ubayda ibn al-Jarrah, another Companion witness to 'Umar's insistence on the day, turned to 'Umar and said, "O son of Khattab! Do you not hear what the Messenger of God says? You had better seek refuge in God against the accursed Satan and criticize your own views if you are to criticize." At this, 'Umar was begin to repeat the words, "I seek refuge in God against the accursed Satan," and even if he was not able to attain repose in feeling, yielded in mind and reason, and thereafter strove to repress his emotions. Waqidi, *Al-Maghazi*, 426; As-Salihi, *Subulu'l Huda*, 5/52–53.

457   Bayhaqi, *Dalail*, 4/147; Az-Zahabi, *Tarikh*, 2/224; As-Salihi, *Subulu'l Huda*, 5/54. Yet another veil to the Unseen realm was lifted and perhaps with these words, he wished to evoke the choices that 'Ali would one day be forced to make in the period beginning with the martyrdom of 'Uthman up until his own martyrdom, especially in the incident of the *tahkim* (arbitration). When that day came, 'Ali was to remember these words and say, "So this is the time that the Messenger of God alluded to."

458   Bayhaqi, *Kubra*, 9/370 (18807)

459   An-Nisa 4:128; al-Anfal 8:61

460   'Umar used to say in reference to this incident: "I hoped that he would take the sword and kill his father with it, but the man spared his father and so the matter ended." Ibn Hanbal, *Al-Musnad,* 31/220 (18910); Ibn Hisham, *Sirah,* 2/197; Waqidi, *Al-Maghazi,* 427; As-Salihi, *Subulu'l Huda,* 5/56.

461   Ibn Hisham, *Sirah,* 2/197; Bayhaqi, *Dalail,* 4/171

462   More commonly known by his honorific title Abu Basir, the name of this Companion was 'Utba ibn Usayd. Waqidi, *Al-Maghazi,* 436; Ibn Hisham, 2/199; Bayhaqi, *Kubra,* 9/227; Ibn Hajar, *Isaba,* 4/433 (5401).

463   The sole exception were those female migrants who escaped the violence and persecution in Mecca to seek sanctuary in Medina. They were exempted from this stipulation on the basis of their not being able to defend themselves in the face of aggression, or endure the oppression. Al-Mumtahana 60:10; Ibn Hisham, *Sirah,* 2/201–202; Waqidi, *Al-Maghazi,* 440; At-Tabari, *Tarikh,* 3/134. Furthermore, their marriage to polytheists or their remaining married to them was also prohibited. However, a condition was set that their sincerity of intention should be checked first (see Al-Mumtahana 60:10).

464   Waqidi, *Al-Maghazi,* 436; Ibn Hisham, *Sirah,* 2/200; As-Salihi, *Subulu'l Huda,* 5/61

465   Waqidi, *Al-Maghazi,* 436; As-Salihi, *Subulu'l Huda,* 5/61. Their intent was obvious. They supposed that Abu Basir could find a way out if he were able to kill the ruthless envoys of the Quraysh on the way back, and suggested it to him as a feasible plan of action. 'Umar was more explicit: "You are a fine man, and you have with you a sword!" As-Salihi, *Subulu'l Huda,* 5/61.

466   Abu Basir was thereafter to follow the coastal road to eventually settle in al-'Is. Waqidi, *Al-Maghazi,* 1/625-629; Ibn Hisham, *Sirah,* 2/200; Ibn Abdilbarr, *Istiab,* 4/1614 (2875); Ibnu'l Athir, *Usdu'l Ghaba,* 3/146

467   *Mustad'af* (pl. *Mustad'afin,* literally means "taken to be weak or helpless") is the term used to refer to those Companions who were unable to migrate to Medina and who were forced to remain in Mecca due to the practice of their faith under difficult conditions, and because of their generally being subjected to torture.

468   Waqidi, *Al-Maghazi,* 436-439; Ibn Sa'd, *At-Tabaqat,* 4/134; Bayhaqi, *Dalail,* 4/175; Ibn Abdilbarr, *Istiab,* 4/1614 (2875); Ibnu'l Athir, *Usdu'l Ghaba,* 3/146

469   Just as this Lesser Pilgrimage is known as 'Umra al-Qada' (the Compensatory

Pilgrimage), it is also sometimes called 'Umra al-Qadiyya (the Pilgrimage of the Pact) by virtue of its role in the treaty, 'Umra al-Qisas (the Retaliatory Pilgrimage) as it was done in response to the previous unfulfilled pilgrimage, and 'Umra al-Sulh (Pilgrimage of Peace) for its leading to peace. As-Salihi, *Subulu'l Huda*, 5/196.

470   Waqidi, *Al-Maghazi*, 501

471   Waqidi, *Al-Maghazi*, 502

472   Waqidi, *Al-Maghazi*, 503; Bayhaqi, *Dalail*, 4/328–329

473   Waqidi, *Al-Maghazi*, 503. As soon as the pilgrimage was complete, the Messenger of God ordered around two hundred of his Companions to proceed to Ya'jaj to assume guard, keeping watch over the weapons and other military equipment, so that the men previously on guard there also might go to the Ka'ba. In this way, all those who had set off with the intention of performing the Lesser Pilgrimage would fulfill their duty. Waqidi, *Al-Maghazi*, 505; Ibn Sa'd, *At-Tabaqat*, 2/93.

474   While Barra was her birth name, God's Messenger gave her the name Maymuna. Ibnu'l Athir, *Usdu'l Ghaba*, 7/262.

475   Maymuna was the maternal aunt of Khalid ibn al-Walid. Ibnu'l Athir, *Usdu'l Ghaba*, 7/262

476   Ibn Hisham, *Sirah*, 2/230; Bayhaqi, *Dalail*, 4/330; Suhayli, *Rawdu'l Unf*, 4/117; Az-Zahabi, *Tarikh*, 2/266; As-Salihi, *Subulu'l Huda*, 11/208

477   With the objection of Meccan leadership, God's Messenger met with Maymuna at a place known as Sarif, outside the boundaries of the Sacred Precinct. After the Messenger's departure from the city, Abu Rafi' escorted her to Sarif, where they set up camp for a day. In a providential twist of fate, Maymuna was to pass away years later in this very same place and was to be entrusted to the town where the Messenger's tent had been pitched. Ibnu'l Athir, *Usdu'l Ghaba*, 7/263.

478   Al-Bukhari, *Jizya*, 19 (3184); Ibn Hanbal, *Al-Musnad*, 30/594 (18635); At-Tabari, *Tarikh*, 3/132

479   It was the month of Sha'ban of the eighth year after Migration and only twenty-two months had passed since the signing of the Treaty.

480   Abdu'r Razzaq, *Musannaf*, 5/374

481   They did not merely join the raid, but provided all manner of aid in weapons, mounts, and arms. Moreover, the leading figures of the Meccan leadership covered their faces and disguised themselves despite the dark of the night, so as to

conceal their complicity and thus not be the party which openly violated the agreement. When they realized that the clans to which they had provided every possible assistance for an attack on the Khuza'a had gone too far, some of them stood back, but there was no way of stopping an assault that had already begun. On top of that, they even hunted down and killed those who fled and sought sanctuary in the Ka'ba—the inviolable territory—or who had concealed themselves among their relatives in Mecca. This was, in short, one of the bloodiest days that Mecca had ever seen. Waqidi, *Al-Maghazi*, 1/318; Ibn Sa'd, *At-Tabaqat*, 2/134.

482　　Abu Sufyan was to chance upon Budayl ibn Warqa at a place called 'Usfan, where he would do all that he could to learn whether the Khuza'a had sent word to Medina before him. Despite all his efforts, he did not get the answer he wanted. So he then went to the place where Budayl's camel had knelt and examined its droppings with the stick in his hand. When he found it to contain date stones, he was to conclude that they had been to Medina. Waqidi, *Al-Maghazi*, 536; Ibn Hisham, *Sirah*, 2/247; At-Tabari, *Tarikh*, 2/154.

483　　Waqidi, *Al-Maghazi*, 532–533

484　　Waqidi, *Al-Maghazi*, 536

485　　Despite all the doors being shut on him, he did not lose hope. Instead, he went to Fatima, the daughter of God's Messenger and the wife of 'Ali, and appealed to her to arrange an opportunity for him to meet with her father. This, too, was to prove fruitless. Such was his desperation on the day that he even hoped for help to come from her son Hasan, who was then but in his infancy. Ibn Hisham, *Sirah*, 2/247; At-Tabari, *Tarikh*, 2/154; Ibn Kathir, *Bidaya*, 4/302; Ibn Sayyidi'n Nas, *Uyunu'l Athar*, 2/214; Suhayli, *Rawdu'l Unf*, 4/148.

486　　Banu Kinana is the main tribe the Quraysh had branched out.

487　　Difficult days were in store for Abu Sufyan, when he returned to Mecca to brief the Meccans on developments in Medina. They were already uneasy because of the delay, presuming that he too had embraced Islam. When he related the situation to them, they voiced their displeasure, leaving Abu Sufyan in a bind. Despair was now billowing through the streets of Mecca, and they said to him: "You have consented to something that no one will settle for. You come back with an outcome of avail neither to you nor us. By God, your protection means nothing, and it is easy for them to violate it! As for 'Ali, he has merely toyed with you!" Waqidi, *Al-Maghazi*, 538; *Sirah*, Al-Halabi, *Sirah*, 3/9; Ibn Kathir, *Bidaya*, 4/302–304; *Sirah*, 3/534; Ibn Qayyim, *Zadu'l Maad*, 3/347; *Jami'*, 190.

488   The Conquest forces are said to have been ten or twelve thousand strong. Ibn
      Hisham, *Sirah*, 2/249, 263; Ibn Sa'd, *At-Tabaqat*, 2/102. It is quite likely that while
      they departed from Medina with a force of ten thousand men, this number
      reached twelve thousand with those who joined the forces en route to Mecca.

489   Al-Halabi, *Sirah*, 3/114; As-Salihi, *Subulu'l Huda*, 5/215

490   Ibn Hisham, *Sirah*, 2/251; Al-Halabi, *Sirah*, 3/113; As-Salihi, *Subulu'l Huda*, 5/216

491   'Abbas who was in Mecca until this date, set off as soon as he learned of the Mes-
      senger's departure from Medina and met up with God's Messenger on the way.
      When God's Messenger saw him, he said, "Just as my Prophethood is the last in
      the line of Prophethood, your migration is the last migration." He then had his
      uncle's load sent off to Medina. So, for 'Abbas, who had until then concealed his
      Muslim identity from the Meccans, a period of openly communicating the mes-
      sage began with the end of his mission in Mecca.

492   Some narrations provide an account of 'Abbas' encounter with Abu Sufyan and his
      friends while he traveled towards Mecca on the mule of God's Messenger. 'Abbas
      is described as conversing with them, and subsequently taking Abu Sufyan with
      him, with Abu Sufyan riding on the back of the mount, to God's Messenger. Ibn
      Hisham, *Sirah*, 5/59.

493   Here, we see 'Abbas, who realized that 'Umar was on his way to seek the Messen-
      ger's permission to kill Abu Sufyan, filled with alarm that all his efforts over twen-
      ty-one years would be destroyed at one stroke, and in an eager flurry, he rushed to
      the Messenger's tent lest he should lose for all eternity the Abu Sufyan in whom he
      had devoted so much of his energy to bring to reason and reconcile. Thus, we see
      'Abbas from this moment on as a staunch believer, seizing an opportunity he had
      for the very first time, and conveying the message of Islam fervently and without
      fear.

494   Ibn Hisham, *Sirah*, 2/251-252; At-Tabari, *Tarikh*, 2/157; Ibn Kathir, *Bidaya*, 4/312;
      Ibn Sayyidi'n Nas, *Uyunu'l Athar*, 2/218; Al-Halabi, *Sirah*, 3/113; As-Salihi, *Subu-
      lu'l Huda*, 5/216

495   As-Salihi, *Subulu'l Huda*, 5/217

496   Ibn Hisham, *Sirah*, 2/252; As-Salihi, *Subulu'l Huda*, 5/217

497   Ibn Hisham, *Sirah*, 2/252; Ibn Kathir, *Bidaya*, 4/312; Ibn Sayyidi'n Nas, *Uyunu'l
      Athar* 2/218; Al-Halabi, *Sirah*, 3/114; As-Salihi, *Subulu'l Huda*, 5/217; Ibn Qay-
      yim, *Jami'*, 193

498   As-Salihi, *Subulu'l Huda*, 5/216

499   Waqidi, *Al-Maghazi*, 552; Ibn Hisham, *Sirah*, 2/252; At-Tabari, *Tarikh*, 3/170; Ibn Sayyidi'n Nas, *Uyunu'l-Athar*, 2/218; Ya'qubi, *Tarikh*, 2/39; Ibn Asakir, *Tarikh* 23/447, 448. The point has also been made that one reason for this declaration was that Abu Sufyan had sheltered God's Messenger years earlier from the hellish schemes of the polytheists. On one of these occasions, Abu Sufyan opened his doors to God's Messenger when he was stifled by all the insults and oppression from the Meccans, and gave him a space where he could at least feel some reprieve from their evil. Ibn Hajar, *Isaba*, 3/413; *Tazhib*, 4/361.

500   Ibn Kathir, *Bidaya*, 4/313; Ibn Sayyidi'n Nas, *Uyunu'l Athar*, 2/220; Al-Halabi, *Sirah*, 3/117; As-Salihi, *Subulu'l Huda*, 5/218

501   Ibn Kathir, *Bidaya*, 4/314; As-Salihi, *Subulu'l Huda*, 5/218

502   Ibn Hisham, *Sirah*, 5/58-61; Ibn Hajar, *Isaba*, 3/413, 414; Akk, *Uzama*, 2/1044

503   Ibn Abdilbarr, *Istiab*, 4/1678; Ibnu'l Athir, *Usdu'l Ghaba*, 3/189

504   Waqidi, *Al-Maghazi*, 552; Tabarani, *Al-Kabir*, 8/8; As-Salihi, *Subulu'l Huda*, 5/218

505   The first division to pass in front of Abu Sufyan was the Banu Sulaym, led by Khalid ibn al-Walid. As they passed, a thousand men repeated in unison the proclamation of God's greatness pronounced by their leader. Waqidi, *Al-Maghazi*, 552; Al-Halabi, *Sirah*, 3/116; As-Salihi, *Subulu'l Huda*, 5/219.

506   Waqidi, *Al-Maghazi*, 553

507   Al-Bukhari, *Al-Maghazi* 48; Waqidi, *Al-Maghazi*, 554; Ibn Sayyidi'n Nas, *Uyunu'l Athar*, 2/221; Ibn Qayyim, *Jami'*, 194

508   Contrary to what is commonly thought, the conquest of Mecca did not take place in January, but in July. Those who assert that it took place in the first week of January do not take into account the intercalation of a month (*nasi*) by the Arabs, and the Hijri to Gregorian conversion. To begin with, it is virtually impossible to determine the year in which the inhabitants of the Arabian Peninsula tampered with the calendar and for which duration. Moreover, accounts of the weather being very hot leading up to Mecca's conquest are well known, as is a narration of God's Messenger, who upon seeing a person who was observing the fast on the journey and trying to keep cool with something like a fan, said, "It is not a part of righteousness to fast while traveling." Al-Bukhari, *Sawm*, 36 (1946); Muslim, *Siyam*, 15 (1115); Nasai, *Siyam*, 48 (2258). The key determinant in the date of Mecca's conquest is Tabuk. As is known, Tabuk took place thirteen months after the conquest. Conquest was on the twentieth of Ramadan and God's Messenger advised his Companions not to fast so that they may be vigorous and remain

strong, and demonstrated that he himself was not fasting on the day of conquest by drinking some water. Muslim, *Siyam*, 16 (1120), 15 (1113–1114); Abu Dawud, *Sawm*, 27 (2365); At-Tirmidhi, *Sawm*, 18 (710); Al-Halabi, *Sirah*, 3/112. While on the return from Tabuk, he observed a Ramadan fast in Medina. As indicated in the Qur'an, the hypocrites of the day criticized the departure to Tabuk, using the heat as an excuse (At-Tawbah 9:81; Waqidi, *Al-Maghazi*, 657). Had this event occurred in January, in the middle of winter, there would not have been such a warning for the Companions not to observe the fast. And if there had been, it would not have been taken into consideration, or would not have been conveyed in the text of the Qur'an. Moreover, Ka'b ibn Malik reports remaining behind on the day of Tabuk, and mentions a time when the fruits had begun to ripen and the shade was appealing. Al-Bukhari, *Al-Maghazi*, 79 (4418); Muslim, *Tawbah*, 9. Abu Khaythama's absence from Tabuk follows similar lines and is based on the same reasons. Ibn Hisham, *Sirah*, 2/325; Al-Halabi, *Sirah*, 3/188. The fruit in Medina was no doubt dates and the season for the ripening of dates is the end of June or the beginning of July. If we are to accept Tabuk as an expedition that took place after mid-June, then the Messenger's return to Medina after close to two months and his observing the fast of Ramadan here coincides with the month of July. Given that the conquest of Mecca took place one year prior to this date and again in the month of Ramadan—namely the twentieth of Ramadan—then its occurring in July and not January is plausible. Another fact corroborating this concerns Badr. There is no doubt in the sources in relation to Badr's having taken place on the seventeenth of Ramadan. The accounts of Badr in these sources place particular emphasis on the heat (Ibn Sa'd, *At-Tabaqat*, 2/17). When this is taken into consideration in addition to the points above, then it becomes clear that it coincided with the end of August. Taking into account the 10–11 day difference between the Hijri and Gregorian calendars and also given the possibility of a few days' time lag, it is not difficult to presume that the first of the nine days of Ramadan in which God's Messenger fasted (which was at Badr) coincided with the end of August, and that the eight days fast he observed thereafter coincided with the beginning of the months August and June. In other words, God's Messenger observed his nine Ramadan fasts in the hottest months and longest days of the year.

509   Waqidi, *Al-Maghazi*, 554; Ibn Hisham, *Sirah*, 2/252; Ibn Sayyidi'n Nas; *Uyunu'l Athar*, 2/219; At-Tabari, *Tarikh* 3/170; Ya'qubi, *Tarikh*, 2/39; Ibn Asakir, *Tarikh*, 23/450; Tabarani, *Al-Kabir*, 8/13; Ibn Athir, *Al-Kamil*, 2/120; Ibn Kathir, *Bidaya*, 4/313; Al-Halabi, *Sirah*, 3/116

510   Just as God's Messenger did not allow for any tension or unease in his audience, he was never silent when people sparked such tension and unease. He openly explained the wrong that had been done and, by punishing the perpetrators, crowned his words with his actions. In this way, he established a climate of transparency, in which no one would have any reason for concern or anxiety. There is no Companion of God's Messenger who did wrong and was shown favoritism or protected against the others, or whose faults were brushed over. What is more, when once approached with such a proposal, he was as angered as he could possibly be, and saying, "By the One who has my soul in His hand, if Fatima were to do that..." drew attention to the causes of destruction of a society, and always spoke in the most direct and unequivocal manner. Al-Bukhari, *Al-Maghazi*, 53 (4304); Muslim, *Hudud*, 2.

511   Waqidi, *Al-Maghazi*, 554; Ibn Sayyidi'n Nas; *Uyunu'l Athar*, 2/221; Ibn Asakir, *Tarikh*, 23/454; Ibn Qayyim, *Jami'*, 194; As-Salihi, *Subulu'l Huda*, 5/221–222. It seems to me that this incident has much to teach us about solving those problems in our day that have become gangrenous and that we have not managed to resolve.

512   By means of the steps that God's Messenger took before tangible action had been taken and when emotion had only just been expressed, he says to us, who constantly make the same mistakes and who cannot seem to get back on our feet, "If you seek to solve your problems which have become affected by gangrene, then be as transparent as you possibly can!" Do not cover up the mistakes of others, though they be those closest to you. For that matter, impose even heavier sanctions for their wrongdoings, however small. When people who are required, by virtue of their position, to display even greater sensitivity and care have such outbursts, subject them to a penalty that everyone can see so that similar wrongs are not repeated by those in similar positions."

513   Ibn Hisham, *Sirah*, 4/22, 23; At-Tabari, *Tarikh*, 2/331, 332; Ibnu'l Athir, *Al-Kamil*, 2/228, 229

514   As a case in point, see Al-Furqan 25:63; Ash-Shu'ara 26:215

515   For a sampling of relevant Traditions, see Abu Dawud, *Adab*, 48 (4895); At-Tirmidhi, *Birr*, 82 (2029); Ibn Majah, *Zuhd*, 16 (4176, 4179); At-Tabarani, 9/94 (8512)

516   Waqidi, *Al-Maghazi*, 555; Bayhaqi, *Dalail*, 5/68; Ibn Kathir, *Bidaya*, 4/315

517   Translator's note: He rode with God's Messenger on the camel's back, behind the saddle, in the manner of a pillion rider (*radif*). Customarily, the *radif* would use a cloth wrapped around the hump of the camel as a saddle.

518   Waqidi, *Al-Maghazi*, 561; As-Salihi, *Subulu'l Huda*, 5/239

519   Waqidi, *Al-Maghazi*, 555; Bayhaqi, *Dalail*, 5/68; Ibn Kathir, *Bidaya*, 4/315; As-Salihi, *Subulu'l Huda*, 5/226

520   Waqidi, *Al-Maghazi*, 555; As-Salihi, *Subulu'l Huda*, 5/226

521   Bayhaqi, *Dalail*, 5/66; Ibn Kathir, *Bidaya*, 4/317; As-Salihi, *Subulu'l Huda*, 5/227

522   Al-Bukhari, *Al-Maghazi*, 48 (4280); As-Salihi, *Subulu'l Huda*, 5/227

523   The words that Jabir heard from God's Messenger on this day reminded him of those which he had heard previously, when in Medina. God's Messenger had said, "If God grants us victory, we will camp at Khayf, of the Banu Kinana, where the Meccan polytheists swore an oath of loyalty to unbelief." On that day, the Meccans had come together and pledged to drive the Muslims out of Mecca and leave them to perish. But fate would now have it that God's Messenger and his Companions come to the same place, that which was foretold by God's Messenger, and from the very place the decree of their death was signed, they entered Mecca in victory. Waqidi, *Al-Maghazi*, 558; As-Salihi, *Subulu'l Huda*, 5/230.

524   Waqidi, *Al-Maghazi*, 558-559; As-Salihi, *Subulu'l Huda*, 5/230–231

525   The saints and people of spiritual knowledge view the Ka'ba as the twin of God's Messenger, for while he is the first light that was created, the Ka'ba was the first place of worship on earth.

526   Ibn Majah, *Iqamatu's Salah*, 76 (1076); Waqidi, *Al-Maghazi*, 584

527   Waqidi, *Al-Maghazi*, 569; As-Salihi, *Subulu'l Huda*, 5/250

528   A single circuit during circumambulation (*tawaf*) is referred to in Arabic as *shawt*.

529   There are also reports that the individual who drew out the bucket of Zamzam water was Abu Sufyan ibn al-Harith ibn 'Abd al-Muttalib. Waqidi, *Al-Maghazi*, 560; As-Salihi, *Subulu'l Huda*, 5/235.

530   Ibn Hisham, *Sirah*, 2/258; At-Tabari, *Tarikh*, 3/174; Ibn Kathir, *Bidaya*, 4/324; Ya'qubi, *Tarikh*, 2/39; Ibn Qayyim, *Jami'*, 197

531   There is a narration to the effect of his participation at Hunayn despite not having embraced Islam and his having professed his belief after the victory here. Waqidi, *Al-Maghazi*, 569.

532   The Messenger of God himself informs us of a person's being cleansed of all sin with their acceptance of Islam. See for examples Ibn Hanbal; *Al-Musnad*, 29/315 (17777); Az-Zahabi, *Tarikh*, 2/271.

533   Al-Bukhari, *Tarikh*, 4/103; Ibn Hajar, *Isaba*, 3/214

534   Ibn Sa'd, *Tabaqat*, 4/44, 45; Ibn Hajar, *Isabah*, 2/1230

535   Al-Bukhari, *Salah*, 4 (357); Muslim, *Salatu'l- Musafirin*, 13 (336); Abu Dawud, *Jihad*, 167 (2763); Ibn Hanbal, *Al-Musnad*, 44/460 (26892); Hakim, *Mustadraq*, 4/45, 53

536   Ibn Hajar, *Isabah*, 1/334-335; Ibn AthirIbn Athir, *Usdu'l Ghaba*, 1/644-645; Ibn Abdilbarr, *Istiab*, 1/179–180

537   Ibn Sa'd, *Tabaqat*, 2/153; Mizzi, *Tahzibu'l Kamal*, 5/296; Ibn Abdilbarr, *Istiab*, 3/1084

538   Gülen, *Hidayet Mektubları (Letters of Guidance, II)* (Aug. 14, 2000, Zaman Daily); tr.fgulen.com/content/view/3238/86

539   Waqidi, *Al-Maghazi*, 579; Ibn Sa'd, *Tabaqat*, 7/293; Ibn Athir, *Usdu'l Ghaba*, 5/410; Ibn Abdilbarr, *Istiab*, 3/53

540   Safwan and those like him from the Hudhayl, Aslam, Banu Bakr, and Quraysh who labored under the delusion of resistance, had also prepared to resist the approaching forces and prevent their entry into Mecca. However, finally, the people who came together for this purpose were a small minority and this completely obliterated any hopes that their leaders had entertained.

541   Ibn Hisham, *Sirah*, 5/81; At-Tabari, *Tarikh*, 3/175

542   Ibn Hisham, *Sirah*, 1/390, 391

543   At-Tabari, *Tarikh*, 3/175; As-Salihi, *Subul'ul Huda*, 5/254

544   Waqidi, *Al-Maghazi*, 573; As-Salihi, *Subul'ul Huda*, 5/254

545   The distance between Mecca and Jeddah is approximately 90 kilometers. At the time, this distance would only be traversed in three days. With faster and stronger riding animals, this time could be reduced to two days. Given that 'Umayr traversed the same distance four more times, this equates to a total time of between 8 and 12 days, and this demonstrates the sacrifice that he made.

546   Waqidi, *Al-Maghazi*, 573; At-Tabari, *Tarikh*, 3/175; As-Salihi, *Subul'ul Huda*, 5/254. There are also mentions in some narrations of God's Messenger having given a piece of his shirt or his cloak. Al-Halabi, *Sirah*, 3/42.

547   Waqidi, *Al-Maghazi*, 573; Ibn Hisham, *Sirah*, 2/262; At-Tabari, *Tarikh*, 3/175; Al-Bayhaqi, *Dalail*, 5/97; Ibn Athir, *Usdu'l Ghaba*, 3/24; As-Salihi, *Subul'ul Huda*, 5/254

548   Ibn Hisham, *Sirah*, 5/81; Abdu'r Razzaq, *Musannaf* 7/169, 170

549   Sanawi, *Hayatu's Sahabiyyat*, 426, 427

550   Al-Halabi, *Sahabiyyutu'r Rasul,* 313. Only after Mecca's conquest was Hind able to realize that her cousin Ramla, whom she insulted so deeply at the time, was right. After that day, she would describe Ramla as more intelligent than herself. Al-Halabi, *Sahabiyyutu'r Rasul,* 313.

551   Ibn Asakir, *Tarikhu Dimashq,* 23/459

552   Al-Bayhaqi, *Dalail,* 5/103; Ibn Asakir, *Tarikhu Dimashq,* 23/457

553   Waqidi, *Al-Maghazi,* 532; As-Salihi, *Subul'ul Huda,* 5/205

554   As-Salihi, *Subul'ul Huda,* 5/255

555   Ibn Sa'd, *Tabaqat,* 8/237; As-Salihi, *Subul'ul Huda,* 5/255

556   Ibn Athir, *Usdu'l Ghaba,* 7/281; Al-Halabi, *Sahabiyyutu'r Rasul,* 40

557   Some sources mention that Hind was on the list. At-Tabari, *Tarikh,* 3/173; Al-Halabi, *Sirah,* 3/135.

558   Al-Halabi, *Sahabiyyutu'r Rasul,* 40

559   Her sister, Fatima bint 'Uqba, was married to 'Aqil, the son of the Messenger's paternal uncle Abu Talib. Especially after Badr, she would make constant mention of her father, uncle, and brother. One day she said to her husband, "Where is 'Utba ibn Rabi'a? Where is Shayba ibn Rabi'a? Where is Walid? Her husband replied, "On your left when you enter the Fire." Enraged, Fatima hurled insults at him, and stormed out. Her husband's words caused their separation and brought their marriage to breaking point. She informed 'Uthman of the situation who sent for 'Abbas and Mu'awiya. The three of them ultimately reconciled the couple. Ibn Sa'd, *At-Tabaqat,* 8/189–190; Al-Halabi, *Sahabiyyutu'r Rasul,* 299, 300. Some sources document that Hind appealed to her brother, Abu Hudhayfa. Hakim, *Mustadraq,* 2/528 (3805).

560   At-Tabari, *Tarikh,* 3/174

561   Ibn Sa'd, *Tabaqat,* 8/188–189; At-Tabari, *Tarikh,* 3/174; Al-Halabi, *Sirah,* 3/138

562   Translator's note: The exact words of God's Messenger were "*Marhaban biq*" or, "Welcome to you. I invite you to safety and spaciousness." For the sake of coherence in the context, I have translated the expression as "Greetings to you."

563   There are accounts to the effect that in the message that Hind sent to God's Messenger with her maidservant, she said, "Our sheep breed little this year. Had I possessed them, I would have given them all to you." To this, God's Messenger is said to have replied, by way of supplication, "May God bless you with your sheep and increase its offspring." The maidservant later used to say that they experienced a

sudden increase in the number of those sheep and their offspring that they had not seen before and that the Messenger's blessing became apparent. Hind referred to the same incident saying, "This is due to no other reason than the prayer of the Messenger of God and his blessing." *She also related a dream in which she saw herself perpetually standing in the sun, with the shade close but always unreachable, until God's Messenger drew near and she was able to enter the shade. She thus expressed her praise to God for guiding them to Islam.*

564   For a comprehensive discussion of Hind, see Kesmez, *Fethin Mü'minleri* (The Believers of Conquest), Isik Yayinlari: Istanbul, pp. 155–190.

565   Umm Hakim, was also the daughter of 'Ikrima's paternal uncle by virtue of her being the daughter of Abu Jahl's brother, Harith ibn Hisham. She was among the women who came to Uhud with the Meccan forces. Ibn Athir, *Usdu'l Ghaba*, 7/309.

566   Abu Jahl's daughter, Juwayriya, decided to accept Islam after hearing Bilal's recitation of the Call to Prayer, and pledged allegiance to God's Messenger at Safa along with the other Meccan women. She later married 'Attab ibn Asid, who had, like her, embraced Islam after the Conquest, and whom God's Messenger appointed as the first Governor of Mecca. Ibn Sa'd, Tabaqat, 8/262; Waqidi, *Al-Maghazi*, 1/846; Ibn Athir, *Al-Kamil*, 1/332.

567   Restoring the rights of those who were wronged was also a duty, and the Messenger of God was the most sensitive in this respect, as the representation of justice was an elemental part of his mission. Included within this mission was demanding justice for those in society who did not have a voice. In explaining this aspect of God's Messenger, 'A'isha states that while he forgave all wrongs that were done to his own person, he was second to none in the sensitivity he showed in the matter of applying sanctions for such crimes which threatened the public. Al-Bukhari, *Manaqib*, 23; Muslim, *Fadail*, 77. In our day, we face serious problems in public life due to our failure to intervene at the right time and punish the offender in such offenses which fall into the sphere of "public law" and which threaten the social fabric. People who lose hope in the central authority seek to take matters into their own hands and generate new problems and complications. It must not be forgotten that such offenses simultaneously constitute a violation of the "Rights of God" (*Huquq Allah*).

568   Twelve people were on the execution list at the time. 'Ikrima was one of them. The other men were 'Abdu'llah ibn Hilal al-Khatal, Habbar ibn al-Aswad, *Huwayrith ibn Nuqaydh, Ka'b ibn Zuhayr, Wahshi*, Miqyas ibn Subaba *and*

'Abdu'llah ibn Sa'd ibn Abi Sarh. *Among the women, were Hind bint 'Utba ibn Rabi'a, Sara mawlat of 'Amr ibn Hashim, Fartana and Arnaba (Qurayba and Qurayna). Their execution was ordered because of their crimes against the* rights of God, and as punishment for the killings they perpetrated. However, the Messenger of God waited for those who would intervene for their pardon. For he did not turn away anyone who came to him to request pardon and immunity, and he pardoned all those whose pardon was sought. Had even Abu Jahl lived to see the day and someone intervened on his behalf, God's Messenger would have forgiven him too. After the Conquest of Mecca, only four of these people were put to death (Miqyas ibn Subaba, Huwayrith ibn Nuqaydh, 'Abdu'llah ibn Hilal al-Khatal, and Fartana), while all the others were forgiven and continued their lives as Companions. Waqidi, *Al-Maghazi,* 556; Ibn Hisham, *Sirah,* 2/256, 257; Ibn Sa'd, *Tabaqat,* 2/103; Hakim, *Mustadraq,* 2/62; At-Tabari, *Tarikh,* 3/172–173; Al-Halabi, *Sirah,* 3/130–135; Ibn Abi Shayba, *Musannaf,* 7/404; Al-Bazzar, *Al-Musnad,* 3/350.

569   They had proclaimed on that day, "You will not enter Mecca by force, ever," and incited the Meccans against them. Although the outcome remained unchanged, some of those from the Hudhayl, Aslam, Banu Bakr and Quraysh who entertained such a fancy, had long before begun preparations to prevent God's Messenger from entering Mecca. Ibn Hisham, *Sirah,* 5/67; Ibn Kathir, *Al-Bidaya,* 4/296.

570   When 'Ikrima, who was dealt a crushing blow on that day, heard the Call to Prayer recited by Bilal from atop the Ka'ba, he said, alluding to his father: "Indeed God has been most generous to Abu al-Hakam, for he will not hear this slave say what he says today!" Ibn Kathir, *Al-Bidaya,* 4/232.

571   Waqidi, *Al-Maghazi,* 572; Ibn Asakir, *Tarikhu Dimashq,* 41/63

572   When 'Ikrima was at sea, he lamented, "Well, by God, if the only thing to deliver me at sea is sincerity in faith, then what else can deliver me on land also! How strange it is that the Arabs, the Sassanids, and even this sailor knows of this!" He had begun to grasp the truth to which he had been called all these years and to which he did not respond, and he was heard to say, "The religion that Muhammad has come with must be the true religion!" He cried desperately, "O God, I promise You that if You save me from my present plight, I will go to Muhammad, place my hand in his and will surely find him full of generous forgiveness and mercy." Abu Dawud, *Jihad,* 117; an-Nasai, *Tahrim* 14; Ibn Athir, *Usdu'l Ghaba,* 4/68; Ibn Asakir, *Tarikh,* 41/59.

573   During one of their stops along the way, 'Ikrima sought to be together with his wife

after a long separation, but received a most unexpected response. His wife refused him—the powerful leader of the Quraysh. 'Ikrima looked sternly at his wife to learn the reason for her refusal, and Umm Hakim replied with stoicism and maturity, "No, for I am indeed a Muslim and you are an unbeliever." These words shocked 'Ikrima. Had he heard these at any other time, everyone would have seen how this incident would have ended, but now everything was different. The woman who had waited attentively on him now stood before him as a completely changed person. 'Ikrima saw firsthand the power and transformational capacity of belief. His wife had shown full strength of will, and this doubled her estimation in his eyes. He said, "Surely, a matter that keeps you from me is an important matter indeed." Waqidi, *Al-Maghazi*, 572; Al-Halabi, *Sirah*, 3/133.

574   Hakim, *Mustadraq*, 3/269; Waqidi, *Al-Maghazi*, 572; Ibn Abdilbarr, *Istiab*, 2/269; Ibn Asakir, *Tarikhu Dimashq*, 41/63

575   God declares, "*And do not (O believers) revile the things or beings that they have, apart from God, deified and invoke, lest (if you do so) they attempt to revile God out of spite, and in ignorance*" (Al-An'am 6:108).

576   Al-Bukhari, *Adab*, 4 (5973); Muslim, *Iman*, 38 (90)

577   In a dream, the Messenger of God had seen himself entering Paradise. Upon seeing a grapevine that appealed to him, he asked, "For whom is this?" he received the answer, "It is for Abu Jahl." He could not make sense of this, however, and thought, "What is a person like Abu Jahl doing in Paradise? By God, he can never enter Paradise." He then related his dream to his wife, Umm Salama. When Abu Jahl's son, 'Ikrima, had become Muslim after the Conquest, God's Messenger turned to Umm Salama and said, "O Umm Salama, this was the interpretation of the dream!" He clearly interpreted the grapevine in Paradise that he saw in his dream as 'Ikrima. He then praised God for making the truth of his dream manifest. Al-Bukhari, *Tarikh*, 3/412; Hakim, *Mustadraq*, 3/271; Ibn Hajar, *Isabah*, 2/1280; Ibn Athir, *Usdu'l Ghaba*, 4/70.

578   Hakim, *Mustadraq*, 3/270; Waqidi, *Al-Maghazi*, 1/850; Ibn Abdilbarr, *Istiab*, 3/1082, 1084

579   Waqidi, *Al-Maghazi*, 573; Ibn Abdilbarr, *Istiab*, 2/270; Ibn Asakir, *Tarikhu Dimashq*, 41/64

580   Ibn Asakir, *Tarikhu Dimashq*, 41/60. It is stated in another narration that 'Ikrima raised the matter with God's Messenger himself. Seeing 'Ikrima to be so injured by these remarks, the Messenger of God turned to his Companions and admonished

them saying, "Do not insult his father, for insulting the dead only hurts the living who are left behind." Hannad, *Zuhd*, 2/561; Hakim, *Mustadraq*, 3/269; Ibn Abdil-barr, *Istiab*, 3/1082.

581   Ibn Asakir, *Tarikhu Dimashq*, 41/60, 61

582   Ibn Athir, *Usdu'l Ghaba*, 4/68; Mizzi, *Tahzibu'l Kamal*, 20/247; Al-Halabi, *Sirah*, 3/40

583   Ibn Hajar, *Isabah*, 3/419, 5/772; Ibn Asakir, *Tarikh*, 41/60

584   At-Tabarani, *Al-Kabir*, 17/371; Ibn al-Jawzi, *Sifatu's Safwah*, 1/730; Az-Zahabi, *Siyar A'lami'n Nubala*, 1/323

585   'Ikrima, fresh from polytheism and until then one of its chief advocates, devoted himself to breaking any idol he came across. Whenever he learned of an idol in the house of one of the members of the Quraysh, he would go there and not return until he destroyed it. This is because he was witness to the following injunction of God's Messenger: "Let those who believe in God either destroy the idols in their houses, or cast them into the fire and burn them" (Ibn Hibban, *Sikat*, 2/60). Hence, he dedicated himself to fulfilling this command of God's Messenger and could not rest until he tore down whatever idol he became aware of. Al-Misri, *Ashabu'r Rasul*, 1/403.

586   At-Tabarani, *Al-Kabir*, 17/371; Al-Haythami, *Majmau'z Zawaid*, 9/385; Ibn Kathir, *Al-Bidaya*, 7/34

587   At the Battle of Yarmuk, 'Ikrima looked as though he was raising the battle anew on the front line. On the battlefield where the Muslim forces were hard pressed after protracted fighting, 'Ikrima saved the day. Striking hard at and plunging into the enemy ranks, he shouted at the Byzantine Roman forces: "Would I fight the Messenger of God in every place, yet flee from you today?" Ibn Asakir, *Tarikhu Dimashq*, 41/69.

588   To those who said to him on the day, "Fear God, think of yourself also, and do not destroy yourself so," he was to respond, smiling a strange bitter smile: "Until but recently I exerted myself for al-Lat and al-'Uzza, fighting for the sake of nothing and doing what I am now doing. So am I now to think of taking care of myself, when I have only just found the opportunity to exert myself for God and His Messenger? No, not now, by God, and not ever! Leave me, so that I may now drink of the cup of eternal life in the way of God and His Messenger." These words are said to have been first uttered on the day of Fahl, and he is reported to have attained martyrdom after uttering these. Ibn Athir, *Usdu'l Ghaba*, 4/69; Ibn Asakir, *Tarikhu*

Dimashq, 41/70; An-Nawawi, *Tahzibu'l Asma*, 1/312.

589 At-Tabari, *Tarikh*, 2/338; Ibn Hajar, *Isabah*, 4/593. 'Amr was 'Ikrima's only son. Ibn Athir, *Usdu'l Ghaba*, 4/70; Ibn Hibban, *Sikat*, 3/310.

590 Al-Bayhaqi, *Shuabu'l Iman*, 3/260; Ibn Abdilbarr, *Istiab*, 2/270; Az-Zaylai, *Nasbu'r Rayah*, 2/318. There were four of them and the fourth was another twenty-one-year enemy of Islam, Suhayl ibn 'Amr. Ibn Abdilbarr, *Istiab*, 2/270.

591 The number of Meccans killed is reported to be three.

592 When God's Messenger later discharged his debt, he said, "What a fine reward of a loan is full repayment and gratitude," and prayed for the blessing of his family and possessions. Waqidi, *Al-Maghazi*, 579.

593 Waqidi, *Al-Maghazi*, 579; Al-Bayhaqi, *Dalail*, 5/99

594 Waqidi, *Al-Maghazi*, 579; Al-Bayhaqi, *Dalail*, 5/99

595 Waqidi, *Al-Maghazi*, 579; Al-Bayhaqi, *Dalail*, 5/99; Az-Zahabi, *Tarikh*, 2/324

596 Ibn Hisham, *Sirah*, 2/276; Ibn Hibban, *Sikat*, 2/66

597 Waqidi, *Al-Maghazi*, 573; Al-Bayhaqi, *Dalail*, 5/99; At-Tabari, *Tarikh*, 3/181; Ibn Athir, *Usdu'l Ghaba*, 3/24; Al-Halabi, *Sirah*, 3/153; Ibn Qayyim, *Zadu'l Maad*, 3/468; As-Salihi, *Subulu'l Huda*, 5/312

598 This figure is put at one hundred coats of mail in another narration. Waqidi, *Al-Maghazi*, 573; At-Tabari, *Tarikh*, 2/167; Ibn Hibban, *Sikat*, 2/67.

599 Ibn Hanbal, *Al-Musnad*, 3/400; Abdu'r Razzaq, *Musannaf*, 7/169, 170; 8/180; Hakim, *Mustadraq*, 2/54; Al-Bayhaqi, *Al-Kubra*, 6/88 Ibn Abdilbarr, *Ad-Durar*, 1/225. In confirmation of this, Safwan ibn Umayya's son 'Abdu'r Rahman related that God's Messenger borrowed weapons from his father. Ibn Abdilbarr, *Istiab*, 2/119.

600 Some sources put the figure of those who participated in Hunayn while they were not Muslims at two thousand. Ibn Sa'd, *Tabaqat*, 2/114; At-Tabari, *Tarikh*, 3/181; Ya'qubi, *Tarikh*, 2/41; Al-Halabi, *Sirah*, 3/153; Ibn Qayyim, *Zadu'l Maad*, 3/468.

601 Ibn Hisham, *Sirah*, 2/278; Ibn Abdilbarr, *Istiab*, 3/1333

602 Waqidi, *Al-Maghazi*, 598; At-Tabari, *Tarikh*, 3/182; Ibn Abdilbarr, *Istiab*, 3/1333

603 Al-Bayhaqi, *Sunan*, 7/19

604 At-Tirmidhi, *Manaqib*, 74 (3942); Ibn Hanbal, *Al-Musnad*, 23/50 (14702); Ibn Hisham, *Sirah*, 2/305

605 Waqidi, *Al-Maghazi*, 627; Ibn Sa'd, *Tabaqat*, 2/116; Ibn Qayyim, *Zadu'l Maad*, 3/473

606 Al-Bukhari, *Jihad*, 24 (2821); Ibn Hanbal, *Al-Musnad*, 27/321 (16756); At-Taba-rani, *Al-Kabir*, 2/130 (1551); Al-Bayhaqi, *Al-Kubra*, 6/547 (12933); At-Tabari, *Ta-rikh*, 3/190; Ibn Athir, *Al-Kamil*, 2/269

607 This expression demonstrates that God's Messenger was not addressing only the believers on the day.

608 He was reminding them of the following Qur'anic verse: "*And know that whatever you take as gains of war, to God belongs one fifth of it, and to the Messenger, and the near kinsfolk, and orphans, and the destitute, and the wayfarer (one devoid of sufficient means of journeying).*"

609 Waqidi, *Al-Maghazi*, 627; At-Tabari, *Tarikh*, 3/190; Al-Bayhaqi, *Al-Kubra*, 6/547 (12933); Al-Halabi, *Sirah*, 3/153

610 Abu Dawud, *Jihad*, 143 (2711); Al-Bayhaqi, *Al-Kubra*, 6/547 (12932); Ibn Sa'd, *Tabaqat*, 2/88

611 Al-Bayhaqi, *Al-Kubra*, 6/547 (12933); As-Salihi, *Subul'ul Huda*, 5/395

612 An *'uqiyya* is one twelfth of a *rotl* (or *ritl*). This standard differed according to the city with the Syrian *rotl* being 3.202 grams, while the Beirut and Aleppo *rotl* was equivalent to 2.566 grams.

613 Waqidi, *Al-Maghazi*, 628; Ibn Sa'd, *Tabaqat*, 2/116

614 Waqidi, *Al-Maghazi*, 628; Ibn Athir, *Usdu'l Ghaba*, 2/14; Ibn Abdilbarr, *Istiab*, 2/714; Al-Halabi, *Sirah*, 3/170

615 Waqidi, *Al-Maghazi*, 629

616 According to some sources, God's Messenger wanted to settle his debt to Safwan in Umayya on this day as well as compensate him for his weapons losses at Hu-nayn and Ta'if, and Safwan embraced Islam as a result of his honesty and scrupu-lousness. Ibn Hanbal, *Al-Musnad*, 24/13 (15302).

617 Waqidi, *Al-Maghazi*, 629; As-Salihi, *Subul'ul Huda*, 5/398

618 Ibn Athir, *Usdu'l Ghaba*, 3/25; Ibn Kathir, *Al-Bidaya*, 4/389; Ibn Hibban, *Sahih*, 11/159; Mizzi, *Tahzibu'l Kamal*, 13/183

619 Hakim, *Mustadraq*, 3/317

620 Waqidi, *Al-Maghazi*, 629; Ibn Sa'd, *Tabaqat*, 2/116;At-Tabari, *Tarikh*, 3/190

621 Waqidi, *Al-Maghazi*, 629; Ibn Hisham, *Sirah*, 2/308; Ibn Sa'd, *Tabaqat*, 2/116; At-Tabari, *Tarikh*, 3/190

622 As-Salihi, *Subulu'l Huda*, 5/396, 399

623   When Hakim ibn Hizam was given one hundred camels on the day, he asked God's Messenger for a hundred more and was given them, after which he asked for another hundred, which he also received. The Messenger of God then said to him, "O Hakim ibn Hizam, indeed this wealth is sweet and most appealing. Whosoever takes it with generosity of spirit, this wealth will be for them a source of blessing and prosperity. Whoever takes it with pride will be deprived of its blessings, like the one who eats constantly and is not satisfied. The hand above (that which gives) is better than the one below (that which takes). When you begin giving, start with your dependents." Hakim ibn Hizam was overcome by shame upon hearing these words from God's Messenger. His face changed color, and he was unable to look God's Messenger in the face. He said, "By Him Who sent you with the Truth, I will not ask for anything or take anything from anyone after you!" Al-Bukhari, *Zakah*, 50 (1472); Waqidi, *Al-Maghazi*, 628–629; Al-Halabi, *Sirah*, 3/170; As-Salihi, *Subul'ul Huda*, 5/397.

He remained true to his word until his death. So much so that if he dropped his walking stick while mounted on his camel, he would not ask anyone to pick it up, but would dismount and retrieve it himself. During 'Umar's caliphate, 'Umar set aside a share from the state treasury for him, but he refused to take it. 'Umar held him up as an example for all others in this regard. Al-Bukhari, *Zakah*, 50 (1472); Waqidi, *Al-Maghazi*, 629; As-Salihi, *Subul'ul Huda*, 5/397. While there are reports that he took the two hundred camels at Ji'rana, there are also reports that he left the second hundred. Waqidi, *Al-Maghazi*, 629; As-Salihi, *Subul'ul Huda*, 5/397.

624   Ibn Hisham, *Sirah*, 2/308; At-Tabari, *Tarikh*, 3/190. Some sources indicate that 'Ala' was given fifty camels. Waqidi, *Al-Maghazi*, 629; Ibn Sa'd, *Tabaqat*, 2/116.

625   When 'Abbas ibn Mirdas received fewer camels than the others, he said, "Is my share and that of 'Ubayd my horse [highlighting his being of the cavalry] to be parceled out between 'Uyayna and 'Aqra', while neither Hisn nor Habis excel Mirdas in assembly, and I am not inferior to either of them? But he whom you demean today cannot again be exalted." The Messenger of God then raised the number of camels that he received to one hundred. Muslim, *Zakah*, 46 (1060).

626   Nudayr ibn al-Harith was the brother of Nadr ibn al-Harith who was slain as a polytheist at Badr. When he heard that God's Messenger had given him a hundred camels, he was greatly moved. But he neither requested, nor needed them. He even saw it as degrading in some way. However, as the recipient of this Prophetic gesture in spite of everything that had happened, he came to God's Messenger and professed his acceptance of Islam. He even presented ten of the camels given to him as a gift to

the man who brought him the news. Ibn Athir, *Usdu'l Ghaba*, 5/306, 307; Ibn Hajar, *Isabah*, 3/1999; Ibn Abdilbarr, *Istiab*, 3/20.

627   Waqidi, *Al-Maghazi*, 635; At-Tabari, *Tarikh*, 3/190; Ibn Kathir, *Al-Bidaya*, 4/389; As-Salihi, *Subul'ul Huda*, 5/405

628   Ibn Hisham, *Sirah*, 2/310

629   Waqidi, *Al-Maghazi*, 630; Ibn Hisham, *Sirah,*, 2/310; At-Tabari, *Tarikh*, 3/191; Al-Bayhaqi, *Dalail*, 5/183; Ibn Athir, *Al-Kamil*, 2/271; As-Salihi, *Subul'ul Huda*, 5/401. Sa'd ibn Abi Waqqas elaborates: "The Messenger of God was distributing things to a group of people while I was sitting among them. But he left out a man whom I admired and did not give anything to him. I went to the Messenger of God and spoke privately to him, saying, 'O Messenger of God, what about that person? By God, I see him to be a *mu'min* (believer).' God's Messenger said, 'Better say I see him a muslim (who have surrendered).' I was silent for a while and then what I knew about him became too much for me and I thrice repeated my opinion to him. Each time, however, he responded in exactly the same way.

On the last occasion he said, 'My giving to another is not a measure of my love, for I give to one man and leave out another I love more than him for fear that they might fall headfirst into the Fire.'" Al-Bukhari, *Zakah*, 53 (1478); *Iman*, 19 (27); Muslim, *Iman*, 68 (150); Abu Dawud, *Sunnah*, 16 (4685).

630   Al-Bukhari, *Al-Maghazi*, 56 (4333); Muslim, *Zakah*, 46 (1061); Waqidi, *Al-Maghazi*, 636; Ibn Hisham, *Sirah*, 2/312; Ibn Sa'd, *Tabaqat*, 2/117; At-Tabari, *Tarikh*, 3/192

631   Ibn Hisham, *Sirah*, 2/309

632   Waqidi, *Al-Maghazi*, 630; At-Tabari, *Tarikh*, 3/191. Some sources state the number of camels as forty. As-Salihi, *Subul'ul Huda*, 5/398

633   Embracing Islam on this day, Abu Mahdhura never cut the hair that God's Messenger had stroked and blessed, instead preferring to grow it for the rest of his life as a cherished reminder. Ibn Hanbal, *Al-Musnad*, 24/92 (15376); Hakim, *Mustadraq*, 3/589 (6181); Abdu'r Razzaq, *Musannaf*, 1/457 (1779); Ibn Khuzayma, *Sahih*, 1/200 (385).

634   Ibn Hanbal, *Al-Musnad*, 24/91-100 (15376- 15381); Muslim, *Salah*, 3 (379); Abdu'r Razzaq, *Musannaf*, 1/457 (1779). During this time, he also taught him the statement that is repeated twice exclusively during the Call to the Morning Prayer: "*As-salatu khayrun min an-nawm*" ("Prayer is better than sleep"), and instructed him in reciting the *iqama*, or commencement call for the Prayer. Ibn Hanbal,

Al-Musnad, 24/94 (15378); Abdu'r Razzaq, *Musannaf,* 1/457 (1779).

635   The Call to Prayer that Abu Mahdhura recited initially with Bilal he was later to
continue on his own. In this way, the sweet sound of the Call to Prayer was to
resound in Mecca by means of Abu Mahdhura, and this would become a tradition
handed down from generation to generation, and the Callers to Prayer in Mecca
would always be chosen from his descendants. Hakim, *Mustadraq,* 3/589 (6182);
Al-Bayhaqi, *Al-Kubra,* 1/578 (1846).

636   Al-Qurtubi, *Jami',* 8/97

637   At-Tabari, *Tarikh,* 2/167; Al-Bayhaqi, *Al-Kubra,* 3/409. God's Messenger later appointed him as Provincial Governor of Janad, in Yemen. He was to die in a fall
from his horse close to Mecca, while on his way to support Caliph 'Uthman who
was under siege. Ibn Abdilbarr, *Istiab,* 3/897; Ibn Hajar, *Isabah,* 4/79.

638   The first child of Hisham ibn al-Mughira and Abu Jahl's paternal half-brother.
His father was also referred to, in reference to his name–as "Abu 'Uthman." His
mother was Bint 'Uthman ibn 'Abdu'llah. No offspring are credited to him.

639   The son of Shifa' bint al-Khalid from the Banu Makhzum, he is reported to have
been killed at Badr by his nephew 'Umar. Nevertheless, his sons, Hisham and
Khalid, came to God's Messenger on the day of Mecca's conquest and became
Muslim, when God's Messenger patted Hisham's chest three times and prayed, "O
Lord, remove suspicion and jealousy from him." Ibn Hisham, *Sirah,* 1/416; Ibn
Athir, *Usdu'l Ghaba,* 2/128; 5/377; Ibn Abdilbarr, *Istiab,* 1/235.

640   The full brother of Abu Jahl, died as an unbeliever at Badr.

641   Abu Jahl's maternal brother and the first of Abu Jahl's siblings to accept Islam.
His mother was Duba'a bint 'Amir. Migrated to Abyssinia to escape Meccan persecution and, on his return after the first migration, was subjected to all kinds
of torture and imprisonment in unrest led by Abu Jahl. God's Messenger offered
supplication for him due to the hardships he endured. A Qur'anic verse was revealed about him and those in his situation: "*Why, then, should you not fight in
the cause of God and of the oppressed, helpless men, women, and children, who cry
out: 'O Lord! Bring us out of this land whose people are oppressors, and appoint
for us from Your Presence a protector, and appoint for us from Your Presence a
helper!'*" (An-Nisa 4:75). Due to the oppression, he was only able to migrate
to Medina after Khandaq. He participated in the Battle of Mu'ta immediately
afterwards. Died in the Damascus surrounds during the Caliphate of Abu Bakr,
either in Mardj al-Suffar or Ajnadayn. Ibn Athir, *Usdu'l Ghaba,* 2/531–532; Ibn

Hajar, *Isabah,* 1/755–756; Ibn Abdilbarr, *Istiab,* 1/351–352.

642　Born of Shifa' bint al-Khalid, 'Ayyash ibn Abi Rabi'a and Salama ibn Hisham embraced Islam and endured the same persecution. When they embraced Islam, God's Messenger had not yet entered the house of Ibn Arqam. Unable to withstand the severe oppression led by Abu Jahl, he migrated to Abyssinia with his wife, Asma' bint Salama, and his son 'Abdu'llah was born there. When he returned to Mecca after this first migration, he suffered torture and persecution. When he set off to Medina, Abu Jahl and his cohorts followed him and forced him to return from Quba'. Following this and owing to the hardship endured by other Companions facing a similar predicament, God's Messenger made a special invocation (*qunut*)—recited in the standing position of the Prayer—for these people who became known as *mustad'afin,* or "the helpless and dispossessed." He was martyred at Yarmuk. Ibn Abdilbarr, *Istiab,* 2/254.

643　The full brother of Abu Jahl and the most active in opposition to Islam of all his brothers. He was so important that poems were composed in his name. He held high standing in his tribe. He fought against Islam at Badr, Uhud, and Khandaq, and wherever Abu Jahl led the polytheists against the believers. He acted as Abu Jahl's agent and instrument of the torture inflicted their own brothers on Salama and 'Ayyash. He accompanied Abu Jahl to Quba' to bring 'Ayyash back to Mecca for persecution. He heads the list of those who carried the banner that Abu Jahl relinquished at Badr, until the conquest of Mecca. He wanted to mount resistance on the day of Conquest also, but went into hiding when he realized it was in vain. Abu Talib's daughter Umm Hani' granted protection to him when 'Ali, her own brother, was on his trail. As a result, he cast aside his bad character traits and habits, and thereafter led a most careful and upright life. The Messenger of God gave him one hundred camels also, as one of the *mu'allafa al-qulub.* From that day forth, Harith ibn Hisham led a very honest and virtuous existence, until his martyrdom at Yarmuk with his uterine brother 'Ayyash ibn Abi Rabi'a. He left thirty-two grandchildren; his grandson Abu Bakr, from his son 'Abdu'r Rahman, is one of the renowned Seven Jurists (*al-fuqaha' as-sab'a*) of his era. Ibn Abdilbarr, *Istiab,* 1/178–180; Ibn Athir, *Usdu'l Ghaba,* 7/309.

644　Khalid ibn Hisham was among those taken captive at Badr—which proved to be the end for Abu Jahl—and was released on ransom. His antagonism was to continue until Mecca's conquest after which he took his place among the *mu'allafa al-qulub.* Ibn Hajar, *Isabah,* 2/250; Ibn Athir, *Usdu'l Ghaba,* 2/144; Ibn Abdilbarr,

Istiab, 1/235. Some sources mention his having died as an unbeliever in accounts of his brother Salama's life. Ibn Abdilbarr, *Istiab,* 1/351.

645 The son of Shifa' bint al-Khalid from the Banu Makhzum, 'Abdu'llah ibn Abi Rabi'a was Abu Jahl's diplomat brother. He went to Abyssinia with 'Amr ibn al-'As to bring back to Mecca the migrant believers in Abyssinia. He is known by the honorific Abu 'Abdu'r Rahman. After Mecca's conquest, the Messenger of God borrowed from him a sum of approximately ten thousand dirhams. In discharging his debt on the return from Hunayn, God's Messenger said: "May God bless your family and your property. Surely, the reward for a loan is full repayment and acknowledgment" (Al-Bukhari, *Al-Kabir,* 5/9–10). He was a sincere Muslim from that day forth. 'Umar appointed him commander of the army. He continued in the same role during the caliphate of 'Uthman and was martyred during a siege. Ibn Athir, *Usdu'l Ghaba,* 3/233.

646 Abu Jahl is said to have had three more sons by the names of Zurara, Tamim, and 'Alqama. Bint 'Umayr ibn Ma'bad bore Abu Jahl's two sons Zurara, who was known by the honorific Abu 'Alqama, and Tamim, known as Abu Hajib, while 'A'isha bint al-Harith was the mother of 'Alqama. Abu 'Alqama (Zurara) was killed at Yemen.

647 Until the conquest of Mecca, Abu Jahl's son 'Ikrima took after his father. After Badr he became one of the leading opponents of Islam. He was one of the foursome who began to undermine and bypass Abu Sufyan, who softened in his stance against God's Messenger following his daughter Umm Habiba's marriage to him. He wanted to offer resistance on the day of Conquest, but fled to Yemen when he realized that he would not be able to do so. He was one of the few individuals who had been condemned to punishment by death on the day. In spite of this, however, his wife and cousin Umm Hakim, who had pledged allegiance to God's Messenger and sought immunity for her husband, pursued him all the way to Yemen and brought him back to God's Messenger, where he embraced Islam. He did not care for the wealth that was offered to him upon his acceptance of Islam, only asking God's Messenger for his prayer and supplication for his forgiveness from God. The promise he made to God's Messenger was that he would exert himself in the name of Islam twice as much as he exerted himself in unbelief. History attests to his having lived as a believer who was faithful to his promise. Having spent the most fruitful twenty years of his life against the Qur'an, 'Ikrima was in his later life to cling onto the Qur'an, place it against his face, and weep inconsolably saying, "The Word of my Lord!" In standing by his word, 'Ikrima went from battle to battle for the sake of his cause giving his

everything, whether physically or by the financial resources at his disposal until he was martyred at the Battle of Yarmuk, in one of the fiercest ever encounters with the Byzantine Romans, along with his son and two uncles.

648 Abu Jahl is reported to have had five daughters by the names of Sakhra, Asma', Hind, Umm Hakim, and Umm Sa'id. Sakhra was born of Arwa bint Abi al-'Is, and was given in marriage to Abu Sa'id ibn al-Harith. Arwa bint Abi al-'Is was also the mother of Asma', and she married Walid ibn 'Abd Shams. Ibn Sa'd, Tabaqat, 5/153. Hind was the wife of Hisham ibn al-'As ibn Wa'il. Ibn Hajar, *Isabah*, 8/193. It is reported that Abu Jahl's daughter Umm Sa'id was more masculine in her walk and bearing. Ibn Hajar, *Isabah*, 8/220.

649 Born of Arwa bint Abi al-'Is, Juwayriya—who is also known as Jamila—is the famous Muslim daughter of Abu Jahl whom 'Ali wanted to take in marriage, but this was not permitted by God's Messenger. She is the narrator of the Prophetic Tradition: "The best of my community are those living in my generation, then those who will follow them, and then those who will follow them." Ibn Athir, *Usdu'l Ghaba*, 1/1326; 7/59 (6803); Ibn Hajar, *Isabah*, 7/559. After the Conquest, the newly appointed Governor of Mecca 'Attab ibn Asid took her in marriage. Following his death, Juwayriya married Aban ibn Sa'id. Ibn Sa'd, *Tabaqat*, 8/262; Ibn Athir, *Usdu'l Ghaba*, 7/54, 57.

650 Ibn Sa'd, Tabaqat, 8/206; Ibn Hajar, Isabah,4/2473. Also known as Safiyya or Hunfa'. Born of Arwa bint Abi al-'Is. She accepted Islam on the day of the Conquest and pledged allegiance to God's Messenger. Subsequently, she married Abu Jahl's old friend Suhayl ibn 'Amr, who was known as the eloquent orator of the Quraysh and who became Muslim after the Conquest. Ibn Sa'd, *Tabaqat*, 5/44. Some sources refer to her marrying 'Usama. This marriage presumably took place following Suhayl's martyrdom. Ibn Sa'd, *Tabaqat*, 8/262. Suhayl ibn 'Amr's son Anas, who had a disability, was born of Abu Jahl's daughter Hunfa'.

651 Asma' bint Mukharriba, is known by the epithet Umm Mujalid and is also referred to Hanzaliyya, in reference to her tribal affiliation. She embraced Islam after the Conquest and passed away close to two years after the demise of God's Messenger (634 CE). Abu Jahl was also occasionally called Ibn al-Hanzaliyya after his mother. This epithet, however, was more often than not used disparagingly. The Meccans who disliked Abu Jahl referred to him by the pejorative "Ibn al-Hanzaliyya" from time to time, thus making their displeasure clear to him. It is striking that while the Messenger of God likens the believer who recites the Qur'an to the citrus fruit, sweet in taste and aroma, he likens the hypocrite who does not recite the Qur'an

to a *hanzala*, a fruit bitter in taste and smell. *Hanzala* is also known as the fruit of Abu Jahl. Al-Bukhari, *Fadailu'l Qur'an*, 17; Muslim, *Salatu'l Musafirin*, 243. In some sources, Asma' bint Mukharriba emerges as the mother of Abu Jahl's son, 'Ikrima, in which case Abu Jahl's wife and not his mother embraced Islam.

652   Ibn Athir, *Usdu'l Ghaba*, 1/645

653   Hakim, *Mustadraq*, 4/265 (5106)

654   'Ikrima ibn Khalid died in Mecca after 'Ata' ibn Abi Raba.

655   Ibn Hisham, *Sirah*, 1/385

656   In depicting his pitiable state, the Qur'an declares: *"May both hands of Abu Lahab be ruined, and ruined are they! His wealth has not availed him, nor his gains. He will enter a flaming Fire to roast; and (with him) his wife, carrier of firewood (and of evil tales and slander). Around her neck will be a halter of strongly twisted rope"* (Tabbat 111:1–5).

657   Ibn Sa'd, *Tabaqat*, 4/44, 45; Ibn Abdilbarr, *Istiab*, 2/251; Ibn Hajar, *Isabah*, 2/1230; Al-Halabi, *Sirah*, 3/139

658   Also reported as having the name Subay'a, Durra embraced Islam in Mecca in spite of her father and her husband Harith ibn 'Amir. She migrated to Medina after he husband was killed at Badr. She remained as a guest in the house of Rafi' ibn al-Mu'alla for some time, and then married Dihya al-Kalbi. Mention is also made of her having married either Usama or Zayd ibn Haritha. Known for her poetic personality, Durra is the narrator of three Prophetic Traditions. Ibn Hajar, *Isabah*, 4/2498; Ibn Athir, *Usdu'l Ghaba*, 7/103, 139.

659   Ibn Hajar, *Isabah*, 4/2578

660   Ibn Hajar, *Isabah*, 4/2478

661   Relevant narrations have been provided in combination. Ibn Hajar, *Isabah*, 4/2498; At-Tabarani, *Al-Kabir*, 24/257 (656); Ibn Abdilbarr, *Istiab*, 4/1835.

662   Became Muslim after being taken captive at Badr and released on ransom. Ibn Abdilbarr, *Istiab*, 3/44.

663   Walid ibn al-Mughira's most active son Khalid ibn al-Walid, embraced Islam after the Treaty of Hudaybiya. Ibn Athir, *Usdu'l Ghaba*, 2/141; Ibn Abdilbarr, *Istiab*, 1/232). However, some sources indicate that he embraced Islam after Khaybar. Ibn Hajar, *Isabah*, 1/469.

664   Among the *mu'allafa al-qulub* and became Muslim after Mecca's conquest. Ibn Abdilbarr, *Istiab*, 3/35.

665 Also known as Lubaba Sughra and is the mother of Khalid ibn al-Walid. One of nine sisters, among whom was Mother of the Believers, Maymuna. Thus, she is also sister-in-law to God's Messenger, 'Abbas, and Ja'far. Ibn Athir, *Usdu'l Ghaba*, 7/247.

666 Wife of Safwan ibn Umayya, embraced Islam a month before him on the day of Mecca's conquest. Ibn Abdilbarr, *Istiab*, 3/250.

667 Became Muslim at Mecca's conquest. Ibn Sa'd, *Tabaqat*, 8/205; Ibn Abdilbarr, *Istiab*, 3/249; Ibn Athir, *Usdu'l Ghaba*, 7/226.

668 Accepted Islam in the year that Mecca was conquered. Ibn Athir, *Usdu'l Ghaba*, 7/406. Wife of Safwan ibn Umayya. Safwan ibn Umayya had six contractual wives. When he came to the presence of God's Messenger, the latter told him that he could only remain married to four, and that he needed to divorce two of them. Ibn Athir, *Usdu'l Ghaba*, 7/397.

669 Umm Habib is also the paternal aunt of Khalid ibn al-Walid. Ibn Athir, *Usdu'l Ghaba*, 7/301.

670 Accepted Islam in the year that Mecca was conquered. Ibn Hajar, *Isabah*, 4/2658.

671 Busra bint Safwan ibn Nawfal was 'Uqba ibn Abi Mu'ayt's uterine sister. Ibn Athir, *Usdu'l Ghaba*, 7/38.

672 Born of the same mother as 'Uthman ibn 'Affan, Walid embraced Islam during the year of Conquest. Ibn Abdilbarr, *Istiab*, 3/46; Ibn Hajar, *Isabah*, 3/2086; Ibn Asakir, *Tarikh*, 63/218; Ibn Athir, *Usdu'l Ghaba*, 5/420.

673 Became Muslim at Mecca's conquest. His son Aban was also a Companion of God's Messenger. Ibn Abdilbarr, *Istiab*, 1/235, 3/46; Ibn Hajar, Isabah, 4/2658; Ibn Athir, *Usdu'l Ghaba*, 2/134; Ibn Asakir, *Tarikh*, 7/364.

674 Embraced Islam with his other brothers, Walid and Khalid, at Mecca's conquest. Washed his hands before coming to the presence of God's Messenger and pledging allegiance to him. Ibn Athir, *Usdu'l Ghaba*, 7/134; Ibn Hajar, *Isabah*, 3/2086; Ibn Abdilbarr, *Istiab*, 2/198.

675 She embraced Islam in the Meccan period despite the oppression and persecution of her father, and migrated to Medina after Hudaybiya. Born of 'Uthman ibn 'Affan's mother. When the Meccans came to ask for her hand in marriage, a Qur'anic verse was revealed in relation to her, and while God's Messenger returned the men to the Meccans, as was stipulated in the Treaty of Hudaybiya, he did not give her up to the Meccan polytheists. Later married Zayd ibn Haritha. Ibn Athir, *Usdu'l Ghaba*, 1/158, 7/376; Ibn Abdilbarr, *Istiab*, 3/283.

676   Ibn Hajar, *Isabah*, 4/2658

677   Mother of Abu Hudhayfa. 'Utba divorced her upon her acceptance of Islam and she married 'Amr ibn Sa'id. She was among those to migrate to Abyssinia. Ibn Athir, *Usdu'l Ghaba*, 7/222.

678   His real name was Musham, and Hashim or Hushaym, Abu Hudhayfa was one of the early Muslims. He was among the first wave of migrants to Abyssinia. He is also the son-in-law of Suhayl ibn 'Amr. Ibn Athir, *Usdu'l Ghaba*, 5/269, 378, 380; 6/68.

679   Considered one of the leading Companions, Abu Hashim's real name was Shayba. He became Muslim at the conquest of Mecca. He was Mu'awiya's maternal uncle, the half-brother with Abu Hudhayfa from his father's side, and the uterine brother of Mus'ab ibn 'Umayr. Their mother was Khannas bint Malik. Mu'awiya once came to visit him, as he had been stabbed, and found him to be weeping. So he asked him whether he wept from the pain, or because of something worldly that he could not acquire. Shaking his head, he replied, "It is neither." He then said that the Messenger of God once said to him, "O Abu Hashim, there will come a time when you will see wealth of the tribes divided among the people, and all you will need of that will be a servant and a mount to ride in the way of God." He then said that the time had indeed come, but that he had accumulated much more than what God's Messenger advised him would be enough, and that this was the reason for his weeping. Abu Hashim lost an eye at Yarmuk. His son Sulayman was also one of the Prophet's Companions. Ibn Athir, *Usdu'l Ghaba*, 2/144, 550, 644; Ibn Abdilbarr, *Istiab*, 3/176.

680   He named his daughter Hind also. Ibn Hajar, *Isabah*, 4/2478; Ibn Athir, *Usdu'l Ghaba*, 7/283. Another one of his daughters, Fatima, was among the first migrants. Ibn Athir, *Usdu'l Ghaba*, 7/283.

681   Also Mu'awiya's maternal aunt, Fatima declared her acceptance of Islam on the day of Mecca's conquest. Ibn Athir, *Usdu'l Ghaba*, 7/223; Ibn Abdilbarr, *Istiab*, 3/249.

682   Ibn Asakir, *Tarikh*, 70/231

683   The wife of Aban ibn Sa'id ibn al-'As. When her husband died at Ajnadayn she returned to Medina and married Talha ibn 'Ubayd Allah. Ibn Abdilbarr, *Istiab*, 3/265; Ibn Athir, *Usdu'l Ghaba*, 7/287; Ibn Hajar, *Isabah*, 4/2663.

684   Abu Sufyan's wife and mother of Mu'awiya. Accepted Islam in the year that Mecca was conquered. Ibn Abdilbarr, *Istiab*, 3/263; Ibn Athir, *Usdu'l Ghaba*,

7/281.

685   Wife of 'Uthman. They migrated together. Ibn Abdilbarr, *Istiab*, 3/217.

686   Wife of 'Ali's other brother 'Aqil ibn Abi Talib. Ibn Athir, *Usdu'l Ghaba*, 7/222.

687   Embraced Islam at Mecca's conquest. Ibn Hajar, *Isabah*, 1/45; Ibn Abdilbarr, *Istiab*, 1/74; Ibn Athir, *Usdu'l Ghaba*, 1/223.

688   Ibn Hajar, *Isabah*, 3/1845

689   Wife of 'Adi ibn Nawfal who became Muslim at Mecca's conquest. Ibn Athir, *Usdu'l Ghaba*, 4/17; Ibn Hajar, *Isabah*, 1/45.

690   Mother of Safwan ibn Umayya. Ibn Athir, *Usdu'l Ghaba*, 7/209.

691   Became Muslim at Mecca's conquest. One of the *mu'allafa al-qulub*. Ibn Athir, *Usdu'l Ghaba*, 1/180.

692   Ibn Abdilbarr, *Istiab*, 2/119

693   Embraced Islam at Mecca's conquest. There are accounts to the effect of 'Umar's having condemned him to exile in Khaybar, and that he in turn joined the Byzantine Romans and converted to Christianity. Ibn Abdilbarr, *Istiab*, 1/399.

694   One of the strongest in opposition to God and His Messenger, Safwan ibn Umayya wanted to resist Meccan occupation, but escaped when he realized that he would not be able to do so. 'Umayr ibn Wahb, who he had sent to assassinate God's Messenger at Badr, brought him back from Jeddah and obtained immunity for him from God's Messenger. When Safwan ibn Umayya requested two months' time to consider the invitation to accept Islam, God's Messenger gave him double. He embraced Islam two months later. His wife Baghum bint al-Mu'adhil also embraced Islam on the day of the Conquest. Ibn Athir, *Usdu'l Ghaba*, 7/39; Ibn Abdilbarr, *Istiab*, 1/397–399.

695   Ibn Sa'd, *Tabaqat*, 8/211; Ibn Athir, *Usdu'l Ghaba*, 7/43

696   Ibn Hajar, *Isabah*, 4/2661

697   Embraced Islam at Mecca's conquest. Ibn Abdilbarr, *Istiab*, 2/37.

698   Ibn Hajar, *Isabah*, 4/2653

699   Ibn Athir, *Usdu'l Ghaba*, 4/39

700   Migrated to Abyssinia and was martyred at Yarmuk. Ibn Athir, *Usdu'l Ghaba*, 4/338.

701   Migrated to Abyssinia. Ibn Athir, *Usdu'l Ghaba*, 5/307.

702   On the day her father was killed, she wrote a letter to the Messenger of God,

expressing her grief in verse. When this letter and poem reached God's Messenger, he wept so much that his beard became wet and said, "Had this poem reached me earlier, I would have forgiven him." Ibn Abdilbarr, *Istiab*, 3/252; Ibn Athir, *Usdu'l Ghaba*, 7/235.

703   One of the *mu'allafa al-qulub*. Accepted Islam in the year of Mecca's conquest and was martyred at Yarmuk. Waqidi, *Al-Maghazi*, 629; Ibn Asakir, Tarikh, 62/101–105.

704   One of the *mu'allafa al-qulub*. Ibn Abdilbarr, *Istiab*, 1/342.

705   Ibn Athir, *Usdu'l Ghaba*, 5/424

706   Migrated to Abyssinia. Ibn Hisham, *Sirah*, 1/206.

707   Ibn Hajar, *Isabah*, 2/1151; Ibn Athir, *Usdu'l Ghaba*, 3/424; Ibn Abdilbarr, *Istiab*, 2/126

708   When God's Messenger saw her as a Muslim, he said, "All praise be to God Who brings forth the living from the dead." Ibn Abdilbarr, *Istiab*, 3/209; Ibn Hajar, *Isabah*, 4/2478; Ibn Athir, *Usdu'l Ghaba*, 7/312.

709   Came to God's Messenger after the Conquest, at Ji'rana, sought his forgiveness, was forgiven, and subsequently accepted Islam. Ibn Athir, *Usdu'l Ghaba*, 5/360.

710   One of the migrants to Abyssinia. Ibn Hisham, *Sirah,*, 1/205; Ibn Sa'd, *Tabaqat*, 4/90.

711   The person responsible for intercepting the daughter of God's Messenger Zaynab and causing her miscarriage. Became Muslim at Mecca's conquest. Ibn Athir, *Usdu'l Ghaba*, 5/426; Ibn Hajar, *Isabah*, 3/2090.

712   His mother was the sister of Mother of the Believers Umm Salama, Qurayba bint Abi Umayya ibn al-Mughira. Embraced Islam at Mecca's conquest. Ibn Athir, *Usdu'l Ghaba*, 3/246; 5/427; Ibn Abdilbarr, *Istiab*, 2/61.

713   Ibn Athir, *Usdu'l Ghaba*, 3/510

714   Accepted Islam in the year that Mecca was conquered. Waqidi, *Al-Maghazi*, 571; Ibn Hajar, *Isabah*, 4/2658.

715   Wife of 'Amr ibn al-'As and mother of 'Abdu'llah ibn 'Amr. His mother was the sister of al-'As ibn Wa'il. Became Muslim at Mecca's conquest. Ibn Athir, *Usdu'l Ghaba*, 7/122; Ibn Hajar, *Isabah*, 4/2514.

716   Ibn Athir, *Usdu'l Ghaba*, 7/350

717   Among the migrants to Abyssinia. Ibn Athir, *Usdu'l Ghaba*, 1/233; Ibn Hisham, *Sirah*, 1/205; Ibn Hajar, *Isabah*, 1/50.

718 Of the migrants to Abyssinia. Ibn Athir, *Usdu'l Ghaba,* 1/430.

719 One of those to migrate to Abyssinia. Ibn Athir, *Usdu'l Ghaba,* 1/382; Ibn Abdilbarr, *Istiab,* 1/360.

720 Among the Companions who migrated to Abyssinia. Ibn Athir, *Usdu'l Ghaba,* 1/430, 2/472; 1/313; Ibn Abdilbarr, *Istiab,* 2/61.

721 Ibn Athir, *Usdu'l Ghaba,* 1/430

722 One of those who migrated to Abyssinia. Ibn Athir, *Usdu'l Ghaba,* 1/430, 3/207; Ibn Abdilbarr, *Istiab,* 1/360.

723 One of the early believers and among the migrants to Abyssinia. Ibn Athir, *Usdu'l Ghaba,* 1/430, 2/389; Ibn Abdilbarr, *Istiab,* 1/360.

724 He was one of the migrants to Abyssinia. Ibn Athir, *Usdu'l Ghaba,* 1/596; Ibn Abdilbarr, *Istiab,* 1/360.

725 One of the early Muslim pioneers in Mecca, and one of those who migrated to Abyssinia. Ibn Athir, *Usdu'l Ghaba,* 1/596; Ibn Abdilbarr, *Istiab,* 1/360.

726 She was among those to migrate to Abyssinia. Came to Medina after Uhud. Ibn Athir, *Usdu'l Ghaba,* 1/689.

727 His son al-'As was killed at Badr. Sa'id, the son of al-'As, also became Muslim. Ibn Abdilbarr, *Istiab,* 1/313.

728 One of the early Muslims and also one of the migrants to Abyssinia. Khalid's daughter Umm Khalid and his wife Umayna bint Khalaf are also Companions. Ibn Athir, *Usdu'l Ghaba,* 2/124; 7/313; Ibn Abdilbarr, *Istiab,* 1/229.

729 One of the migrants to Abyssinia. Ibn Abdilbarr, *Istiab,* 2/161.

730 Ibn Abdilbarr, *Istiab,* 2/161

731 Embraced Islam prior to the conquest of Mecca. Ibn Abdilbarr, *Istiab,* 1/313.

732 One of those who God's Messenger commanded to record everything in writing. Ibn Abdilbarr, *Istiab,* 2/97.

733 Ibn Sa'd, *Tabaqat,* 8/206

734 One of the first to believe. Migrated to Abyssinia. Came to Mecca when he heard that God's Messenger had migrated to Medina and was held prisoner by his tribe. Was only able to reunite with the Messenger of God after Khandaq. Hakim, *Mustadraq,* 4/262 (5099); Ibn Hisham, *Sirah,* 1/207; Ibn Abdilbarr, *Istiab,* 3/33; Ibn Athir, *Usdu'l Ghaba,* 5/375.

735 In the eighth year after the Migration, in the month of Safar, Khalid ibn al-Walid

and 'Uthman ibn Talha came to God's Messenger and embraced Islam. One of the four individuals considered prodigies among the people of the time and is a Companion who made a huge contribution to Islam in later years. Ibn Athir, *Usdu'l Ghaba*, 4/232–234. His son 'Abdu'llah accepted Islam before him. 'Abdu'llah sought permission to write everything he heard, and God's Messenger granted him permission to record the Prophetic Traditions saying, "For I speak nothing but the truth." Ibn Athir, *Usdu'l Ghaba*, 3/345; Hakim, *Mustadraq*, 4/262 (5099).

736   Hakim, *Mustadraq*, 4/262 (5099)

737   Abu Sufyan and his sons Mu'awiya, 'Utba, Yazid, 'Anbasa, Ziyad, as well as his daughters Durra (also known as 'Azza or Khansa'), Ramla (also Hind, best known by her honorific Umm Habiba and is one of the Mothers of the Believers), Hind, Hamna, Habiba, Juwayriya, Umayna, Zaynab, Umm Hakam, and Sakhra embraced Islam. Ibn Sa'd, *Tabaqat*, 7/284, 285; 8/190-191; Ibn Asakir, *Tarikh*, 70/219; Ibn Athir, *Usdu'l Ghaba*, 7/132, 307; Ibn Hajar, *Isabah*, 4/2497.

738   Like their father, Hakim ibn Hizam's sons 'Abdu'llah, Hisham, Khalid, and Yahya, came after Mecca's conquest and became Muslim. His wife, Zaynab bint al-'Awwam ibn Khuwaylid, the sister of Zubayr ibn al-'Awwam, was also Muslim. His brother Khalid was among the early Muslims. Hakim, *Mustadraq*, 4/611 (6097); Ibn Athir, *Usdu'l Ghaba*, 2/118; Ibn Hajar, *Isabah*, 4/2523; Ibn Abdilbarr, *Istiab*, 1/237, 1/235, 2/50.

739   This is to say, the Abu Jahls of the time rushed to judgment, acting upon the force of their emotion, became the victim of these, and failed to avail themselves of the opportunity that came right to their door, and repeatedly at that.

740   Al-Bukhari, *Fadailu'l Qur'an*, 6 (4707); *Tafsir Surah* 54/6 (4876); An-Nasai, *Fadailu'l Qur'an*,1/65; Abdu'r Razzaq, *Musannaf*, 3/352; Ayni, *Umdatu'l Qari*, 20/21; Ibn Hajar, *Fathu'l Bari*, 1/319; 9/39

741   Az-Zarkani, *Manahil*, 1/185–232

742   Al-Bukhari, *Mazalim*, 4; *Ikrah*, 7; Abu Ubayd, *Al-Amsal*, 142

743   God's Messenger made this statement when he noticed slight tension between the one of the Helpers and one of the Migrants during the Banu Mustaliq campaign, wanting to prevent the spark from growing into a full-blown conflict that would involve all the Helpers and Migrants, as used to be the case during the Age of Ignorance. The matter thereby ceased to be a problem. Al-Bukhari, *Mazalim* 5; Muslim, *Birr* 62 (2584), 63; Ibn Hanbal, *Al-Musnad*, 3/323 (14507); Al-Bayhaqi, *Sunan*, 10/231; Al-Baghawi, *Sharhu's Sunnah*, 13/96–98.

744   These four esteemed individuals mentioned by God's Messenger were Mu'adh ibn Jabal, 'Abdu'llah ibn Mas'ud, Ubayy ibn Ka'b, and Salim, the freed slave of Abu Hudhayfa. Al-Bukhari, *Manaqibu'l Ansar*, 16 (3808); Muslim, *Fadail*, 22 (2464); At-Tirmidhi, *Manaqib*, 38 (3810); Ibn Hanbal, *Al-Musnad*, 11/76 (6523).

745   At-Tirmidhi, *Manaqib*, 33 (3790–3791); Ibn Majah, *Fadail*, 17 (154)

746   Ibn Hanbal, *Al-Musnad*, 36/333 (22007)

747   Things turned out exactly how God's Messenger had foretold. Mu'adh returned to Medina immediately after receiving the news of the Messenger's demise and visited him at his grave and Mosque, just as he had said. Ibn Sa'd, *Tabaqat*, 3/441; Al-Faraj, *Ashabu'n Nabiyy*, 406.

748   Ibn Hanbal, *Al-Musnad*, 1/320 (188); At-Tirmidhi, *Tafsir*, 6 (3043); Ibn Sa'd, *Tabaqat*, 2/144

749   Muslim, *Fitan*, 5 (2889); Abu Dawud, *Fitan*, 1 (4252); At-Tirmidhi, *Fitan*, 14 (2176); Ibn Majah, *Fitan*, 9 (3952)

750   Some narrations contain the phrase "this affair," while some refer to, "this religion." Ibn Hanbal, *Al-Musnad*, 4/103 (16998); Hakim, *Mustadraq*, 4/477 (8326); Al-Bayhaqi, *Kubra*, 9/181 (18400). Others still contain both these expressions. Al-Haythami, *Majmau'z Zawaid*, 6/7 (9807); At-Tabarani, *Musnadu'sh,Shamiyyin*, 2/79 (951). One narration includes the expression, "the word of Islam." Ibn Hanbal, *Al-Musnad*, 6/4 (23865).

751   Ibn Hanbal, *Al-Musnad*, 4/103 (16998); 6/4 (23865); Hakim, *Mustadraq*, 4/476 (8324), 477 (8326); Al-Bayhaqi, *Kubra*, 9/181 (18399, 18400); Al-Haythami, *Majmau'z Zawaid*, 4/15; 6/7 (9807); 6/14; 8/262, 263; At-Tabarani, *Al-Kabir*, 2/58 (1280); *Musnadu'sh Shamiyyin*, 2/79 (951); Ibn Munda, *Iman*, 2/982 (1085); Ibn Hibban 15/91 (6699); Al-Hindi, *Kanzu'l-Ummal*, 1/469 (1345). Its transmitter Tamim al-Dari makes the following addition after narrating the Tradition: "I observed this in my own family: those who were graced with Islam attained good, honor and esteem, while those of them who chose to remain in unbelief attained ignominy, humiliation, and were forced to pay the *jizya*." Ibn Hanbal, *Al-Musnad*, 4/103 (16998; Hakim, *Mustadraq*, 4/477 (8326); Al-Haythami, *Majmau'z Zawaid*, 4/15; 6/7 (9807); 8/262, 263; At-Tabarani, *Al-Kabir*, 2/58 (1280).

752   It is also apparent that God's Messenger expressed similar sentiments to his daughter Fatima on the return from the Farewell Pilgrimage. As was always the case, he first went to the Mosque where he offered the supererogatory Prayer of Thankfulness, and then called upon his daughter. When she saw her father, for

whom she had been waiting for such a long time, she was overtaken with joy. So much like her father in compassion, Fatima at once began to experience jubilation and sorrow and was not able to contain her emotions. She wept inconsolably. At this, God's Messenger turned to her and said, "My beloved daughter, why are you weeping?" She said, "You who are dearest to me! I see you, your color pale, you beard disheveled and your clothes worn and shabby. It is clear that you have suffered much!" He looked at her with compassion, and said tenderly, "Do not weep, for God has sent your father with such a mission that the day will come when He will affect every house of mud or brick, and every tent of animal hide and hair, within the reaches of night and day (i.e. whether urban or rural), bringing to it either honor or humiliation, until this mission is fulfilled just as night (inevitably) comes." Hakim, *Mustadraq,* 3/169; Al-Haythami, *Majmau'z Zawaid,* 8/262, 263; At-Tabarani, *Al-Kabir*, 22/225, 226 (595, 596); *Musnadu'sh Shamiyyin,* 1/299, 300; Abu Nuaym, *Hilyah,* 2/30; 6/123.

753   The Companions remaining in the Hijaz were barely ten percent.

Event	# of Muslims	# of Enemy	Casualties		Prisoners of War	Duration (hours)	Total Time (hours)	Death Penalty	BATTLES AND EXPEDITIONS DURING THE TIME OF THE PROPHET
			Muslim	Enemy					
BATTLES WITH MAJOR CONFRONTATION									
Badr	314	950	14	70	70	3	20	0	Muslims departed from Medina on the 8th or 12th of Ramadan; the battle took place on Friday 17 Ramadan; Muslim army 300, 313, or 318 vs Meccans which were around 1,000 men. According to Ibn Kathir, Muslim martyrs are 11, Meccan casualties are 39, 40, more than 70 or 88.
Uhud	700	3,000	70	23	0	5	7	0	Departure on the 3rd or Friday 14 Shawwal. Battle took place on the 11th or Saturday 15 Shawwal. Those martyred at Uhud are said to be 44, 49, 65, or 68. The figures for the Meccan casualties are 16, 19, or 22.
ACTIVITIES WITH MINOR OR NO CONFRONTATION									
Khandaq	3,000	10,000	6	5	0	n.a.	30	0	According to other reports casualties for Muslims are 4 or 5, for non-Muslims 3, 4, or 8, and the duration is 15 days.
Hunayn	12,000	20,000	4	1	6,000	4	4	0	With the 2,000 Meccans who joined the ranks despite the fact that they were not Muslim, this figure reaches 14,000. While the sources do not indicate how many people were killed from the enemy, there is a report to the effect of a woman being killed where Khalid ibn al-Walid was present.
Conquest of Mecca	12,000	n.a.	2	12	0	n.a.	9	4	The reported number martyred was 3. While the sources concentrate on 12 casualties, the figures 13, 24 and 28 have also been suggested. One of those receiving capital punishment for a crime was a woman.
Ta'if	12,000	unknown	12	0	0	n.a.	18	0	The siege is reported to have lasted for 15 or 30 days.
Tabuk	30,000	n.a.	0	0	0	n.a.	50	0	No confrontation
Second Badr	1,500	n.a.	0	0	0	n.a.	15	0	No confrontation
COUNTER-INSURGENCY OPERATIONS									
Banu Qaynuqa	unknown	unknown	1	1	700	unknown	15	0	
Banu Nadir	unknown	unknown	unknown	unknown	0	unknown	6	0	Some sources suggest that the siege lasted 15 days.
Banu Qurayza	3,000	unknown	2	unknown	0	unknown	15	400	Some sources record 3 people as martyred. The woman killed, by the name of Nubata, was executed in retaliation for the Companion she had killed. The figures for those killed from the Banu Qurayza are put at 600, 700, 750, 800 or 900.
Khaybar	1,600	10,000	15	93	0	unknown	30	1	The number of martyrs is indicated to be 18 or 21. A woman by the name of Zaynab received capital punishment for poisoning a Companion.
Wadi al-Qura	1,585	unknown	0	11	0	unknown	4	0	
Fadak	100	unknown	0	0	0	unknown	unknown	0	
Tayma'	unknown	unknown	0	0	0	unknown	unknown	0	

Event	# of Muslims	# of Enemy	Casualties		Prisoners of War	Duration (hours)	Total Time (hours)	Death Penalty	Patrols/Expeditions
			Muslim	Enemy					
Bi'r al-Ma'una	70	unknown	69	0	0	unknown	unknown	0	Figures suggested for the Companions martyred are 21 and 39.
Raji'	10	100	10	0	0	unknown	unknown	0	The number of Companions martyred is reported to be 6 or 7.
Abwa' (Waddan)	70	unknown	0	0	0	unknown	15	0	
Buwat	200	100	0	0	0	unknown	unknown	0	
Dhu al-'Ashira ('Ushayra)	150	unknown	0	0	0	unknown	30	0	Some sources put the number of the Companions at 200.
Sawiq	200	100	2	0	0	unknown	5	0	They were martyred beforehand.
Banu Sulaym	200	unknown	0	0	0	unknown	15	0	Three days spent in Kudr.
Buhran	300	unknown	0	0	0	unknown	10	0	Reported to have continued for two months.
Dhat al-Riqa'	400	unknown	0	0	1	unknown	15	0	Known to have lasted 30 days, and the number of Companions martyred is put at 700 or 800.
Dumat al-Jandal	1,000	unknown	0	0	1	unknown	25	0	Captive, embraces Islam.
Banu Lihyan	200	unknown	0	0	0	unknown	14	0	
Ghaba (Dhu Qarad)	400	unknown	1	4	2	unknown	5	0	Two people are said to have been martyred. One of the captives, Furat ibn Hayyan, embraces Islam. Some sources put the number of captives at 1. The death toll on the enemy side is given in some sources as 3.
Ghatafan	450	unknown	0	0	0	unknown	11	0	Some sources suggest that it lasted for one month.
Hamra' al-Asad	630	3	0	0	0	unknown	5	1	Killed as a war criminal. The number of people killed is also put at 2 and both these were case of the punishment of war criminals.
Banu Mustaliq	700	unknown	1	10	0	1	28	0	A person is killed mistakenly. Ibn Hisham puts the death toll at 3 people.
al-'Is	30	300	0	0	0	unknown	unknown	0	
Rabigh	60	200	0	0	0	unknown	unknown	0	
Kharrar	21	unknown	0	0	0	unknown	unknown	0	The reported number of Muslims is 21.
Batn Nakhla	12	unknown	0	1	2	unknown	unknown	0	The Muslims are reported as numbering 8 or 13.
Banu Sulaym and Ghatafan	200	unknown	0	0	0	unknown	unknown	0	
Qarada	100	unknown	0	0	2	unknown	unknown	0	One of the captives becomes Muslim.
Qatan	150	unknown	1	0	0	unknown	unknown	0	
Qurata'	30	unknown	0	12	0	unknown	19	0	Two expeditions were dispatched to Qurata'. One person is killed in the first, while 11 people are killed in the second.

Event	# of Muslims	# of Enemy	Casualties		Prisoners of War	Duration (hours)	Total Time (hours)	Death Penalty	Patrols/Expeditions
			Muslim	Enemy					
Ghamr	40	unknown	0	0	0	unknown	unknown	0	
Dhu al-Qassa	10	100	9	0	1	unknown	unknown	0	Captive, embraces Islam. Two further expeditions, the first of ten and the second of forty men, are carried out to the same place. 9 Muslims are martyred in the first and one person is taken prisoner.
Jamum	unknown	unknown	0	0	1	unknown	unknown	0	
al-'Is	170	unknown	0	0	2	unknown	unknown	0	Mention is made of prisoners, but no figures given. One of the prisoners is the Prophet's son in-law, Abu al-'As ibn al-Rabi'. The other is al-Mughira ibn Mu'awiya ibn Abi al-'As.
Taraf	15	unknown	0	0		4		0	
Hisma	500	unknown	0	2	100	unknown	unknown	0	The captives consisted of women and children.
Khabat (Sif al-Bahr)	300	unknown	0	0	0	unknown	unknown	0	
Wadi al-Qura	unknown	unknown	0	0	0	unknown	unknown	0	
Dumat al-Jandal	unknown	unknown	0	0	0	unknown	unknown	0	
Fadak	100	unknown	0	0	0	unknown	unknown	0	
Madyan	2	unknown	0	0	0	unknown	unknown	0	Prisoners are taken.
Turaba	30	unknown	0	0	0	unknown	unknown	0	
Najd	30	unknown	0	7	0	unknown	unknown	0	
Fadak (Banu Murra)	30	unknown	1	0	0	unknown	unknown	0	The number of martyrs is purportedly 29.
Banu Kilab	unknown	unknown	0	1	0	unknown	unknown	0	
Mayfa'a	130	unknown	0	1	0	unknown	unknown	0	While there are casualties, the exact number is not given. The casualty indicated in the table is the individual who, despite his pronouncement of the Declaration of Faith, was killed by Usama ibn Zayd.
Jinab	300	unknown	0	1	2	unknown	unknown	0	Both captives become Muslim.
Banu Sulaym	50	unknown	49	0	0	1	unknown	0	
Fadak (Banu Murra)	200	unknown	0	1	0	unknown	unknown	0	
Kadid/Banu Mulawwih	10	unknown	0	0	0	unknown	unknown	0	
Ka'b Ibn 'Umayr/Dhat Atlah	15	unknown	14	0	0	unknown	unknown	0	
Siyy	24	unknown	0	0	0	unknown	15	0	
Mu'ta	3,000	200,000	12	0	0	unknown	unknown	0	
Dhat al-Salasil	500	unknown	0	0	0	1	unknown	0	There is also indication of there being no confrontation.
Khabat (Sif al-Bahr)	300	unknown	0	0	0	unknown	unknown	0	
Khadirah	15	unknown	0	1	0	unknown	15	0	The number of Companions is indicated in some sources as 14 or 16.

Event	# of Muslims	# of Enemy	Casualties		Prisoners of War	Duration (hours)	Total Time (hours)	Death Penalty	Patrols/Expeditions
			Muslim	Enemy					
Idam/Idm	8	unknown	0	0	0	unknown	unknown	0	1 person is killed. It is stated that the 94th verse of the Qur'anic chapter An-Nisa' was revealed in connection with this incident.
Dhat al-Salasil	unknown	unknown	0	0	0	unknown	unknown	0	
Banu Sulaym	unknown	unknown	0	0	0	unknown	unknown	0	
Banu Kath'am	20	unknown	0	0	0	unknown	unknown	0	
Yalamlam	200	unknown	0	0	0	unknown	unknown	0	
'Urana	300	unknown	0	0	0	unknown	unknown	8	
Awtas		unknown	0	0	0	unknown	unknown	0	
Banu Jazima	350	unknown	0	0	0	unknown	unknown	0	Waqidi mentions close to thirty captives being killed during this expedition, upon the command of Khalid ibn al-Walid.
Banu Suda'	unknown	unknown	0	0	0	unknown	unknown	0	
Banu Tamim	50	unknown	0	5	41	unknown	unknown	0	The captives comprised 11 women and 30 children.
Tabala	20	unknown	1	1	0	unknown	unknown	0	There are women captives.
Banu Haritha ibn 'Amr	unknown	unknown	0	0	0	unknown	unknown	0	
Jinab	unknown	unknown	0	0	0	unknown	unknown	0	
Habasha	300	unknown	0	0	0	unknown	unknown	0	
Dumat al-Jandal	420	unknown	0	0	0	unknown	unknown	0	
Judham	unknown	unknown	0	4		unknown	unknown	0	
Banu Sulaym/Baliyy	unknown	unknown	0	0	0	unknown	unknown	0	
Qurata	30	unknown	0	0	0	unknown	unknown	0	
Banu al-Harith ibn Ka'b	400	unknown	0	0	0	unknown	unknown	0	
Yemen (Mudhij)	300	unknown	0	20	0	unknown	unknown	0	Prisoners are taken.
Jurash	unknown	unknown	0	0	0	unknown	unknown	0	
Najd	unknown	unknown	0	0	0	unknown	unknown	0	
Wadi al-Qura	unknown	unknown	0	0	0	unknown	unknown	0	
Kadid	20	unknown	0	0	0	unknown	unknown	0	

Counter-insurgency operations: These were conducted against the tribes which violated the Medina Charter. They betrayed the alliance and took the side of Meccans who were attacking Medina. They provoked Meccans to war, provided reinforcements, and attempted to assassinate the Prophet. It is important to note that the revolting tribes did not only revolt to the Prophet but to the state they established together with other tribes. This is why other tribes did not choose to take side with them and remained loyal to the pact.

Patrols/Expeditions: Many of these expeditions were mainly conducted to patrol the borders of the new state and to ensure security. These patrols/expeditions proved very useful in a land which suffered from tribal warfare for many decades, and gang raids and violence were the norm or perceived as a sort of sport.

Index

A

'Abbad ibn Bishr 145

'Abbas (the Prophet's uncle) 22, 75, 88, 95, 99-108, 111, 123, 132, 161, 170-173, 175-177, 187, 191, 216, 221-223, 230, 231, 248, 249, 274, 280, 282-284, 293, 303, 309, 316, 323

'Abd al-Muttalib 16, 17, 39, 87, 100, 187, 248, 282, 307

'Abdu'llah ibn 'Abbas 95, 111, 132, 230

Abdu'llah ibn Abi Rabi'a 215, 216, 224, 229, 320

'Abdu'llah ibn Jahsh 73, 123, 267, 285, 293

'Abdu'llah ibn Rawaha 52, 78, 79, 104, 158, 159, 271

Abdu'llah ibn Ubayy 82, 136, 137

'Abdu'r-Rahman ibn 'Awf 31

Abraha 16, 67

Abraham, the Prophet 15, 78, 142, 187, 250, 294, 295; Station of 187

abtar 233, 234

Abu al-'As 76, 81, 141, 269, 277

Abu al-'As ibn al-Rabi' 76, 269

Abu al-Bakhtari 58, 232, 254, 264

Abu al-Shahm 46, 83, 278

Abu Ayyub al-Ansari 117, 118

Abu Bakr 65, 78, 97, 104, 119, 138, 166, 173, 175, 177, 183, 215, 222, 223, 249, 259, 271, 299, 318, 319

Abu Basir 152, 153, 154, 155, 156, 300

Abu Burqan 86

Abu Dharr 31, 251, 279

Abu Hafs 102

Abu Hudhayfa 69, 70, 102, 150, 232, 262, 282, 309, 324, 329

Abu Jahl 10, 17-21, 23-25, 34, 35, 50, 53-55, 66, 70, 75, 101, 102, 108, 109, 125, 134, 137, 141, 160, 164, 192, 193, 202, 205, 206, 208, 209, 211, 212, 215, 221, 224, 229, 230, 232, 239, 248, 249, 252, 254, 262, 270, 285, 287, 310-312, 318, 319-321, 322; family of 229

Abu Jandal 149, 150, 151-153, 156

Abu Lahab 23, 25, 101, 106, 108, 191, 230, 231, 252, 322; family of 230

Abu Qatada 40

Abu Sufyan 18, 19, 20, 39, 80, 81, 104, 108, 110-113, 119, 123-126, 128-131, 155, 156, 162-181, 198-203, 219, 220, 233, 258, 265, 273, 275, 276, 284-288, 291, 302-304, 307, 320, 324, 328

Abu Talib 17, 21, 141, 184, 192, 309, 319

Abu Wada'a 79, 82, 272

Abyssinia 16, 26, 111, 132, 194, 198, 276, 285, 286, 288, 318, 319, 320, 324-327

Addas 138

Age of Happiness 9, 48, 49, 63, 240, 241, 280

Age of Ignorance 22, 24, 61, 100, 165, 212, 240, 241, 250, 267, 328

Ahl al-Qalib 68, 71

Ahzab 43, 119, 258

'A'isha, the Prophet's wife 119, 121, 136, 141, 240, 254, 266, 310, 320

Akhnas ibn Shariq 18, 19, 20, 153, 155

'Ali ibn Abi Talib 25, 27, 38, 65, 66,

97, 100, 102, 141, 146-148, 162, 166, 167, 192, 222, 251, 252, 262, 264, 271, 278, 298, 299, 302, 319, 321, 325

aman 58, 141, 297

'Amr ibn 'Abdu'llah 80

'Amr ibn Umayya 111, 127, 128, 268

Ansar 76, 119, 329. *See also* Helpers

'Aqaba 100

Aqil ibn Abi Talib 81, 105, 325

'Aqiq Valley 83, 122

'Arafat 12, 243, 244, 245, 246

ashnaq 15, 249

'As ibn al-Wa'il 25, 108

Aws tribe 51, 52, 282

aysar 15, 249

ayyam al-'Arab 41. *See also* Heroism

'Ayyash ibn Abi Rabi'a 97, 193, 214, 230, 319

Aziz ibn 'Umayr 77

B

Badr, the battle of 10, 41-43, 48-50, 52-54, 56, 58, 63-78, 80-82, 93, 101-106, 110, 112, 115, 125, 126, 141, 146, 150, 164, 167, 192, 194, 195, 198, 203, 212, 217, 229, 231-233, 237, 253, 257-259, 262, 264, 266, 267, 269, 270, 272-277, 280-282, 285, 287, 293, 294, 296, 305, 309, 316, 318-320, 322, 325, 327; Second 43, 49, 258, 259

Banu 'Abd Manaf 21, 170

Banu Bakr 163, 308, 311

Banu Ghatafan 45

Banu Hashim 16, 17, 22, 58, 99, 102, 159, 175, 248, 270

Banu Khaybar 45

Banu Makhzum 16, 75, 124, 125, 208, 270, 318, 320

Banu Mustaliq 83, 120, 121, 292, 328

Banu Nadir 44, 45, 83, 114, 116, 259

Banu Nufatha 163, 165

Banu Qaynuqa 44, 45, 46, 51, 83, 259

Banu Qurayza 44-46, 51, 52, 63, 83, 84, 114, 116, 259, 261, 262, 265, 266, 289, 298

Banu Qusayy 21

Banu Umayya 16

Barley Army 126

Barra 161, 278, 301

Becca 159, 181

Bilal al-Habashi 188

Black Stone 159, 187, 191, 231

Budayl ibn Warqa 168, 173, 302

Busr ibn Sufyan 86, 268

Byzantine Empire 43, 132, 212, 261, 313, 321, 325

C

Caesar 100

Call to Prayer 160, 171, 223, 224, 310, 311, 318

Chosroes 100, 260

Confederate 43, 51, 83, 114, 258

conquest of Mecca 12, 47, 49, 50, 60, 61, 62, 93, 108, 168, 181, 193, 229, 233, 234, 256, 262, 267, 280, 304, 305, 319, 320, 324, 327

D

Dahna 89

Damascus 6, 104, 112, 162, 163, 239, 249, 285, 318

Dar al-Nadwa 15, 16, 17, 21, 22, 99, 180

Day of Judgment 31, 84, 141, 218, 232
Day of Resurrection 61
dhimmi 141
Dhu al-Majaz 23, 24, 57
Dihya al-Kalbi 116, 231, 322

E

ethos of Islam 7

F

Fadak 45, 260
Fakhita bint al-Walid 202
Farewell Sermon 12

G

Gabriel, the Archangel 31, 32, 36, 38-40, 51, 65, 78, 79, 85, 109, 110, 111, 116, 151, 241, 245, 267, 268, 271, 283
ghazwa 46, 47, 72

H

hadith qudsi 67
Hafsa, the Prophet's wife 119
Hakam ibn Qaysan 73, 74, 82, 268
Hakim ibn Hizam 53-55, 58, 168, 170, 173-175, 216, 221, 233, 262, 293, 316, 328
Hamza 38-40, 193, 194, 201-204, 262, 267, 271, 293
Harith ibn Abi Dirar 83, 120, 121
Hasan ibn Thabit 183
Hashemites 18
Hatim al-Ta'i 84
Hawazin 50, 72, 86-89, 192, 215, 217-219, 224, 293
Helpers 26, 88, 177, 328
Heraclius 132, 295
Heroism 41
hijaba 15, 143, 248

Hind 39, 123, 164, 179, 198-205, 232, 233, 265, 288, 309-311, 321, 324, 328
Hudaybiya 46, 47, 50, 60, 80, 94, 96, 97, 114, 139, 142-151, 153, 155, 156, 162, 163, 165, 166, 173, 259, 264, 322, 323
hukuma 15
Hunayn, the battle of 42, 43, 50, 62, 63, 72, 85, 192, 215-218, 220, 221, 223, 237, 259, 265, 268, 293, 307, 314, 315, 320
Huwaytib ibn 'Abd al-'Uzza 143, 161, 163, 215, 216, 221, 224
Huyayy ibn Akhtab 114-116, 119, 289, 291
Hypocrites 136

I

Ibn 'Abbas 95
idolatry 23
'Ikrima ibn Abi Jahl 98, 99, 163, 193
ISIS 7
Israfil, the archangel 66

J

Jannat al-Baqi 244
Jaysh al-Sawiq 126
Ji'rana 72, 86, 89, 217, 218, 220, 223, 316, 326
Jonah, the Prophet 138
Judaism 115, 117
Juwayriya bint al-Harith 83

K

Ka'b ibn Asad 114
Khadija 25, 53, 100, 109, 174, 182, 183, 244, 252, 269, 292
Khalid ibn al-Walid 47, 62, 63, 77, 98, 109, 114, 123-125, 161, 182, 183, 194, 212, 221, 249,

261, 265, 270, 284, 293, 301,
304, 322, 323, 327
Khalid ibn Hisham 75, 81, 221,
229, 270, 319
Khallad ibn Suwayd 45, 64
Khandaq, the battle of 50, 52, 72,
110, 146, 167, 192, 194, 237,
258, 259, 318, 319, 327
Khawwat ibn Jubayr 52
Khaybar 10, 45, 46, 51, 107, 114-
116, 118, 127, 218, 258, 264,
265, 278, 281, 288-290, 322,
325
Khazraj tribe 52, 100, 147, 161,
177, 179
Khubayb ibn 'Adi 74
Khuda'a tribe 15, 50, 60, 61, 214,
248, 264

L

Lat 24, 57, 208, 313
liwa' 15, 248

M

maghazi 42, 73, 252
Majanna 23, 126
Malik ibn 'Awf 62, 85, 86, 89, 221
Marr al-Zahran 126, 157, 158, 168,
174, 176, 179-181
mashwara 15, 249
Maymuna, the Prophet's wife 123,
161, 263, 301, 323
Meccan administration 15, 16
Mecca's conquest 33, 40, 50, 83, 98,
113, 168, 183, 184, 192-194,
224, 231, 255, 279, 284, 297,
304, 309, 318-320, 322-326,
328
Migrants 88, 159, 166, 177, 184,
328
Migration 44, 101, 115, 134, 139,
232, 233, 285, 288, 301, 327

Mika'il, the archangel 66, 78, 266
Mosaic Law 51
Mount Qu'ayq'an 160
Mu'adh ibn Jabal 51, 52, 76, 243,
244, 329
mu'ahad 141, 297
mu'allafa al-qulub 219, 222, 269,
319, 322, 325, 326
mubaraza 212
Mughira ibn Shu'ba 17, 18, 135,
296
Muhammad, Prophet, al-Amin 11;
mosque of 43, 85, 134, 212,
242, 276; strategy of 41, 102,
105; the Trustworthy 11, 15,
17, 111, 112, 122, 157, 172,
185, 200, 201, 208, 209, 216,
217
Muhammad ibn Maslama 156, 157,
187
Mujadhdhar ibn Dhiyad 58
munafara 16
Mus'ab ibn 'Umayr 77, 285, 324
Musaylima the Liar 194, 298
mustad'afin 95, 155, 277, 319
Mu'ta, the battle of 48, 261, 318
Mut'im ibn 'Adi 80

N

nadwa 15
Najd 84
Najran 135, 296
Negus of Abyssinia 111, 132, 285,
286, 295
Nineveh 138

P

Paran mountains 159, 160, 182
People of the Book 33, 242, 243
People of the Well 68, 71
Pilgrimage, Compensatory 123,
161, 259, 270, 300; Farewell

234, 243, 248, 257, 329;
Lesser 142, 156, 279, 294,
300, 301
Prophetic methodology 11, 179

Q

Qaswa' 158, 177, 182
Quba' 192, 284, 319
qubba 15, 249
Quraysh 16, 21, 35, 40, 50, 53, 54,
67, 68, 73, 77, 87, 96, 99, 102,
107, 108, 126, 137, 142-145,
149-155, 157, 159, 162, 163,
165, 167-169, 177-181, 183,
185, 186, 188, 191, 210, 217,
229, 248, 249, 264, 266-268,
271-273, 298, 300, 302, 308,
311-313, 321
Qusayy ibn Kilab 15, 108, 248

R

Raji' incident 74
Ramadan 42, 134, 181, 257, 304,
305
Ramla bint Abi Sufyan 111, 125,
286
reconciliation 7, 11, 115
rifada 15, 143, 248

S

Sa'd ibn Abi Waqqas 76, 222, 252,
269, 317
Sa'd ibn Mu'adh 51, 52, 76
Sa'd ibn 'Ubada 52, 147, 161, 166,
177, 178
Safiyya, the Prophet's wife 39, 40,
114, 116-118, 119, 123, 288-
291, 295, 321
Safiyya bint 'Abd al-Muttalib 39
Safwan ibn Umayya 98, 99, 108,
109, 112, 114, 124, 127, 160,
163, 183, 194, 195, 197, 202,

215-217, 220, 224, 234, 249,
275, 293, 314, 323, 325
sariyya 47
Shayba ibn Rabi'a 25, 35, 69, 70,
102, 163, 198, 221, 232, 251,
255, 271, 272, 282, 283, 288,
309, 311, 324
sifara 15, 249
siqaya 15, 99, 143, 248, 249
Suhayl ibn 'Amr 77, 81, 98, 108,
114, 127, 128, 143-145, 147-
150, 154, 160, 161, 183-186,
188, 224, 233, 234, 267, 276,
293, 314, 321, 324
Suhayl ibn Bayda' 79, 81, 271, 280

T

Tabuk expedition 43, 49, 132, 136,
259, 263, 304, 305
Ta'if 35, 43, 72, 80, 85, 86, 89, 137,
217, 218, 259, 315
Tayma' 45, 260
Thaqif 86, 134, 137, 138, 217
Thumama ibn Uthal 84, 130
Trench, the battle of 83, 125, 296

U

Ubayy ibn Khalaf 56, 57, 82, 123,
232, 293
Uhud, the battle of 37-40, 42, 43,
48, 50, 56, 63, 71, 72, 74, 106,
110, 125, 135, 146, 167, 192,
194, 198, 201-203, 221, 233,
237, 244, 254-256, 258, 259,
265, 272, 284, 285, 296, 310,
319, 327
'Ukaz 23
'Umar 55, 70, 71, 77, 78, 97, 102,
104, 119, 134, 136, 145, 146,
149, 152, 159, 166, 169, 170,
177, 202, 203, 222, 229, 230,
245, 249, 259, 270, 271, 275,

282, 291, 299, 300, 303, 316,
318, 320, 325
Umayna bint Abi Sufyan 112
'Umayr ibn Wahb 81, 82, 194, 195,
197, 275, 325
Umayya ibn Abi Hudhayfa 75
Umayya ibn Khalaf 35, 70, 108, 232
Umm 'Abdu'llah bint Abi Umayya
86
Umm al-Fadl 99, 106, 280
Umm Habiba 110-112, 123, 125,
129, 165, 285-287, 291, 320,
328
Umm Hakim 109, 202, 205, 206,
208, 213, 284, 310, 312, 320,
321
Umm Hani' 141, 192, 297, 298, 319
Umm Jamil 108, 231
Umm Salama 75, 124, 125, 132,
212, 312, 326
'Umra al-Qada' 46, 300. *See also*
Pilgrimage, Compensatory
uqab 15, 248
'Uqba ibn Abi Mu'ayt 25, 34, 35,
232, 252, 323
Usama ibn Zayd 33, 181, 188, 321,
322
Usayd ibn Hudayr 62, 63, 147, 177,
275, 276
'Utba ibn Rabi'a 25, 35, 53, 54, 55,
69, 70, 102, 105, 164, 191,
204, 231, 232, 253, 262, 300,
309, 311, 324, 328
'Uthman ibn 'Abdu'llah 73, 318
'Uyayna ibn Hisn 88, 216, 221, 222,
223
Uzza 24, 57, 143, 161, 163, 208,
215, 216, 221, 224, 313

W

Wadi al-Qura 45, 260
Wahb ibn 'Umayr 275

Wahshi 39, 193, 194, 310
Walid ibn al-Mughira 17, 25, 77,
108, 109, 123, 125, 232, 249,
270, 293, 322
Walid ibn al-Walid 77, 81, 97, 124,
270, 293
Walid ibn 'Uqba 35, 253
Walid ibn Walid ibn al-Mughira 77

Y

Yamama, the battle of 103, 130
Yarmuk, the battle of 193, 212, 214,
230, 284, 313, 319, 321, 324,
325, 326
Yemen 194, 205-208, 213, 243, 318,
320

Z

Zamzam 16, 21, 187, 248, 307
Zayd ibn Harith 25, 36, 74, 188,
261, 267, 322, 323
Zayd ibn Dathinna 74
Zaynab, the Prophet's wife 24, 141,
232, 253, 265, 269, 277, 285,
288, 290, 291, 293, 326, 328
Zubayr ibn Awwam 39, 40, 183,
184, 328